RETURN

DIVINE
SOPHIA

"This book reveals the unique place of the Isis tradition and the true purpose and significance of Mary Magdalene. Thoroughly researched and very readable, this book draws the reader into the fascination and deep symbolism of this subject: a wonderful book to enjoy and treasure."

STUART WILSON, COAUTHOR OF *POWER OF THE MAGDALENE*

"Tricia has done it again. She writes for a new time, and the glorious homecoming of Sophia, the wisdom of the essential feminine essence. Travel with this world renowned teacher to the heart of the mysteries of the quantum field where the great masters dwell and return with newfound knowledge, purpose, clarity and love."

ALAN STEINFELD, FOUNDER OF NEWREALITIES.COM

"I strongly recommend a close reading of Tricia McCannon's book. Her personal journey reveals the suppression of the divine feminine aspect within the world's religions and may well point the way to a more truthful, equitable, and peaceful future."

JIM MARRS, *NEW YORK TIMES* BEST-SELLING AUTHOR

"This book is a revelation for the soul and the missing link to help us end the dark agendas of the patriarchy. It is an incredible and brilliant piece of work. Read this book!"

LAURA EISENHOWER,
FOUNDER OF COSMIC GAIA SOPHIA SEMINARS

"This powerful and transformative book is the proverbial cracking of the Cosmic Egg. Incredibly well researched and emotionally moving, this book has the power to bring us all to a new paradigm for world healing."

COLIN TIPPING, AUTHOR OF *RADICAL FORGIVENESS*

RETURN OF THE
DIVINE
SOPHIA

Healing the Earth
through the
Lost Wisdom Teachings
of Jesus, Isis, and
Mary Magdalene

TRICIA McCANNON

Bear & Company
Rochester, Vermont • Toronto, Canada

Bear & Company
One Park Street
Rochester, Vermont 05767
www.BearandCompanyBooks.com

Bear & Company is a division of Inner Traditions International

Library of Congress Cataloging-in-Publication Data
McCannon, Tricia.
  Return of the divine Sophia : healing the earth through the lost wisdom teachings of
Jesus, Isis, and Mary Magdalene / Tricia McCannon.
     pages cm
  Includes bibliographical references and index.
  Summary: "An initiatic journey into the Mysteries of the Goddess and humanity's
return to an age of peace and celestial light" — Provided by publisher.
  ISBN 978-1-59143-195-4 (pbk.) — ISBN 978-1-59143-776-5 (e-book)
  1. Goddess religion. 2. Goddesses. 3. Jesus Christ—Miscellanea. 4. Isis (Egyptian
deity). 5. Mary Magdalene, Saint—Miscellanea. I. Title.
  BL473.5.M335 2015
  204—dc23
                                                                    2014030472

Printed and bound in the United States by McNaughton & Gunn, Inc.

10 9 8 7 6

Text design and layout by Debbie Glogover
This book was typeset in Garamond Premier Pro with Goudy Oldstyle Std,
Decoration Pi, Shelley Script Lt Std, and Gill Sans MT Pro

To send correspondence to the author of this book, mail a first-class letter to the
author c/o Inner Traditions • Bear & Company, One Park Street, Rochester, VT
05767, and we will forward the communication, or contact the author directly at
www.triciamccannonspeaks.com.

This book is dedicated to my mother,
Carolyn Hayes McCannon,
who has tirelessly supported me with
the beauty of her spirit.
She embodies all of the best qualities
that a mother can have:
wisdom, patience, love, and understanding.

It is also dedicated to my two sisters,
who have each played a role
in my own search for Truth
as they have followed their own spiritual callings.

Finally it is dedicated to Shasta,
and to all of the mystics, masters, priests, priestesses,
shamans, and medicine men and women who,
throughout the centuries,
have kept the great spiritual Mysteries alive
so that we, in our time,
can benefit from their sacrifices and teachings,
and reclaim our true divinity
while still living in this world.

Contents

Part Three

THE RETURN

Acknowledgments

No one ever takes a journey of this magnitude without standing on the shoulders of others great in stature. While the list of those who have paid the price for remembering the ancient paths of illumination are too numerous to name, in this generation I wish to acknowledge the legacy of Lady Olivia Robertson and her scholarly brother, Lawrence Durdin-Robertson, who began the modern day movement of the Fellowship of Isis in Clonegal, Ireland, many decades ago. I had the chance to be initiated by Lady Olivia in her castle while she was still alive, and she was a powerful voice for the remembrance of the Great Mother in our times. Along those lines I also wish to honor the courage of historians Barbara Walker, Merlin Stone, Riane Eisler, Jennifer and Roger Woolger, Monica Sjöö, Barbara Mor, Andrew Harvey, Anne Baring, and Z. Budapest. Your discoveries about the true nature of human history have changed the world.

I wish to also thank my beloved illustrator girlfriend, Sylvia Laurens, who has spent many long hours listening to me read and believing in this work; my steadfast roommate Pam Iams, who spent many nights preparing dinner while waiting for me to come down from my attic office and eat; my fellow priestess, Nicki Scully, who recommended Bear & Company so warmly; and my terrific agent, Devra Jacobs, who is a joy to work with. I would also like to thank the great staff at Inner Traditions and Bear & Company: Jon Graham, my acquisitions editor, whose vision for world enlightenment is vast and wide; Meghan MacLean, Jeanie Levitan, Jessica Wimett, and Diana Drew, each of whom are part of my wonderful editing team; and finally Peri Swan for the wonderful cover design of the book. My heartfelt thanks to all of you! Your professionalism, support, and optimistic spirits make birthing a book of this magnitude a sheer joy!

And finally, I thank my teacher, Shasta Zaring, whose insights are a prominent part of this narrative. Shasta Zaring is a priestess and the Keeper of the sacred space of the Goddess Garden Atlanta, a temple of the Goddess in contemporary times. She creates Women's Intertribal Medicine Wheel Circles, Moon Circles, and Sisterhood Circles. She can be reached at: www.goddessgardenatlanta.com.

Introduction

Today, perhaps more than any other time in human history, we are seeing the rebirth of a unity consciousness that incorporates many ancient streams of knowledge with the desire to write a new destiny for the human race. This rekindling of ancient wisdom with modern-day mysticism is being brought about by the quest to bring a deeper meaning into a world that appears to have lost it; a fast-paced, materialistic world that seems to be obsessed with violence, death, and killing. Perhaps one of the reasons this resurgence is needed is that we can see how badly the world needs balance. We feel it personally in the stress of our daily lives, the imbalance of our relationships, and the ecological crisis of the Earth herself.

Yet in the midst of this chaos a new kind of human being is emerging, a being that I call *Homo luminous;* a man or woman of inner light who may perhaps be the next step in our evolution as a species. These are people who yearn to create the type of world where war, pollution, and struggle are things of the past; who have an innate sense of the sacredness of life and are committed to finding a way back to it. If you are reading this book, you may be one of these people. As forerunners

1

to this more enlightened kind of human, we seek to move past the distractions in our outer world to find a more eternal truth. We want to transcend the chaos of our heavy-handed politics, our materially co-opted media, our patriarchal religions, and the dysfunctional patterns of our relationships that have been handed down by our families. We are people who search for the beautiful, the true, and the eternal. These luminous human beings know that in order to bring a new and better world into being, we must somehow align ourselves with these more eternal principles, if the world we are living in now is ever to heal.

But discovering what has caused this imbalance in the world is not an easy task. Untangling the strings of history, culture, religion, and power is not something generally discussed on the evening news. This book is a journey toward unraveling these elements of cultural belief that have caused us to fall out of rhythm with the cosmos. By understanding how our past has shaped our present, and how our theological beliefs have programmed our societies, we can then choose whether to continue the path we are on, or rewrite our own destinies.

The Mysteries of the past hold keys to recovering this inner balance that can help us to transform our world. These ancient teachings were taught within the great Mystery Schools some four thousand years before the birth of Jesus, and some four hundred years after the crucifixion. Sages associated with these Mystery Schools saw the universe as infinitely vast, and also profoundly personal, embracing the concepts of both God Within and God Without, concepts that we now call Immanence and Transcendence. They integrated the disciplines of philosophy, religion, and science into one unified field, and they honored the Creator of the Universe as the Divine Father and Mother of All.

At the heart of this wisdom is an inner alchemy that Jesus called the Way. It is a path of integration and transformation that embraces both the Divine Masculine and the Divine Feminine within the heart. It is the inner path of sacred union taught by Jesus and by Mary Magdalene, but these teachings have also been taught by Thoth, the god of wisdom in ancient Egypt; by sages in Taoism and the Sufi world; and in the Old

Religions of the Goddess, with people who lived close to the land and the natural cycles of nature. Intrinsic to the Way is the reclaiming of the Divine Father/Mother God within the heart. This creates a wave of enlightenment for ourselves and our societies, giving us the power to change our world.

Many of these secrets were encoded in the language of sacred myth and story so that they would not be forgotten, yet most of us can no longer translate the meanings behind this symbolism, steeped as we are in a less than enlightened society. It is only now, as we embrace the sciences of astronomy, cosmology, genetics, biology, and quantum physics, that we are really beginning to understand how these "myths" are founded on deeper truths. This book is a journey into the teachings of the Goddess, the inner alchemy of sacred union, the wisdom of the masters, and the path that will lead us back to wholeness as a planet.

As a longtime student of these Mysteries, I am pleased to take you on a journey into the heart of this wisdom. To do so I must go back to the beginning of my own journey, and the discovery of the Divine Feminine. I will share parts of my story that will help you to discover a hidden world of wonder, beauty, and infinite possibilities—a world that the most famous mystics have taught their disciples in secret. I encourage you to take the journey with an open mind, to consider that the innate imbalance we see in the world around us is the result of something precious we have forgotten, and that must now be remembered. This wisdom lies at the heart of all great religions, and its discovery is the path of the true initiate.

PART ONE
The Departure

Humanity has imagined her as the immensity of cosmic space,
* as the moon, as the earth and nature.*
She is the age-old symbol of the invisible dimension of soul and
* the instinctive intelligence that informs it.*
We live within her being, yet we know almost nothing about her.
She is everything that is still unfathomed by us about the
* nature of the universe, matter, and the invisible energy that*
* circulates through all the different aspects of her being.*
She spins and weaves the shimmering robe of life in which we live
* and through which we are connected to all cosmic life.*

ANDREW HARVEY AND ANNE BARING,
THE DIVINE FEMININE

1

A Priestess of Isis

In the beginning there was Isis, Oldest of the Old.
She was the Goddess from whom all becoming arose.
As the Creatress, she gave birth to the sun when he rose
upon this earth for the first time.

BARBARA WALKER, *THE WOMAN'S ENCYCLOPEDIA*
OF MYTHS AND SECRETS

I sat up abruptly in bed, still in the other world. The blue-black shadows on the bedroom wall looked almost like the hieroglyphics I had seen painted on the walls in the dream. Where was I now? Oh, I was asleep in the dormitory of some college. I had returned to school for my master's degree. Now I remembered. I turned my head, slowly remembering the strange extraterrestrial language that had appeared on all four walls of the room only moments ago. They had looked like codes or symbols, some kind of light geometries written vertically on the walls of the small college dorm room. As I fastened my eyes back on the walls, I could still make out the faint inscription of some of the symbols.

How could they still be there? I wasn't still dreaming, was I? They seemed like characters in some ancient Egyptian language, and I zeroed in on them. My eyes came to rest on one in particular. It was a circle with a dot at the center. *What did it mean?* Abruptly I heard the answer in my head. *This is the beginning of all things, the beginning and the ending, the alpha and the omega.*

I lay back down. *How did I know this?* It felt like a galactic language, universal among higher life-forms. Somehow I knew that this symbol was a code for something much more ancient than our human tongue. It came from the language of light, the language of the angels.

Suddenly I could not keep my eyes open. I slid back into sleep on the dormitory bed, succumbing once more to the dreamtime. Hours later I awoke, disappointed to see that the astonishing writing had disappeared from the walls. Sitting up in bed, trying to remember, I finally forced myself to my feet. I hurriedly dressed and went down to the school library, a vast, wood-polished sanctuary with rows and rows of research books. I was determined to find some reference to the one symbol I could recall, the circle with the dot at the center. I was deep in study when a student assistant found me. "Excuse me, miss, but there's a phone call for you," he said.

"For me?" I queried. That was odd. No one even knew I was here. *How could there possibly be a phone call for me?* Surprised, I followed the young man back to the front desk. "Yes?" I said into the mouthpiece of the library phone. "May I help you?"

"Is this Tricia McCannon?" the female voice on the other end of the line asked. The voice was cool, even, and familiar.

"Yes. But who is this?"

"We have called to tell you that your dreams are real," she said quietly.

"What?" I uttered in astonishment. "Who is this?"

There was a moment of hesitation. "I am from the priestesses of Isis, and that's all I am permitted to tell you at this time." The click of the phone was audible as she hung up. Unable to speak, I stood there

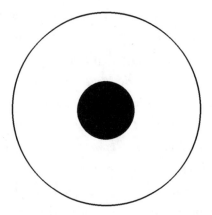

Figure 1.1. The circle with the dot at the center has long been a symbol used by the ancients for the sun and the creation of the cosmos. It is the Bindu point of light, found within the Hindu tradition, which marks the location of the Inner Sight. When activated this inner vision allows us to pull back the veils to behold the Inner Worlds of the Divine.

astonished for the longest time, looking at the phone. *Whoever were the priestesses of Isis, and why were they calling me? Furthermore, how did they even know about my dreams?* I conjured up the symbols in my mind. The writing was so familiar. Years later I was to discover that this symbol was the ancient glyph for the sun, the first principle of life. It was the shape that the *Om* sound created when chanted. It meant the Christ, the limitless light, the *Ain Soph Aur.* It was also one of the members of the Council of Nine.

The phone beside the bed rang insistently. Without thought I reached over to pick it up. This time, as I opened my eyes, I realized that I was at home in Atlanta. I was in bed. There was no library, no college campus, nothing except my strangely lucid dream. It had all taken place in the "inner worlds." Now I was back in the world of photography, advertising, and work, and it was dawn. As I replaced the handset on its cradle, I slowly realized that I had had a dream within a dream, and there had been a double message within it—the priestesses of Isis and some kind of language. I knew it was important, but I had no idea what it meant.

THE HIGH INITIATE APPEARS

I was still trying to make sense of these things as I got into my teal Honda sedan the next day and left for work. *Who were the priestesses of Isis, and why had they contacted me? Was this some sort of secret cult from Egypt? Did they still exist today?* I started the ignition. *And why had I remembered that symbol?* I slipped my car into gear, deep in the mystery.

Two months later the answers began to arrive. I had stopped for lunch at a new restaurant, and there was a long wait. To pass the time, I wandered into a beautiful gift shop called Illumina. As I opened the door onto a richly appointed carpet, the store's exquisitely lit crystals and one-of-a-kind jewelry looked unlike anything I had ever seen before. Immediately, my eyes landed on an Egyptian statue. Transfixed, I went to stand before it, letting my eyes sweep over the smooth black sculpture of a beautiful Egyptian woman with two tall feathers at the crown of her head. The saleswoman behind the counter leaned forward onto the highly polished glass, fixing me with her eyes. "Do you like Egyptian things?" she asked in a voice softly modulated with power. I turned at the sound. She was probably forty-five with a long mane of thick salt-and-pepper hair and a strong, attractive face. Her eyes were gray and piercing.

I stammered, feeling a bit self-conscious. "Yes, in fact, I've been having dreams about the priestesses of Isis."

Her eyes widened slightly and then seemed to grow sharper, as if she were seeing something around me for the first time. She extended her hand slowly, never blinking for a moment. "Welcome to Illumina. My name is Shasta."

I took her hand. "Hi, I'm Tricia," I said, feeling electricity go through me.

"Would you like to tell me about your dreams?" she suggested.

I blushed. "Well . . . I'm not sure I even understand my dreams." I looked away self- consciously, trying to decide how much to reveal. After all, since I had been working for many, many years with masters in my dream state and had been clairvoyant from the time I was a child, I certainly couldn't assume that a perfect stranger would follow my line of thinking. "I'm not sure you'd understand them, either," I added lamely.

Her eyes brightened, and a mysterious smile played about her lips. "Let's just say, I might. I'm a high initiate of the priestesses of Isis."

2

The Magic House
by the Grove

I am nature, the Universal Mother,
Mistress of all the elements, primordial child of time,
Sovereign of all things spiritual,
queen of the dead, queen of the immortals,
The single manifestation of all gods and goddesses that are.

APULEIUS, *THE GOLDEN ASS*
(TRANSLATED BY ROBERT GRAVES)

A week later I pulled into the dead-end street hidden in one of the oldest sections of the city of Atlanta. This was the address Shasta had given to me, after extending an invitation for me to visit. It was a short road, perhaps less than fifty yards, and it appeared to end in a tangle of vines and bushes. I parked on one side of the road, staring straight ahead of me. The house was supposed to be there. I read the address again, checking to be sure I was on the right street. But all I could see was a forest of kudzu, trees, and vines. Suddenly, as if a veil had been removed from my eyes, I realized that I was looking at a little white cottage hidden among the greenery. It looked like a fairy house: Shells, crystals, flowers, and bones were strewn down the path that led to the front door. The wooden porch was full of deerskins, Indian blankets, rocking chairs, baskets of gourds, and Native American dream catchers.

To one side of the front yard were four old metal chairs, overgrown with ivy. A hand-knotted rope with brass bells served as the doorbell, and on the front door, behind the dilapidated screen, swung a wooden heart. I stepped cautiously up onto the porch, looking at everything with wonder. Very different from my own lovely, artistic, but very neat and proper house, this cottage felt very much alive. Its magic was palpable. I sent out my inner senses, and it felt like decades of history were sequestered here. Ghosts of ancient wise women whispered in the air. A "spirit house," I thought, feeling the power of the ancestors gathering around me as if they knew I had come. I felt as if I had just arrived in some Hans Christian Andersen fairy tale, and as I pulled on the bell rope, I realized that I was in completely uncharted territory.

Shasta came to the door. She practically purred as she led me into her quaint little cottage, humming with energy. My eyes drank in everything. The first room was completely empty, except for an old stone fireplace and four altars, one at each of the room's corners. I got a glimpse of a large, coiled, stuffed snake mounted high in one corner, a large statue of Mary in another with roses at her feet. In a third corner a cat-headed, stained-glass goddess about four feet tall stared back at me. *Who was she? Egyptian!* I thought, and then I was past her living room and moving into her kitchen.

"Would you like some tea?" Shasta asked in a softly modulated voice. A white cat jumped down from the kitchen counter, looked up, and mewed. There were four white wicker chairs with a small coffee table between them nestled beneath a set of double-wide windows. This was clearly where she ate, read, and even served guests. Two other cats, looking profoundly pleased with their lounging activities, yawned up at me.

Shasta moved one of them from a chair. "Sit down. I'll put on the tea."

While she was busy in the kitchen, I looked around, trying not to be rude. The cottage was laid out in a simple square pattern. At the left front was the living room, with the kitchen to the rear. On the right side of the house, I guessed, was probably Shasta's bedroom and somewhere tucked toward the back right was a bathroom. "I have several herb choices," she said across the countertop. "I make them fresh from my garden. Would you like some dandelion or catnip tea? I grow it wild here."

I had never even heard of catnip or dandelion tea before. "Either one would be nice," I mumbled. I had only had herb tea made from a Celestial Seasonings box.

Figure 2.1. The magical house in the grove.
(Illustration by Sylvia Laurens)

"When the tea is finished steeping, we'll go out and sit in the garden." Through the side windows I could see that the garden was wild with kudzu. I could also see a little area where the land had been cleared and vegetables planted, but beyond that almost everything looked half hidden in green—the trees, the rocks, even the arched arbors of this magical little valley. From here it looked like an enormous green vortex where the Earth dropped away into the center of the yard, leaving the entire perimeter rimmed with trees. Wild roses covered the old fence around the property, making her house almost invisible to those not trained to know what they were looking for.

"This grove is hundreds of years old," Shasta explained as she saw me studying it. "Women have been coming here for centuries to pray. I am the keeper of the grove, along with my old friend Jeremy."

"Jeremy?" I asked.

Her chin gestured to the little hidden house on the other side of the sanctuary. I had not seen it before. "He is the guardian of the grove, just as I am the priestess." I wondered if he was half as fascinating as she was. Shasta poured the hot water from the kettle into our cups of dandelion. "Do you like honey?"

I nodded. "Shasta, do you have a restroom I can use?"

She smiled, gesturing. "Go back through the living room into the healing room. It's on the opposite side of the house."

I wandered through the rooms, my eyes large as saucers. I saw turtle shells, snakeskins, cow skulls, and fur throws. There were baskets of gourds in several corners and a bookcase of well-loved books. This time, as I passed the altar with the beautiful cat-headed being, I studied it more carefully. It looked majestic and proud, definitely Egyptian. In a second corner I realized that a white wolf pelt was draped beneath a white cow skull. *What could that mean?* One thing I knew, though: the whole place felt alive. As I entered her bedroom, which she had called the healing room, I noticed how pristine it was. Lace, candles, and rattles lay near the mirror above the dresser, and a large double bed with a white lace bedspread stood against one wall with a couple of overstuffed chairs.

Then I was at the door to the bathroom. From the moment I entered it, I could tell that the house was watching me. A strange sort of power emanated right through the floorboards. There was one window that threw triangles of light into the room, and the afternoon sun was subdued. Everything was white except the walls; the fixtures, the towels, the rugs. But the walls were painted purple with strange swirling symbols, spirals, and portals on them. I felt as if I knew these images. *Were they part of the language I had seen in my dream?* A shiver went through me. This was a place of power. It felt as if the living intelligence of the land was here, like some ancient being was watching. I knew that whatever energy the grove had, this room was one of its exit points, and it seemed as curious about me as I was about it.

Shasta was ready with the tea when I returned.

"Interesting bathroom," I commented dryly.

She gave me a sideways glance. "I thought you'd like it." She held my eyes for a moment.

"It was watching me," I said.

She smiled. "Yes, I know. This grove lies at the intersection of two blind springs, springs that run underground but do not surface. This creates a powerful magnetic field through which River Woman can speak. Come. We'll go out into the garden." Shasta opened the door and stepped outside onto the porch into the afternoon sun. The light seemed to glisten off the railing, the teacups, even her earrings. I took a deep breath and followed.

River Woman, I thought, contemplating the meaning of her words. *Who was River Woman?* I thought she meant the primordial intelligence of the water itself. As I thought of the water all over the world having an active intelligence, I realized that water passed through everything—cities, mountains, meadows, towns. Water even passed through the ocean and the sky as rain. Water passed through humans and animals and returned to the Earth. If water could communicate its vast wisdom to someone who truly knew how to listen, one could learn a great deal simply by sitting beside the water.

Shasta seemed to be reading my mind. "In the ancient days the women made their homes near water. This was not only practical; it was also for understanding. A wise woman from the village would go down to the water and listen each day. In this way she would hear news from the spirit of the water about all that was happening in other villages upstream. She would know before anyone arrived to tell the elders. This is part of the teachings of River Woman."

I nodded, not even sure how to respond. It was an entirely new way of thinking. "Think about it," Shasta went on. "If all water is connected to the great ocean, then everything is connected. This is why the Goddess was always called la Mer, Mari, Mary, or the Great Mother. She is the ultimate healer. On a planet like this one, a water planet, one can sit in this grove and learn a lot about what is happening all over the world just by being still."

We picked up our mugs, descended the steps, and entered the magical glade. I followed her silently through the foliage into the back. Three huge grandfather oaks oversaw the little valley, and beyond it were even more woods, buffering her from the world. From one oak hung a rope swing. The grove looked for all the world as if we had stepped into an eighteenth-century painting. Several alcove gardens could be seen hidden in the foliage, and now Shasta led me into one of them. A statue of Maria of the Woods, overhung with altar offerings and half-melted candles, attested to the fact that other initiates had visited here. Mardi Gras beads, ceremonial objects, and prayer ties all hung from the trees, and a loose assortment of benches, rugs, tables, and candles were half obscured beneath the canopy of foliage. An aura of reverence emanated from the place.

"Mary is the patron saint of our woods," Shasta explained. "Many people have gathered here to speak to her." I nodded, not even able to formulate a question. Despite my years of spiritual training, this was all new to me. The healing energies of sacred ritual were gathered in the silence. "Shall we sit?" Shasta asked, leading me toward a wicker sofa where I could see down into the little bowl-shaped valley for the first time. There was a fire pit and four altars, one for each of the directions. I could feel the power rising from the ground like a pulse. I knew that if I were left alone in this grove, I would be able to hear the Earth speaking.

Suddenly I spotted three huge cauldrons turned upside down in the circle. The sight sent a shiver through me. I knew from my Christian upbringing that witches used cauldrons. "What are those?" I said, pointing at them dubiously.

She laughed, amused by my fundamentalist sensibilities. "Don't be afraid," she reassured me, patting my arm in a matronly manner. "Cauldrons are only iron kettles, you know. People have cooked in them for centuries." I smiled sheepishly, feeling chagrined. My Southern Baptist training was rearing its head. "The cauldron, you see, is like the womb of the Earth, the womb of women everywhere. It is dark and round and mysterious, and from it life springs, even if that life is only a well-cooked stew." She laughed, and I laughed with her, half embarrassed, half still ill at ease. *What had I gotten myself into?*

"The Earth is the same as the cauldron, Tricia. The nurturing power of the feminine grows something wonderful from the dark womb that is our Mother Earth. Although most people take this for granted because they are disconnected from the natural world, it is still true. The Mother gives us everything: air, food, water, all our plants, our trees, our wood, our fabrics, even our animals. It's all offered from the bounty of the Mother. Life germinates in the womb. This is true for all creatures. It is part of the Great Mystery of life, death, and rebirth. Cauldrons represent the alchemical laboratories that symbolize the nature of women and sacred life. This is also why the cauldron was used in alchemy."

"Alchemy?" I swallowed, my adrenaline humming. "What do you mean 'alchemy'?"

She laughed, seeing my discomfort, but her voice was patient. "Alchemy is transmutation," Shasta explained. "Personal inner transmutation, or chemical scientific transmutation—it's all the same. The alchemy of transformation is always done with the four elements, because that is the paintbox of the Divine."

I held her eyes but didn't speak, thinking about her words. *The paintbox of the Divine. What a strange thought, but true,* I realized. I wanted her to go on.

She sighed. "Let me ask you a question, Tricia. What do you think the world is made of?" I looked around at the trees, the sky, the bench, my own clothes. I wasn't sure what she wanted me to say. "Elements," she said plainly. "Lots of elements, like those you find on the periodic table. And each of these elements is composed of some combination of air, earth, fire, or water, aren't they?"

Yes, I thought, *that was true, wasn't it?* It was all some proportion of these four simple elements, plus the element of life or Spirit that animated it. When Shasta put it like this, it was easy to follow.

She continued. "So all science is the study of the elements and how they respond to one another, whether it is the science of chemistry, biology, astronomy, physics, or even medicine. From herbology to pharmaceuticals, we are talking about how things combine, how they transmute and change and interact with one another. That's alchemy, isn't it?"

She was right, I realized. Science is basically the empirical study of how the universe works, how it combines and operates within our ability to perceive its laws.

Shasta went on. "But there is a deeper level of working with the elements that is known as the Great Work. This is the alchemy of the human soul, and it is done within the laboratory of time." I opened my mind to let these ideas come in. "The past, the present, and the future—these were all known in ancient mythology as the three Fates, the three Norns that sit beneath the One World Tree."

"The One World Tree?" I asked.

"A symbol of the Absolute behind it all." I looked at her hard, trying to follow what she was saying. She smiled, as if dismissing a subject that was too large for the moment. "Anyway, that is what we do here in this grove—transformation, connection; prayer, ceremony; the alchemy of connecting the soul with the Divine behind it all."

The magician's quest, I thought, *the Philosopher's Stone*—these were part of the secret societies connected with the search for the Holy Grail. I knew that for centuries there were legends of medieval alchemists who had sought the formulas that would turn lead into gold, create the fountain of youth, and allow them to attain immortality. These were clearly a metaphor for something far deeper.

Shasta went on. "Whenever someone goes to church to worship, the church uses these same elements, don't they? The Catholic fathers took this knowledge of ritual and ceremony from the priestesses long ago because it engages the inner senses as well as the outer ones." I thought about what she was saying. *Yes, they did use air, earth, fire, and water.* These four elements were part of every religious ceremony I had ever attended. The burning of incense used both air and fire; so did the lighting of candles. Water was intrinsic to baptism and the sprinkling of "holy water," which represented cleansing. Drinking wine and eating the communion wafers were part of the Earth, as well as the golden chalice. That sacred cup could represent anything, from the act of receiving, to the womb of the Holy Mother herself. At the Eucharist we even say, "Take. Eat. This is my body that was given for you and for all men . . ." Shasta was right. This was how all the most beautiful ceremonies were done in virtually every religion.

"They use the four elements because they work," she said. She opened her hands and gestured around the yard. "Now look around you. This is the Goddess's true cathedral, Tricia, made of the natural elements. This is why our ancestors built campfires and sat around them. It wasn't just to stay warm or to cook food; it was to dream with the fire. Anyone who has gone camping knows this. When we stare into the flames, we enter an altered state, a place where our vision takes us beyond the mundane things of life into the dreamtime." She looked out at the grove. "Those cauldrons are merely holders for the alchemical fire of transmutation, like the chalice. It's as simple as that."

I took a deep breath. Her words were part of something I had always felt, as if nature itself were the real holy place, not a house of worship. I realized then that my silly fears were part of a rigid prejudice against all other faiths, spawned by my own Christian upbringing. It was based on ignorance. We had always been taught that anything "Earth-centered" was evil, although, stepping back from it now, I realized that this was patently absurd. The Earth was the only reason any of us had life at all! Each day we ate from her, drank from her, and breathed her air. How could anyone consider that "evil"? It was like separating yourself from the sacredness of God.

Even though I thought I had "graduated" long ago from the overt oppression of the church, clearly there were still pockets of its upside-down logic left in my psyche. As beautiful as organized religions can be, I had long ago realized that the church separated people by assigning judgment and blame. I had long been on a path of listening to that inner voice that speaks to all of us who come in purity of heart. Yet until that moment, I hadn't realized how firmly the fear of witches had been implanted in me.

"Are you a witch?" I blurted out, blushing scarlet with my own lack of tact.

She laughed and shook her head, unruffled. "No, a witch is a person trained in the Wiccan path. That is not my training. My path is the path of the Goddess. I am a priestess of the Divine Mother in all her forms, but my personal circle is Isis, Quan Yin, and Sekhmet, the cat-headed being that you saw inside. The Wiccans work with both male and female deities."

"Is that why you have three cauldrons?" I asked, trying to keep any distress from my voice.

She smiled. "Yes, they represent the Triple Goddess." I had no idea what she was talking about. She saw that and went on. "These are the three stages of life that every woman lives through—the maiden, the mother, and the matron. These complete the wheel of life, death, and rebirth. The Divine Mother encompasses them all."

Hmm . . . I had a lot to learn. "But what about God?" I asked a bit petulantly. "Where does God fit into all this?"

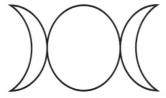

Figure 2.2. The Celtic symbol for the Triple Goddess represents the three major phases of life: the maiden, the mother, and the matron, referred to by the patriarchy as the Crone. For men these are the youth, the man, and the sage. In this symbol we see three of the eight major phases of the lunar cycle, expressing the first and last crescent moons with the full moon at the center.

Her eyes blazed. "Tricia, the male version of the Creator has had plenty of press these past few thousand years. There are many advocates for a vengeful, punishing god, a god who separates and divides, who judges and condemns, a god who destroys or conquers everything that will not submit." I felt the power touch her like a flame. "I, for one, choose life. I choose a Creator who unites. I choose peace and unity, not division and war. Our world has seen enough of that to last many lifetimes."

She was right. Condemnation, punishment, original sin, blame, and shame seemed to be at the root of all the patriarchical religions, from Islam to Christianity. They said they revered women, and yet they oppressed them. They said they were bringing forth the teachings of the prophets of love, yet they were more than eager to tell you that you would go to Hell. To me, something was fundamentally wrong with any version of the Creator who would only bless one group and send the others into oblivion. Yet this was the world that we had been born into, a world where men taught oppression in the name of God. And their way was taking the entire planet down a path of abuse. We saw it in the exploitation of children, the killing of animals, and the pollution of natural resources. They gave no thought to the generations that would come after; their only concern was their own profits right now.

I remembered then the creed that our Native American ancestors had tried to live by: "Make no decision that does not serve seven generations forward." This ensured that we would become wise stewards of the land and the people. I flashed on the words of the Bible: "And the tree shall be known by its fruit." Well, our culture and its fruits clearly sprang from a warped and twisted tree.

Shasta's voice cut in, pulling me from my contemplation. "But who remembers the Great Mother who actually creates everything, the one who gives everything on this planet life? Who honors her?"

Tears sprang to my eyes. I could think of nothing to say.

"All things are born of woman, Tricia," Shasta continued in a voice soft with power. It was so plain a truth that I could not believe it had never occurred to me before. *She was right.* Nothing would be born or live without the creative power of the female. "Show me one living creature born of man. It doesn't happen. The best we can offer is androgynous earthworms."

I laughed out loud. The image of men claiming supreme dominance as huge aggressive earthworms was just too fantastic. The laughter broke the tension. After a moment Shasta joined me, and I knew we were visualizing the same thing.

"Honestly, Tricia, in all the cosmos it is only the Mother who is the Life Giver. How can God be a male, I ask you? Males do not give birth, do they?" I looked at her, and beneath the mirth there was a serious glint in her eyes. "She is both the Queen of Heaven and the Mother of Earth, but she has been forgotten by her children, dishonored and mistreated. When you come here to this grove, you honor her."

I looked out on the ragged beauty of the half-wild garden hidden by the kudzu. Just like the Goddess, I thought, hidden unless you had the eyes to look for her. Shasta's words brought an entirely new way of thinking into my world. I realized then that, in some strange way, I had always accepted God as being male. I had accepted the inner picture of some guy with a long, white, flowing beard, who judged and punished us if we didn't do as he said.

"Shasta," I turned, knowing my prescient gifts were speaking. "I know that the time will arrive when I will come here to study with you, but that time is not yet. There are other things I must do first. But I am sure this is why the priestesses of Isis contacted me in that dream." She nodded. "So when I am ready, will you teach me?"

A mysterious smile played around her lips. She fixed me with her piercing eyes. "So shall it be. And in the years to come, may you discover for yourself the answers to who the Great Mother truly is."

3

The Feather of Truth

I had not yet found a place upon which I could stand.
I conceived the Divine Plan of Law and Order, Ma'at, to
make all forms.
I was alone. I had not yet emitted Shu, nor had I yet
emitted Tefnut,
nor existed any other who could act together with me.
EGYPTIAN BOOK OF KNOWING THE CREATIONS
OF RA AND OVERCOMING APOPHIS

One might think that I would have dived easily into the study of the
Goddess, but in truth, I was afraid. While the idea of becoming an initiate of any golden path of wisdom strongly appeals to any seeker of truth, I
knew that the path to enlightenment has never been easy. Thus, I stepped
back from taking the plunge. There were several reasons for this. The
first was that I was a commercial advertising photographer and had a successful business in the "real world." My spiritual studies were private, and
even though I had strong natural gifts of clairvoyance and clairaudience

(inner sight and inner hearing) and frequently saw information about other people with my spiritual vision, I had always kept my esoteric interests private. To begin a study of the Divine Feminine would be a big step for me, and I wasn't sure how it would impact my worldview. Secondly, I knew that any true spiritual commitment can completely change your life, and at the time when these events began to unfold, my spiritual training had already moved in another direction with an extraordinary group of spiritual masters I had encountered at the age of nineteen. These powerful but elusive sages taught a process of meditation called "soul travel," which allowed seekers to begin to experience the Higher Worlds for themselves, to activate their subtle spiritual bodies and use them to travel in the unseen realms of God, while still maintaining our lives in a three-dimensional world. I was already being guided by wise, enlightened teachers, and I had just received my third initiation.

The third reason that I stepped back from Shasta's invitation was my own Christian background. As a mystic who had seen and heard and felt the invisible worlds of Spirit from the time I was a child, I knew that my studies were already beyond the bounds of my family's conservative belief systems. My dad had been raised a Baptist, and my mother was a Methodist, yet none of the ministers I queried at our local churches seemed to know about the spiritual beings of light that I studied with at night in my dreams. They looked outside themselves for answers, relying on scripture to tell them what to say. I could see that there was no direct connection with the living intelligence of the Divine, and thus, even within the houses of God's worship, the light was dim.

As a child, I also noticed a great hypocrisy within the church. On the one hand, church leaders seemed to honor Jesus, the God of unconditional love, yet on the other hand, they taught the doctrines of blame and guilt, fear and damnation from their pulpits, threatening punishment to all who did not conform. They also seemed to cultivate a rivalry between the various factions of their own Christian creeds while preaching to their congregations, "Judge not, least you be judged." This made no sense to me. How could the God of unconditional love be the fearful, angry God of wrath? How could they preach tolerance and forgiveness, yet make other people their enemies?

Perhaps discouraged by these same observations, my mother took it upon herself to find a gentler approach to Jesus that we could all identify with. When I was ten, she discovered a sweet Episcopalian parish about five miles from our house. I was confirmed there at the tender age of thirteen. I loved the sacred rituals with their formal robes and wafting incense. The gatherings were kind and heartfelt, and I was grateful not to hear the threat of fire and brimstone every Sunday. I knew even then that each of us comes into the world again and again to perfect our inner natures, and that love and kindness are the keys to shaping our inner natures in the divine image. No matter what the pomp or circumstance of a religion, it is in the province of the heart that real wisdom dwells.

So at the time that I met Shasta, my older sister and her preacher husband had become fundamentalists, my dad was still a Baptist, and my younger sister and my mother were Evangelists. They believed that Jesus was the only spiritual teacher who had ever told the truth, the only guide to salvation. I believed that there have been many great spiritual avatars and masters who have come to this planet. Jesus was the latest, and perhaps the greatest, world teacher, the one who had come to bring the message for the Age of Pisces, a 2,160-year cycle that had begun about a hundred years before he was born. From what I could see, that message had been corrupted, and even as a child, I felt the great imbalance that the male-dominated patriarchy had imposed on the world. So I was leery about pursuing a path that might take me even further from my family's beliefs.

THE MAGICAL WORLDS OF SPIRIT

Born with the gifts of inner sight and hearing, I spent the best days of my childhood in a forest across from my parents' house, communing with the trees and magical springs that bubbled up from the Earth. This was the church of God that I knew and loved, and it was in that forest that I wrote my first poems to God, listening to that small still voice that speaks within. There I learned to see the fairy realms and elemental spirits that oversee the plant and animal kingdoms.* Like the guardian angels of the human world, these elemental spirits supervise the world of nature. And sometimes, when I was very still, I could even hear the trees talking in the rustling of the leaves. But these flashes of knowing swept in and out, born on the wings of their own mysterious currents. I did not know how to control these gifts; they came and went as they would.

I know now, years later, as a longtime initiate of the Mysteries, that the gifts of inner sight, hearing, feeling, and knowing are just part of the naturally unfolding gifts of every spiritual aspirant. The masters teach that there are thirty-three of these inner gifts, which we acquire on our spiritual road to God, including the gifts of healing, telepathy, levitation, and lucid dreaming.† But since there was no one there to teach me, except the tall forest angel that appeared from time to time, I spent my time in the woods in prayer, hoping fervently that someone wiser than I would come along to connect the dots. Little did I know that the great Vairagi masters, who had heard that call, would arrive to initiate me into their teachings when I was nineteen years old

THE VAIRAGI MASTERS

The Vairagi are an unbroken line of spiritual adepts whose purpose is spiritual liberation of the soul within this lifetime. Like Jesus, they are interested in helping people free themselves from the burden of the

---

*The elemental spirits, or devas, are nature spirits from the angelic kingdoms that serve in accordance with God's will to assist nature.

†The four main gifts are clairvoyance (inner sight), clairaudience (inner hearing), clairsentience (inner feeling), and claircognitive ability (or inner knowing). Each of these gifts may develop in a different order, according to the personal history, experience, and life plan of a seeker. Other gifts include mind-to-mind communication, such as telepathy; the ability to move objects with the mind, also called telekinesis; plant and animal communication; and the gift of lucid dreaming, which allows us to develop a conscious gateway into the inner planes.

worlds of suffering. I had first met these elusive adepts in the spring of my sophmore year of college at Florida State University. They were the great spiritual teachers I had prayed for in my early years. Not only did they understand how the multidimensional planes of the universe are layered, but they knew the spiritual mechanisms that allow us to travel from one dimension to another. Discovering the Vairagi was like finding the road map to creation.

The name *Vairagi* derives from the Sanskrit root *vairag,* meaning "detachment." This name lies at the heart of their mission, for these sages have become detached from the affairs of the world and follow a path of inner truth. Unlike those of us still ensnared in our emotions, minds, sexuality, or materialism, they focus on the inner landscapes of Heaven, transcending the physical plane through soul travel.

The Vairagi teach that the three purest aspects of God are love, sound, and light—the trinity of creation itself. Love is the force that binds the universe together, the very fabric of creation. It is the essence from which all things are composed, the constantly moving adamantine particles that are the living body of the cosmos itself. Sound is the mechanism through which all worlds come into being, the underlying vibration that creates and sustains all things. In Freemasonry this is called the "lost note." This essential knowledge has been rediscovered by our physical sciences today and is referred to as string theory.

"In the beginning was the Word" begins the Gospel of John. This is the sound current that has been known as the *Aum,* the *Shabda,* the *Vani,* the *Nada,* and the Music of the Spheres.* Many of us have heard the roar of this current in the moments before we drop into sleep. Through specific exercises, the Vairagi teach the aspiring initiate to surf these sounds toward the center of creation. We find a reference to this in Edmond Bordeaux Szekely's *Essene Gospel of Peace.*

---

*Science now calls these sound particles *phonons,* which become light particles or *photons.* They are joined together by gluons, the wave form of sound transitions, into the wave form of light.

And when the sun is high in the heavens, then shall you seek the *Holy Stream of Sound*. In the heat of noontide, all creatures are still and seek the shade; the angels of the Earthly Mother are silent for a space. Then it is that you shall let into your ears the *Holy Stream of Sound:* for it can only be heard in the silence . . .

Truly, this is the Voice of God, if you did but know it. For as it is written, *in the beginning was the Sound, and the Sound was with God, and the Word was God.* I tell you truly, when we are born, we enter the world with the Sound of God in our ears, even the singing of the vast chorus of the sky, and the holy chants of the stars in their fixed rounds; it is then that the Holy Stream of Sound transverses the vault of stars and crosses the endless kingdom of the Heavenly Father.[1] (emphases mine)

The Vairagi teach that creation is divided into many dimensions, all vibrating at slightly different frequencies. The *Aum* is the mechanism that allows each dimension to come into existence. Sound organizes atoms into the shapes that we recognize, creating form, mass, height, and weight, yet this sound is beyond duality, emanating from every atom. Through the hearing of this cosmic vibration, we can establish a direct contact with Christ consciousness itself. As the divine vibration moves out through the worlds of form, it generates friction, creating suns and stars and the entire spectrum of visible light, and it has been said that the sun itself is a visual expression of this Word.[2] Sound brings all things into being from a state of "potentialized possibility." This is why it has long been said in magic that to know the "true name" of a thing is to be able to command it.

This brings us to light, the transmitter of heat, warmth, and illumination. Without light nothing would have life. Thus, the ancients saw the sun as a visible symbol for God itself, the unmanifested Source behind all things. It was this profound image that I had seen painted on the walls of the dormitory room in a dream so long ago, the ancient symbol for the sun. The ancients believed that there is both a physical and a spiritual sun, the supreme benefactor of the material and spiritual worlds. The Mayans call this the *Hunab Ku,* a term meaning "one meaning and one measure," one heartbeat behind it all. This is the Great Central Sun or the "Light that lights the Worlds." Paracelsus, the famous alchemist of the fifteenth century, wrote: "There is an earthly sun . . . and there is an Eternal Sun, which is the source of all wisdom, and those whose spiritual senses have awakened to life will see that sun and be conscious of His existence; but those who have not attained spiritual consciousness may yet feel His power by an inner faculty which is called Intuition."[3] Franz Hartmann, the German theosophist and friend of renowned theosophist Madame Helena Blavatsky, writes:

> The Sun is the Center of Power or Heart of things. The Sun is . . . the symbol of Wisdom . . . a storehouse of power. Each living being contains within itself a centre of life, which may grow to be a Sun . . . The terrestrial Sun is the image or reflection of the invisible celestial Sun; the former is in the realms of Spirit while the latter is in the realms of Matter; but the latter receives its power from the former.[4]

Hence throughout the centuries, many knew that the spiritual realms are the true world of cause, while the physical world is the ground of effect. In simple terms, this means that our thoughts, beliefs, and words have the power to change our reality. Our cultures are generated by what we think, feel, and do, shaping the very foundation of the world we experience.

So some twenty-five years ago, when I first met Shasta, this was the path that I was traveling. About Isis, I knew only that she had been a great queen of Egypt, and that, along with her husband Osiris and her son Horus, she had been part of the most famous trinity in all of Egypt for over seven thousand years. Legends surrounded her—myths of courage, resurrection, and eternal life—but I had not delved into these matters too deeply then. I was deep in the lessons of my third initiation with the masters of the Far East. So now let's talk about the awesome power of initiation itself.

THE RELUCTANT INITIATE

There is a classic story about a young seeker who was eager to have his second initiation. He had come to his master full of ambition, and he wanted to advance quickly up the ranks. Every day he would say to his teacher, "Give me my second initiation, please. Give me my second initiation, please. I beg of you!"

"All in time," his patient master would reply, "all in time."

But in the chela's mind it was not fast enough.* He ranked all initiates according to their initiation levels, so whenever he met any of the other disciples he would ask, "What initiation are you?" This told the chela whom he should be friends with, and whom he should try to emulate.

Some would nod and say proudly, "I am a second initiate!"

Others would scratch their chins and say thoughtfully, "I am a third initiate."

Still others would take a deep sigh and say quietly, "Hmm . . . I am a fourth initiate."

The older ones would smile kindly, shake their heads, and say in compassionate tones, "Yes . . . I am a fifth initiate."

One day, as the chela sat in audience with his master, he watched as another disciple was summoned. As the student bowed in respect before his teacher, the master spoke: "Zut-su, it is now time for me to offer you your sixth initiation. Are you ready?"

"Oh, no, master!" the older disciple protested. "Please don't give me another initiation, master. I beg of you!"

The young chela was shocked. As Zut-su left the master's building,

---

Chela is a name for a spiritual student, initiate, or aspirant.

the boy ran after him and caught him by the arm. "Why?" he stammered incredulously. "Why would you turn down such an opportunity? That is all any of us want—to become great masters!"

The wise student smiled down at him and said, "When I entered the master's teachings during my first initiation, I left my family's business and gave up my inheritance, thus learning to place the inner world above the outer one. During my second initiation, I let go of my wife and children, who could not find their way to any spiritual path, let alone mine, and thus I learned detachment, and to allow others to pursue their own evolutionary paths. During my third initiation I came down with a crippling disease, and discovered that beneath it was my own suppressed rage from childhood, and the anger at losing my family. I released it, and I healed. Then in my fourth initiation, my house was swept away by a flood, and I went to live in the forest, learning to eat the seeds and berries. There I learned humility, appreciation for animals and plants, and to move into sympathetic resonance with nature. Finally, during my last initiation, I died twice and came back from the dead, becoming a 'twice born.' Now I am just beginning to walk the path of my true immortality."

The young chela's mouth hung open. It was a moment before he could even gather his wits. "But why . . ." he blurted out before he could stop himself. "Why do you keep going at all?"

Zut-su smiled. "Because in losing all these things, I have found something greater."

The chela could barely utter the words. "But what . . . what is that?"

"I have found myself."

THE CATALYST EVENT

So what propels us to begin the search for a deeper truth? What sets our feet on the path to awakening? For some it is a tragedy, a change of life so profound that it sweeps away all the old, comfortable answers we have relied on to understand the world. Whether it be the death of a child, the end of a marriage, the dissolution of a career, or the wiping away of our dreams through some financial crisis, the usual answers will not suffice. Pain becomes the catalyst that mobilizes us to take action, and we search for something greater than the predictable version of reality we have been inculcated with since childhood.

For some it is like a siren's song in the quiet moments when we are most alone. It hovers like an unspoken yearning behind the day-to-day busyness of our lives, a longing ancient beyond years. This is the cry of the soul calling for itself. It whispers of a time when we knew more, understood more, and were connected to our eternal self. It is the remembrance of an age when growing up meant growing into mastery, and wisdom was the real goal of life. But the modern mind, now trained by the distractions of our swift and superficial societies to ignore such whispers, brushes it aside, until finally the mechanisms of pain and suffering force us to listen. So it was for me.

Many things had to change in my life before I was ready to step onto that path with Shasta, so it was to be nearly five long years before I began my studies with her. My engagement to a music producer in Britain had ended in heartbreak, and I had returned to the States on my knees in prayer. I entered a dark night of the soul where I remained for nearly a year and a half while trying to rebuild my photography business, my home, and all the things that I had abandoned when I left for England. This is the mystical death that precedes resurrection, where one descends to the depths of one's sorrow or pain; a time of crisis where the seeker must be willing to endure this dying to the old self, that precedes spiritual rebirth. Out of the ashes came a new beginning. Each day, as I knelt by my altar to pray, I began to hear angels' voices raised in song, constantly praising the Divine. In the process, my inner spiritual gifts of clairvoyance and clairaudience took a leap to another level.

Later I was to learn that this process of dying to the old self is considered essential to the path of enlightenment. Tau Malachi, a modern-day Christian Gnostic, writes: "Dying is part of living. You cannot have one without the other. Everything is interconnected and interdependent, it is the nature of things ever-becoming. You must learn to accept and embrace the whole of life and the whole of yourself if you would discover the Spirit and Truth. The Light and the Darkness must be joined and you must realize the Sacred Unity."[5] Only later did I realize how true this was, and this wisdom was at the very heart of the Great Mother.

The ancients have called this powerful process of dying and being reborn "initiation," and like the reluctant initiate Zut-su, it is always about letting go of what we have once held dear to find a more enduring path. In Christian terms it is "being born again," since the death of the ego allows a powerful shift in consciousness that then propels us toward a greater spiritual awakening. The structures that had once supported our life come crashing down, and in their place, something greater is born. Like Zut-su, this "ego death" ultimately leads us to our higher self.

In my meditations I began to hear angels singing in constant praise of the Divine; I heard messages about the nature of love and spiritual surrender; and I began to actively discourse with these higher spiritual beings of light. People began asking me to do readings for them, and my clairvoyant abilities increased as I began to see the past lives of those around me, as well as the arc of their present missions here on Earth. I found myself tracking the reasons behind their blocks and traumas and relationships and fears backward through time. For the first four years I did these readings without ever charging money. But in time there was such a demand for my sessions that it began impacting my ability to respond to my photography/advertising clients. And as with all gifts of the Spirit, when we serve from a place of the heart, our gifts have a life of their own. In time my desire to help others allowed me to discover the core wound behind my clients' loneliness, separation, and abandonment issues, and I realized that at the root of all this suffering was our inability to realize that we are never alone and that we have never been abandoned by God. During these readings I also began to see angels around people, wonderful spirit guides who were completely committed to the enlightenment of my clients. Some of these guides were there to help heal families, relationships, or careers. Others were there as sources of inspiration for someone's artistic or creative talents. Some were connected to a person's spiritual mission, while other guides had been part of their spiritual team for many lifetimes. All this made me start to wonder about my own guardian angels, and at one point I realized that while I could see other people's spirit guides quite well, I had no idea about my own. How could I find out who they were? Who could help me with this dilemma? I could think of no one better suited to guide me on this path than Shasta.

SEEING THE UNSEEN

I arrived at Shasta's house apprehensive, but excited. It had been almost five long years since our first encounter, and although I had never approached her for a private session, we had continued to stay in touch. We often crossed paths at the symposiums that I had produced in the Atlanta area on a variety of scientific, paranormal, and metaphysical topics. Was it possible that Shasta would be able to help me make a breakthrough now? If I could see other people's guides so clearly, why couldn't I see my own? Having worked closely with the Vairagi masters for over a decade, I had never questioned who my spirit guides were. I had simply assumed that these masters were my only teachers, but that couldn't be right. Each of us has at least two—and sometimes three— spirit angels or guides who have agreed to help us accomplish our life's goals. Certainly I had the right to know my own allies, didn't I?

Shasta met me at the door of her little cottage and led me inside. We sat in the kitchen, and I laid out my problem. "Why can't I see my own guides?" I asked in frustration. "Especially when I can see everyone else's? I want to know who is helping me from the Otherside!" She listened quietly, then took me by the hand, leading me into the healing room.

"Lie down," she instructed, pointing to the bed. She handed me two large double-terminated crystals, one for each hand, then placed a silk pouch over my eyes. "Now I want you to simply breathe," she instructed, her voice a soothing balm. "I am going to move some energy blocks out of your field, and then we'll see where this takes us." As she began to work, my muscles relaxed, and my mind slipped into a quiet state. I began to see flickering lights floating all around me in my inner vision. The faces of many different kinds of beings appeared and disappeared, as if greeting me in turn. Angels, animals, masters, and even Egyptian divinities floated in and out of my consciousness. Nature spirits and elementals swept in, and I could hear melodies from the higher levels like a choir of angels' voices playing on the radio, its volume moving up and down like a wave. After a while I lost all track of time. Then the separate images stopped, and all I could see was golden light.

I didn't know how much time had passed before Shasta touched me on the hand. She took the two crystals from my palms and slowly lifted the eye pouch. I could vaguely see from the shadows in the room that it was now late afternoon. "Everybody is here," she said in a quiet voice. "The angels, the masters, the fairies, the elementals, the gods and goddesses. The question is who do you want to work with? They are all interested in you."

I sat up slowly blinking. "Really? I saw them. Or at least I think I did. There were a lot of lights."

Shasta smiled. "Yes, I know."

"What do I do now?" I asked, swinging my legs over the side of the bed.

"Go home and call them in. Decide who you want to work with."

"I . . . I only want to work with the highest energy," I said. She helped me up and handed me an orange.

"Eat this before you drive. You are not back in your body yet, and you will need to be grounded to get home." I nodded. *What did she mean, go home and decide who you want to work with? What were my choices? Oh . . .* I guess she had already told me that.

Slowly I walked back to my car, deep in thought; it was now dusk. I sat in the front seat and ate my orange. Then I drove home slowly. Two weeks later my two spirit guides arrived and completely changed my life.

AURIEL AND RIGEL:
THE MOTHER AND FATHER OF CREATION

Their names were Rigel and Auriel, and they told me that they had been with me since the beginning of time. They are aspects of the Divine Father and Mother, and I would like to introduce you to these profound presences now, although we will be encountering them in various ways throughout this book. Auriel is the Mother, and Rigel the Father, of all that lives and breathes. Of course, they have been known by many names throughout the centuries in religions across the world, but no matter what they are called, they are the same eternal Presences at the heart of creation itself.

Rigel appears as a large golden eagle whose wings span the universe. This is doubtless a metaphor for the One who can see into every mind and heart, and yet is above them all. While Rigel communicates to me through both words and form, it is always through the power of direct transmission or frequency that he comes into my field. Many seers have beheld this same transcendent eagle as a symbol of the Divine Father, including mystics within the Native American traditions, as well as the Egyptians, Plato, Carl Jung, and the Yaqui shamans of Central America.

Auriel is the Divine Mother of Love whose sweet energy leads us back to the heart. She first appeared as a moving wave form of light and sound—a fountain of loving pink and gold energies. I could see no defined form when she first appeared, but as the months and years passed, I was to discover that she took endless forms in all the great traditions of the world. "I am the doorway of eternity," she told me, "the White Dove of hope that enters every age as a promise of that which can be. I am the dreams of the holy, and the vision of men of reason. Mine is the blue cloak of daybreak, the bird's song at morning. Mine is the mantle of the evenings and the starlight of Heaven's hem. I am the first thought that ever was, the portal to your own becoming. I am the snowflakes on your frozen lashes and the tears of your sorrow. I am she who is always present—waiting endlessly, loving endlessly, hoping endlessly that my children will awaken."

In the many years that I was to study with her, she always entered my heart with great compassion and kindness. Hers were the tears of the suffering of humanity, and she gave me many discourses about the nature of human pain.

One day she said to me, "Who has told you that your lives were meant for suffering and pain? I have not. Who has told you that you must toil beneath the yoke of sacrifice? I have not." I saw in my inner visions the suffering of humanity and the self-imposed struggle we all place on ourselves every day. But Auriel continued. "It is my will that you rejoice in one another, and share joy as the effervescent sparkle of light shimmering at the fullness of the water's edge. That you honor my fields and crops, my fruits and flowers, and bless them with your energy as they have blessed you with theirs." Her powerful presence seemed to enter my heart and expand it with compassion. I saw vast fields of flowers, orchards, wheat, and corn, and sunlight over golden plains.

"It is my will that you acknowledge the four-footed, the winged, the small and the furry, the hoofed and the clawed, and the tribes of your brothers and sisters who live at your sides. If you could but remember the languages that they speak, you would know who they are beside you—no less, no more, but part of yourselves. These are my other children, as surely as you." I saw a stag appear in the woods with his large antlered head and noble countenance. Then other animals appeared around him—deer, rabbits, raccoons, wolves, bears, pumas, tigers, even elephants, and I knew that many of these animals were going extinct through the greed, brutality, and hunting of man.

"It is my greatest hope that you might learn to live with one another in compassion and tolerance, for you are no longer little children. The squabbles of your adolescence should have been left behind long ago." I knew that the Mother was speaking about the spiritual maturity of our societies that seemed to simply repeat the same patterns over and over again—the same imperialistic governments, the same war mongering, the same tyrannical obsession with greed and negative control that has caused cycle after cycle of self-destruction. She was right—we should have outgrown these games of victim and victimizer long ago.

"There is only one God," she said, "and that God is love. It matters not what you call it. The Source of Sources expresses itself through everything and everyone, coursing through the universe as a sacred sound, filling every vessel. I am that vessel and all that is created moves through me."

THE PORTAL OPENS

Perhaps because of these profound teachers and my own surrendered state, my spiritual gifts made a quantum shift. Now, when I pulled up each of my clients' soul records, I could follow their journeys back through time, tracing the connections between husbands and wives, parents and children, or any individuals who had known each other in the past. I could find the soul-mate agreements that bound them and understand why these individuals were in each other's lives again. I also began to see not only angelic protectors around my clients, but sometimes shamanic animals, creative muses, or even masters. All these were spiritual allies from the Otherside who had come to support my clients as part of their "spirit team."

But on occasion I would see a different kind of guide that I can only describe as a divinity, or a god or goddess. The first time this happened I was in San Diego reading for three lovely, creative women. One of these women was overlit by Aphrodite, the Goddess of Love, a presence well known in the Mediterranean. In the second reading I saw a beautiful Middle Eastern desert goddess who hovered over my female client and told me her name was Ishtar. I saw her walking on the desert sands, and I felt that she had known great loss and pain that somehow had to do with losing her love. She was a protective goddess for tribal people, even men in battle. She showed me her symbols—a crescent moon and the planet Venus—but I had never heard of her before.

The third woman was overseen by a goddess who called herself

Ma'at. She arose from the rich, deep Earth as a primordial principle of the Mother herself, and seemed to come from Africa. Of course, I had heard about Aphrodite in high school, but I had never heard of Ma'at or Ishtar. Each of these goddesses seemed to be a massive benevolent energy with her own symbols, personality, and gifts. *How was it possible, I asked myself, that such beings still existed, unless they lived in a higher realm? Were they some kind of archetypal deities who oversaw human-kind's development? Did they exist independent of human thought, or were they the residual imprint of long-lived extraterrestrial gods or goddesses from our past who had once existed on our planet?* They seemed completely interactive and present with me, but drawing on my own worldview, I could not understand how they could exist in the contemporary world. I realized that I would have to find out more about them when I got back to Atlanta.

THE FEATHER OF MA'AT

When I returned to Atlanta, I made a trip to my local Barnes & Noble. In the bookstore I spread out the books I had collected around me in a circle. They came from a variety of departments. There were coffee-table books on the gods and goddesses of ancient Egypt, Rome, and Greece, and other books on angels, the Great Mother, and related topics. I flipped open the Egyptian coffee-table book, looking for the section on goddesses. Ma'at was the first to appear. With her dark brown skin and deep, wise countenance, the book said that she had come from Nubia. The book opened to the page with her picture, and I looked down, stunned. Here was the spitting image of the Egyptian statue that I had seen all those years earlier in Illumina, the store where I had first met Shasta. One tall feather arose from her head, held in place by a simple headband. "Ma'at, the Goddess of Cosmic Truth," I read beneath the picture: *Hmm . . . What did that mean?*

Next I opened historian Barbara Walker's *Woman's Encyclopedia of Myths and Secrets.* It was a thick book that Shasta had recommended, a veritable encyclopedia of hidden history. Her listings were alphabetical. I flipped to the Ms and found Ma'at. "An Egyptian Goddess and the personification of Truth. The original name is based on the universal Indo-European mother syllable *Ma,* which meant simply 'Mother.'"[6]

Holy cow! I sat back in my chair. *This was an interesting coincidence, to say the least!* Not only did Ma'at represent the pursuit of spiritual truth, but her presence was like a signal leading to the deeper Mysteries.

Figure 3.1. Ma'at is the Egyptian Goddess of Cosmic Truth, who rules all cycles of life, death, karma, and rebirth. (Illustration by Tricia McCannon)

Was Ma'at how we had gotten the original word for mama? *Was Mary's name also derived from this same source? Was Ma'at the Holy Mother herself?* I closed my eyes, recalling the smooth ebony statue I had seen in the store with the two tall feathers extending from her headdress. I summoned up the image of the goddess who had appeared in my reading. She was the quintessential grandmother of wisdom. She arose from the Earth, ancient as time. Ma'at had told me that she was connected with the rhythms of the universe and had shown me a single feather that seemed to represent morality, law, or truth. *Is that what her two feathers had meant?* I continued down the page excitedly. "Ma'at's symbol," I read, "was the feather against which she weighed each man's heart-soul in her underground Halls of Judgment." *There it was! The feather!* I continued to read. "Thus the plume of Ma'at itself became a hieroglyph for truth. The same feathers of truth were worn by other aspects of the Goddess, such as Isis, who was the same lawgiving Mother . . ."[7]

I paused to breathe this in. *Isis? . . . Ma'at was connected to the priestesses of Isis who had called me to join them long ago? What did all this mean?* The memory of the statue of Ma'at rose in my mind. The Goddess of Truth had been there from the beginning! I focused my eyes on the page once again, my mind now racing. I read: "Ma'at's laws governed all three worlds,* and thus she was known as the 'lady of Heaven, queen of the Earth, and mistress of the Underworld.' Ma'at was the lawgiver of archaic Egypt." My heart jumped. *Did the book say anything about Nubia?* In my vision I had seen her arise from the rich soil of Nubia. I read on. The book quoted a writer who compared his own countrymen to the honest Ma'at-worshipping tribes of Nubia. *Holy smokes! There it was!*

Ma'at was apparently deeply involved with the Weighing of the Heart ceremony between lifetimes. On Judgment Day, Egyptians believed that they stood before the throne of Osiris, the Egyptian God of resurrection, and allowed their hearts to be weighed against the feather of truth. If your heart was as light as a feather, then you got

---

*Universal truth rules all three worlds: the Upper World, the Middle World where we live, and the Underworld.

to enter Heaven. But if you still had a heavy heart, an angry heart, or an unforgiving heart, then you had to return to Earth to resolve your karma. This all happened in the Halls of Amenti, the antechamber of Heaven, with the forty-two lords of karma present. As the soul protested its innocence before the Councils of Light, Thoth, the scribe of the gods, wrote the results in the Book of Life. These were some of the things each soul had to declare:

I have not been a man of anger. I have done no evil to mankind. I have not inflicted pain. I have made none to weep. I have done violence to no man. I have not done harm unto animals. I have not robbed the poor. I have not fouled water. I have not trampled fields. I have not behaved with insolence. I have not judged hastily. I have not stirred up strife. I have not made any man to commit murder for me. I have not insisted that excessive work be done for me daily. I have not borne false witness. I have not stolen land. I have not cheated in measuring the bushel. I have allowed no man to suffer hunger. I have not increased my wealth except with such things as are my own possessions. I have not seized wrongfully the property of others. I have not taken milk from the mouths of babes . . .[8]

Holy cow! I couldn't think of anybody who lived that honestly! The Egyptians must have had very high moral standards. I opened a third book. It was called *Angels and Archetypes,* and the table of contents revealed an entire chapter on Ma'at. Below her picture were these words:

Ma'at, the *netert* goddess that personifies the principle of Cosmic Order, the concept by which not only men, but also the gods themselves were governed . . . She represents the embodiment of accuracy, honesty, fairness, faithfulness, authenticity, legitimacy, integrity and justice . . . the essence of rhythm . . . the divine order of the Universe that has reigned since the beginning . . . Ma'at is the motivating force in the Universe that drives us to become conscious, for in essence, the Universe is pure consciousness itself. One who achieves "Double Ma'at" is one who has merged their individual consciousness with Cosmic consciousness.[9]

I sat back, trying to take this in. This was saying that all cosmic order in the universe, symbolized by Ma'at, followed the principles of divine law to bring us back into alignment with the Creator. This meant that all the karmic challenges we go through are all part of the mechanism of Ma'at that will allow each of us to reach mastery someday. Perhaps this goddess had appeared in my life long ago to remind me of something I had forgotten, and this was somehow connected to the priestesses of Isis.

I must call Shasta, I realized. Only she might have the power to help me unravel this puzzle. *Who were the priestesses of Isis? What was it about the gods or the goddesses that was so important? If these beings had lived long ago, how was it possible to interact with them in current time, to have them appear as spirit guides or teachers?* I didn't know. Despite my fear of stepping outside my comfort zone, I knew that it was finally time for me to search for answers.

PART TWO
The Journey

Soul of my soul, Heart of my heart,
I hear you, I long for you, I follow you
Through all the Shadows into the Light.
You are with me, though I know it not.
You have never forsaken me—not once—
Though I have lost my way.
You are the Question and the Answer,
The Song and the Calling,
And if I can only remember who You are,
Then I will remember my Name.

TRICIA MCCANNON

4

The Great Medicine Circle and the Four Gates of Heaven

The Grail of the Feminine urges us to open our minds to a
*   new vision of reality,*
A revelation of all cosmic life as a divine unity . . .
It is to be born into a world lit by an invisible radiance,
Ensouled by Divine Presence,
Graced and sustained by incandescent light and love.

ANDREW HARVEY AND ANNE BARING,
THE DIVINE FEMININE

Five years had passed since I had been to the magical little house in the forest, and I saw as I stepped out of the car that Shasta's cottage had barely changed. The crisp golden leaves of late Indian summer sparkled against the blue sky, and I could feel the pull of the grove's wild beauty calling. I was here to ask Shasta to convene a sacred circle for me, for I was ready to study with her. I felt that for all the knowledge that

I had gained, there were questions that perhaps only she could answer.

I took my time walking to the far side of the house, feeling the sacred energies gathered in the grove. I saw that Shasta had added an herb garden to her vegetable garden beside the house, and from the top of the hill I could see new sanctuaries hidden amid the foliage. Statues of goddesses and arbors of honeysuckle hid secret alcoves. The fire pit that lay at the lowest point of the medicine circle was now half hidden by kudzu, and there was no sign of the three cauldrons I had seen years earlier. I wondered idly what had become of them. I made my way to a cluster of chairs and waited for Shasta to join me. I suspected that she knew why I had called. A flock of butterflies fluttered around me, a symbol of transformation and change. Well, perhaps these butterflies knew more than I did, for whatever happened now would certainly change my life forever.

Shasta came out of the house with two large mugs of tea. She handed me one in silence and led the way down toward the fire pit, toward the medicine circle. She drew me wordlessly to the eastern altar, and we stood before a marble slab that had been raised several feet into the air to create a platform. Upon it stood a life-sized statue of an Asian woman draped in gold. Beside this was a smaller statue of Isis with her outstretched wings, and then, completing the trinity, was a medium-sized statue of Mother Mary. She let me have a moment to breathe it all in, and then she began.

"In the Goddess path all ceremony is done in a sacred circle. That is because the circle is the totality of the all. The circle is not hierarchical. It is cyclical, like the universe. Everything moves in a circle—the seasons, the planets, the constellations in the sky. We are all part of this sacred circle, and this is why sites like Stonehenge and Avebury were laid out in a circle. The path of the circle, the Goddess of the All, links us to the heartbeat of the cosmos." She let these words sink in, and I felt myself falling back into connection with something I had known long ago. "In the sacred language of light, the circle with a cross at the center is the symbol for the soul. It is also the symbol used in astrology for planet Earth, telling us that we are linked to Mother Earth from the very beginning. Native Americans call this the great medicine circle, a symbol for balance and mastery. They believe that all people are flawed in some way; thus the medicine circle, which is connected to the Great Mystery, the Source of all things, gives us a way to come back into balance with ourselves and heal our wounds."

I followed her words carefully. I knew some of this, of course, but I had never heard it put this way. The four arms of the cross represented the four elements, the four directions, and, of course, the four aspects of our natures: physical, emotional, mental, and spiritual. In the union of all four of these elements, mastery is found.

Shasta went on. "When you enter a sacred circle, you begin in the East and travel sunwise or clockwise. The East is the gate of new beginnings, the place of the rising of the sun and of illumination. It is the place of hope where Mary the Mother sits, the Virgin at the beginning of time. It is the place where Horus arises with his great wings of truth, turning the universe. It is the home of the sweet goddesses of love." I nodded, taking in the bowl of pink roses on the open altar. "It is said that long ago, during the time of Atlantis, the Earth spun in the oppo-

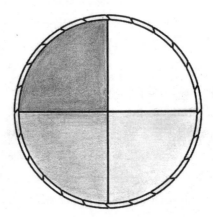

Figure 4.1. The circle with the four quadrants is called a medicine wheel or circle because it is the union of body, emotions, mind, and spirit that allows us to come back into balance and heal our wounds.

site direction, and the sun rose in the western gate, but now we travel the circle sunwise, as the light moves in the sky."

I was not completely surprised by what she said. I had studied the legends of Atlantis, Lemuria, and Tibet, and knew the theories about magnetic pole shifts. Scientists have now discovered that the magnetic poles of our planet have reversed many times during Earth's long, convoluted history. Sometimes this pole reversal is gentle, and sometimes catastrophic. *Was it possible that such reversals had actually caused a change in the rising position of the sun?*

Shasta continued. "There are only a few shamans who can work the wheel counterclockwise, and these are usually Celtic or Native American medicine people. They are *hyokas,* 'shamans who walk backwards,' and can thus unwind karma. I teach my students to travel from east to west in the circle, honoring the natural harmony of life." As I studied the eastern altar, my eyes drank in the red and gold candles, the ribbons on the trees, and the sweet fragrance of roses. I could indeed sense a Presence here. Shasta watched me carefully. I wondered why Mary and Isis were on the same altar.

"Mary and Isis are one," she murmured, as if reading my mind. "These are the sweet Goddesses of compassion and wisdom." I gave her a puzzled look. *Mary and Isis are one . . . just what did that mean?* "Isis is the template for Mary. The first images of Isis holding her son Horus are the templates for the Madonna and Child. Both Isis and Mary are mothers of compassion who brought saviors into the world in a time of darkness."

The idea of a great cosmic play seemed to be at work here, I thought, as if these vast archetypal energies come again and again into the world to act out similar dramas with different characters in different eras. I digested her words without speaking. Then I lifted my chin toward the Asian woman draped in gold. "Who is she?"

"Ah . . . Quan Yin, the lady of boundless compassion. She was born from the tears of an Avalokiteshvara, a bodhisattva from the heavenly realms. Her consort is Father Heaven. He is said to have lived with her

Figure 4.2. Quan Yin, the Goddess of Boundless Compassion, was born from the tears of the most illuminated saints. Her mission, like that of Mary and Isis, is to relieve the suffering of humanity. The dragon symbolizes the conquering of our lower instinctual nature, synonymous with our reptilian brains. Once the serpentine forces of kundalini are mastered, this energy can rise from the base of the spine into the higher spiritual centers, allowing us to travel outside of our bodies through the Great Cosmic Seas. (Illustration by Tricia McCannon)

as the jewel in the lotus." *Oh! She is like Auriel,* I thought, *the Divine Mother of Compassion.* I had heard of the Hindu prayer *Om Mani Padme Hum.* This prayer literally meant, "I salute the jewel within the lotus of the One." Contained within this phrase were also the seed syllables *Ma* for Mother, *Pa* for Father, and *Hu* for human being, and this mantra started with the original seed syllable of creation, *Om.*

Figure 4.3. Aphrodite, the Goddess of Love, arises from the Cosmic Waters at the beginning of time. The lotus blossom, like the seashell, is a depiction of the opening of the Great Cosmic Egg from which the universe is born. (Illustration by Tricia McCannon)

"Isis, Mary, and Quan Yin are the sweet Goddesses of healing who nurture the world," Shasta explained. She then lifted her hands, and her voice rose, softly modulated with power. I felt the energies in the garden shift, and the plants seemed to quiver around us. "Hail Quan Yin, hail Mary, hail Isis." *Were these beings coming into the grove now?* I wondered. "We ask that you bless this one, your daughter, who has come before you seeking today. May you guide her in the right way, and lead her on a path that is right for her and for all whom she touches."

After a long moment Shasta lowered her arms and drew me silently to the next altar. This was the southern gate. The altar had two platforms, one higher than the other, and the bottom one was draped in a red satin cloth. Red candles formed a semicircle of light, around a small globe of the Earth and an empty turtle shell. There were also many sea-shells gathered here, along with the translucent skin of a snake. I didn't understand any of these symbols. Why would anyone have dead animal skins and turtle shells on an altar? "Whose altar is this?" I asked awkwardly.

"Shell Woman's. Turtle Woman's. Gaia's—the Earth herself. The South is the altar of all great goddesses who come from the sea. This is the altar of the ground we stand upon, and it also honors the Earth's oceans. White Shell Woman is the protector of the dolphins and the whales, and of all the animals of the Earth. She lives in the South Seas with the turtle."

A picture of Botticelli's *Birth of Venus* painting arose in my mind. *Was she talking about Aphrodite? What did that have to do with the snake? Was it the snake from the Garden of Eden that had tried to seduce Eve? But if so, what was it doing here in the garden of the Goddess?* My mind was trying to catch up. I lifted my chin. "What is that serpent doing here?"

Shasta smiled. "That's Uatchet Buto [pronounced OO-chat BOO-toe], perhaps the most ancient of all the goddesses. She represents the kundalini energy of the universe. This is the chi that runs up the spine, moving through every one of the body's energy centers until it reaches the forehead, the seat of the Inner Sight. In its untransformed state it is the serpent that must be conquered, concerned with survival issues only. But in its awakened state it is the spiritual initiate who has embraced the kundalini life force and harnessed it for knowledge. Uatchet Buto represents life, death, and transformation—part of the natural cycles of Earth. Like the Ouroboros, or the snake biting its tail, Uatchet Buto symbolizes the alpha and the omega, the beginning and the ending of all things. Egyptian legends say that this goddess existed before all the gods and goddesses put together."

Okay . . . a serpent . . . Well, it was certainly a different interpretation from the Adam and Eve story I had learned in Sunday school, but did that make it any less valid? After all, weren't all these just

Figure 4.4. Uatchet Buto is the kundalini life force of creation. Here she is depicted as the Ouroboros, the snake biting its tale, an ancient symbol that represents the vast cycles of the world ages and the beginning and ending of time. (Illustration by Tricia McCannon)

symbols or parables for the archetypal principles that move through the universe? So I guess the ancients used the snake because it was the only animal that shed its skin while it was still alive. It seemed like a perfect symbol for being born again. Along with raising the kundalini energy through the body, it was one of the most ancient symbols for the initiate's path—life, death, release, and rebirth. And didn't the caduceus, the medical symbol for healing, have two snakes entwined around it? That came from Egypt. I knew it represented the male and female nervous systems that ran up the spine, known in Sanskrit as the *ida* and the *pingala*.

These two currents crisscrossed at each of the seven major chakras of the body, the seven energy centers where the world of Spirit connects with the world of matter. The spiritual masters teach that in order to fully activate our mastery we have to first clean out, then activate all seven chakras. Then we can balance the yin and yang currents within us.* My mind flashed back to the pharaohs. Didn't the rulers of Egypt

---

*The word *chakra* is Sanskrit for "wheel." It refers to the energetic points where our spirit interfaces with matter in our body. There are seven major chakras that run from the base of the spine up to the top of the head, and many minor chakras located in places like the palms of the hands and the soles of the feet.

Figure 4.5. The caduceus has long been a universal symbol for healing and illumination. It represents the sympathetic and parasympathetic nervous systems that travel up the spine on either side of the central nervous system. All three of these must be activated to reach enlightenment.

wear a serpent at the front of their crowns? Maybe they were trying to say that they had activated their kundalini and acquired this mastery. *Hmm . . . Maybe the mystery of the serpent was deeper than I had thought.*

HEALING AND HUMAN BIOLOGY

Next Shasta drew me toward the western gate, and I saw the cat-headed Egyptian goddess that I had glimpsed so long ago in her living room. "What is her name again?" I asked.

"Sekhmet. She is a galactic goddess. She didn't come from our world at all."

Apparently not, I thought to myself, sizing up her strange cat head. She didn't look like anybody I had ever seen. But I could well imagine that there were many kinds of beings on other planets that looked different from us, and why not? Human life could have arisen on other worlds and been blended with other species besides primates. After all, if alien visitation reports are true, then there is an insectoid type of human out there, as well as a reptilian species, and several variations on the human type. Why couldn't there be a strain of feline humans as well?

Shasta raised her brows. "I am a priestess of Sekhmet."

"Oh," I said softly. "Tell me about her."

She smiled quietly, and I wondered just what she was thinking. "Legend tells us that once, long ago, the gods summoned Sekhmet to cleanse our planet of the genetic abominations created by the scientists in Atlantis. When the gods could not subdue the half-human monsters, they asked Sekhmet to do it. According to the stories, she wiped them out and protected Earth; thus she is considered both a warrior and a protectress. Sekhmet was known as a great healer in Egypt, and even today her small temple stands behind the great Temple of Karnack in Luxor, for she is very much alive on the inner planes."

"Do you have this power—to heal, I mean?"

Figure 4.6. Sekhmet is a Fire Goddess who activates the kundalini power of protection and life itself. She is the Egyptian Goddess of Healing and War. (Illustration by Tricia McCannon)

Shasta assumed a cryptic expression. "All priests and priestesses develop some kind of healing ability. This is a natural attribute of women. We are by nature life-givers and nurturers because the Divine Mother lives within us." I wondered then if she was speaking of something hidden within our genetics or merely a principle, but before I could ask, Shasta went on. "The Cosmic Mother has been revered in cultures around the world long before the patriarchical gods were even born, Tricia. This is because each human being's biological origin is always female before it becomes male."

"What?" I raised my eyes in astonishment. *What was she saying?*

"Look it up. I'll show you the references."

"I don't understand," I stammered. "Please say it again."

"Biology has confirmed that every living creature begins as a female. All mammals are biologically female first. Becoming a male is an added hormonal development."[1]

My mind reeled in disbelief. *How was this possible? This was the exact opposite of what we had been taught in the Bible!* In fact, this was one of men's great claims to superiority—that they had been created first! Judeo-Christian theology teaches that Adam was created first in the image of God, and that Eve was taken from Adam's rib, almost like an afterthought. This is one of the many justifications that the male-dominated church has used for centuries to make women feel that they were inferior, and created just to do a man's bidding. If science actually reveals that we all began as biologically female, then the patriarchal religions have been lying all along. They have completely subverted the natural order. What they told us was a fabrication designed to manipulate women for their own political purposes! How could this theology continue to be taught if it contradicted a biological fact?

Shasta was still speaking. "Long ago human beings knew that everything was born of woman, so the Great Mother was honored as the Creator of the all. This is why they called the heavens the Milky Way, the source of the Mother's Milk. They knew that everything emerged from her. Egyptians referred to her as Hathor, the Cow Goddess of

Figure 4.7. Nuit is the Egyptian Goddess of the Night Sky. We travel through the body of her infinite stars when we leave this world and journey into Heaven. (Illustration by Tricia McCannon)

Milk and Honey, or Nuit, a term meaning 'night' in French. Nuit is the Mother of the Starry Skies. It is in her body that we travel after death through the sea of the galaxy. And even before the creation of the heavens, there was Nun, the primordial Ocean of Mercy."

Years later I would discover that this ancient Egyptian description of the Cosmic Ocean is a realm where scientists believe there is no polarity, where atoms are squeezed so tightly that the electrons are pushed out of their orbits and can move around freely, a place beyond all polarity. In Egypt, Nun was this Great Cosmic Ocean from which all being arose. It is the undefined, undifferentiated energy before creation.[2]

Shasta continued. "It is from Mother Earth that everything comes, every piece of wood, coal, iron, or wool—every animal and plant—but our society has forgotten this. When we dishonor the Mother, we dishonor all that holds the universe in balance."

We were now standing at the western gate and I saw a large wooden medicine shield nailed to a post. It was painted black and red, and the altar below was also black. There was a large spiderweb on one side of it. "The West is the place of women," Shasta explained, "the place of hidden power. It is the seat of the secret societies, the Mysteries, all that is hidden, so we paint it black. Like the secrets of wisdom contained within the Black Madonna, it is the vessel of life that is veiled from sight. Although the patriarchy has tried to destroy her, the priestesses of Isis have long been the caretakers of these secrets. This is where the deepest Mysteries were passed from mother to daughter, generation to generation, a vast lineage of underground wisdom."

In later years I was to realize just how true Shasta's words were. The source of all great spiritual traditions flowed from the wisdom cultures of Egypt, India, and China, and as this wisdom spilled out into the world, it had birthed the mystical teachings of the Druids, Mayans, Essenes, Greeks, Therapeutae, Sufis, Magi, Kabbalists, and the Gnostic Christians and Rosicrucians. It had also influenced the inner teaching circles of the Native Americans. But as the Age of Darkness fell, this secret stream had been nearly strangled by the church. The world had been steeped in religious wars, book burnings, and ignorance, and the deeper teachings had been forced underground. Long ago the wise teacher Thoth, God of wisdom in ancient Egypt, had predicted this fall in a Hermetic writing called *The Lament:*

There will come a time when it will be seen that in vain have the Egyptians honored the divinity with pious minds and with assiduous service. All their holy worship will become inefficacious. The gods leaving the earth will go back to heaven; they will abandon Egypt; this land, once the home of religion, will be widowed of its gods and left destitute. Strangers will fill this country, and not only will there no longer be care for religious observances but, a yet more painful thing,

Figure 4.8. Thoth, the God of Wisdom, holds a book of knowledge in his lap and a merkaba field and ankh—the symbol of eternal life—in his hands. He sits upon the Eye of Horus, or the Eye of Illumination, in front of a full and crescent moon, one of his many symbols. (Illustration by Tricia McCannon)

> it will be laid down under so-called laws, under pain of punishments, that all must abstain from acts of piety or cult towards the gods . . .[3]

Who would preserve this knowledge once it was lost? I wondered. *How could we reclaim it today?* I realized then that there had to be people like Shasta out there, people like me—souls who were actually the reincarnation of ancient initiates—alive in our time. They had begun to awaken their own memories and recapture what had been lost through all the centuries of death and destruction. Was this the reason that the priestesses of Isis had called me years ago?

Over time I was to learn that as the destruction of each great civilization approached, the Mystery Schools sent initiates into other lands to set up centers of wisdom in places around the globe. But again and again the powers of politics, greed, and ignorance had sought to wipe out these streams of wisdom, so that now all that remained were the broken fragments of legend and crumbling stone. I knew intuitively that this deeper wisdom was somehow woven into the heart of the Goddess, and if we only had the keys to decode her symbols, we could awaken to the wisdom behind them. But in those early years I did not yet know the language of hermetics that had been taught by the masters, nor did I realize that there were other spiritual initiates who still honored the Divine Mother, even in the mystical orders of patriarchal societies.*

THE LAST GATE

I followed Shasta solemnly to the last gate, trying to absorb the truth behind her words. "We are now in the north gate, the place of the teachers," she said. A white wolf pelt lay over the cool white alabaster slab. A bleached cow skull rested on top of it and statues of white angels flanked it on all sides. I was deep in my own thoughts and did not speak. After a moment Shasta began. "The North is the place of the teachers. It is the home of the masters, the wise ones who oversee our planet. It is the home of Sophia, the Goddess of Wisdom, and Ma'at, the Goddess of Truth. It is the abode of the arctic wolf and of White Buffalo Calf Woman, the Star Woman who brought balance to the native peoples. It was she who taught them how to commune with the spirit world in the sweat lodge. She who taught them to dance their

---

*Examples of these are the mystical Sufi, whose religious symbol is the winged heart, a statement about the power love has to release us from our suffering. The heart has always been a symbol of the Divine Mother. Other examples are the Rosicrucians, a sect of mystical Christians whose symbol is a rosy heart fixed upon a cross. The rose is a symbol of the eternal soul trapped on the grid of time and space. It is the power of the Goddess of Love that releases us from this cross of matter.

prayers around the Tree of Life in the sundance ceremonies, and she who brought the sacred pipe, or *chanupa,* to the tribes."

"Who is White Buffalo Calf Woman?" I asked. The name seemed strange and mysterious to me.

"The Star Woman who teaches the balance of life—that all beings are part of the same great circle, *O mitakuye ayasin*—all my relations—the four-footed, the winged, the tree people, the stone people, the balance of all kingdoms. She knows that we must honor the balance of the wheel of life, or we will destroy ourselves."

I absorbed the power of these words in silence. When I did not speak, Shasta took me by the hand. "Come, let us talk now, let us step through the pillars of initiation and take our seats in the place of eternal silence." She led me quietly through an archway that I had not noticed before. It was covered in greenery, and I imagined that in the spring it would be full of roses. We settled onto a nearby bench, close enough to the circle that I could still feel the pulsing of the wheel. "Now, Tricia," she said softly, "tell me what it is that I can do for you."

"I am ready to study with you," I said without preamble.

Shasta sat in silence for a few minutes, choosing her words with care. "Good. Then I will convene a circle. I teach only women, you know." I was not surprised. "This will change our relationship," she said solemnly. "I will no longer be your friend. I will be your teacher. I know that you have been trained in other paths, but you will become a novice to the Goddess now. Then, if you wish, you may take your vows to become a priestess a year and a day after the training is complete." I nodded, taking this in. "We will begin in late winter and go for four full seasons. How else can you learn to live the life of a priestess if you do not mark the yearly changes?" The question was rhetorical. "We will also meet on the eight High Holy Days. I will give you a schedule." Shasta stood up and embraced me then, kissing me on each cheek. I could already feel our relationship shifting. "In the meantime, you might want to take some time away from your busy schedule to do a little bit of research. You're certainly going to need it."

5

The Circle Convenes

To the one who comes forth from heaven, "Hail!" do we say . . .
Loftiness, greatness, reliability are hers, as she comes forth radiantly in the evening.
A holy torch that fills the heavens; Her stance is like the Moon and the Sun . . .
On Earth she is enduring, mistress of the lands . . .

EXULTATION OF INANNA,
FROM THE SUMERIAN CITY OF ERECH

February 2. Brigit's Day. I could just make out Shasta's cottage against the gloaming indigo twilight sky as I parked on the dead-end street that led to her house. Inside the windows I could see candlelight winking through the windows. Tonight was the first meeting of the sacred circle, and I was nervous. As I made my way slowly up the shadowed walk onto the wide wooden porch, I could feel my heart beating in my chest. I opened the front door to see a cheerful fire blazing in the fireplace of the living room, and candles illuminating the altars in the corners of the room. In front of the merry crackle of the winter's fire were a dozen women seated in a circle on the floor. They looked up as I entered and smiled, and I wondered whom I might know in this circle. I took my seat quietly on the large open cushion that was waiting for me, feeling the deep magic of the house enveloping us in its arms.

"You are in perfect time," Shasta said, indicating that we should all go around the circle and introduce ourselves. My eyes registered the long feminine skirts and shawls that many of the women wore, but I was dressed in leggings, boots, and a sweater, my normal garb for a winter's day. This show of graceful femininity was quite a change from the male-dominated world of photography and advertising that I was used to in my daily life. Even as a clairvoyant who did readings for others, I always dressed in a practical nongirly way. Like many people I knew, my life seemed to straddle two worlds—my Clark Kent world of photography, art direction, and advertising and my spiritual world, where I helped people in need through my readings.

As I entered Shasta's living room I counted thirteen women in all—twelve around the one teacher. That was the same number that Jesus had used, putting himself at the center of the circle like the sun in the middle of the twelve signs of the zodiac. *Interesting coincidence,* I reflected, wondering if the number of women gathered here had been deliberate or a divine act of providence.

As the ladies began to introduce themselves I learned that these were intelligent, articulate women who ranged from homemakers to directors of multinational companies. There was Meg, a short, slender blonde who worked as a liaison in international affairs in Washington, D.C.; Claudia, a stylish makeup artist from Los Angeles with an Emmy Award under her belt; Susan, a sexy sales representative; Donna, an accountant; Alexis, a shy tomboy with freckles; Emerald, a large, overweight head secretary at a law firm; and Sara, a bright massage therapist and singer. These were all smart, attractive women who had been on their own spiritual journeys for many years.

SOPHIA, ISIS, AND MARY

When we had finished with our introductions, Shasta greeted us warmly. "Welcome to the Circle of the Goddess. Tonight we begin a journey into the heart of the Mysteries. This path is a journey of self-discovery not only about ourselves, but about the hidden history of our planet. The Goddess teaches a path of the heart, a path that all life is sacred, and that the intelligence that moves through the universe moves through each of us as well. This path honors the living energies of the Earth and the spiritual beings behind the cosmos. It honors the energetic connections between all people, animals, and how we are all linked together in a symbiotic web of light."

As she spoke I could feel that connection with my inner senses, not only to the women in the circle, but to all the people I loved, no matter where they lived across the planet.

"Throughout the centuries, the Goddess has been known by many different names in many different cultures. In Christianity she is called Mary, the great mother of compassion. In Judaism she is known as Sophia, the Goddess of Wisdom. In India, China, and Japan, she is Lakshmi, the Mother of Generosity who dwells in the Great Cosmic Egg with Vishnu, her eternal mate. She is also Sarasvati, the Goddess of Creativity, and Durga, the vanquisher of demons. She is named Parvati, the Mother of the Universe, and Kali, the great transformer who rules the cycles of death and rebirth. In China she is embodied in Quan Yin, the bodhisattva of children, and in Japan she is Amaterasu, the Goddess of the Sun. These are only a few of her many faces."

Shasta looked around the circle. Our eyes were wide with wonder. I had never even heard of most of these goddesses, although I had seen pictures of a few of them.

"Honoring the Goddess was the first theology of our ancestors. They believed that the Creator of the universe is female, but in the last few thousand years people have forgotten who she is, and so now the world has fallen out of balance. Our path is about remembering her place in creation and restoring balance to the world." Emerald and Meg were nodding. "The path of the Goddess teaches us to attune to the invisible world of Spirit, and the connections behind all that we see. To become a priest or a priestess, a healer or a shaman, is to learn to walk between the worlds, to become a mediator between the realms of Spirit and the realms of the mortals. It is not about leaving the physical worlds behind or denigrating the worlds of matter. It is rather about seeing the sacred worlds of Spirit beneath the visible world and rejoicing in it. This physical body is the vessel we are given in this life to communicate with the 'seen and unseen' forces of the Divine, and long ago it was believed that the female was the natural mediator between Earth and sky, the physical and the spiritual realms. Thus we are about establishing a conscious partnership with the Divine, and learning to take responsibility for our own lives. In the end this path is also about discovering the divine spark within every creature and within every one of you." Her words fell into a deep place within me.

"The Goddess gives birth to all that lives, and she takes back into herself all that ever was. She shows us the cyclical patterns of life and regeneration, and she is forever in a state of change. Thus the Indians called her Changing Woman, for she rules all the cycles of time. We women have all the same characteristics as the Goddess. We bleed, we give birth, we nurture the unborn, we tend to the dying, and we celebrate the many natural transitions of life."

Yes, I thought, birthdays, graduations, funerals, and the birth of children were all things that my mother had honored, even though I sometimes forgot them. And holidays—my mother was the first to call the family together around Thanksgiving, Christmas, or Easter dinners, or to send a thoughtful card or a gift for a nephew's graduation.

"In Egypt she was known as Isis, She of Ten Thousand Names and Ten Thousand Faces, the female *I am* principle of the Great Mysteries. Her true name was Au Set, and her husband was Au Sar, the ancient name for Osiris. Isis was also called Iahu, a term meaning 'high dove,' and Isa, the first of all created beings. She was a sister, daughter, mother, wife, a widow, and a queen. When she fled from the dark forces that swept Egypt during the reign of Set, her evil half-brother, she even became a refugee. Then, along with her young son Horus, Isis became the savior goddess whose cunning and insight helped to rescue Egypt from 350 years of darkness."

Our faces were rapt with attention. We could almost see the images that her words painted, and I felt that Isis was so real, so easy to relate to, as if she could have been any one of us. "Isis lies within every woman, and every woman is Isis, for we each have the potential to experience all these aspects of ourselves—daughter, sister, lover, wife, mother, and wisdom keeper. Isis established the first Mystery Schools in Egypt, and then, assisted by her father Thoth, her husband Osiris, and later her courageous son Horus, these teachings were brought to other lands and cultures. When Osiris was murdered by Set, Isis brought up Horus in secret so that he would one day be strong enough to challenge his uncle. Those who followed her became known as the 'Sons of the Widow,' one of the titles still used by Freemasons, even today."

The Sons of the Widow . . . I pondered the depth of what that phrase implied. It seemed to exude the sorrow of her loss, and the spirit of her husband as an eternal presence beside her.

"The spiritual temples of Isis taught that there is one great Creator behind all the many faces or facets of the gods and goddesses, and that the divine spark that dwells within the gods dwells within us as well. The Mystery Schools taught that it is the balance between the male and the female that brings us to mastery. If we neglect either side of our natures, we cannot achieve it. But because the Divine Mother has been forgotten for so many centuries, this garden is dedicated to Her." The light from the fire danced across her face as we drank in her words.

"For over seven thousand years Isis was worshipped in temples across the world, from Egypt to Britain, Rome to Turkey. She was the faithful wife, the courageous mother, the great queen, the gifted healer, the wise teacher, and the great civilizer. And for the last two millennia she has continued to be honored as Mary Magdalene, another widow once married to a great world savior."

A collective gasp echoed through the room. *Mary Magdalene? What did she have to do with Isis?* "As you will learn, Mary the Magdala, or Mary the Great, was trained as a priestess of Isis in the temples of Egypt. The knowledge of who she really was, the female equivalent or partner of Christ, was forced underground by the patriarchy, although Jesus had called her the 'Apostle who knew the all.'" All of us in the circle seemed to be holding our breath. "In all the great temples of wisdom, there were always two levels of learning—the outer or lesser Mysteries, and the inner or greater Mysteries. In the Christian teachings Peter was entrusted with the outer Mysteries, while Mary Magdalene was the teacher of the greater ones. But these teachings of balance between the masculine and the feminine—and her role—were suppressed by the orthodox church. And because of that suppression, the true secrets of mastery are largely unknown to us today."

You could feel the entire circle exhale, and my mind began to race. At the time when I first began to study with Shasta in 1985, the Gospel of Philip had not yet been published, nor had many of the hidden gospels, discovered in the writings of the Dead Sea Scrolls, been published. Margaret Starbird's *Woman with the Alabaster Jar* (1993) and Dan Brown's *Da Vinci Code* (2004) had not yet been released. These books examined the revelations that Mary Magdalene had been the wife or spiritual companion of Jesus and had been entrusted to impart his deeper wisdom in the years after the crucifixion. In the Gospel of Philip we read about how Jesus used to kiss Mary on the mouth, and that his love for her was deep and abiding.

> Of all his disciples he loved his companion, Mary Magdalene, the most, and kissed her. The disciples asked, "Why do you love her most?" He answered. "When a blind and sighted man are both in darkness they are equal. When light dawns, he who can see will know the light: he is who is blind will stay in the dark."[1]

Yet at that time this was a totally new concept, and largely unknown to the world. My mind grappled to understand the meaning of Shasta's words. "Like Isis, Mary Magdalene became the Black Madonna, the hidden Goddess of Wisdom who must reemerge so that the world might return to balance." *I will have to learn more about this,* I thought, wondering how I could begin to discover the hidden history of the Magdalene. Later I would learn that the "Sons of the Widow" was a title used by the early Gnostic Christians, followers of Jesus and Mary Magdalene. Both Isis and Mary Magdalene had been widowed through the loss of their enlightened husbands.

Shasta lifted her chin, directing Emerald to stir the fire. The popping of the logs sounded loud in the chilly room. When the fire had begun to burn brightly again, Shasta resumed. "We will speak more of these subjects in the months to come, but tonight we begin our year of study on the Eve of Candlemas, one of the eight High Holy Days of the year." Shasta picked up an unlit box of candles beside her, passing it around the circle. We each took a candle and then passed it to the next person. "In the Celtic world February second was the Festival of Brigit, a Triple Goddess with three major forms—the maiden, the mother, and the matron. Brigit governed the arts of healing, knowledge, agriculture, and smithcraft, and she was also the patron Goddess of Writing. Her temples at Kildare in Ireland had clear running springs, and a fire that was constantly maintained in the temples by the priests and priestesses, like the ever-burning shrines of Vesta, the vestal virgins in Rome. This fire was dedicated to truth, illumination, and knowledge."

Shasta lit her candle, and then reached over and touched the flame to the wick of the candle that Claudia held. Claudia offered its bright fire to Meg, passing the light around the circle. "Later when the Catholics could not get rid of Brigit, the bride, her history was rewritten by the church. She was turned into a Christian saint named Bridget, and nunneries were set up in her name. Worship of her became mixed with worship of both Mary the Mother and Mary Magdalene, since both women had spent time in Britain among the Druids. Bridget, the

Figure 5.1. Brigit, the Celtic Goddess of Illumination, governs healing, smithcraft, agriculture, and knowledge. She is therefore a Triple Goddess, who is associated with both fire and water. Her major sanctuaries at Kildare, Ireland, kept the eternal flame of wisdom alive for centuries. Later this same divinity became known as Hestia in Greece and Vesta in Rome. Her shrines were attended by the six vestal virgins who were entrusted to keep the fires of illumination alight for all of humanity. These fires were extinguished by order of the Catholic Church in 382 CE. (Illustration by Tricia McCannon)

bride, became known as the Queen of Heaven, mother of my sovereign, prophetess of Christ, and mother of Jesus. Like the two Marys, Bridget was both a bride and a mother."

The flame had almost reached me. I touched my unlit candle to Sara's and watched the living flame leap to my wick. "Bridget's symbols are the sacred flame of illumination and the waters of eternal healing, symbols that were also sacred to Isis." Shasta looked around the circle at the illuminated faces of the women. "Tonight, we light these candles for them—for Brigit, Isis, Mary, and Mary Magdalene, the hidden brides whose light must be rekindled in the world."

I had heard of St. Bridget in England. I wondered if she was really Isis the widowed bride, and if she had become Mary Magdalene, the hidden bride of Jesus. But whoever she had been originally, the church had rewritten her history, and through the repetition of her story, her original identity had been subsumed. It seemed as if the old adage, "If you can't beat 'em, adopt 'em" was at work here. Or in this case, they had seized the energies of the existing deity and pretended that it was their own. Later I would learn that this is exactly what the church had done with many of the ancient deities and temples, having seized over five hundred temples to the ancient Mother across Britain, France, Italy, Greece, Germany, Spain, and Portugal. They had even done this in Egypt and throughout the Mediterranean, using the original temple locations where the ley lines of the Earth crossed, to harness their power for themselves and rename them in the new religion.[2] Most of these centers had been dedicated to the Mother of the All, like Chartres Cathedral in France, once a place of worship for Isis and Horus. Now they were dedicated to Mary and Jesus, or to Mary Magdalene. Well, at least they still acknowledged the sacred feminine, I thought, even if they had maligned it. I reflected on how Brigit's holiday fell in the winter season of darkness when native peoples must have despaired of ever seeing the sun again. Brigit was the bringer of hope and light. Perhaps now, when the world has forgotten the light of the feminine face of God, we could help her to return.

Shasta was speaking again. "We light candles to Brigit as a way of affirming that, despite the seeming darkness, we believe that light and love and truth will return, and that all the people of the Earth will one day awaken from their spiritual slumber." It seemed to me that our tiny flames symbolized the hope of women everywhere that there would soon come a time when women were not beaten, marginalized, or oppressed. Our candles in that tiny room were like the kindling of hope that the light would dawn once again for women across the world, and with it healing would come to the Earth.

"Let us go around the circle now and share a blessing for the world."

Claudia spoke first. "I just wish that people were kinder to one another." We took a breath. *That would be nice,* I thought. Kindness and tolerance were not so easy to come by.

Meg lifted her candle. "I wish that women could be treated fairly across the world, not made to hide their faces with burkas and face veils, and be forced to have clitorectomies."

I had heard of this barbaric practice among the Muslim nations. Many men in Africa and the Middle East continued to force their daughters to have their sex organs of pleasure surgically removed so that they would only be good for serving the man's pleasure, not their own. It was a horrible custom, and it took away a woman's enjoyment of sex. Furthermore, they had convinced the older women to do it to their own daughters as if it were for their own good. *Barbaric!*

Sara spoke next. "If I could wish anything, it would be to put an end to sexual slavery. Children are sold into slavery every day across the world, and women are kidnapped and forced to become prostitutes to serve men and then die. This has got to stop!"

Holy smokes! This was getting deep. As bad as things sometimes seemed for women in "free" countries, they were a million times worse for women in other parts of the world.

Emerald spoke next. "I just want to get equal pay for equal work, if you know what I mean." We all laughed. Leave it to a legal secretary to bring things back to basics.

Susan spoke next. "I would just like to offer my blessings to all the women who have been abused by men through domestic violence—the runaway girls, the beat-up wives, and the girlfriends who are too afraid to leave their boyfriends because they don't have enough self-esteem." Yes, I knew that statistics show that a woman is raped somewhere in North America every thirteen seconds, and that does not include the countries where women are more oppressed.[3] Statistics from the U.S. Department of Justice show that intimate-partner homicides make up 40 to 50 percent of all murders of women in the United States.[4]

I took a breath. Now it was my turn, and I wasn't even sure what I wanted to say. I had always been the tomboy in my parents' house and had refused to let myself be defined by what being "just" a woman meant. "I would like to give a blessing to people like Shasta, who are carrying this ancient knowledge forward and who are here to share it with us today."

I know my words were lame next to all the amazing things that the other women had said, but they just felt right to me. If Shasta were not around to make us aware of another perspective, then we might not even realize that the things that were happening to women in the world were essentially wrong. This information was critical for us to awaken. I barely heard what the other women said as we completed our ritual. When we were done, we put our candles into holders at the center of our circle, then took a deep breath.

"Tonight I wish to share some of the precepts of the Goddess path," Shasta said. "As you begin to examine your own belief systems, you may want to consider these." Several of the women pulled out notebooks, but Shasta stopped them. "No, just take this in and let it live within you." We put our pencils down. "First, the path of the Goddess teaches us that we are each responsible for our own spiritual development. You are responsible for deciding who or what the Divine is for you, and forming a relationship with that Presence. No one can do this for you but yourself. Like all relationships, this takes time and effort, but you will find that what you put into it is what you will get out of it. The more time you spend in nature, in contemplation, or in self-discovery, the more quickly you will grow. This means that the path of enlightenment is up to you." I nodded. I had already discovered that the constant chatter of our daily lives continually tried to pull us into mayhem and distraction. By creating an altar in my home, I was reminded to spend more time cultivating this active connection with Spirit.

Shasta continued. "The path of the Goddess teaches us that all things contain a spark of the infinite, and thus all beings are sacred. Since consciousness can communicate with consciousness, each part of the whole can communicate with every other part, whether we are talking about a plant, an animal, a rock, or the elements. These parts often cooperate with one another to accomplish very specific ends, like the spirit of the herbs for healing or incense for sacred ceremony. Our thoughts can interface with everything around us—the stars, the moon, the Earth, the elements. By honoring their sacred gifts, they can assist us in our journey. This is an interactive process." She paused to look at us. "Are you following me?" We nodded, afraid to interrupt her train of thought.

"The path of the Goddess also embraces the belief that consciousness survives beyond death, and that nothing of Spirit is ever really lost. Matter converts to energy, and back again, the fundamental discovery of physicist Albert Einstein—$E = mc^2$. We grow, we evolve, we change, and yet as souls we are eternal. This is the wisdom of Changing Woman, who rules all the cycles of life. When we die, we open a door into another dimension, and we pass into it. When we are born, we open a door into this world, and we return to live in a physical body. This was taught within the Eleusian Mysteries of Greece. The lesser Mysteries were dedicated to the Divine Mother and Daughter, Demeter and Persephone, just as the second level of the Mysteries were dedicated to the Father and Son. Do any of you know the story of Demeter and Persephone?"

Shasta looked around the circle. Several of the women shook their heads. *Wasn't this the story of how the Greeks explained the four seasons?* I thought. In fall and winter Persephone descended into the Underworld. Then in spring and summer she returned to her mother Demeter, who was so happy to have her daughter back that spring came into bloom.

"Myths and stories are tales used by the ancients to encode a deeper level of knowledge because even if the meaning got lost, the story would be remembered. While the uninitiated know only the surface meaning, the initiated understand the real significance behind the legend. So when we seek to understand a Goddess or her wisdom, we begin by learning her story. In this tale, it is also helpful to know that Persephone was also called Koré [pronounced CORE-ā], or Kernel, the small seed that falls from the wheat's shaft, the seed that is the innocent virgin of potential that lies inside of us, the kernel that comes from the Tree of Life."

Hmm . . . the Tree of Life . . . A subject I would have to explore in more depth.

"In the Greek story, Persephone, the daughter of Demeter, was out in the fields picking flowers one day when suddenly the ground opened up around her. Hades, the lord of the Underworld, emerged with his golden chariot and twelve black horses. Swooping up the innocent maiden, Hades carried her down into the Underworld. Demeter, not knowing where her daughter had gone, searched everywhere, but could not find her. Over time, she grew sick with worry, so the plants began to die. For one full year the Earth fell into drought, and eventually even the gods themselves were suffering. They petitioned Demeter to bring back the bounty of the Earth, but without Persephone, Demeter had no reason to bring back the Earth's bounty.

"Eventually, Thoth, or Hermes, the Greek God of wisdom, told Demeter that Persephone was in the Underworld, and Demeter demanded that Hades release her. But because her daughter had eaten six red pomegranate seeds during her year of captivity, the gods decreed that she must remain in the Underworld for six months of the year. The other six months she could return to her Mother in Heaven." Shasta looked around the circle. "So what is the meaning of this story?"

We all exchanged glances. The only thing that I could think

Figure 5.2. Demeter helps her daughter Persephone to escape Hades in the Underworld with the assistance of Thoth/Hermes, messenger of the gods. (Illustration by Tricia McCannon)

of was what I had been taught in high school—this was how our ancestors had explained the seasons. Some of the other women made halfhearted suggestions, but I could see from Shasta's stillness that we had not decoded its meaning. At last she sighed. "This is a meta-phor for each of us, a parable about our cycles of rebirth." *Rebirth. What did she mean?* "Half the time we live in Heaven with God the Mother. The other half of the time we descend into the physical

worlds and forget who we are." *Ah!* This was a metaphor for the evolution of the soul!

"Our world is the realm of light and shadow, the Underworld, a
land of illusion and confusion. We are living in the Underworld today.
When we return to our Mother, the Queen of Heaven, we return to the
realms of celestial light."

Oh! I had never understood this parable before because I had always
thought of God as male. Wow! It had been right in front of me the
whole time!

"What do the pomegranate seeds represent?" Claudia asked.

Shasta looked around the room. "Does anyone have any ideas?"

Were they good seeds or bad? I wondered. *Was Persephone supposed to*
eat them or not? At last Shasta answered. "They are the seeds of karma
that each of us sows when we come into this world of shadows." This
took a moment to sink in. "The seeds remind us that we can trap ourselves in this world through fear and desire, and thus we must return
to be reborn on the wheel of life." Donna and Alexis shifted in their
seats, perhaps thinking of actions that had bound them to the wheel.
"The seeds are sweet, but they can also bind us to the great wheel of
Awagawan, the Wheel of Life, Death, and Rebirth." She let a full minute go by while we all digested this.

Shasta unwound herself from the floor. "Now let us get up and
dance. We will dance our joy that we are here on Earth at this time
and that we are waking up. Let us experience the sweetness of life without being bound to the wheel. So in this ceremony, we will return the
pomegranate seeds to the center, symbolizing our liberation from past
karma." Slowly we all got to our feet. Shasta picked up a basket of rattles and passed them around. Then she turned on some music. I took a
rattle and began to dance, not sure what I was doing. But as the music
seeped into my blood, I begin to move into an altered state. We spun in
circles around the room as the chant moved over us:

*Dissolve the seeds of time and space, return them to the light
with grace.*

*Remember who we've always been, reclaim the Soul that lies
within.*

*Bring light into the worlds of form, that who we are might
be reborn.*

I felt the spirits of other dancers, time out of mind, who had been here before us.

Finally, Shasta brought us into a sacred circle again when the dance was over, and we laced our arms around one another's shoulders. "Tonight is a good beginning. In the months ahead I encourage each of you to learn more about how the Divine Mother and her history has been hidden from the modern world. We will meet again in four weeks' time, just before the season of Eostara, the ancient Mother of Rebirth, the time of new beginnings. In the meantime, I suggest you do some reading and find some answers for yourselves."

I looked around the circle, feeling blessed to be among such wonderful sisters of light. "In the Goddess tradition," Shasta said, "we close our circles by saying, 'The Circle is open, but unbroken. Merry meet, merry part, and merry meet again. Blessed be.'"

6

Rewriting
Religious History

∽ᔕᔕᔕ∽

The ancient God of Israel is harsh and relentless . . .
Israel should bring forth a God whose heart is not a jealous
  heart,
and whose memory of their shortcomings is brief:
one who would not avenge Himself upon them even to the
  third and fourth generation.

KAHLIL GIBRAN, JESUS THE SON OF MAN

I had no idea what the other women might study, but for me, since
my roots lay in Christianity, I decided to try to find out more about
how the Goddess had gotten lost in my religion. Yes, of course I knew
about Mary, the Holy Mother, and the badly judged Mary Magdalene,
but I couldn't figure out how or why the Jews had become so patriarchal, especially since there were so many wonderful Jewish people living in the world today, and so many thriving, balanced cultures in the

Mediterranean at the time the Hebrews settled there. But since Judaism was the culture that Jesus had been born into, and his apostles were largely Jewish, I knew that Judaism had heavily influenced the version of Christianity that has been transmitted to us today.

I figured one of the best places to start was an objective review of Jewish monotheism. After all, its stories were in the Old Testament and make up over half the Bible. Today with the contributions of many highly trained archaeologists, linguists, historians, and scholars, much has been uncovered about the origins of Jewish history that contradicts the events recorded in the Old Testament. So in this chapter, we want to first take a look at who wrote the Old Testament, then begin to examine the historical evidence for its claims.

THE TIME LINE OF THE
OLD TESTAMENT WRITINGS

First, biblical scholars now know that most of the books of the Old Testament were not compiled for at least five hundred to seven hundred years after the Exodus took place, circa 1250 or 1300 BCE. This dating is based on an analysis of linguistic dialects of Hebrew used in the various centuries, the dates of events in the passages, and a comparative review of historical events happening in the area at the time. According to biblical scholars, the Old Testament stories were continually edited until about 100 BCE, when the Jewish canon finally settled into a more stable set of beliefs, stories, and religious practices.[1] This was a huge surprise to me. I had always thought that the Old Testament had been written a thousand years earlier.

While there are a host of archaeologists and historians who weigh in on this subject, the consensus is that the first possible period when these books could have been written was just before, or just after the Jewish exile in 586 BCE. Some historians, such as Morton Smith, place the bulk of the Old Testament writings as late as 500 BCE, while others, such as William Albright, assign very late dates to many of these writings, placing Chronicles as late as 400 BCE, Ecclesiastes in the 200s BCE, and the writing of books such as Proverbs, Isaiah, Ezekiel, Habakkuk, Song of Songs, Jubilees, and parts of Daniel between 600 and 200 BCE.[2] Traditional history tells us that northern Israel, whose capital was Samaria, fell to the Assyrians in 722 BCE, while southern Judea, the location of King Solomon's Temple, fell to the Babylonians in 586 BCE. This means that most of the Old Testament books were created sometime between 750 and 200 BCE. So the early accounts of Genesis, Exodus, and the Jewish settlements in the land of Canaan would have been written some five hundred to nine hundred years after the actual events they chronicle took place!

Like so many other people across the world, I had always assumed that the first five books of the Bible were written by Moses at the time of the Exodus. After all, they are called the Five Books of Moses, implying that they were written by Moses himself during his forty years of wandering in the desert. But this is not true. These first five books of the Old Testament—Genesis, Exodus, Leviticus, Numbers, and Deuteronomy—were written in various stages and political climates over a period of about seven hundred years after the events they relate. Together these five books are called the Pentateuch, and they also compose the Jewish Torah, covering key events like the creation of Adam and Eve, the story of the Great Flood, the genealogy of Abraham, Joseph in Egypt, and, of course, the famous Exodus from Egypt. But as the majority of biblical scholars now acknowledge, the Pentateuch was not written by Moses at all and is now believed to have been created at least four to five centuries after Moses lived.[3] Hebrew scholar and biblical historian Richard Friedman gives us a glimpse into how scholars arrived at their understanding of the dates of the Bible's composition through linguistic methods.

> The method that produced this picture has come to be known as Higher Criticism and the picture itself has come to be known as the Documentary Hypothesis. Its root idea is that the Torah was

not written by one person, Moses, but was a product of several source works that were combined by editors to form the Five Books of Moses.

The four largest of these source works are known classically by the symbols J, E, D, and P. The works that are known as J and E have been regarded as the earliest, written in the tenth to eighth century B.C.E.; D comes next in the late seventh century; and P has been regarded as the latest, from the sixth or fifth century.[4]

This model is now being taught at universities and seminaries, and many priests, rabbis, and ministers are familiar with it. Scholarly analysis of the Pentateuch has revealed that about 60 percent of it was written by two separate authors whom researchers now refer to as J and E. The J material uses *Jehovah* or *Yahweh* as the name for God, while the E material uses the term *Elohim*. The term *El* means "Shining One," while *Elohim,* the plural form, is literally translated as "the Shining Ones, or the gods."[5] *El* is a suffix that can be found in the names of angels such as Gabri-el, Rapha-el, Micha-el and Uri-el, revealing that all these heavenly messengers were part of a band of "Shining Ones," large beings with a radiant countenance who appeared as messengers of the gods.

The Hebrew names *Jehovah* and *Yahweh* are both derived from the same four-consonant tetragrammaton, *IHVH* or *YHWH,* depending on which reference book one reads, which is Jehovah's name without the vowels (*I* or *Y* is used here instead of *J* since there was no *J* in the Hebrew language at that time). By placing various vowels between these consonants, we transform the tetragrammaton into both *Yahweh* and *Jehovah*.[6] Hebrew mystics tell us that these four letters represent the four directions, the four elements, the four races, and the four corners of the world. They are also abbreviated symbols for the four divine elements, which the Kabbalah, the mystical writings of the Jews, tell us are an intrinsic part of the deity. These four elements are Hokhma (Wisdom), Binah (Understanding), Tiferet (Beauty), and Malkhut

(Kingship). Wisdom is identified with the Father, Understanding with the Mother, Beauty with the Son, and Kingship with the Daughter. These four divine attributes form the Kabbalistic tetrad.[7]

Biblical historian Richard Friedman, professor of Hebrew at the University of California in San Diego, tells us that most scholars believe that the author of the J (Jehovah) books came from the Southern Kingdom of Judea sometime between 848 and 722 BCE. This means they were written over five hundred years after Moses lived. The author of the E (Elohim) books is believed to be a displaced Levite from the Northern Kingdom of Israel, who wrote between 922 and 722 BCE, which would mean these books were composed between three hundred and five hundred years after Moses. When combined, these two books form about 60 percent of the Pentateuch, which biblical scholars now refer to as the JE material. This compilation of J and E materials did not occur, most scholars believe, until just before Israel fell to the Assyrian invasion in 722 BCE, some five hundred years after the Exodus.[8] Yet the final editing of the Pentateuch did not take place until two or three centuries later, when the Jews had left their exile in Babylon in 518 BCE and returned to their lands to build the Second Temple in Jerusalem under the supervision of the Persian empire.* This is when the stories of the Garden of Eden and the Great Flood were added, as well as the other 40 percent of these religiously worshipped books. These stories of the Garden of Eden and the Great Flood were taken by the priests of Yahweh from much earlier Babylonian tales acquired by the Jews during their time of captivity in Babylon. The priests of Yahweh then adapted them, creating their own versions with a patriarchal slant, and inserted them into the earlier Hebrew histories to create the illusion of a historically linear time line.

---

*Today many biblical scholars believe that one person or a team of editors integrated the old and new material together seamlessly, making them appear to be one linear text. They call this person or team the Redactor. It is believed that the Redactor may have also added various verses and chapters to the older literature to promote this retelling of history, including chapter 15 of Numbers, the Feast of Booths, and verse 39 of Leviticus 23, which focuses on observances relating to the Sabbath.

These revelations derived from biblical research were a profound shock to me; after all, I had been taught from an early age to revere the Bible as a book of complete and utter truth. But it also made me realize that great literary license had been taken in the retelling of history and events in our distant past, not to mention God's Holy Word.

As I began to examine the Old Testament more closely, I also noticed that there were two versions of some of these stories. For example, there are two versions of the creation of the world and its life-forms in Genesis, the story of Noah and the ark, the covenant between God and Abraham, the naming of Abraham's son Isaac, Isaac's journey to Mesopotamia, and many others. How could this happen? According to Professor Friedman, it's because at one time there were two completely separate Jewish states—Judah and Israel. They had two different kings, two different temples, and two different sets of high priests. This lasted for about two hundred years (920–722 BCE). When the northern and southern states were reunited under one king, there was an obvious difference in their stories, due to the biases of the different priests. For over two hundred years the cultures had progressed down separate paths, and since neither side wanted to compromise, both versions of the stories were placed side by side in the Old Testament without any explanation. In other places the different stories were woven together as if they were one. So for millennia we have been left with holy scriptures that have glaring inconsistencies and contradictions based on the politics and beliefs at the time they were written.

This illuminates two different forms of Judaism that developed during this period of separation. Professor Friedman explains, "One culture, those who referred to God as Elohim, maintained their belief that there were numerous gods of which their god was one. The other culture had elevated their one god to a higher status and the other gods to minor players with little power. These they referred to as angels. In time, this is the view that prevailed and became the 'orthodox' belief system."[9]

So what about the rest of the Old Testament? I wondered. Who wrote those books, and when were they written? Today scholars have divided most of its creation into two additional designations, D and P. D stands for Deuteronomists, the traditional members of the Jehovah-worshipping sect who wrote the books of Deuteronomy, Joshua, Judges, Samuel, and Kings. Joe Lewels, author of *Rulers of the Earth*, states, "These writings present a rather bulky history that goes back to the time of Moses and reinterprets events from their perspective."[10] Historian Morton Smith says that these books are compilations of a single system of laws, customs, prophecies, and histories that basically demanded the worship of Yahweh alone. These books banned inter-marriage with other tribes, required the recitation of Hebrew law, suppressed the worship of all other divinities except Yahweh, and promoted different customs from those followed by the Jews in earlier centuries. Archaeologist William Dever writes that the Deuteronomists' writings are "largely propaganda" designed to give "theological legitimacy to a party of nationalist ultra-orthodox reformers known as the Yahweh-alone party."[11] Professor Friedman speculates that the D books were all written by one person, or by a school of scribes with one overriding objective—to promote the singular worship of Yahweh alone, essentially suppressing the existence of all other gods and goddesses as if they had never existed.

Finally, we arrive at the P section, which was developed after the Jews were released from their exile in Babylon. Much of this material was rewritten from earlier Babylonian or Assyrian sources to substantiate the theme of God's punishment of humanity and the supremacy of the singular cult of Yahweh. These stories are part of what historians now call the P material for "priestly" because they were added by the priests of Jehovah around 500 or 400 BCE, again after the Babylonian exile. These writings include the stories of Abraham, Jacob, the Exodus, the Flood, and Adam and Eve, as well as the other material previously mentioned in the Pentateuch. Interestingly enough, these "made up" or readapted stories compose nearly half of the Pentateuch, including eleven chapters out of the fifty in Genesis, nineteen of the forty chapters in Exodus, twenty-eight out of the thirty-six chapters in Numbers, and the whole Book of Leviticus![12]

This means that the Hebrew stories of creation and the Exodus were not even composed until nearly eight hundred years after the Exodus. And as we shall see, there is strong evidence that these books were created with the specific agenda of suppressing all other sects except their own. Professor Richard Friedman tells us the Redactor was able to cut and interweave the text in the books "intricately," making them appear to be one long narrative.[13]

The rest of the P material focuses on rules and regulations about how to make the proper sacrifices to Jehovah, while rejecting any mystical communication with God via dreams or with angels or talking animals.[14] Since the writing style of the P literature follows the same approach as the JE materials, scholars now believe that the writers of these books had a copy of the JE material on hand to emulate. All this explains why, despite the attempts to give an impression of unity to the Old Testament, there are so many internal inconsistencies.

TO RETHINK A WORLD

So why does any of this matter to us today? Because most of us who have been raised in the Christian, Jewish, or Muslim faiths, collectively known as the Abrahamic faiths because of their common ancestor, Abraham, have been taught that the Bible represents the holy "Word of God." In other words, it is not only true but it is a mandate from God himself. If biblical research reveals that these books are, in fact, the social or political creations of the priests of Yahweh, who took great literary license with history to advance a particular political agenda, then perhaps we should take a step back and rethink our worldview.

The events in the Bible, and the moral lessons they impart, have been used for centuries to legitimize the supremacy of these respective religions. But any objective analysis of these lessons reveals that they teach aggression, intolerance, and the destruction of any other philosophies except their own, all at the behest of Yahweh. Consequently, these judgmental attitudes have been adopted by the Jews, the Muslims, and the Christians, resulting in millions of deaths in "holy wars." Without realizing it, most of us have unconsciously accepted the attitudes and mandates put forth by these dualistic religions, since, for centuries, the Bible has been presented to us as verifiable fact. However, in recent decades, much evidence has emerged that suggests that some of these Old Testament accounts cannot be true. Many of these stories have been highly embellished or were totally manufactured as instruments of social and religious control, with the Jewish people themselves being the first victims of this subterfuge. While it is certainly possible that some of these events did take place, with such a large gap of time between the actual events and the written accounts, some major discrepancies are bound to have occurred.

Archaeologist William Dever writes in his book *Who Were the Early Israelites and Where Did They Come From?:* "The biblical writers and editors had some genuine sources, but they did not hesitate to manipulate them. They did this not only with exaggerations and embellishments, but also with additions and even outright inventions, in order to make the stories serve their own ideological agenda . . . This may be called 'historicized myth' and that is how modern, liberal, critical scholarship regards the Hebrew Bible . . ."[15]

MOSES AND THE HYKSOS KINGS

So let's examine just a couple of examples of how ancient history and modern-day archaeology do not match up with these Old Testament accounts. The first is the case of Moses, a deeply venerated figure in Jewish history, yet there is no mention of this seminal spiritual leader when we examine the records of any of the kingdoms that surrounded Israel. This includes Sumeria, Babylon, Persia, Assyria, and Canaan, which were all countries whose residents interacted with the Jews for centuries. As the founding patriarch of a tribal people and a religion,

*Figure 6.1. Moses has long been
a venerated figure in history.
But is the story we've been told
about him the real one? Note the
two horns on the top of his head,
indicating that he is an initiate of
the ancient wisdom. This statue by
Michelangelo sits in the Vatican.*

one would certainly think that Moses would have made his way into the histories of at least a few of these other cultures, but he doesn't.

However, in Egypt there is a rather lengthy reference to Moses in the accounts of Manetho, the high priest of Heliopolis, the City of the Sun. These accounts came to light during the era of Ptolemy II Philadelphus (283–247 BCE), the second Greek king of Egypt, who asked Manetho to compile a detailed list of Egypt's ancient kings and histories. While the original document has now vanished, the account was quoted extensively by the well-known Jewish historian Flavius Josephus when these documents still existed in the first century of the

Common Era. As we shall see, this version of Moses is quite different from the one that appears in the Old Testament.

It begins with a king named Amenophis. Since this name comes from the line of Egyptian kings at the time of, and just prior to, the monotheistic king Akhenaten, it seems to coincide with known history. Akhenaten's original name was, in fact, Amenophis IV, and his father's name was Amenophis III. Their reigns were in the same time period as Moses, between 1300 and 1200 BCE. In this historical account, King Amenophis decided one day that he wanted to behold the gods for himself, so he went to an oracle to find out how such a thing could be accomplished. The oracle who prophesied for him, whose name was also Amenophis, told the king that if he would expel all the lepers from Egypt, the gods would allow him to see them face-to-face. However, the oracle also warned that if the king did expel the lepers from the country, they would forge alliances with outside forces and return to take over Egypt for thirteen years. A perilous prophecy indeed!

So King Amenophis rounded up all the sick, deformed, and leprous people and sent them far away from the major cities to a remote part of Egypt on the west side of the Nile. According to these ancient documents, there were eighty thousand of these people. "There were some of the learned priests that were polluted with the leprosy; but that still Amenophis, the wise man and the prophet, was afraid that the gods would be angry at him and at the king, if there should appear to have been violence offered them [the ill or infirm]."[16] So the king did not oust them from the country completely but sent them west of the Nile to work in the quarries. At length, having mercy on them, "The king was desired that he would set apart the city of Avaris, which was then left desolate of the shepherds, for their habitation and protection; which desire he granted them."[17]

The people then selected a leader, "a ruler out of the priests of Heliopolis, whose name was Osarsiph, and they took their oaths that they would be obedient to him."[18] Osarsiph's name was also Moses or Mouses. *Mouses* signifies a person who is preserved out of water, for the

Egyptians called water *Mou*.[19] Osarsiph is a derivative of Osiris or *Osar,* a name that actually means the "good shepherd." This priest, Osarsiph, had been trained in the temples of Heliopolis, the highest teaching temples in Egypt, and even the accounts of Manetho acknowledge Moses to have been a wonderful, divine person.[20] Unfortunately, Moses also had contracted leprosy, so he was one of those rounded up to be exiled. Yet such was his bitterness at this turn of events that when he and the other lepers entered the city of Avaris, Moses "gave order that they should use the multitude of the hands that they had in building walls about their city, and make themselves ready for a war with King Amenophis, while he did himself take into his friendship the other priests and those that were polluted with them, and sent ambassadors to those shepherds who had been driven out of the land by Themosis to the city called Jerusalem."[21]

These neighboring shepherds were the descendents of the old Hyksos kings who had invaded Egypt about four hundred years earlier from the regions of Syria and Palestine. *The Encyclopedia of Ancient Egypt* tells us that Josephus, the Jewish historian of the first century CE, equates them with the Semitic marauders who five centuries earlier, around 1750 BCE, had invaded Egypt with some three hundred thousand warriors, desecrating its temples and granaries, and adopting the evil gods Set and Apophis as their deities.[22] Set is the personification of chaos, death, and darkness, and Apophis is the many-headed serpent that the soul encounters during its passage through the Egyptian Underworld. Apophis represents all our doubts, fears, and unresolved sins. The six Hyksos kings, as they later came to be called, occupied northern Egypt for over a hundred years, settling the town of Avaris (now modern-day Tell el-Dab'a) and making it their capital. They also overran the Egyptian capital of Memphis and took possession of the pyramids and many of the northern cities of Egypt in their bid for power.

During this invasion, the legitimate Egyptian king withdrew to the city of Thebes in the south, now called Luxor. There, he continued the spiritual traditions of the seventeenth dynasty. However, the

Hyksos invaders decided that they wanted the spiritual secrets of Egypt, as well as its land, harvests, and material wealth, so they sent assassins to Thebes to threaten the high priest, his two assistants, and the true Theban king. When the assassins could not wrestle these secrets from the priests, they murdered them. This is the premise of Christopher Knight and Robert Lomas's best-selling book *The Hiram Key*, which chronicles the archaeological discoveries of the mummified bodies, tracing these corpses back to this crushing incident in Egyptian history. The murder of the Theban king prompted the Egyptian people to rise up and overthrow the usurpers, finally ejecting them from their lands. So this is the backstory of the city of Avaris, and the nomadic shepherds Moses marshaled as allies to begin his siege of Egypt. Today many scholars believe that the Hyksos tribes were the precursors of the Hebrews because these marauders were called *Habiru,* the root word for the name "Hebrew."*

MOSES AND THE EGYPTIAN ACCOUNTS

Let's fast-forward now some four hundred years later to the time of Moses. It is sometime around 1300–1250 BCE. Osarsiph, or Moses, makes laws that forbid the worship of any of the Egyptian gods, and he also gives his people permission to eat many of the foods that the Egyptians are forbidden to eat, particularly meat. Moses also makes an alliance with the surrounding tribes to plan a war on Egypt. "He also promised that he would bring them back to their ancient city and country Avaris, and provide a plentiful maintenance for their multitude; that he would protect them and fight for them as occasion should require, and would easily reduce the country under their dominion."[23] These

---

Habiru was a derogatory name given to the nomadic and seminomadic invaders, Semites and non-Semites alike, who infiltrated Palestine from the north in the centuries between the ousting of the Hyksos kings and the time of the Hebrew settlements in Canaan. In Mesopotamia and the Middle East, the term referred to loosely organized and unorganized immigrants. (D. Winton Thomas, ed., *Documents from Old Testament Times* [New York: Harper Torchbooks, 1895], 41–42.)

nomadic tribes totaled some two hundred thousand able-bodied men, and they agreed to join Moses and his people in a revolt against Egypt.

Now these two forces combined, totaling around three hundred thousand, returned to Egypt, and laid waste its temples. They occupied the country for some thirteen years, just as the oracle of Amenophis had predicted. "They did not only set the cities and villages on fire, but were not satisfied till they had been guilty of sacrilege, and destroyed the images of the gods, and used them in roasting those sacred animals that used to be worshipped, and forced the priests and prophets to be the executioners and murderers of those animals, and then ejected them naked out of the country."[24]

Finally, King Amenophis, who had fled to Ethiopia with his five-year-old son, Ramses, returned to challenge Osarsiph some thirteen years later. King Amenophis brought his 250,000 troops back to Egypt and eventually drove Moses and the invading tribes out of Egypt for good. The account ends by telling us: "It is also reported that the priest, who ordained their polity and their laws, was by birth of Heliopolis, and his name Osarsiph from Osiris, who was the god of Heliopolis; but that in original when he was gone over to these [other] people, his name was changed, and he was called Moses."[25] Having been driven out of Egypt, this entire group of invaders then decides to relocate to Canaan, where they will build their new home in the land of the Canaanites.[26]

Whew! Intense, isn't it? This is quite a different story of Moses from the one we all heard in Sunday school class or in the synagogue, isn't it? As you will recall, the Old Testament scriptures claim that Moses was the adopted son of the pharaoh, and actually of Hebrew descent. When Moses discovers his half-Hebrew parentage, he murders an Egyptian military officer and flees Egypt, fearing that he will be arrested for his crime. Moses lives peacefully for many years in Ethiopia with his black wife and children, until Yahweh finally calls him back to Egypt. In these Hebrew scriptures, Yahweh then demands that Moses tell the pharaoh to let the Hebrew slaves leave Egypt. When the pharaoh refuses, this contest of wills brings down the ten deadly plagues on Egypt, including the death of each firstborn son, which later became the celebration of the Jewish Passover.* In this biblical version, through the many torments that Moses unleashes, the pharaoh capitulates and agrees to let Moses lead his people out of Egypt but then changes his mind and pursues the Hebrews, causing the destruction of his armies during the closing of the Red Sea. The victorious Hebrew slaves escape to freedom. This is the version of the story as we know it today.

Despite the obvious differences in these two stories, there are still some common elements. Osarsiph or Moses is still a highly educated priest, who may well have been related to the royal family, since he was being trained in the highest temples of the land. We do not know if he was originally from Egyptian or Hebrew stock, and he may have had both bloodlines. Essenes at the time of Jesus believed that he was the full-blooded son of the pharaoh's daughter, who had had an affair with a Hebrew slave; thus he had many of the privileges of a prince but would never have been allowed to rule.[27] In the Old Testament account, Moses also has a physical deformity, but it is not leprosy; it is a speech impediment. The writers of Exodus, crafting their story some four hundred to five hundred years later, would have found stuttering much more acceptable to Jewish nationalists, since Hebrew law later forbade any of their kings to rule if they had leprosy. But in the original story, the "slaves of Egypt" were not slaves at all; they were sick, leprous people sent to the quarries to work, and judging by their numbers, they may have also included people with other deformities or illnesses. One could certainly argue that being uprooted from their homes would have made them angry, but since they are given free rein to settle in Avaris and build their own city, not to mention having lots of time to plan their attack on Egypt, these people were essentially free to pursue their own fates.

The ten deadly plagues of Egypt may have taken their source mate-

---

*The ten plagues were rivers that turned to blood, frogs, lice, flies, murrain (a disease of animals), boils, hail mixed with fire, locusts, darkness, and the death of the firstborn males.

rial from the thirteen years of desecration and plunder caused by the rebels in the Egyptian temples. And in recent years there has been evidence that the volcanic eruption on the Greek isle of Thera (now known as Santorini) may have been responsible for many of the plagues attributed to Moses. This would include the molten lava that tinged the Nile red, the frogs leaping out of the boiling waters, the lice and flies, and the flights of migrating locusts, not to mention the hail mixed with fire that could have been carried on the winds across much of the Mediterranean Sea.

The final ousting of Moses and his Semitic invading forces from Egypt after their thirteen-year siege was later rewritten by Hebrew writers into the story of Exodus we know today, generating the tale of the poor, oppressed slaves leaving Egypt with the Egyptian pharaoh in pursuit. However, in the Old Testament version we know today the pharaoh pays with his life as the waters of the Red Sea wash over him in death, sending a message to any kings who would dare to oppose the Israelites that they will pay with their lives if they challenge the Jews. Clearly, in the Hebrew retelling of this story, King Amenophis has lost the favor of God, or the gods, forever.

JOSEPHUS AND MANETHO'S ACCOUNTS

While the meticulously kept records of Egypt were destroyed in the many centuries of Christian and Arabic plundering, this account still existed in the first century CE. Many excerpts from this document were painstakingly transcribed by the Jewish historian Josephus, who tried to argue against them. We must remember, however, that when Josephus wrote the *History of the Jews* it was many years after the destruction of King Herod's Temple in 70 CE, when the Jews were out of favor with Rome. Josephus, who was living at the Roman emperor's palace at the time, sought to present the Hebrew people as an intelligent, cohesive nation, since the Romans largely despised them as rabble rousers. So certainly, Josephus would have argued against any history that portrayed the Hebrews as a group of ragtag, leprous, invading nomads. That would not have left a very good impression. However, the history that Manetho produced for Ptolemy II, the second Greek king of Egypt, was written some nine hundred years earlier at the time the events occurred, while several centuries had passed by the time that the Hebrew authors of the Old Testament finally wrote their version, which is presented in the Pentateuch today.

SOME LOGISTICAL QUESTIONS ABOUT HEBREW HISTORY

Two last comments about Moses. First, the Jews did not start celebrating Passover until 621 BCE,[28] a custom introduced some six hundred years after Moses. So we might suggest that if historic events had unfolded just as the Old Testament writers claim, then the Passover celebration would have been initiated centuries earlier when the Jews first settled in Canaan. Biblical scholars believe that this tradition was started by the priests of Yahweh to anchor this new version of history within their tribe. This date of 621 BCE falls about a hundred years after Israel was defeated by the Assyrians (722 BCE) and about forty years before the takeover of Jerusalem by the Babylonians (586 BCE). Some six hundred years after the Exodus and the real events behind the Moses story, this may be one of the first strong indications that the priests of Yahweh were winning in their bid for political power.

Second, it is clear that in this re-creation the authors of the Old Testament took great pains to cast Moses as a divinely anointed person. While Moses was obviously a highly intelligent, learned priest and strategist, as with all folk heroes or founders of religions, a mythical story must be created to burnish his image. In that age, "divinely appointed messengers of God" typically had certain archetypal elements associated with them, and we see these added in the Bible. You will recall the story of Moses being found as a baby in the bulrushes of the Nile by the pharaoh's daughter. This is the story that was told of Horus, the divine

Egyptian savior. It is also the story of Sargon, the famous Akkadian king. Isis discovers Horus in the bulrushes of the Nile, just as Ishtar discovers Sargon in the reeds and rushes of the Mesopotamian riverbanks.

In the symbolic language of the Mysteries, this myth was meant to convey the presence of a universal savior sent from the Mother Ocean, then sanctioned by the Great Goddess, giving the hero legitimacy and power. Joseph Campbell, the well-known historian, points out that the roots of this Egyptian and Hebrew story can be traced back to the original Sumerian version, famous across the entire Mesopotamian world.[29] So the writers of the Old Testament sought to duplicate specific Mystery elements in their stories in order to establish Moses's divinely appointed right to rule.

PEACE OR WAR
AMONG THE CHOSEN PEOPLE

Let's look at another major discrepancy between the Old Testament accounts and the archaeological discoveries in the land of Canaan. Canaan, incidentally, encompasses the modern-day countries of Lebanon, Syria, Jordan, and Israel, so it is quite a large territory. This was the major trade route between the Mediterranean countries of Italy and Greece, the Persian Gulf, and the vital corridor between Egypt and Mesopotamia. The name *Canaan* actually comes from one of Noah's grandsons, Canaan, the son of Ham.

Ancient history tells us that the Canaanites were peaceful people who honored both male and female deities, and their agricultural communities were thriving when the nomadic Hebrews arrived. The history of this area goes far back into the Bronze and Iron Ages, when a variety of Semitic tribes from Mesopotamia and the Syro-Arabian desert had settled the land. "The Canaanites migrated from the Arabian desert no later than 3000 B.C. They built a magnificent civilization and invented three different alphabets, one of which (the Phoenician) became the ancestor of practically all those in the

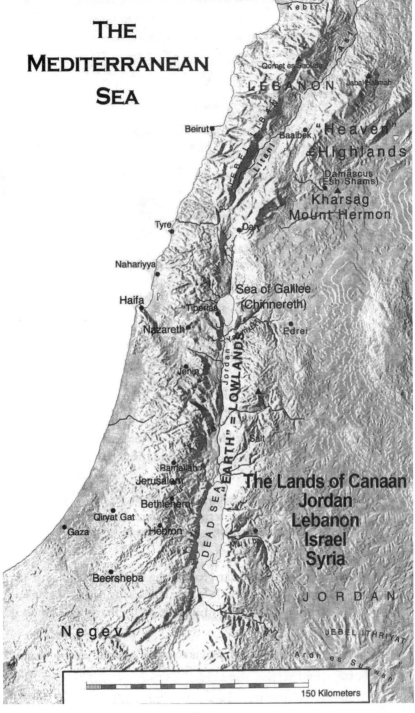

THE
MEDITERRANEAN
SEA

Kebir

Qomet es Saouda

L E B A N O N   Jabal Halimah

Beirut

Baalbek   "Heaven"

=Highlands

Damascus
(Esh Shams)

Kharsag

Mount Hermon

Tyre   Dan

Nahariyya

Haifa   Tiberias   Sea of Galilee
(Chinnereth)

Nazareth   Edrei

Jenin

Salt

Ramallah
Jerusalem   The Lands of Canaan
Bethlehem   Jordan
Qiryat Gat   Lebanon
Gaza   Hebron   Israel
Mujib   Syria

Beersheba

J O R D A N

Negev   JEBEL ITHRIYAT

Ardh es Suwan

150 Kilometers

*Figure 6.2. A map of Canaan and the Levant, which encompassed the
modern-day countries of Jordan, Syria, Israel, and Lebanon.*

Western world. Their literature contained notable epics. Their laws and religious practices deeply influenced the Hebrews who, in turn, have influenced the modern world."[30]

The cities of Ugarit, Tyre, Sidon, and Byblos were known to be thriving ports by the time of the Hebrew settlement in Canaan, and it would have been easy for the Hebrews to have adopted the religion of the people already settled there as a way of assimilation. "These tribes had a greater affinity with the Semitic peoples who were already living in northern Mesopotamia. Canaanite mythology shares many stories and images with Mesopotamia and Egypt."[31] These discoveries certainly go along with the idea that Moses and his people might have settled into this land far more peacefully than we hear in the Bible, since they were all of a similar racial heritage. Archaeologist William Dever also tells us that the liturgical calendar and sacrificial system adopted by the Hebrews was actually the same as that of the Canaanites,[32] and Professor Bernhard Lang writes that during the many years of the Israelite monarchy, identified in the Bible between 1020 and 586 BCE, the Israelites continued to be indistinguishable from their neighbors in terms of worship.[33]

Anne Baring and Jules Cashford, authors of *The Myth of the Goddess,* write about this area in the first few centuries of the Hebrew settlements:

When the Hebrews entered Canaan, they did not find a sparsely populated land with primitive people, but a country with a powerful religion and cultural traditions in which queens took the role of high priestesses, and ordinary women were priestesses. Strong and wealthy cities had long been established in Canaan that had trading connections with Egypt, Babylonia, and the Hittite kingdom in Anatolia [modern-day Turkey]. Canaanite rulers had often married princesses from these foreign courts, and the early Hebrew kings followed this tradition.[34]

Exodus 33:3 tells us that when the Jews entered the land of Canaan they found great cities "overflowing with milk and honey." The Canaanite cities worshipped both the Divine Male and Female in the names of Asherah, Astarte, or Ashtoreth, and her son Tammuz. Asherah was also the mother of the Babylonian Goddess Ishtar, who was married to Tammuz. Ishtar's long devotion to her husband Tammuz had turned him into a fertility god, and throughout the entire Middle East, numerous cities celebrated the death and rebirth of Tammuz each year at Easter, much as today we celebrate the sacrifice and resurrection of Jesus.

Tammuz, or Dumuzi, as he was called in Mesopotamia, was the green God of agriculture, the "ever dying and renewing god," whose blood had been spilled to bless the land. Like Jesus, his death was seen as a deliberate sacrifice for the people, and it was believed that each spring, after a celebration of three days he would rise again when new life came to the crops. For the ancient people, the celebration of this yearly rite of death, rebirth, and resurrection was similar to our celebrations of Easter each year. We grieve on Good Friday, then we celebrate the resurrection of the risen lord three days later. In those early pre-Christian centuries this fertility passion play took the form of a young man who was chosen to represent the sacrificial king, Tammuz. First he was anointed with holy oil by the queen. Then he was sacrificially slain. Mourners then laid his body to rest in a cave, representing the womb of the Mother Earth, where he would be reborn. For three days and three nights he stayed in the cave while processions of women grieved over his death. Then, three days later, the young man rose and emerged from the cave, heralding the birth of the new crops.

Authors Anne Baring and Jules Cashford explain how the Hebrews came to adopt these local customs of the Canaanites. "These goddesses were adopted by the Hebrew tribes when they settled in Canaan, for like the Semitic invaders who had preceded them, they took over the mythology and the cult sites as well as the seasonal feasts and ritual customs of the Canaanite people . . . In Canaan, as in the surrounding countries, the mythology of the goddess and her son-lover was the most deeply rooted aspect of religious belief because it was closely associated with the seasons of the agricultural year, and more widely, with the archaic rituals of fertility and regeneration."[35]

This neighborly account of the Jews' settlement in Canaan is very different from the version that we read in the Hebrew scriptures. In the biblical version, Jehovah instructs the arriving Jews to annihilate the surrounding communities as a religious mandate, legitimizing the slaughter of innocent people. In Deuteronomy 10:15–17, we read ". . . thou shalt save alive nothing that breatheth, but thou shalt utterly destroy them, namely the Hittites, and the Amorites, the Canaanites, and the Perizzites, the Hivites, and the Jebusites, as the Lord thy God hath commanded thee." The Book of Joshua (6:21–24) records that at Jericho " . . . they utterly destroyed all that was in the city, both man and woman, young and old, and ox, and sheep, and ass, with the edge of the sword . . . and they burnt the city with fire, and all that was therein." The Book of Ezekiel (9:6–7) tells us, "Slay utterly old and young, both maids and little children, and women . . . fill the courts with the slain." All in all, the Old Testament claims that the Hebrews destroyed over forty different cities in this area.[36]

ARCHAEOLOGY
AND THE PROMISED LAND

However, archaeologists tell us that there were three major waves of settlement in Canaan during this period, and none of them shows any signs of invading warriors or battles. This directly contradicts what the writers of the Old Testament tell us about the hordes of murdering Israelites, led by Joshua and his legions. Archaeologist William Dever chronicles the extensive excavations in Canaan that have sought evidence of these Old Testament battles. According to him, in the area now believed to be the original region of Israel, there arose some three hundred small agricultural hilltop villages during the thirteenth and twelfth centuries BCE, each one being no more than four or five acres wide. Most were located

Figure 6.3. The balanced synergy of the male and female energies can be seen easily in the six-pointed Star of David, revealing that at one time the Jews honored both the male and female faces of God equally. It is this merger or synthesis that allows us to come into mastery.

on top of hills or in fertile valleys close to water in the central hill country north of Jerusalem. None of them had any defensive walls, but there was a "notable absence of pig bones in the excavations," Dever notes, revealing that these were Jewish settlements, since eating pork was prohibited among the Hebrews.[37] "Of the supposed forty cities, only two or three are even potential candidates for some form of conquest, as most of the other cities either didn't exist in that period, or if they did, show no destruction. Most are new sites in an area that was essentially unpopulated, so there was no need for conquest."[38]

So what is the truth of these events, and why does it matter to us today? First, it would be wonderful to believe that the Hebrew people did not break every one of the Ten Commandments at the behest of their own God by killing, stealing from, and annihilating those in communities who had done nothing to them. It makes no sense for a God to issue moral commandments, then immediately order the people who follow that God to break every one of them. We can also see from the esoteric emblem of the six-pointed Star of David or Seal of Solomon, that the Hebrews honored both the male and female aspects of God in balance in the early centuries of their teachings. This is revealed by many of the sacred emblems of King Solomon, who ruled at the time of their Golden Age.

So perhaps the real question we should be asking is why such gruesome tales of war and pillage would be told to a people in a body of religious literature, especially if they aren't true? Today we can only speculate as to the answer. Perhaps the Jehovah sect of the Levite priests, who wrote these books some seven hundred to a thousand years after the Exodus, wanted to portray a fiercesome and punitive God that should not be questioned. If the accounts of bloodshed in the Old Testament are true, not only did these nomads murder tens of thousands of people living in harmonious communities without any provocation, but in some cases they took the virginal daughters of their murdered enemies captive, raped them, and forced them to live as sexual slaves. In the Book of Numbers we read:

> And they warred against the Midianites as the Lord commanded Moses; and they slew all the males. (31:7) . . . And the people of Israel took all the women [of] Midian captive and their little ones, and took the spoils of all their cattle, and all their flocks, and all their goods. And they burnt all their cities wherein they dwelt, and all their goodly castles, with fire . . . (31:9–11)
>
> [Yahweh says,] "So therefore kill every male among the little ones, and kill every woman that has known man by lying with him. But all the women and children that have not known a man by lying with him keep alive for yourselves." (31:17–18)

In the Book of Isaiah we hear a similar story of the murder and rape of other innocents:

I have commanded my sanctified ones, I have also called my mighty ones for My anger, even them that rejoice in my exaltation. (13:3) . . . Wail, for the day of the Lord is at hand! It will come as destruction from the Almighty. Therefore all hands will be limp, every man's heart will melt, and they will be afraid. Pangs and sorrows will take hold of them. (13:6–8) . . . I will punish the world for its evil, and the wicked for their iniquity; I will halt the arrogance of the proud, and will lay low the haughtiness of the terrible. (13:11–12) . . . Everyone that is found shall be thrust through; and everyone who is captured will fall by the sword. Their children also will be dashed to pieces before their eyes; their houses will be plundered and *their wives ravished.* (13:15–16) (emphasis mine)

This is misogyny at its worse. And as if murder, imprisonment, and rape were not enough, we have lots of examples of people being burned alive as punishment.

"Therefore behold, the days come," saith the Lord "that I will cause an alarm of war to be heard in Rabbah of the Amorites; and it shall be a desolate heap, and *her daughters shall be burned with fire:* then shall Israel be heir unto them that were his heirs," saith the Lord. (Jeremiah 49:2) (emphasis mine)

These destructive commandments, whether given by the actual Yahweh, or later created by his priests, sent a frightening message to everyone that cruelty, savagery, and punishment are the right paths to take. Imagine the level of psychological shock, horror, and damage to these poor women, and then the children who were later born into the Hebrew tribes from their mother's rape. These same self-righteous attitudes were then adopted by the Christian and Muslim faiths in later centuries, sending both of these originally inspired spiritual paths down a trajectory toward destruction and jihad.

THE HEAVY HAND OF YAHWEH

Let's take a look now at some of the other unprovoked punishments that Yahweh imposed, even on his own people. In Leviticus we read about two of Aaron's sons, Nadab and Abihu, who were making offerings to Jehovah by laying incense on a fire pan outside of the tabernacle tent, and suddenly "fire came forth from the Lord and consumed them; thus they died at the insistence of the Lord" (Leviticus 10:1–2).[39] These were sons of Aaron, the high priest, and they had undoubtedly been trained to perform these duties already. So was this a deliberate act of punishment, and, if so, for what? Death seems like a pretty severe penalty to impose when they were only honoring their God.

Then after the Philistines had captured the Ark of the Covenant and returned it to the Hebrew tribe, the people gathered to celebrate its return. But according to 1 Samuel 5–7, Jehovah wiped out some 50,070 of his own people because they dared to look upon it.

> Then he struck the men of Beth Shemesh, because they had looked into the Ark of the Lord. He struck fifty thousand and seventy men of the people, and the people lamented because the Lord had struck the people with a great slaughter. (1 Samuel 6:19)

For heaven's sake! Doesn't this seem a bit counterproductive? These were God's own people celebrating the return of a device that would allow them to talk with their God more directly. So perhaps we are actually looking at an extraterrestrial technology in both of these cases that has backfired in some way. But for Jehovah, or the priests of Jehovah, to admit error would be to admit that Jehovah is not the all-powerful, all-knowing God of all.

Our next incident comes from the Book of Ezekiel. This is when King David was close to death and chose to "number" or count his people. According to the Old Testament, Jehovah then sent a "plague" that wiped out some seventy thousand of the Jewish people, and this plague only ended after David had pleaded for his people's lives. Now perhaps Jehovah did send a plague, but for what reason? On the other hand, maybe this was just a ploy by the priests of Jehovah to bully the tribes and ascribe a natural—albeit unfortunate—occurrence to the wrath of a punitive god. In this account Jehovah says to his own people:

> I shall judge you, and I shall pour out my wrath upon you, breathing the fire of my fury upon you! I will hand you over to men of ravaging, craftsmen of destruction. Fuel for the fire shall you be and through the land shall flow your blood. You shall not be remembered, for I, the Lord, have spoken. (Ezekiel 21:31–32)

In Leviticus (26:14–33) we also learn of the contract that Jehovah makes between himself and the Hebrew nation, and a dire and fierce threat it is.

> If you disobey me . . . I will appoint terror over you, wasting disease and fever which shall consume the eyes and cause sorrow of heart. And you shall sow your seed in vain, for your enemies shall eat it. I will set my face against you, and you shall be defeated by your enemies. Those who hate you shall reign over you, and you shall flee when no one pursues you. And after this if you do not obey Me, then I will punish you seven times more for your sins. I will break the pride of your power; I will make your heavens like iron and your earth like bronze. And your strength shall be spent in vain; for your land shall not yield its produce, nor shall the trees of the land yield their fruit. Then if you walk contrary to Me and are not willing to obey Me, I will bring on you seven times more plagues, according to your sins. I will also send wild beasts among you, which shall rob you of your children, destroy your livestock, and make you few in number, and your highways shall be desolate. And if by these things you are not reformed by Me, but walk contrary to Me, then I also will walk contrary to you, and I will punish you sevenfold for your

sins. I will bring a sword against you that will execute the vengeance of My covenant. (Leviticus 26:16–25) . . . You shall eat the flesh of your sons and the flesh of your daughters. I will destroy your high places and cut down your incense altars, and I will heap your carcasses on the lifeless forms of your idols; and My soul shall abhor you. (Leviticus 26:29–30) . . . I will scatter you among the nations and draw out a sword after you; Your land shall become a desolation and your cities a ruin (Leviticus 26:33).

Sheesh! This kind of threat would frighten anyone, especially if those making the threat had the clout to carry it out. This kind of cruelty does not sound like the work of an all-loving God, but rather like the threats of a tribal god, similar to the many other tribal gods who oversaw this entire region. Or perhaps they are the politically manufactured lies of priests hungry for power and promoting their own agenda. Carl Jung, the famous psychologist, writes of Yahweh's character in the Bible:

The absence of human morality in Yahweh is a stumbling block which cannot be overlooked . . . We miss reason and moral values, that is, two main characteristics of a mature human mind. It is therefore obvious that the Yahwistic image or conception of the deity is less than that of certain human specimens; the image of a personified brutal force and of an unethical and non-spiritual mind, yet inconsistent enough to exhibit traits of kindness and generosity, beside a violent power drive. It is the picture of a sort of nature-demon and at the same time of a primitive chieftain aggrandized to a colossal size, just the sort of conception one could expect of a more or less barbarous society.[40]

Today most of us forget that the three Abrahamic faiths of Christianity, Judaism, and Islam all spring from this same heavy-handed, fear-based root. Thus the knee-jerk reaction to the mere mention of any other "god" (or goddess) has Yahweh's threat of impending doom behind it. And even though these religions claim to be followers of the one powerful, unifying God, they spend much energy talking about his rival, Satan. This polarization taught within the Yahweh sect was reinforced after the Hebrew exile ended. At that time, the Persians financed the Jews' rebuilding of the Second Temple in Jerusalem, and only then did a codified writing, like the Old Testament, begin to be put together.

Unfortunately, the Hebrews' patron, the leaders of the Persian empire, had become very dualistic themselves at that time and were following the teachings of Zoroaster. Zoroaster taught that the world was engaged in a constant battle between good and evil, exemplified by the gods Ahura Mazda and Ahriman, similar to our modern-day conception of God and Satan. However, Ahura Mazda was also not the ultimate God, for there are many glyphs of Ahura Mazda shown as a

Figure 6.4. The Persians honored Ahura Mazda as the symbol of a righteous god. Here he is seen flying in a round disc with landing struts over the canopy of King Darius, revealing his true identity as one of the many Anunnaki gods of Sumeria and Persia. (Illustration by Tricia McCannon)

human being in a hovering spacecraft or a round disc with flying wings holding a ring of kingship. His clothes, hair, beard, and hat all look exactly like the earlier gods of the Sumerian, Assyrian, and Akkadian civilizations that we will address in the next chapter.

Furthermore, Zoroastrian philosophy predicted an impending apocalypse between the forces of light and darkness. This Armageddon approach was then adopted by the Jews in Jerusalem, when they became locked in their own power struggles with the Roman empire. This philosophy of impending doom and conflict was then passed on to the Essenes, who recorded it in the book called *The War of the Sons of Light against the Sons of Darkness*. This book was found among the Nag Hammadi texts in 1945.

Later, this same apocalyptic scenario became part of Christian beliefs through the Book of Revelation, believed to have been written by the apostle John on the island of Patmos some fifty years after Jesus's death. Yet the Book of Revelation actually derives from a far earlier writing found among the *Essene Gospel of Peace*. John, if he ever did write down his own version of this earlier manuscript, would have been repeating his knowledge of a far earlier Essene book. Today these original writings can be found in the *Essene Gospel of Peace,* Book 2,[41] and are part of a series of several largely unknown books written by the Essenes and by Jesus that were first released in English in the mid-twentieth century. These six slender volumes are compilations of Essene writings that have all been translated from their original Aramaic by historian, philosopher, and philologist Dr. Edmond Bordeaux Szekely. Dr. Szekely, who speaks eleven languages, had access to these documents when he studied at the secret archives of the Vatican, and based on these writings, these books were finally published.

While the conflict described in the Book of Revelation has already occurred, by adopting the philosophy of eternal conflict as a future revelation, we have created centuries of doomsdaylike fear. Millions of Christians have waited for the hammer of judgment to fall, almost praying for a final holocaust or armageddon. Unfortunately, by promoting this fear-based philosophy, Christianity has continued to act as a mechanism for the same kind of judgmental, religiously justified violence we see portrayed in the Old Testament writings.

In summary, it is clear that the tribal God of the Old Testament is not the same deity that Jesus espoused. Jesus's God was a God of love, forgiveness, and peace, while Jehovah's priests taught punishment, death, and damnation. This is important to keep in mind as we realize that Christian theology has propounded two completely different messages—vengeance and judgment versus forgiveness and love. These two different versions of the Creator, one expressed in the Old Testament and one in the New Testament, are diametrically opposed, and this may explain some of the many reasons why our faiths have seemed so distorted and confusing.

Most of us raised in the Judeo-Christian world have not understood this clearly because these two different approaches were joined together under one heading—the Holy Bible. Once we step back to grasp the social, political, and religious agendas of the various sects involved in the creation of the Abrahamic faiths, we take the first step toward becoming deprogrammed from this mythology. Then, by realizing that there are vast discrepancies in the events in the Old Testament, which are not supported by historical, physical, or archaeological evidence, we can begin to gain enough perspective to realize that the stories we watch on television or in the movies about the Bible may not actually be true. While the Bible may have many excellent moral lessons and pieces of genuine history woven into it, it is also a conglomeration of both fact and fiction that has been served to us on a silver platter. We cannot accept it as a total reality when we weigh all these factors.

Finally, understanding that there is a vast philosophical difference between the God of love and the God of fear is the first step in realizing that all of us have a choice today about what kind of world we want to live in. Will it be a world of judgment, killing, and violence or a world that follows the path of acceptance, understanding, and peace, exemplified by the teachings of Jesus? The choice is ours.

Goddesses in
Hebrew History

Queen of Heaven, Goddess of the Universe,
The One who walked in terrible chaos and brought life by
*   the law of love,*
and out of chaos brought us harmony,
and from chaos She has led us by the hand.

"POEM TO ISHTAR"

While it is clear to anyone raised in the Judeo-Christian-Muslim world
that the gender of Yahweh and Allah is decidedly male, I couldn't figure out how or why this had come to be. In truth, the Divine Power
that creates all things must contain currents of both male and female
and is beyond the petty designation of one gender over another. I knew
that in the empires of the ancient world there had been many names
for both the gods and goddesses, so what had happened to this more
balanced approach? These civilizations had endured for thousands of

years in prosperous, enlightened societies that had birthed the foundations of the arts and sciences we know today. So what had changed this
fundamental balance between the sexes? What had caused the world
to become so aggressively male, and with such dire consequences? How
had religions ceased to honor the Divine Feminine aspect of God, and
was there ever a time when the Hebrews had honored her?

I decided to dig a bit more deeply into the hidden history of the
Jews. What I discovered next astonished me. The monotheism that
we take for granted today in Judaism did not exist for the first thousand years of the Jews' tribal existence. For centuries, the Hebrews had
honored numerous gods and goddesses, and the worship of the Divine
Feminine had only been eradicated about four hundred years before
the birth of Jesus. This is reflected in the teachings of the Northern
Kingdom of Samaria, whose leaders had referred to their creator gods
as the Elohim, the plural form of *El,* the Shining One. Joyce and River
Higginbotham write about this in their book *Christ to Paganism:*

> Most people are unaware that monotheism within Judaism devel-
> oped as a minority movement and remained a minority for hundreds
> of years, becoming a majority only in the fifth century B.C.E. or
> perhaps even later. Many people do not realize that throughout most
> of this time temples, shrines, priests, and ordinary people were rou-
> tinely polytheistic in their practices and observances, and were gen-
> erally not interested in monotheism. All archaeological findings to
> date, and they are numerous, support the existence of routine poly-
> theistic practices in the region, both in the temples and among the
> populace.[1]

Historian Morton Smith writes about the archaeological site that
researchers now believe was once the original location of King Solomon's
Temple. Amid these ruins were images of several gods and goddesses,
including Tammuz, the Mesopotamian grain god, who, like Jesus, was
said to have died for three days and come back from the dead, and

Shamash, the Mesopotamian sun god whose numerous worship sites have been found in several holy areas around Jerusalem, dating from the ninth and eighth centuries BCE. In addition, every major archaeological excavation found in Palestine to date has uncovered statues of female figurines dating from between 2000 and 600 BCE.[2] These figurines were used by women in prayer to aid them in times of childbirth. Hebrew scholar Raphael Patai, author of *The Hebrew Goddess,* writes:

> In view of the general human, psychologically determined predisposition to believe in and worship goddesses, it would be strange if the Hebrew Jewish religion, which flourished for centuries in a region of intensive goddess cults, had remained immune to them. Yet this [male monotheism] is precisely the picture one gets when one views Hebrew religion through the polarizing prisms of Mosaic legislation and prophetic teaching. God, this [patriarchal] view maintains, revealed Himself in successive stages to Adam, Noah, Abraham, Isaac, and Jacob, and gave His law to Moses on Mount Sinai. Biblical religion, in this perspective, is universal ethical monotheism, cast in a ritual-legal form.[3]

Based on extensive excavations across the Levant, Patai goes on to tell us:

> The chief of all the gods was El, the father god, often called "bull of his father." His wife Asherah, also referred to as "Lady Asherah of the Sea," was the mother of all other gods whom she suckled at her breasts. Their son Baal, also called Aliyan, Prince, King, and Rider of Clouds, was the god of rain, and fertility who periodically died and again came to life. Their daughter Anath, usually referred to as the Virgin or Maiden Anath, or simply as The Girl, was a goddess of love and female fecundity, as well as of the war and the hunt, who enjoyed fighting as much as she did love-making, was bloodthirsty, tempestuous and unrestrained.[4]

As we will discover, these four gods and goddesses made up a tetrad of male and female figures, filling the spiritual roles of father, mother, daughter, and son, and each of them played major roles in Jewish culture. Echoes of these four deities can also be found in Hindu, Norse, Greek, Roman, and Egyptian theology.

ASHERAH: THE WIFE OF JEHOVAH

While the concepts of a Divine Mother and Father were intrinsic to many ancient cultures, each region had its own name for these deities. In her primordial expression the Great Mother is she who has birthed the universe, the one from whose body the Cosmic Egg was born; keeper of animals, nature, and humankind. Among the Hebrews she was called Asherah or Ashtoreth, the Queen of Heaven, the wife of El. Asherah was worshipped alongside El or Yahweh for centuries, and a Sumerian inscription, dating back as far as 1750 BCE, refers to Asherah as the wife of El, the father god of the Canaanite pantheon—a much earlier version of Jehovah. The term *Elohim,* meaning the "gods" (plural), was one of the two names used in the first five books of the Bible, or the Pentateuch, to designate the original creators of humankind. The prefix *El* means "the Radiant or Shining Ones" and was used in Akkadian, Sumerian, and the Old Welch and Irish tongues. The Anglo-Saxon version is *Aelf,* and the English is *Elf,* later associated with the immortal shining elves of Celtic legend.[5] Since the Hebrews also referred to the deity that Moses spoke with as the *Anokhi,* a word similar to the *Anunnaki* gods and goddesses known throughout the entire Mediterranean world, Asherah and Jehovah may well have been the Mother and Father gods of ancient legends.

We know from numerous tablets found in Ugaritan in Syria that the Goddess Asherah was the major female deity of the cities of Tyre and Sidon, going back to at least 1300 BCE, before the Jewish exodus. In a temple shrine called Ta'anach in Judea, archaeologist William Dever writes about the discovery of a winged sun disc dating from at least the tenth century BCE. This emblem is similar to the many winged discs found throughout Egypt, Persia, and all of Mesopotamia and is the symbol of the tall, long-lived Anunnaki gods who arrived on Earth in oval spaceships, just as in modern times we see round or disc-shaped UFOs in the skies today. At this same site, researchers also found molds for making terra-cotta goddess figurines, and a striking statue of a nude woman standing between two lions. This is Asherah, the lady of the lions. She is identical to the goddesses Astarte, Ashtart, and Ashtoreth (her Hebrew name), as well as the Canaanite Goddess Qeresh. All these expressions of feminine goddesses are depicted riding on the back of a lion, or standing beside lions or horses, or with one or two graceful ibexes, sometimes seen framing either side of the goddess,[6] revealing her role as Mother of the Animals. This symbology can also be found in India and Rome with the two Goddesses Durga and Cybele, linking this powerful female divinity to the sun, and the courage and heart of

Figure 7.1. Asherah playing with two horses. Notice the wheat in her hands that links her to the agricultural cycles of fertility.

Figure 7.2. Asherah is sometimes depicted on the back of a lion, a symbol of both courage and war, linking this goddess to both Durga in the East and Cybele in Rome. Here she is flanked by two women, possibly handmaidens.

the lion. Later this lion symbology would be adopted by the Hebrew house of David, and the lions of Judah became a symbol for their highest rank of kingship.

As the wife of Jehovah, Asherah was associated with Jove and Hera. *Jehovah* is another name for *Jove,* the "god most high" in Greek mythology. Jove was the same deity as the Roman Jupiter and the Greek Zeus, the king of the gods. Jove, Jupiter, or Jehovah would certainly have been bold enough to command the people to "have no other gods before me," since all other gods would have been subordinate to his rule. In Greek theology, Jove was married to Juno, just as in Roman mythology this same god, known as Zeus, was married to Hera. So these are undoubtedly the same deities that the nomadic Hebrew people came to refer to as Jehovah and Asherah for, as we shall see, their attributes are virtually identical.

Zeus and Hera were the married king and queen of the gods, who were known for living in high places, such as Mount Olympus, Mount

Figure 7.3. Zeus and Hera were the "gods most high," the King and Queen of the gods, who were also known as Jove and Juno or Jehovah and Asherah. (Illustration by Tricia McCannon)

Sinai, Mount Hermon, and Mount Carmel. In both Old and New Testament accounts, Moses and many of the other Hebrew prophets were often called to the mountaintops to talk with their God, and in this way they let their wishes be known for the rulership of their tribes. Jove's totem was the sacred bull, while Hera's was the heavenly cow—a symbology carried over from the Age of Taurus, the bull, an age that spanned the centuries between 4400 and 2150 BCE.[7] Jove or Zeus was the lord of the thunderbolt, and his appearance was often accompanied by roaring flames and thunder, all qualities reported in the stories of Moses, who met Jehovah on top of Mount Sinai.

In Exodus 19:16–18 we read, "Then it came to pass on the third day, in the morning, that there were thunderings and lightnings, and a thick cloud on the mountain; and the sound of the trumpet was very loud, so that all the people who were in the camp trembled. And Moses brought the people out of the camp to meet with God, and they stood at the foot of the mountain. Now Mount Sinai was completely in smoke, because the Lord descended upon it in fire. Its smoke ascended like the smoke of a furnace, and the whole mountain quaked greatly." All this sounds a great deal like a large spaceship or rocket ship with its accompanying fire, smoke, and roar.

In both Roman and Greek mythology Hera, Jove's wife, was protective, wise, and just, but also known for her terrible temper in the face of her husband's many sexual exploits. While these two gods may have lived in harmony for many centuries, it is clear that the fury of their celestial divorce was played out through the polarization of the priests of Jehovah, who ultimately decided to destroy the Goddess and her temples of worship and either demonize, conscript, or suppress all the sacred symbols associated with her worship.

ASHERAH: QUEEN OF HEAVEN

The name *Asherah* actually means "holy queen" and is a fitting title for Hera. In Jerusalem she was also worshipped for centuries by the

names Asherah, Anath, Mari, and Miriam, and this title of spiritual
honor in connection with the many Marys in the Bible was then passed
down into both Jewish and Christian faiths. From the fifteenth century BCE onward, Asherah was the chief goddess of Tyre and also bore
the title Qudshu, or "holiness." Then, from the thirteenth century BCE
onward, she became the most important goddess of the Canaanite pantheon. Scholars know from the immense library of thirteenth-century
cuneiform tablets found in Ugarit, Syria, that, along with her daughter
Anath or Ishtar, Asherah was the most important goddess of the entire
northwestern Semitic pantheon.

As a consequence, there were many sanctuaries built to both
Asherah and Anath throughout the ancient world. Her sanctuary
of Beth-Anath, meaning the "House of Anath" in Hebrew, is mentioned in the nineteenth chapter of the Book of Joshua.[8] Some of the
early Israelite chieftains even called themselves her sons, among them
the Hebrew warrior Shamgar ben Anath (meaning "Shamgar son of
Anath") from the Old Testament Book of Judges (3:31), who "slew
of the Philistines six hundred men with an ox goad," or the jawbone
of an ox. As the Mother of Wisdom, Asherah's oracular centers were
renowned, and her diviner priests had the power to see far into the
future. In fact, the priests of Asherah and of Ba'al were both highly
gifted in the arts of dreaming and prophecy, and thus became a powerful threat to the priests of Yahweh, who wanted total control of the
people. Yahweh's priests even ordered the murder of any prophets or
dreamers who might arise among the Hebrew people, seeking to control the minds of the people even in their dreams. This persecution
was one of the dangers that John the Baptist faced many centuries
later when he began to prophesy about the coming of the messiah.
The priests of Yahweh had decreed:

> If there arise among you a prophet, or a dreamer of dreams and
> giveth there a sign or a wonder, and the sign or the wonder comes
> to pass, whereof he spake unto thee saying, "Let us go after other

Figure 7.4. Asherah, the Queen of Heaven, was linked to the Tree of Life, to the garden of the gods, and to Hera's much-beloved peacocks. (Illustration by Tricia McCannon)

gods, which thou hast not known, and let us serve them . . ." that prophet or that dreamer of dreams, shall be put to death . . . So shalt thou put the evil away from the midst of thee. (Deuteronomy 13:1–2, 5)

I dare say that if the prophets had encouraged the people to simply worship Jehovah and his priests, they would never have been put to death.

One of Asherah's titles was "She who gave birth to the seventy deities of Heaven," revealing her role as the overseeing goddess of all the other gods and goddesses on Mount Olympus.[9] Sumerians called her *Ashnan,* meaning the "strength of all things," and "kindly and bountiful maiden."[10] The Canaanites named her *Rabbatu athiratu yammi,* "lady who transverses the seas," and it is from this title that we get the title *rabbi* today.[11] So pervasive was her worship that she was known by many names in many lands, including *Lat, Elat, Elath,* and *Allat,* which literally means "goddess,"[12] and it is from *Allat* that the Muslims later derived the name of *Allah* for their masculinely based God. However, like the female angel Gabriel, who originally brought the inspired teachings of Islam to Muhammad on the mountaintop, centuries of patriarchal followers would later turn this female messenger into a male. Similarly, the morning star and the crescent moon were both originally symbols of Ishtar. Today these same goddess symbols of the crescent moon and star have now been adopted by the Muslim followers to represent their male-dominated religion, completely inverting their original meaning, which was linked to Venus, the morning star, and the lady of love.

THE SACRED WATERS AND THE SACRED TREE

Asherah was identified with the rivers and the sea, just as Mary and Isis would later be referred to as Stella Maris, or "Lady of the Sea." Asherah was called Athirau-Yammi or "She Who Walks on the Sea," a link to her connection with the life-giving waters of the Cosmic Ocean. "Anyone who truly grasps the goddess's complete nature can master the whole universe," writes Dr. Patai, "because he becomes one with her. In her resides all love. Her devotees call upon her as children addressing their mother, and she cherishes them, taking them to herself, so that they at last become one with her, experiencing a flood of supreme joy, and tasting boundless, intense bliss."[13]

The Goddess was also the "bread of life" who brought sustenance to humanity, so Hebrew women made special cakes or loaves of bread in the shape of the crescent moon, which today are called croissants. These cakes were also made in the shape of the Goddess herself and, like today's communion wafers, were ritually blessed and eaten by the priests and the people in ceremony.[14] In fact, the very word *eucharist* derives from the term *charis,* which is the name of a goddess, and simply means "grace."[15]

Asherah was the protector of animals, children, and women. Thus, the places most hallowed to her were the forests, springs, and sacred groves. The grove or the garden represents the birthplace of animals and plants and the inner sanctum of nature herself. It is linked to the idea of the Garden of Eden, where men and women come into sacred union with one another. In her sacred groves, her priests and priestesses taught the arts of carpentry, brick making, and building shelters, and one of her titles was "She Who Builds." Asherah was perennially linked to nature, so her shrines were built on hilltops and wooded knolls, where the carved asherim trees were erected, all dedicated to the Great Mother.[16] These sacred wooden totem poles were called asherim and were planted in the ground as symbols of the Tree of Life. In early times they often stood next to altars dedicated to Tammuz or Ba'al, and later a statue of Asherah was set up in the Jerusalem Temple itself. These sacred wooden totem poles were symbolically connected with both the Mother and the Son who gave his life for humanity. In Greek mythology, the golden apples of the Hesperides grew in Hera's sacred garden, produced by magical trees that provided bounty for the community. In Egypt the sustaining energies of the Tree of Life were linked to both Isis and Hathor, who are sometimes depicted leaning from this tree to offer a drink of water to wandering souls during their journey through the Underworld.

Since all these asherim trees were destroyed by the priests of Yahweh in the many centuries of patriarchal suppression, today we can only guess what these sacred trees looked like. We know they were wooden and may have been carved in the shape of a woman. They were placed in the groves of the Goddess and inscribed with sacred symbols. During

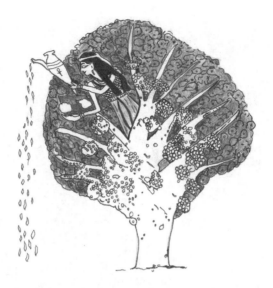

Figure 7.5. In her role as Isis or Hathor, the Goddess of Healing, she leans from the Tree of Life to offer water to the souls who have died as they journey through the Underworld after death. (Taken from the Egyptian Book of the Dead)

the annual rites of Anath and Tammuz, Asherah's women wove woolen bands of mourning to dress the wooden poles, wrapping these bands around the asherim trees each spring in memorial.

The Tree of Life the asherim symbolized is a mystical symbol found throughout the world in many religions. The Tree of Life has many symbolic meanings linked to our immortality, the Source of creation, and the Way of the return to the heavens. It was also the sacred tree on which the Divine Son dies in his many incarnations as Krishna, Adonis, Quetzalcoatl, and others, just as today the cross has become a symbol of the tree on which Jesus sacrificed himself for the world. In earlier centuries, the Tree of Life was associated with the sacrifice of the great lord Osiris in his service to humankind. Like the Christian cross, it was linked to the Egyptian ankh and became a symbol of eternal life. All these symbols remind us that the link between Heaven and Earth is intimately tied to both the Divine Mother of Compassion and the sacrifice of the Divine Son, and their appearance in our world is designed to bring spiritual illumination.

Figure 7.6. A Masonic apron whose symbology is based on the King Solomon's Temple. Notice the two columns of initiation that represent the male and female, with the sun, the moon, and the morning star symbolizing the union of the two polarities—male and female—that ultimately brings the initiate to enlightenment.

Historians tell us that once, long ago, these carved asherim pillars stood on either side of the altar of Jehovah in King Solomon's Temple. It is believed that their design may have been similar to the staff that Moses carried with its serpentine, spiraling snake. You will recall from biblical accounts that the people of Israel were once dramatically healed simply by gazing upon Moses's serpent staff, reminding us of the earlier meanings of enlightenment once assigned to the serpent. We see a symbolic depiction of these same two serpents on the columns of the

Masonic apron climbing up the pillars as spiral vines of ivy. This is reminiscent of the structure of our DNA and our serpentine nervous systems. In the background are the sun and the moon, ancient symbols for the male and female polarities that must be integrated to achieve spiritual mastery.

It is clear that at one time the Hebrew people understood these Mysteries, for within the Holy of Holies in King Solomon's Temple were two large winged human figures called cherubim—one male and one female—entwined in an embrace of conjugal love. Anthropologist Raphael Patai, author of *The Hebrew Goddess,* writes: "The Cherubim . . . continued to figure prominently in the Temple ritual down to the very end of the Second Jewish Commonweath (70 CE). Moreover, in their last version the Cherubim depicted a man and a woman in sexual embrace . . . their presence in the Holy of Holies, the innermost sanctuary of the Temple, and the ritual significance attributed to them, are invariably referred to as a most sacred mystery."[17] So at one time the Jews honored both the male and female aspects of God and understood that the union of both polarities are needed for the sacred alchemy of enlightenment. Yet despite the beauty and wisdom behind these traditions, in 2 Kings we read how the priests of Yahweh destroyed these asherim trees in all the groves and tried to suppress the worship of the Holy Mother. "You shall not plant for yourself an Asherah, any tree, beside the altar of Yahweh your god which you shall make for yourself. Neither shall you set up a pillar, which Yahweh your god hates" (Deuteronomy 16:21–22).

A TIME LINE OF HER WORSHIP

Around 950 BCE Asherah's worship was made official during the reign of the great King Solomon. The Book of Kings reports that while King Solomon loved Yahweh, he also "sacrificed and burnt incense in high places," telling us that these hilly knolls were worship sites to the Goddess. Although the priests of Yahweh revealed as little as possible about their competition, it is clear from these veiled references that we are speaking of the Divine Mother.

Anthropologist Raphael Patai postulates that the worship of Asherah may have first come to Israel through one of Solomon's seven hundred wives or three hundred concubines, since many of these marriages were political in nature. King Solomon's son Rehoboam reintroduced the worship of one aspect of the Goddess back into the Temples of Judah, while Solomon himself constructed a great temple to Asherah to honor the wife of Jehovah. But since the God and the Goddess were both honored in balance throughout the entire region of Canaan, it is likely that this worship had been a religious custom adopted by the Jews long before even King Solomon's time.[18] A hundred years after Solomon's reign, the worship of the Divine Mother was still going strong when King Ahab (who reigned from 873–852 BCE) married Jezebel, a princess of Sidon, and we know that the worship of the Goddess endured until 722 BCE, when the Northern Kingdom of Samaria fell to the Assyrian army. The cult of Yahweh would later claim that Samaria had been conquered because the Samarians worshipped the Divine Mother. The worship of the Goddess was still practiced as late as 621 BCE in Beth-el when Josiah, the King of Judea, destroyed altars to Asherah that had been established some three hundred years earlier by King Jeroboam. Even then, at least one statue of the Goddess survived, but in the Book of Kings we read that King Josiah purged Beth-el of all altars in high places "and burned the Asherah" (2 Kings 23:15). And from Old Testament accounts (1 Kings 15:13), we can determine that the priests of Yahweh were still struggling to oust Asherah from Judea when Maacah, the Israelite queen, was on the throne. Queen Maacah came from Samaria where Goddess worship had long been an accepted custom. When the queen tried to tell the people of Jerusalem that Asherah should be honored as the Mother Goddess, the priests of Yahweh claimed that only the Father deity had made life.[19]

Raphael Patai tells us that during the 370 years that King Solomon's Temple endured, for almost two-thirds of its duration (236 years), a statue of Asherah was kept in the Temple as part of the religion led by the Jewish king, the court, and the priesthood, and that she was opposed by only a few prophetic voices over a relatively long period of time.[20] Archaeologist William Dever reveals the discovery of a tomb at Khirbet el-Qum with an inscription to "Yahweh and his Asherah," as well as the discovery of a second jar dating to the ninth century from Kuntillat 'Ajrud that states, "I bless you by Yahweh and by his Asherah."[21] This means that for centuries the Jews honored both the Divine Mother and Father, although this balance of power was fiercely opposed by the sect of Yahweh. Despite the intense political opposition to the worship of Asherah by this small band of priests, her name is mentioned a total of forty times in the Old Testament, and Astarte's name appears some nine times.

Whether we call these beings Jehovah and Asherah, Jove and Hera, or the Divine Father and Mother of Creation, they were symbols of the universal principles of male and female essential to the dance of creation. Just as the male and female aspects of life fuel the physical and spiritual worlds with their electromagnetic energies, it is this partnership of duality in union that produces new life.

THE HOLY FOUR:
MOTHER/FATHER/DAUGHTER/SON

At the time that these many forms of worship were percolating in the Israeli kingdoms, there were also many sects that honored the Divine Daughter and Son. While Jehovah and Asherah were the Father-Mother gods of Israel, Anath was the Daughter, an incarnation of the Babylonian Goddess Ishtar or the Sumerian Goddess Inanna. Anath had a twin brother named Shamash (from the Hebrew word *shemesh,* meaning "sun"), just as Inanna had a twin brother named Utu. Both brothers were sun gods, and, like Yahweh or Zeus before them, Shamash and Utu were both Gods of thunder. Many shrines to the worship of Shamash as well as the Goddess Anath have been found scattered among the remains of several ancient Hebrew sites.

Figure 7.7. Ishtar visits Tammuz in South Africa. Notice the presence of the palm tree, representing the mystical symbol of the Tree of Life. Also note the lion at his feet, one of the earliest symbols for the christened king. Jesus would later inherit these same symbols. (Illustration by Tricia McCannon)

Then there was Tammuz, the much-loved fertility god who was Ishtar's beloved husband. In Canaanite lands, Tammuz was sometimes called Ba'al, a term that simply meant "master" in Hebrew, a title similar to *Adonis,* a Hebrew word that meant "lord." However, the worship of Ba'al became demonized by the priests of Yahweh, while the title *Adonis* was converted to the plural form of "lord," *Adonai,* used in Hebrew prayer. *Ba'al* is related to the Celtic word *Bel,* meaning light. As the Bible reflects, the priests of Ba'al were targeted by the Yahweh priests as well, perhaps in part because this divine pairing of Ishtar and Tammuz, or Anath and Ba'al, symbolized the deep and complex relationship between the all-loving Divine Goddess and her sacrificial lover and king. Tammuz was the progenitor of the dying, resurrected god, whose sacrifice is fully chronicled in the powerful story of Jesus; thus Tammuz was loved throughout the entire Mesopotamian world. Tammuz was the noble sacrificial priest-king who symbolically gave his life for his people, and whose death and resurrection were tied to the prosperity of the land. His blood was shed so that the crops might grow each year in the continued cycles of life, death, and rebirth.

These two divine couples, Mother-Father and Daughter-Son, are even woven into modern-day Christianity, although it is much harder for us to discern them. As we shall see, the existence of these "sacred four" was taught by Jesus, and this knowledge lies deep at the heart of the Gnostic faith. Their presence was even encoded into the tetragrammaton YHWH. A passage from the Zohar, or the Jewish Book of Wisdom, reads: "The letter Y brought forth a river which issued from the Garden of Eden and was identical with the Mother. The Mother became pregnant with two children, the W who was the Son and the second H who was the daughter, and she brought them forth and suckled them . . . These two children are under the tutelage of the Father and the Mother . . . After the Mother gave birth to the Son, she placed him before her, and this is why the first H in the name YHWH must be written close together with the W. The Son received a double share of inheritance from his Father and Mother, and he, in turn, nourished the Daughter. This is why when writing the Tetragrammaton in sacred texts, one must bring the W and the second H close together."[22] Another passage from the Zohar tells us that "the letter Y is called Father and stands for wisdom; the first H is the Supernal Mother called Understanding; and the W and the second H are the two children, a son and a daughter, who were crowned by their Mother."[23]

While Jehovah, Asherah, Ishtar, and Tammuz may have been exceedingly long-lived extraterrestrial world civilizers, the concepts that they taught are eternal. We see in many cultures that the gods often tried to employ myth, story, and symbol to convey to humanity eternal principles, selecting for example, certain symbols to represent certain qualities: illumination for the sun god; self-sacrifice for the fertility god; wisdom for the mother principle; and loyalty, passion, and fecundity for the daughter principle. If the gods' only purpose had been to be idolized and worshipped, certainly they would have chosen to be visible to their followers, allowing themselves to be publicly revered, like movie stars. Instead, these celestial teachers carefully selected certain complex hermetic symbols to convey powerful esoteric truths about the nature of the universe to their younger, less informed human cousins and, in so doing, passed on their wisdom.

While today most of us are oblivious to such esoteric symbolism, remnants of this way of teaching can still be found in modern-day religions. Christianity uses a cross to represent eternal life and resurrection, a dove to symbolize the Holy Spirit, an eagle for the Divine Father, and a lion for the solar power of the Divine Son. Today, we can see echoes of this knowledge hidden beneath the trinity of the Father, Son, and Holy Ghost, three of the four divine principles of creation. While most of us are familiar with the Father and Son, the Holy Spirit is more elusive. She is the Shekinah, the feminine breath of God that moves throughout the galaxies as the carrier wave of light and sound that allows the universe to come into being. The Holy Spirit is the flame that descended over the apostles, anointing them with the gifts of healing and prophecy. In this great trinity of Father, Son, and Daughter, only the Divine Mother herself has been forgotten, thinly concealed in her guise as the Virgin Mary.

THE SEXUAL RITES OF UNION

Let us now take a look at one of the most controversial aspects of ancient worship—the sacred rites of sexual union hidden at the heart of the Mysteries. As we have seen, the presence of the male and female cherubim in the Holy of Holies, overseeing the Ark of the Covenant, tells us that at one time the Hebrew tribes honored the alchemy of sexual union. This act symbolized a spiritual technology of transformation that must take place within each one of us to awaken to mastery. For many centuries, this spiritual tie took place as part of the Goddess celebrations each year. In Samaria and Judea it was dedicated to Anath and Tammuz (or Ba'al), the daughter and son of the tetrad.

Anath is celebrated throughout all of Mesopotamia, the Indus Valley, the Mediterranean, and much of the Levant. She was famous in many forms as Inanna, the warrior Goddess; Ishtar, the protector Goddess; and Aphrodite or Venus, the Goddess of Sexual Love. In the Ugaritic myths, her titles were the "maiden Anath" or the "virgin

Anath," and, like Ishtar (one and the same), she was called "Lady of heaven, Mistress of all the gods."[24] Over time Anath also assumed many of the original titles of Asherah and later came to be associated with the famous goddess Cybele in Rome, as well as Mari, Miriam, and Astarte. Multifaceted and complex, Anath was the Goddess of Love, War, and Growing Things; thus she is sometimes depicted wearing a lion's head to represent her royalty and fierceness.

Throughout the Levant Anath's annual festivals were centered on the rescue of Ba'al, her husband, from the Underworld, just as in the Mediterranean Ishtar's celebrations were focused on rescuing Tammuz from Hades. As noted on page 98, this powerful annual celebration, held each year at the opening of the planting season, was similar to Easter.

This act of fertility was also played out throughout all of Canaan and the Hebrew lands in sexual rites that were considered liturgical celebrations. During these holidays, men or women could engage in sexual relations with anyone they chose, reenacting the ritual of union between the sexes. In this capacity the man became an expression of the virile forces of the God, while the woman became an expression of the fertile energies of the Goddess. This energetic coupling was one of the most deeply rooted aspects of religious belief linked to the Goddess and her husband-son-lover and was undoubtedly a form of sympathetic magic meant to increase the fecundity of the land. It is also well known that the ecstasy of sexual union can provide a powerful biochemical gateway into mystical states of consciousness, allowing the participants to temporarily dissolve their egos and melt into the bliss of love. Celebrated in its highest form, sex allows us to experience a deep and transcending love for one another. If suffused with the spirit of love, sex has the power to heal, to nurture, and to activate the kundalini life forces, activating the spiritual forces that can awaken the Third Eye. Elsewhere in the world—in India, for example—we can find similar celebrations played out between men and women in ecstatic, tantric union as a form of prayer.

Sexual tantra has long been practiced in the East as a means of raising the kundalini life force. The basic principle behind it is that women possess more spiritual energy than men, so a man could achieve realization of the Divine through sexual and emotional union with a woman. This fundamental rite involved controlled sexual intercourse, or sex without male orgasm. The theory behind it was that a man must store up his vital fluids, rather than expending them in ejaculation. Through tantric training, he could learn to absorb back into his body the fluids engendered by his partner's orgasm through his penis. Theoretically, the vital fluids would then be stored in his spinal column, moving up through his chakras to his head and flowering forth with the inspiration of divine wisdom. Tantric scriptures that explain these practices are based on the worship of the Goddess, together with the philosophies underlying these rites.

Thus, according to this philosophy, sex has the power to produce ecstatic states of consciousness. But this was not a view that the priests of Yahweh supported or encouraged. This approach revealed the power of women as catalysts for this kind of higher consciousness and threatened the social control of organized religions because these sexual experiences had the power to produce direct illumination. Sexual tantra also threatened the power of the patriarchy by giving women equal sexual rites. So the priests of Yahweh rejected the principle of sexual equality embodied by the Goddess, inveighing against the Goddess and turning women who disobeyed them into whores.

Biblical researchers Joan Norton and Margaret Starbird write: "Since time immemorial, the mystical experience of union with the Divine has been expressed in the vocabulary of marriage and sexual ecstasy. One of its most beautiful expressions is found in the Hebrew Bible's Song of Songs, where the bride and bridegroom extol one another's virtues in erotic language, celebrating their passion with mutual admiration. This is the language of lover, the beloveds trysting in the garden."[25]

This sacred union represents the merger of the yin and the yang within ourselves, one of the prime teachings of the Mystery Schools.

Figure 7.8. Each year the annual festivals of Ishtar and Tammuz marked the renewal of the crops, the seasons, and renewed life. At a practical level, they used the sympathetic act of lovemaking to stimulate the fertility and nourish the Earth. (Illustration by Tricia McCannon)

This was also taught by Jesus in his parables of the bride and the bride-groom. This spiritual marriage of alchemy is what Jesus refers to in the Gospel of Thomas when he tells his disciples how to become self-realized human beings. "When you make the two One and the inner as the outer and the outer as the inner, the above as the below, so that you make the male and female into a single One, in order that the male isn't made male and the female made female . . . then shall you enter the kingdom" (22:9–21). This is about bringing the masculine and feminine polarities into balance within the self, which allows us to open the portals of Heaven. This sacred union is the mechanism for achieving true enlightenment. This may well be the real reason that the patriarchal powers chose to avoid, ignore, malign, suppress, or misinterpret these deeper teachings: If the people could achieve spiritual mastery on their own, that would render the priesthood obsolete.

Catholic priest and theologian Jean-Yves Leloup writes about how the knowledge of the Sacred Marriage was once part of the wisdom teachings of the ancients, and represents the two parts of ourselves that must eventually be reconciled to achieve mastery. "Some have seen Plato's teaching as an evocation of the androgynous nature of humanity—at once male and female—kind of a primordial wholeness for which we have a nostalgic longing. Erotic love would thus appear to be a desperate yearning for our missed half. In Greek mythology and thought, the separation of man and woman is seen as a punishment. In Hebrew thought, however, this same separation is seen as a gift of the Creator."[26]

Yet this kind of powerful religious rite was deeply threatening to the priests of Yahweh. Theirs was not a God of bliss, but rather a God of fear and vengeance. While these rites had obviously worked for centuries to create harmonious, prosperous, nonwarlike cultures, the very premise of the Sacred Marriage is based on equality between men and women, so it was not to be tolerated by the patriarchy.

While much can be said about the mystical power of allowing oneself to become a channel for unbridled passion, love, and devotion, today most of us would hardly even know how to approach this kind of exalted sexual experience. After all, we have been programmed for over two thousand years with a plethora of negative emotions regarding sex. These include lust, guilt, shame, incest, obsession, manipulation, and repression, resulting in the multimillion-dollar porn industry that thrives today. So untangling ourselves from these culturally ingrained misalignments may take some time, as we strive to get back to a place of healthy sexuality, where we can enter the sacred temple of the self in true spiritual communion and love and share it with another.

At its most basic human level, this celebration might have provided a social mechanism for married people to have a sexual experience with someone other than their own spouse. It may have been a safety valve built into ancient cultures for curtailing the kind of rampant infidelity and high divorce rates we see in our own cultures today. However, these rites could also be celebrated with one's own wife or husband, keeping the vows of fidelity intact.

From history it is clear that these ecstatic sexual rites were very threatening to the priests of Yahweh. First, they equalized the playing field between men's and women's sexual freedom. Second, they ushered in an ecstatic spiritual experience with which the male priesthood could not compete. And third, they endangered the patriarchical lines of property, succession, and ownership. As long as a man had complete fidelity from his wives and concubines, he could ensure the parentage of his children. But if there were ever a moment when the woman had the same privileges as the man, then his genetic line could not be guaranteed. Under Hebrew law, if a woman engaged in sexual relations with any man except her own husband, even a man who had raped her, she was burned to death or stoned.

These taboos are all related to power, money, and control. For centuries, the rites of succession had been passed through the female line. The man who ruled beside the queen—her husband or brother—was of her own choosing. And since all could observe when the queen bore children, it was her daughter who inherited the throne. In turn, that daughter chose the next king as her husband, selecting the most worthy man as her consort. As we have learned, this partnership model had created centuries of prosperity and happiness. But in the patriarchical system only men could own property, control religions, or decide the fate of women and children. Women had no say in their own fate. This is the primary difference between the matrilineal and patriarchal systems.

ALCHEMICAL MASTERY

Anthropologist Raphael Patai writes that from the beginning, there were two images of the deity in the temple of Jerusalem—Yahweh and his consort, the Goddess. Later, once all images of the Divine had been forbidden by the priests, Yahweh's image disappeared, leaving only the two human cherubim made of olive wood and covered in gold leaf, whose vast wings covered the Ark of the Covenant itself. These cherubim stood fifteen feet tall, and their wingspans stretched the entire thirty feet of the Holy of Holies, overseeing the sanctuary where the Ark was kept.[27] Throughout the Levant, other pairs of such winged figures have also been found, some both male and female; others only female. One such set was discovered on a plaque from the palace of King Ahab of Israel, showing two female beings facing each other, kneeling with outstretched wings and a flower in their hands. These female cherubim remind us of the two Egyptian Goddesses Isis and Nepthys, the two sisters who guarded the tomb of Osiris, the lord of resurrection. Like the male and female cherubim, Isis and Nepthys represent the solar and lunar aspects of the Divine Mother, hermetic symbols of the spiritual technologies of enlightenment. Their wings surround the djed pillar, a symbol of the power of Osiris, who, like Jesus after him, was perennially linked to the Tree of Life, the Way of the Return, and the regenerating power of the soul itself.

Similarly, in temples in Assyria we also find two such winged figures protecting the Tree of Life, and these are both male and female. The importance of this sacred alchemy between the sexes seems to have come to the Jews from Moses when he brought his wisdom out of Egypt. Moses had twelve such pairs of protective winged cherubim sewn onto the fabric of his desert tabernacle: ten pairs on the various curtains of

Figure 7.9. Like the winged figures from the Temple of Solomon, Isis and Nepthys flank the djed, a pillar that symbolizes the Tree of Life and the union of the solar and lunar energies in perfect union. (Illustration by Tricia McCannon)

Figure 7.10. The Ark of the Covenant is flanked by two golden winged figures representing the lunar and solar energies needed to attain enlightenment. These symbols are derivatives of far earlier Mysteries found in Egypt, Sumeria, Babylon, and Assyria.

the tabernacle; one pair embroidered on the veil that hid the Holy of Holies, concealing the statues of the male and female cherubim in sacred embrace, and another pair hovering over the Ark itself.[28] This means that the great Hebrew sages once understood the inner alchemy of spiritual mastery that allows us to make a direct connection with the Source.

However, as the priests of Yahweh became increasingly patriarchal and controlling, they claimed that there was only one aspect of God, Yahweh, and that no other gods would be tolerated. To explain their own sacred symbolism within the Holy of Holies, they told the people of Israel that they were the bride of Yahweh, dismissing the true meaning of alchemical union. Later, we would see this same misinterpretation of the Sacred Marriage imposed by the Catholic Church on the teachings of Jesus, shifting the original teachings of the bride and the bridegroom to mean union with the church. At a personal level, this completely distorts the wisdom of inner alchemy needed to achieve mastery. At a cultural level, it creates a great imbalance in our cultures, our religions, and our relationships as we minimize, suppress, dismiss, or obsess over the feminine sex.

It is clear to anyone who observes the world of nature that both genders are needed equally to birth something new. Anne Baring and Jules Cashford, authors of *The Myth of the Goddess: Evolution of an Image,* a study chronicling the disappearance of the Divine Feminine in masculine theology, write: "After the destruction of the First Temple and the building of the Second Temple, the cherubim in the Holy of Holies were believed to reflect the male and female aspects of Yahweh [or God]. Later still, before the destruction of the Second Temple, figures of the male and female cherubim embracing, which stood in the Holy of Holies, reflected the union of Yahweh with the community of Israel, [that were] now depicted as his bride."[29]

All true initiates know that a knowledge of this alchemical marriage lay at the heart of the great spiritual Mystery Schools and was the goal of those who pursue the "Great Work." This is the alchemical process of the Philosopher's Stone, a process of turning lead into gold and a metaphor for awakening the divine supernal Self within the amnesia of the little egoic self. Past sages realized that uniting the male and the female within the self was the true path of mastery. So they created three successive levels of initiation to teach these principles. The first level was dedicated to the Divine Mother and Daughter; the second level to the Divine Father and Son, and the third was the union between the two. The first level of initiation included a study of the realms of nature: knowledge of the stars, the animals and plants, herbs and trees, and the development of one's healing gifts. It also encompassed a knowledge of the cycles of birth, life, death, and rebirth, and the Great Mother who oversees them all in the endless cycles of change found in the natural world.

The second level of initiation was dedicated to the Father and Son. It included the study of history, law, philosophy, astronomy, astrology, sacred geometry, mathematics, construction, music, and the power of the Word. It also called for the development of the inner senses and control of the elements. This phase embraced the knowledge that the Father periodically returns to Earth as the Divine Son, the agent of enlightenment for each World Age. This soul is called the *Aion,* the great solar lord who ushers in each World Age. Historically, he dies on the "cross" of matter, since the secular powers of the world oppose his message of spiritual liberation. His many incarnations include world saviors, such as Prometheus, Tammuz, Adonis, Osiris, Orpheus, Krishna, Mithra, Quetzalcoatl, and, most recently, the beloved lord Jesus.

The final level of the Mysteries taught the integration of the male and female aspects of ourselves, a union that ultimately brings us to mastery. This is called the Hierogamos, or Sacred Marriage. While it appears that at the time of Solomon this knowledge was still being honored, it was later suppressed by the priests of Yahweh. It remained lost until the time of Jesus, who taught the marriage of the bride and bridegroom. However, with the demotion of the sacred feminine by the Roman Catholic Church, this spiritual technology was lost to us once again, obliterating the path to personal mastery.

THE SHIFT TO AN ALL-YAHWEH SOCIETY

For the Jews, the final shift to a single masculine god occurred when the Persian king Darius swept into Babylon and freed them in 538 BCE, ending the Jewish exile. While only a third of the Hebrews decided to return to Canaan from Babylon, history records that the Persians were instrumental in rebuilding the Jewish strongholds in Canaan, forcibly transporting subjects to many areas that were underpopulated in order to impose economic and imperial Persian policies on their conquered lands. By the mid-400s BCE, the Persians had built a chain of fortresses across this region to protect their trade routes, and they funded the rebuilding of Jerusalem with Persian gold. The Second Jewish Temple was built there in 516 BCE, along with a series of new cities. The Persians also enforced their own legal codes throughout the region they controlled.

But the Jews, like the Persians, fell under the sway of Zoroaster's dualistic theology. Zoroaster preached about the two gods Ahura Mazda and Ahriman, forerunners to our own Christian versions of God and Satan. Ahura Mazda was the good god who inspired people to live moral lives. Ahriman represented all that is evil in humanity. He is the negative ruler of this world. This kind of thinking polarizes everything that does not conform to one's worldview as the "work of the devil." This attitude then crept into Jewish theology with devastating consequences. Thus, the period following the rebuilding of the Second Jewish Temple appears to be one of highly dualistic thinking and increasing patriarchal control.[30]

> The Persian domination of Judea's religious life meant that a strict Zoroastrian type of monotheism replaced the more tolerant old religion that prevailed in the First Temple. Despite a great deal of covert resistance, after the return of the Jews from their Babylonian exile, the Hebrew Goddess and all her tantric works were demonized. Her groves were cut down and her women's orders dissolved.
>
> Monotheism further purged the Jerusalem ideology of its cus-

tomary hierarchy of divinities under the one God, banning its agricultural Ba'als and Ba'alats, its god-kings and soothsaying prophets, and its families of nature gods, devas and angels; and wedded it instead to the idea of a single great God of Heaven: male, omnipotent, and implicitly superior to the deities of all other races.

Reformed Judaism was thus born under the domination of a theocratic priesthood deeply resented by many Jews for casting off Israel's ancient and much beloved agricultural Mysteries.[31]

Today historians believe that this transposition of Yahweh's functions into that of the *Elohim* did not happen until after the Babylonian exile ended in the sixth century BCE. Biblical historian Philip Davies describes how the influx of so many different immigrants to this area of Canaan resulted in the Hebrew implementation of many strict laws, the establishment of castes, and the promotion of a religious agenda that "constitutes a massive exercise in self-definition, in which I take the creation of the biblical literature to be a further enterprise."[32] Davies postulates that "the literate elite, which comprised about 5% of the population, generated an identity through literature and chose the name Israel to represent the people designated by Yahweh to inhabit the area, bind it to a covenant, and distinguish it from other peoples."[33] Davies believes that this period constitutes the earliest plausible context for the creation of the biblical Israel and the Old Testament literature—in other words, the Bible. In the Higginbothams' *Christ to Paganism* we read:

> According to the Old Testament, when [the prophet] Nehemiah came to Jerusalem from the Persians in the mid 400's B.C.E., he began sweeping reforms to reintroduce or enforce Yahweh alone worship, some of which had to be implemented by force. Polytheism and blended practices were eventually abolished, and the Yahweh alone group became the majority. For the first time, worship of Yahweh became the nation's religion.[34]

THE VICTORS WRITE THE HISTORIES

When we consider that the writers of the Old Testament were the political victors in a war fought for control of the Hebrew people, the later stories of male aggression that promote the use of violence and vengeance make sense. It is not that the early stories of murder and theft ordered by Yahweh were necessarily true, although they might have been. However, for Yahweh's priests, these other sects could not be tolerated. In the first Book of Kings (1 Kings 18), Elijah, a priest of the cult of Yahweh, murders some 450 prophets of Ba'al, revealing the absolute ferocity of this sect. That is a lot of priests to murder, especially ones who honor the God of love. I am pretty sure that the destruction of those prophets ended the formal worship of Tammuz in Jerusalem!

It is clear from the information now being discovered in archaeological digs and historical research that for many centuries the Hebrews practiced a more balanced kind of worship. The God and the Goddess were deeply established in the lives of the Hebrew people from the time of their settlement in Canaan, circa 1250 BCE, to the time of the Babylonian exile in 586 BCE. "From about 300 BCE—after the post-Exilic reforms of Ezra—She seems to vanish, although, curiously, Her image still remains in the Holy of Holies of the Second Temple."[35]

Some fifteen hundred years later, the Goddess reappears in the kabbalistic Jewish communities of medieval Spain and southwestern France. This time she comes in the form of the Shekinah, the Holy Spirit, also called the Matronit, the lady and the queen. Viewed as a divine intercessor between humanity and a wrathful, judgmental male deity, the Shekinah is ultimately linked to Isis, Mary, Sophia, and Mary Magdalene, all known as the Queens of Heaven.

In light of these new discoveries it seems clear that at least some of the Old Testament was created many centuries after the events that they claim to portray in order to forge a sense of unity among the many diverse groups that composed the Hebrew nation. Since many of these writings were fabricated, edited, or highly embellished by the priests of

Yahweh, we can now consider much of what we know about the Bible in a completely different light, especially since many of these events directly contradict historical evidence.

The priests of Yahweh had several reasons for these fabrications. First, they needed to create a national identity after years of being dispersed by conquering armies. Second, by choosing one God instead of many, they could more easily control the people. Third, by selecting a powerful male deity, it was easier for them to justify the succession of lands, titles, and religious control, and give these powers entirely to men. Fourth, by generating their own warlike versions of the settlement stories in Canaan, they gave the people a sense of "heroic victory" around which the nomadic tribes could rally. They also simultaneously imposed the message that those who opposed this God would be punished for many generations to come.

Even though these conquest stories of murder, rape, intolerance, and plunder directly contradict the Ten Commandments given by Jehovah, they are still stories of victory promulgated by the elite priesthood. This intolerant approach to religion teaches a highly toxic value system while simultaneously instilling the fear of God's retribution in the people. Thus, the priests of Yahweh were able to convey two major messages in one: the ability of the people to be victorious if they obeyed the priests and the threat of punishment to those who did not. This schizophrenic approach was unfortunately inherited by the newly emerging Catholic Church, resulting in no less than eight "holy crusades" and the horrific deaths of millions, all in the name of the Prince of Peace. This mentality is crazy-making, especially since these actions are a complete violation of the prime directives of both Yahweh's Ten Commandments and Jesus's admonitions to "love our neighbors as ourselves."

Footprints
of the Mother

Humanity has imagined her as the immensity of cosmic
space, as the moon, as the earth and nature.
She is the age-old symbol of the invisible dimension of soul
and the instinctive intelligence that informs it.
We live within her being, yet we know almost nothing
about her.
She is everything that is still unfathomed by us about the
nature of the universe, matter and the invisible energy
that circulates through all the different aspects of her
being.
She spins and weaves the shimmering robe of life in which
we live and through which we are connected to all
cosmic life.

ANDREW HARVEY AND ANNE BARING,
THE DIVINE FEMININE

As I entered more deeply into an understanding of these Mysteries, over the next few years I was to learn about a completely different type of human history from what we are taught about in school today. Through the writings of brave pioneers, such as archaeologists Marija Gimbutas and Alexander Marshack; historians Barbara Walker, Riane Eisler, and Merlin Stone; international authors Andrew Harvey and Anne Baring; and ceremonial teacher Z. Budapest, I learned that for hundreds of years our modern-day society has been a victim of a political and religious cover-up, designed to conceal a time when human beings lived in more egalitarian and humane societies. Before the warmongering ages of the patriarchy descended, there were earlier eras on this planet that honored the Divine Mother as the Creatrix of life. These societies had a completely different paradigm for human partnership from what we have today. Merlin Stone, author of the seminal books *When God Was a Woman* and *Ancient Mirrors of Womanhood,* writes:

> In prehistoric and early historic periods of human development, religions existed in which people revered their supreme creator as female. The Great Goddess—the Divine Ancestress—had been worshipped from the beginnings of the Neolithic periods of 7000 B.C. until the closing of the last Goddess temples, about A.D. 500. Some authorities would extend Goddess worship as far into the past as the Upper Paleolithic Age of about 25,000 B.C. . . .
>
> Archaeological, mythological and historical evidence all reveal that the female religion, far from naturally fading away, was the victim of centuries of continual persecution and suppression by the advocates of the newer religions which held male deities as supreme. And from these new religions came the creation myth of Adam and Eve and the tale of the loss of Paradise.[1]

This hidden era of Earth's cultures stretched back for literally thousands of years and encompassed great civilizations in the Middle East, the Mediterranean, Egypt, Africa, India, Britain, Polynesia, Europe, and the North, South, and Central American continents, all of which had once honored the Great Mother as the Creatress of all. In time, I came to realize that most of the inequities we find in our world today are a direct result of this forgotten aspect of the Queens of Heaven, which set us on a course that threw our core values and ourselves out of balance.

Our male-dominated approach has led to the rape and pillage of our planet's resources, the creation of hierarchical financial institutions that oppress the poor and support the rich, and the clear sense that we are losing touch with our true place in the cosmos. For although many of us may have an innate sense, even a long-buried memory, of a time when men and women lived together in mutual respect and harmony, much of the history, religion, and values we have inherited have been written by the victors of a patriarchal war who have felt highly threatened by the true events of our ancestral past.

As I began to discover these hidden records, I was stunned at how far back they went. Barbara Mor and Monica Sjöö, authors of *The Great Cosmic Mother,* explain the magnitude of the lost centuries of human history: "It is important for us as human beings, to really grasp the time dimensions involved here; that God was considered Female for at least the first 200,000 years of human life on earth!"[2] And, "in fact, the only image of the Creator ever painted on rock, carved in stone or sculpted in clay for a period of about 30,000 years, was that of the Divine Mother."[3] While this statement seems almost incomprehensible to those of us raised in conventional contemporary societies, once we examine the anthropological evidence it becomes an indisputable truth. In a world where we have all been conditioned to expect violence, war, and competition as the norm, few of us can even conceive of a planet where human beings can live side by side in harmony with one another.

So how did this imbalance come about? How did the patriarchy gain power, and how does half the human race claim the right to suppress or belittle the other half? What happened to our understanding of the universe, which led to one sex being forced into subservience, while the other half claims to be superior? Why are the only role models that we have of women in Judaism, Christianity, and Islam the obedient virgin, the penitent prostitute, or the innocent Eve who has been blamed for humankind's expulsion from Paradise? Inculcating these kinds of limited archetypes sends a message to women everywhere that if they stray from the conventions established by men, they will be either condemned or cast out of society. So I began to examine the archaeological evidence of more ancient cultures where men and women had lived together in harmony. Let's take a look at the data that supports this hypothesis, and its implications for contemporary life.

THE WORLD OF ARCHAEOLOGICAL EVIDENCE

One of the first people to discover the evidence for Goddess-based cultures was archaeologist Marija Gimbutas. Raised in Lithuania, Gimbutas studied in Austria, Germany, and finally the United States. She became a graduate fellow at Harvard University in 1950, where she taught for twelve years. In 1963 she moved to the University of California at Los Angeles, and in 1967 she began her own archaeological excavations in Yugoslavia, Greece, and Italy; these lasted for fifteen years. Having been raised in the old country of the Lithuanian countryside, where the culture was not completely Christianized until the fourteenth century, she had grown up with many symbols still present of the ancient Mother religion that once existed in her own country. This had prompted her to become a folklore specialist and a linguist fluent in more than twenty-five languages.[4] So unlike her American-born colleagues, Gimbutas had an innate understanding of the symbolic language of the Goddess that she had learned in childhood.

Between the years of 1967 and 1980, she was the project director at five major Neolithic digs in southeast Europe. During the many years of her excavations in the Mediterranean, particularly Greece, Bulgaria, Yugoslavia, and Turkey, Gimbutas's teams began turning up artifacts that represented the Divine Mother, and Gimbutas was able to interpret them. Circles, spirals, vulvas, snakes, birds, fish, wavy lines, and laby-rinths were all present on the walls, floors, and pottery that they found, as well as numerous Venus-like figurines. Gimbutas recognized all of these as part of an intricate symbol language once used by our ances-tors, linked to the idea of a feminine Creator. Her understanding of this symbol system created a bridge between archaeology and mythol-ogy, as she came to the conclusion that the art of Old Europe reflected a mythopoetic perception of the sacredness and mystery of the natural world expressed through "a cohesive and persistent ideological system."[5] During the course of her many excavations, she discovered images of the Great Mother going back well beyond thirty-five thousand years. These discoveries were first brought to light in 1974 with the publication of her celebrated book *Goddesses and Gods of Old Europe—6500–3500 B.C.: Myths and Cult Images*. Gimbutas went on to publish several more books on this subject, including *The Living Goddess, The Language of the Goddess, The Civilizations of the Goddess: The World of Old Europe,* and *Bronze Age Cultures in Central and Eastern Europe*.

THE CULTURE OF THE GODDESS

In her books Dr. Gimbutas reveals that these earlier matristic cultures lived in balance both with one another and with the land. They cultivated healthy male and female relationships, which resulted in peaceful agrar-ian societies of craftsmanship, ritual, art, and the renewal of the Earth. The reins of leadership were usually held by a woman, who was both the queen and high priestess, and her brother or husband often ruled beside her. The lines of succession and property were usually passed through the mother's line, while the uncle or husband helped to train the next genera-tion and ruled beside her. While a man could certainly have merit, skill, and status in his own right, it was his marriage to the queen, the sovereign of the land, that granted him kingship. "As a general rule society was built around the woman, even on the highest levels where descent was through the female line. A man became king or chieftain only by a formal marriage and his daughter, not his son, succeeded so that the next chieftain was the youth who married his daughter . . ."[6]

Matristic Goddess cultures were always associated with the cultivation of food, and the agricultural knowledge of herbs, roots, plants, healing and other medical aids, as well as the invention of writing, arts, weaving, textiles, and the very foundations of civilization itself. "Among their many advanced achievements were pottery, weaving, writing, complex calendrical and mathematical systems, astronomy and astrology, painting, basket making, domestication of animals, cultivation of grains and seeds, masonry, and sacred architecture."[7] They were keepers of story, history, and sacred rites, and they also maintained temples of worship that honored the sacred in all things.[8]

"The priestesses long presided over religious practices. Woman was the natural intermediary with divinities, the greatest of whom was woman deified . . . the participation of men in the cult was, like the association of a god with a goddess, a late development. Their part in the religious ceremonies was always a subordinate one, even when the king became the high priest of the bull."[9] These cultures were not militaristic; they used weapons only for hunting, consistently choosing the most beautiful sites in which to live. "In these communities no weapons have been unearthed, no defensive earthworks found, and there is no evidence of an oppressive ruling hierarchy or of social conflict."[10]

Figure 8.1. This Neolithic fertility goddess statue found in Dobrogea, Romania, dating from 5000 BCE, combines aspects of both male and female forms within it.

This societal model of balance between husbands and wives or brothers and sisters is what anthropologists now call a "partnership model." This is quite different from the dominant patriarchal cultures we have been living under for the past twenty-five hundred years. These harmonious societies of shared leadership resulted in centuries of prosperous agrarian societies and virtually no war. In their excavations, anthropologists have found streets lined with spacious houses in towns of several thousand inhabitants, where there were no tribal gods, only a universally worshipped Mother Goddess or God/Goddess Creator that expressed the principle of male and female union. While some of these statues were created solely in the voluptuous image of the Divine Mother, others show a round female body and the narrow, pillarlike head of a male; in other words, a Creator of balanced androgyny.

> The key finding is that women participated as fully as the men in all aspects of their religious and intellectual life. With equal authority and creativity, women played essential roles in religious rituals and acted as partners in evolving the spiritual philosophy on which their civilization was built.
>
> Not until the invasions of the patriarchal Kurgan peoples from the north imposed male dominance on the populace, bringing war and national power struggles to the region and competing gods to their temples, did the men and women of Old Europe demonstrate antagonism and disunity. Until then they appear to have built the framework and evolved the structural principles of their society together with great success, each modifying and balancing the extreme tendencies of the other.[11]

In essence we are talking about a partnership model that is quite different from the dominator model we have had for some twenty-five hundred years. Marija Gimbutas explains the difference between these two kinds of civilizations in their use of symbolic language, revealed some fifty years after her archaeological excavations:

The symbolic systems are very different [between the matristic and patriarchal cultures]. All of this reflects the social structure. The Indo-European social structure is patriarchal, patrilineal and the psyche is warrior. Every God is also a warrior. The three main Indo-European Gods are the God of the Shining Sky, the God of the Underworld, and the Thunder God. The female goddesses are just brides, wives or maidens without any power, without any creativity. They're just there, they're beauties, they're Venuses, like the dawn or sun maiden.

So the system of what existed in the *matristic* culture before the Indo-Europeans in Europe is totally different. I call it matristic, not matriarchal, because matriarchal always arouses ideas of dominance and is compared with the patriarchy. But it was a balanced society; it was not that women were really so powerful that they usurped everything that was masculine.

Men were in their rightful position, they were doing their own work, they had their duties and they also had their own power. This is reflected in their symbols where you find not only goddesses but also, gods. The Goddesses were creatrixes, they are creating from themselves. As far back as 35,000 B.C., from symbols and sculptures, we can see that the parts of the female body were creative parts: breasts, belly and buttocks. It was a different view from ours—it had nothing to do with pornography.[12]

Today researchers in this area are beginning to realize that many of our social, political, and economic problems have been created because of this more aggressive, winner-take-all, dominator model. These problems include the classic triangle of the persecutor, rescuer, and victim mentalities that are often generated by the power of caste, hierarchy, abuse, and oppression. Scientist James DeMeo says, "There's no clear and unambiguous evidence for the existence of warfare, sadism, traumatization of babies, subordination of women, nor any of the trappings of patrism anywhere in the world prior to around 4000 BCE. None!"[13] And since this patriarchal model has been the mind-set that has generated the problem, these imbalances in our thinking and culture cannot be resolved by using this same model. We can only heal our society if we are willing to make a paradigm shift in the coming age to a collective life of greater cooperation.

STATUES OF THE GODDESS

During her many years of research, Dr. Gimbutas discovered many ancient statues of the Divine Mother, the earliest of which is the figurine called the Acheulian Goddess. This hand-sized statue is dated somewhere between 230,000 and 800,000 years ago and was discovered in the Golan Heights region of Israel, once known as Berekhat Ram. Carved from scoria stone, it was found in organic matter that has now been carbon-dated to at least 232,000 years ago and may, in fact, be far older. The Acheulian Goddess is one of over 130 such statues that have been recovered to date[14] and is believed to come from an area inhabited by a hominid tribe that predates even the Neanderthals. This tells us that over two hundred thousand years ago, our ancestors believed that God

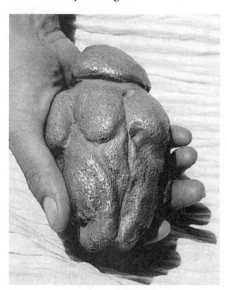

Figure 8.2. The Acheulian Goddess statue, found in the Golan Heights region of Israel, is dated between 230,000 and 800,000 years ago.

Figure 8.3. The Willendorf Goddess, dated around forty thousand years ago, is a symbol of the fecundity of the life-giving, voluptuous Goddess.

was a female, the "One who Birthed the Universe." Some researchers have called this powerful figurine the earliest manifestation of a work of art.

Before the discovery of the Acheulian Goddess, the earliest known statue of the Divine Mother was the "Venus of Willendorf," a voluptuous female figure only 4⅜ inches high, carved out of bone and known to be about forty thousand years old. Found in 1908 in Austria near the Danube River by archaeologist Josef Szombathy,* the Willendorf Goddess is one of several powerful images representing and revering the fertility of the Great Mother.

Some of these figures also resemble the many figures of the Goddess found throughout the Near East,[15] especially in Lebanon, Syria, Palestine, Anatolia (now modern-day Turkey), Iraq, and Jericho. These Goddess figurines also appear in Australia, China, Africa, Sumeria, Turkey, and Egypt,[16] and continue to be discovered even today, dating

---

*The Willendorf Goddess was found in an Aurignacian loess deposit about ninety-eight feet above the Danube River near the Austrian town of Willendorf.

back between 24,000 and 18,000 BCE.* In the ruins of Çatalhöyük, Turkey, for example, there are hundreds of female figurines found all over the site, as well as Goddess symbols painted on the walls, including artistically drawn cow heads that clearly resemble the organs of female reproduction. There are also models that show women baking bread in the temples. Interestingly enough, the women and children are buried *inside* the city, while the men are buried *outside* it.[17] Similarly, in an ancient Chinese city dated to 7500 BCE, archaeologists have found a female spirit temple clearly marked as such in the ancient Chinese characters. Its altars still have seeds on them that, when planted, germinate into plants even today.[18]

Finally, no discussion of Goddess carvings would be complete without including the Laussel Goddess. This carving was found over the entrance to a cave of initiation in the Dordogne region of Laussel, France, not far from the Lascaux caves. Inside this cave are images of a tantric sexual couple, as well as birthing images of the Goddess with a male consort. The Venus herself is a voluptuous figure who points to her pregnant tummy with one hand and holds a sickle moon with thirteen lunar notches marked on it in the other. In addition, these images, dating back to the Paleolithic era, clearly reveal that our ancestors understood that reproduction occurs through the sexual union of a man and a woman. So while the Goddess was the initiator of these Mysteries, revealed in her image over the doorway, the male is honored as the consort of the Goddess.[19]

The Goddess of Laussel was discovered in 1911 by J. G. Lalanne. In the carving above the cave's entrance, the figure holds a horn in her hands, a symbol long linked to the all-pervading Mother goddesses of Mesopotamia, Egypt, Crete, and India. This is linked to the sacred cow, a symbol that was connected to both Hathor or Isis in ancient Egypt, Inanna in Sumeria, Aditi in India, and Asherah by the Jews. The sickle half-moon of the horn she holds becomes the chalice of creation, the

---

*Among the areas where statues of the Goddess have been found are Dolni Vestonice, Moravia, now located in the Czech Republic; Lespugue, France; and Laussel, France.

Figure 8.4. The Laussel Goddess oversees the entrance to a cave of sexual initiation. The thirteen notches in the crescent moon reveal the knowledge of the thirteen lunar menstrual cycles that women go through each year. Inside are men and women's figures, revealing the understanding of the role that both men and women play in the process of procreation.

womb from which all things are born. Throughout the world the moon has long been linked to many female deities, including Diana, Artemis, Aphrodite, Mary, Isis, Selene, Hera, and Juno—all of whom were once called the Queens of Heaven.

SYMBOLS OF THE GODDESS

During her many years of research, Dr. Gimbutas came to understand that throughout all of Neolithic Europe a shorthand script of ideograms was being used to signify the presence of a divinity that was uniquely feminine. She separated these symbols into various categories, representing water and rain; the moon and agricultural cycles; and the continuous rotation of life itself, like the spiral motions of the galaxy (see figure 8.5). Vs were the portals of rebirth, while zigzags and meanders were associated with the oscillating energy of the Holy Spirit on which all sound and light travels. The Hebrews called this undulating wave form the Shekinah, the feminine Spirit of God. Christians call it the Holy Spirit. *Spirit,* or *Ruach* (literally "wind"), is feminine in Hebrew and its symbol is the dove, another image long connected with the Goddess in cultures around the world. In the New Testament we read about a dove descending on Jesus at his baptism, giving the blessings of the Holy Spirit. Yet long before Christianity, the dove symbolized Isis, Aphrodite, and Ishtar, all of whom represented the Mater Magna or Great Mother.[20] This was true across the Aegean, and even the Mayan ruins at Uxmal in Mexico had a "house of the doves."[21] Historically, the dove and the serpent were both linked to the Holy Mother,[22] a fact that Jesus doubtlessly understood when he coupled these animals together in the admonition: "May ye be gentle as doves, and wise as serpents" (Matthew 10:16), indicating a far older meaning behind both of these hermetic emblems.

Gimbutas developed a novel interdisciplinary approach she called archaeomythology, which combines archaeology, linguistics, historical ethnology, mythology, folklore, and comparative religion. She discov-

Figure 8.5. Four versions of the spiral of creation, also known as the Fibonacci Spiral or the Golden Mean Section. The spiral can be found in many ancient sites, from Persia to England, Italy to Greece.

ered symbols of the Goddess that include the four quarters of the world, the fish, and the Great Cosmic Egg—all aspects of gestation and new life. The fish is the ichthys (figure 8.6) taught by Jesus to his students, representing the portal from which we all are born. This almond-shaped symbol is the shape of the vesica piscis (figure 8.7), formed through the merger of the male and female circles to create a perfect portal through which Spirit can enter the worlds of matter. It is also the seed syllable of creation. That is why this is the shape of all seeds, a woman's yoni, and the end of a man's phallus, from which the seed of life emerges. When turned horizontally, the vesica piscis becomes the eye of Ra or Horus, the opening of the inner light, which represents awakening of the spiritual sight. All these symbols are linked to the continual circle of life, death, and renewal and were intrinsically connected in the ancient world to the Great Goddess herself.

Figure 8.6. The ichthys was the symbol Jesus used to represent the path of the return to union with the Divine. This symbol can only be created by the merger of the male and female in perfect harmony.

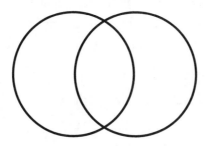

Figure 8.7. The vesica piscis is created through the overlapping of two perfect circles, representing the balance between the male and female that allows creation to come into form.

THE GREAT MOTHER OF ALL

Anthropologist Mircea Eliade, author of the book *From Primitives to Zen,* is known for her worldwide perspectives on shamanic indigenous cultures. Dr. Eliade writes that the first peoples of Earth saw the Great Mother as the source of all nourishment, protection, power, and mystery. She was both the Mother of Birth and the Queen of the Dead.[23] Consequently, their greatest initiations were held in caves or clefts that were entry points to the Earth's body. Birth, life, death, and rebirth were all attributed to her, and burial and entombment were a symbolic prayer for rebirth. The deceased person was laid into the grave in a fetal position, as if being returned to the womb of the Earth to be reborn.

Later megalithic ages found villagers chiseling out "porthole tombs" for this same purpose, just like the caves where Jesus and Lazarus were laid to rest at death. These represent the Mother's womb, and in some cultures, like the Celts of Scotland, the word for "cave" (*wamba*) is almost the same as the word for "womb" (*wame*).[24] Throughout the ancient world, caves were used as places of initiation, as both male and female shamans pulled back the veils to commune with the Otherside. This same connection is made in the entombment rites in the Valley of the Kings in Egypt. Large caverns were dug out of the mountains, and at the entrance to the tombs were painted images of Nuit, the Mother of the Cosmos. Nuit's star-filled body stretched across the walls to the innermost chambers. It was thought that she, and she alone, had the power to escort the soul through the afterlife, just as today many Christians hope that Jesus will take them into Heaven.

GODDESS OF THE COSMOS

In *The Hero with a Thousand Faces,* Joseph Campbell writes: "The mythological figure of the Universal Mother imputes to the cosmos the feminine attributes of the first, nourishing and protecting presence . . . In the Tantric books of medieval and modern India the abode of the goddess is called Man-dvipa, 'The Island of Jewels.'"[25] Campbell goes on:

> Her couch and throne is there, in a grove with wish-fulfilling trees.
> The beaches of the isle are golden sands. They are laved by the still
> waters of the ocean of the nectar of immortality. The goddess is red
> with the fire of life; the earth, the solar system, the galaxies of far
> extending space, all swell within her womb. For she is the World
> Creatrix, ever mother, ever virgin. She encompasses the encompass-
> ing, nourishes the nourishing, and is the life of everything that lives.
> She is also the death of everything that dies. The whole round of
> existence is accomplished within her sway . . . She is the womb and
> the tomb . . . Thus she unites the "good" and the "bad," exhibiting
> the two modes of the remembered mother, not as personal only, but
> as universal.[26]

Hesiod's *Theogony* calls Gaea (Gaia) the deep-breasted Earth, "the
firm seat of all things forever," who, after emerging out of an ocean of
chaos, brought forth the sky, the mountains, and the sea. A sanctuary
to Gaea stood near the entrance to the Acropolis in Athens, and also in
Olympia, the site of the annual athletic games. Romans worshipped her
as *Terra Mater,* the great "Mother Earth," and her symbols were perennially linked to the healing waters of the Cosmic Ocean. One of her

*Figure 8.8. The scalloped seashell has long been a symbol of the
Goddess, who was seen by ancient cultures as arising from the
primordial Cosmic Waters. Not only is it found in motifs across
the ancient world, but it was incorporated in the designs of many
Christian and medieval paintings and stained-glass windows.*

symbols was the undulating sea serpent upon which the universe floats, and today images of Quan Yin, Mary, and Isis are sometimes shown riding on the back of this cosmic dragon. Springs, pools, and fountains were dedicated to the Great Mother, stretching from Sumeria to Asia, Palestine to Rome. She was Sulis Minerva in Britain, Goddess of the Healing Waters, and today her centers can still be found in the city of Bath. In Cyprus, Greece, and Turkey she was Aphrodite, who arose from the Cosmic Waters at the beginning of time. Isis, Mary, and Quan Yin all sail upon this same great ocean, and each of them was in turn called the "Queen of Heaven," "Mistress of the Oceans," and "Star of the Sea."

LADY OF THE ANIMALS

In Paleolithic cultures the life-giving nature of the Mother has long been linked to animals, who were regarded as her children. The Latin poet Lucretius writes, "She alone is called Great Mother of the gods and Mother of the Wild Beasts, and maker of our bodies."[27] These more balanced cultures believed that all things have a right to life—animals, forests, birds, and swimming creatures, but in a "superior" patriarchal system we are told to subdue the Earth and " . . . to have dominion over the fish of the sea, the fowl of the air, and over every living thing that moveth upon the Earth" (Genesis 1:28). However, in egalitarian societies all creatures were seen as an expression of the Mother's regenerative powers. Each is important to the circle of life or everyone will perish.

Shamans, priestesses, and medicine people dreamed with the animals, listening to the invisible rhythms of the Earth.[28] Even today Brazilian medicine people tell us that because their trees and animals are being destroyed, the elders can no longer dream. Without dreaming, the tribe loses its direction. Only their own animals, which belong to their native forests, can give them the right dreams. "The animals are our brothers, the rivers are our veins, they run with our blood; if you block them and dam them, you stop the flowing of blood in our veins and then the heart stops."[29]

Figure 8.9. Diana, or Artemis, was the maiden Goddess of Animals. She was a protector of women, children, and nature itself. (Illustration by Sylvia Laurens)

The Roman Diana, or the Greek Artemis, was the lady of wild things, the keeper of the forest, and her emblem was the stag. Rhiannon and Epona were linked to the white horse in Britain, and Hera was symbolized by the royal peacock and the ibis deer. As Athena, the Greek Goddess of Wisdom, she was synonymous with the owl, the clairvoyant who is able to see what others cannot. In Asia, the Goddess Lakshmi, protectress of home and fortune, is flanked by two mighty elephants who shower her with life-renewing water. And as Isis in Egypt, she was symbolized by the graceful soaring kite, a bird similar to her husband's sharp-eyed falcon.

Three animals, in particular, were most sacred to the Great Mother: the lion, the cow, and the serpent. In Egypt, Sekhmet and Bast had lion's heads, while Freya drove a chariot pulled by cats in Norse culture.

Figure 8.10. Isis or Hathor, the Goddess of Wisdom and Healing, wears the headdress of the cow as she blesses the queen with the ankh of eternal life. (Illustration by Tricia McCannon)

Cybele, the great Goddess of Rome, was often shown flanked by lions that drew her golden chariot, and in the city of Çatalhöyük in modern-day Turkey, going back to 7000 BCE, there is a shrine wall that depicts the Goddess sitting on her throne flanked by two leopards.[30] These leopards were said to have sat beside her when people came for justice and would growl if they smelled the fear of those who lied, helping the queen to render fair judgment. Even the Egyptian name for cat was *mau,* not only an imitation of *meow,* but a derivative of the mother syllable, *ma.*[31]

The cow was very sacred to the ancient Mother. From the isle of Crete to the sanctuaries of Egypt, the Temples of the Goddess were often adorned with crescent horns because this symbol resembles the shape of the fallopian tubes and the uterus of women's reproductive systems. Like the symbol of the moon, the horns of the cow held endless possibilities as the generating chalice of rebirth. In Sumeria, Ninharsag

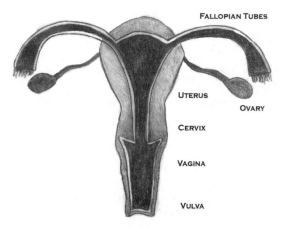

Figure 8.11. The female organs of procreation resemble the shape of a cow's head and horns, thus making the cow eternally sacred to the Goddess. (Illustration by Tricia McCannon)

and Inanna were referred to as the "great cows," who brought milk and honey to humankind. According to Hindu mythology, all gods and goddesses reside in the body of a cow.[32] The Indian name for the cow is *gavu mata,* which contains the seed syllable for "mother," *ma.*[33] The cow is associated with many great divinities, including Lakshmi, the Mother of Compassion, as well as the great avatar Krishna and his wife Sita. In Native American cultures, the cow is honored as White Buffalo Calf Woman, a Goddess figure who came to Earth to teach the balance between the animals, rocks, trees, and humans, reminding human beings of our place in the eternal circle of life.

THE SERPENT OF ENLIGHTENMENT

The serpent represents the kundalini life force of the universe, linked to the changing cycles of time. The Mayans thought of the Milky Way as a long, horizontal serpent, with a head on either end.* The "helical rising" of the serpent's head occurs in the first week of August, a time once

---

*The two-headed serpent that stretches across the galaxy appears in relics of both the Mayan and the Incan civilizations.

sacred to Isis. The helical setting occurs at Candlemas on February 2, another of the eight High Holy Days of the calendar year.[34] In her circular form, she is the Ouroboros, the snake biting its tail, a symbol of the endless rounds of time as one age ends and another begins. She is the one who turns the galaxy and has the power to shed her skin and be reborn. The kundalini is also connected to the Goddess energies found coiled at the base of the spine. The kundalini life force is not only activated in sexual relations and in giving birth, but is fundamental to enlightenment. "The snake and its abstract derivative, the spiral, are the dominant motifs of the art of Old Europe," writes Dr. Gimbutas,[35] reminding us that throughout Mesopotamia, statues of the Goddess have been found holding two snakes in her hands. These

Figure 8.12. Athena, the Greek Goddess of Wisdom, Diplomacy, and Battle is often depicted with the shield and snake, representing the kundalini life force energies of awakening. (Illustration by Tricia McCannon)

two serpents represent the sympathetic and parasympathetic nervous systems, ruling the conscious and autonomic functions that allow the kundalini to rise to the top of the head and awaken our inner sight.

In Egypt this snake was the cobra Goddess Uatchet Buto, symbolizing the original chi force of creation. Serpents were also linked to Asherah or Ashtoreth, the Hebrew Mother Goddess; Athena, the Greek Goddess of Wisdom; and the oracles of Delphi in Greece and Sais in Egypt. In some temple precincts, serpents were even kept at the temple enclosures as a way of staying attuned to Earth currents. Snakes are also highly sensitive to the tellurgic energies of the Earth, and their activities can be used to predict coming earthquakes.[36] Since the original temples of the ancient world were deliberately mapped on key geodesic points, or ley lines, this constant attunement to their energies allowed the electromagnetic energies of the Earth to be harnessed as a conduit between Heaven and Earth.[37]

At the oracle of Delphi, the priestesses who entered these altered states to prophesy were called *pythias,* a derivative of *python,* telling us that they had learned to lift their kundalini energies into their spiritual eye. We find this same enlightened serpent rising up the shield of Athena, the Goddess of Wisdom, in ancient Athens. Researchers have even suggested that through the use of venom, the oracular priestesses were able to enter a trancelike state, giving them access to these other realms. Later this serpent symbology, representing spiritual wisdom, would be reversed in the Hebrew story of the Garden of Eden. Echoes of this reversal can be seen in the tales of Zeus, who slays the serpent Syphon, or the killing of the python by Apollo. We also see it in the destruction of the serpent Ladon by Hercules, and in Jehovah's killing of the Leviathan, a sea monster with many heads. Ironically, Ladon was said to have guarded the Tree of Knowledge in the garden of Hera, the Mother of the gods, giving us clues about how our Old Testament accounts have been distorted over time.

Glimmers of the snake's original meaning can be found in the caduceus, a worldwide emblem for healing. This good serpent also appears in the story of Moses and his serpent staff, a symbol of spiritual power. Likewise, we have drawings of Aesculapius, the father of ancient healing, who had a staff with a single serpent coiled around it, indicative of initiation and health. These stories allow us to peek behind the veils to see that the snake was once a powerful symbol of wisdom before its meaning was corrupted.

According to the Dartmouth Bible, a slightly abridged version of the King James Bible, the Ark of the Covenant, which was kept in the Holy of Holies in King Solomon's Temple in Jerusalem, originally held the brazen serpent staff of Moses. This was the staff that had guided the Jews out of Egypt, and it had a serpent coiled around its length, representing the kundalini forces of enlightenment as they traveled up the spine. Joseph Campbell writes that this staff "was worshipped in the very temple of Jerusalem along with an image of his spouse, the mighty goddess, who was known there as the Asherah."[38] The asherim, you will remember, were the wooden staffs or trees dedicated to the Divine Mother. This serpent staff was only removed from the Hebrew temple during the persecution of King Hezekiah around 700 BCE, when the priests of Yahweh destroyed it. The corruption of wisdom that followed completely distorted the original meaning of both the serpent and the Tree of Life, both emblems perennially linked to the Goddess as a symbolic road map of the path to enlightenment. The priests of Yahweh

Figure 8.13. Moses's serpent staff represented the power of awakened initiation known in the Mystery Schools of Egypt and Greece. It became part of the wisdom of the founding of the Hebrew nation through Moses, until the priests of Yahweh perverted its true meaning. (Illustration by Tricia McCannon)

then invented a story about the evil nature of the serpent and the Tree of Knowledge, which caused the expulsion of Adam and Eve from the Garden of Paradise, blaming this fall from grace on women. This distortion of the true meaning behind these sacred symbols represents a total inversion of the emblems of wisdom that were once part of our spiritual heritage—symbols that emerged from healthier partnership societies.

LADY OF THE HARVEST

The Great Mother was also called the Mother of Plants and the Goddess of Vegetation. While men hunted for food, women searched for berries, herbs, seeds, and roots. Over time these women began to plant their seeds, discovering the art of agriculture. This female invention, based on generations of experimentation with seed cultivation, cutting and grafting, and grain storage, brought about the Neolithic Revolution circa 10,000 BCE.[39] In her book *When God Was a Woman,* Merlin Stone writes:

> Here it was the women who showed themselves supreme; they were not only the bearers of children but also the chief producers of food. By realizing that it was possible to cultivate, as well as to gather, they had made the earth valuable and they became consequently, its possessors. Thus they won both economic and social power and prestige.[40]

Thus the women sparked the change from hunting and gathering tribes to agricultural societies that planted and harvested their food. In Neolithic cave paintings we even see images of the Goddess with a plant growing from her yoni, marking her as the generator of all growing things. Stone writes: "The earliest agriculture must have grown up around the shrines of the Mother Goddess, which thus became social and economic centers, as well as holy places and were the germs of future cities."[41]

Figure 8.14. Demeter is the Lady of the Harvest, the bringer of corn and wheat to the people. In Rome she was known as Ceres, Goddess of the Cereals, but her real identity is Isis, the Egyptian Goddess of Wisdom, who saved the seeds of wheat that grew along the Nile, forever immortalizing her in human memory. (Illustration by Tricia McCannon)

As Isis she was the Lady of the Harvest, the Goddess who had brought the gift of wheat to humanity, just as in the Native American world she was Corn Woman, "the bringer of maize." So powerful were these acts of generosity that the Goddess became immortalized as Virgo, the virgin, whose astrological sign occurs in September, the month of harvesting wheat. Isis then became known as Demeter, or Ceres, the Mother of Cereals in Greece and Rome. Virgo the Queen is depicted holding a staff of enlightenment in one hand and a bundle of wheat in the other, presiding over all physical, intellectual, and spiritual acts of regeneration. Later, Mary the Mother would be given the month of September to celebrate her birthday, which according to the church, falls on September 8.

THE ETERNAL TRIAD

The Great Mother was seen as a triad of constantly evolving stages—cyclical, not linear—like nature itself. She ushers the soul into a higher phase of existence, blessing each stage along the way. This includes life, death, and rebirth. The Goddess encompasses all things within herself: yin and yang, masculine and feminine, light and dark.[42] Her lunar phases represent the cycles of birth, life, and death, reflecting the three phases of a person's life—the maiden, the mother, and the matriarch, or the youth, the man, and the sage.

Unlike the warrior gods who stood outside creation, ordering and punishing, the Mother was alive within her own creation, taking responsibility for the many cycles of life. She exists *within* the matrix, and all things are woven within her. She is not absent from the world, but alive within everything, in both seen and unseen dimensions, and these realms all share in the sanctity of the original Source. Such an image helps us to honor the sacred in everything, fostering compassion and kindness to all.

THE DESCENT OF THE WARRIOR CLANS

Today archaeologists tell us that the demise of the great Goddess cultures began in Turkey and Greece. Excavations in this region are revealing much information about the Neolithic Aegeans, the earliest inhabitants of the Greek peninsula, but there is still much that we do not know. But based on the artifacts we have uncovered, we know these cultures were matrilineal, honored the yearly cycles, and maintained a partnership model of leadership between men and women. They thrived between 2500 and 1600 BCE, a period now called the Bronze Age.

So what changed this idyllic model of society? Archaeology tells us that some thirty-six hundred years ago a group of fierce warrior clans swept down into the Mediterranean from the North, bringing with them their brutal storm gods and violent weapons. There are several

Figure 8.15. The savagery of the Age of Conquest destroyed the peaceful partnership villages and replaced them with violence, war, and a male-dominated political system. In the Greek world, this was epitomized in story and legends. Here the male hero Perseus cuts off the head of Medusa. (Illustration by Tricia McCannon)

theories as to who these tribes were. Some believe they were the Kurgan tribes from the south of Russia, known for their domestication of the horse and their use of chariots. Others believe they were the warmongering Achaeans who swept in from the North and the South, flourishing between 1600 and 1150 BCE throughout the Mediterranean. These were the aggressive, seafaring kings whose naval wars inspired Homer to write *The Iliad* and *The Odyssey*. Others believe they were the Semitic nomads who invaded Egypt about 1800 BCE, later known as the Hyksos kings. This group of marauders threw Egypt into chaos for a hundred years. But whoever these invaders were, they brought with them an oppressive superiority and patriarchal mores that crushed the more peaceful agrarian cultures. These violent intruders raped and impregnated the women, slaughtered the men, and sent those who escaped scurrying for their lives. They imposed their own system of violent values and weakened the matrilineal traditions that had been passed from mother to child for thousands of years, beginning the destruction of all women's rights and the rise of the patriarchal regimes of power.

> Toward the close of the Bronze Age and more strongly, with the dawn of the Iron Age (1250 BCE in the Levant), the old cosmology and mythologies of the Goddess Mother were radically transformed, reinterpreted, and, in large measure, suppressed by those suddenly intrusive patriarchal warrior tribesmen whose traditions have come down to us chiefly in the Old and New Testaments and in the myths and stories of Greek mythology.
>
> Two extensive geographical territories were the source lands of these insurgent warrior waves: for the Semites, the Syro-Arabian deserts, where, as ranging nomads, they herded sheep and goats and later mastered the camel; and, for the Hellenic-Aryan Kurgan marauders, the broad plains of Europe and southern Russia, where they had grazed their herds of cattle and early mastered the horse.[43]

Ann Baring and Jules Cashford, authors of *The Myth of the Goddess: Evolution of an Image,* writes that the matriarchal practices of leadership, healing, and shamanism were suppressed by these invaders, and that slowly the patriarchy won.

> Indo-European tribes, in ever increasing numbers, forced their way into Mesopotamia, Anatolia, and lands stretching eastward to the Indus Valley. At the same time Semitic tribes moved into Mesopotamia and Canaan from the Syro-Arabian desert. The descendants of the old Paleolithic hunters in their tribal homelands of the vast grassy steppes north of the Caspian and Black Seas have now become warriors and we can trace their path of conquest as

they appear as Hittites in Anatolia and Syria; Mittani, Hurrians and Kassites in Mesopotamia; Achaeans and then Dorians in Greece; and Aryans in the Indus Valley. Wherever they penetrated, they established themselves as the ruling caste and their appearance is marked by a trail of devastation: in Anatolia alone some 300 cities were sacked and burned, among them Troy (2300 B.C.E.) and this pattern was repeated from Greece to the Indus Valley.[44]

The sky gods of these tribes lived on mountaintops and in clouds, hurling thunderbolts at those who would not obey them. They brought with them a sense of superiority, "a deep sense of the futility of life, the finality of death and a fundamental conviction of human guilt."[45]

As one might imagine, these sky god cultures preached a paradigm of oppression, conquest, and opposition, in which the world of nature was intrinsically separated from the spiritual realm of the gods. Attitudes toward life and death were fundamentally altered as people experienced life as violent, unpredictable, and untrustworthy. People no longer felt safe in the countryside or in villages but came to seek refuge in cities girdled by immense walls, where they could be protected by warriors. An elite group of warriors sprang up, demoting farmers, artisans, and peasants to the level of serfs. The character of both the culture and the mythology of gods and goddesses changed radically. Dominance and warfare infected society with the barbaric ambitions of territorial rulers who had a compulsion to conquer and enslave other people. The killing of others became a sign of superiority, and "might" became the measure of "right."

This model of society is radically different from the world of the Goddess, where moral order and responsibility are based on the eternal sacredness of life. "Early humans didn't see themselves as separated from nature and other beings. There is no sense of hierarchy or caste operating in the early epochs, no sign of slavery or inequality. The changeover that marks the beginnings of Western culture, five thousand years ago, was a lethal separation from nature and the body in favor of the dominion of the ego over everything."[46] Joseph Campbell writes:

> Where the goddess had been venerated as the giver and supporter
> of life as well as consumer of the dead, women as her representa-
> tives had been accorded a paramount position in society, as well as
> in cult. Such an order of female-dominated social and cultic custom
> is termed, in a broad and general way, the order of Mother Right.
> And opposed to such, without quarter, is the order of the Patriarchy,
> with an ardor of righteous eloquence and a fury of fire and sword.[47]

Many scholars now believe that the later theatrical dramas of
ancient Greece, such as *Agamemnon, Electra,* and *Orestes,* all reflect
this transition from a loving Mother-Son relationship to one of murder,
betrayal, and social demotion.* These Greek tragedies all center around
a son who either kills his mother or engages in sexual relations with her,
and then finds that his life has been ruined. This is a direct reversal of
the earlier Sister-Brother or Mother-Son harmonious rulership models
found across the Mediterranean, where men and women lived together
peacefully with one another. The Goddess was the loving mother of the
hero son, or she was his wife or mate, and together they gave birth to
the holy daughter. It was this union that made the bounty for the land.
Examples of this partnership model can be found in the stories of Isis
and Horus in Egypt, Ishtar and Tammuz in the Levant, Cybele and
Attis in Rome, and Sita and Rama in India.

BROKEN INTO PIECES

As the powers of the goddesses waned, so did the rights of women.
Where once women had had the right to own property, transact

---

*Throughout Egypt this connection with the natural world is easily seen in the hiero-
glyphs for the goddesses, and it can also be seen in the symbols of Hermopolis, where
the cult of Thoth was centered. The snakes were used as a symbol for the female aspects
of creation, and the frogs for the male aspects.

business, and inherit property from their families on equal terms with men, after 2300 BCE the status of women slowly deteriorated. In the Akkadian North of Sumeria, which later became known as Babylonia, the Semitic tribes regarded women as merely the possessions of men. "Fathers and husbands claimed the power of life and death over daughters and wives. Sons inherited from their fathers, whereas daughters inherited nothing, and could be sold into slavery by their fathers and brothers. The birth of a son was hailed as a blessing while a daughter could be exposed to die."[48]

These changes in attitude about the importance of women and their understanding of the universe also caused fundamental changes in the way that people looked at life and death. Death became regarded as the absolute end of life, something dark and terrifying to be feared. The ancient knowledge of rebirth went underground, and the cycles of divine order were lost. In the male-oriented myths, all that was good and noble was attributed to the new heroic gods of war, and the dark, mysterious powers of nature were left to women. The Mother Goddess, once venerated as the Giver of Life and the Welcomer of the Dead, was thrown down. The circle of life was broken, and people no longer understood that the womb and the tomb were all part of the natural cycles of life. In addition, the material realm became the only realm of importance, as we disconnected from our understanding of how the unmanifested realms of Spirit help to generate this world. Nature was now something to be dominated, conquered, and harnessed. Trees and animals had no essential value, except as timber or food. Man became the sole determiner of everyone's life, and all was in service to him.

Over the next two thousand years, the Goddess would be slowly dismembered by the patriarchy, shattered like a beautiful vase that has been broken into pieces. For the goddesses that remained, one aspect of her nature would be pitted against another. Aphrodite, the Goddess of Sexual Love, was pitted against Hera, the married Queen of Heaven, vying for the attention of a male. Athena, the Goddess of Wise Civilizations, was now at odds with Aphrodite, the Goddess of Love, fighting over the city of Troy. In time, with the rise of the Abrahamic religions, the Great Mother was either totally extinguished or split further into pieces. In Christianity she became the Good Mother or the Lady of Sexual Pleasures, but she was never allowed to be both, confusing both men and women alike. This polarity is exactly what we find in the stories of the obedient Virgin Mary and the penitent Mary Magdalene. As Jennifer and Roger Woolger write in their book *The Goddess Within:* "Each of the departmental goddesses is now cut off from the original Mother, and they are from this point onward divided against themselves. Here, very dramatically, is the historical origin of the deepest aspect of the goddess's wounds."[49] Once the fracturing of the Goddess began as the patriarchy came to control most of the world, the continuity of life itself was broken and, with it, our sacred connection to Mother Nature.

Then beneath the negative projections of Hebrew, Muslim, and Christian archetypes, these pieces became further divided. It seemed that each woman had to choose between being an obedient wife, a virginal maiden, a self-sacrificing mother, or a woman of ill repute. If a woman was too independent in her thinking, she was cast as Eve, the disobedient wife. If she rebelled against male authority, she was turned into Lilith, the first wife of Adam, who refused to obey her husband's sexual commands. So strenuous was this condemnation of women that in the Dark Ages Lilith was cast as Satan. Never mind that these fables of man's "divine right to rule" were fabricated by patriarchal men during the construction of the Old Testament documents around 500 BCE. While perverting the symbols of the feminine face of the Divine, they cut down her forests, leveled her sacred trees, and demonized those aspects of Mother love that they could not eradicate. And by justifying their suppression of women as the "will of God," they made half the world's population subservient to the other half.

Finally, the patriarchy turned the wise herbalist into the withered hag, transforming grandmothers into symbols of evil. *Hag,* by the way, derives from a root word meaning "holy woman" or "sacred grove," revealing the deeper links of this currently pejorative word to the healing priestesses of old.[50] But in the Middle Ages the patriarchal interpretation of the Wise Woman was abandoned, and the elderly woman lost the grace of male protection since she was no longer useful to a man's political or sexual agendas. If her husband or sons were killed in war, she had no one to speak for her. She was turned out of her house and her only recourse was to take refuge in the woods, where the church depicted her as good for nothing but gathering sticks.

In Europe the one bastion of influence that older women still retained was that of the midwife or healer. Her understanding of plants had come down from her ancestors. But with the rise of the male-dominated church, even the medicine women were replaced by the "all-knowing" male doctor. Thus the wise woman was persecuted for her gifts of herbal wisdom and turned into the witch. For over a thousand years she became the target of fear, suspicion, and torture, accused of causing the deaths of those she sought to save. In the most brutal eras of the Inquisition, there were somewhere between five million and nine million women put to death by the church for the crime of being attuned to the natural energies of the Earth.[51] Never again would the Goddess be allowed to reign as the Great Mother. She was erased as the Queen of Heaven, the Creatrix who had birthed the universe.

Jungian psychologist James Hillman says that in creating this extreme polarization between a negative, condemning, judgmental God and a banished, loving mother, we have actually denied ourselves a healthy spiritual life. Some historians have even likened this to the fracturing of a horrible divorce. The male and female aspects of ourselves no longer speak to one another. Humanity, as the poor child, is left destitute with only an angry Father as a parent. He forbids the children to speak of their loving Mother and tells them that she must be banished as if she has never been. "By worshipping the Father principle alone, and suppressing or belittling the feminine, we have done serious damage to our individual and collective psychic health. And this is to say nothing of . . . the planet earth."[52] These wounds have been sustained for over three thousand years in a battle waged by the patriarchy over the feminine. Roger and Jennifer Woolger observe:

> With only a father to guide us, despite his love, we have become hardened, relentlessly heroic, and grimly puritanical in our efforts to forget the lost security and sensual trust in the Earth the Mother once gave us. Long ago, we dimly sense, there was a primordial unity, when an Earth Mother and a Spirit Father enjoyed a happy and harmonious union. But that paradise is lost, and in our estrangement we have been forced to swallow the embittered propaganda of a guilty, yet all-powerful Father.[53]

CULTURAL SUPERIORITY

While today's modern religions congratulate themselves on outgrowing the polytheism of our childish past and graduating into a more mature monotheism, in truth, by refusing to acknowledge the divine spark in everything around us, we cripple our ability to relate to the Divine in all its forms. We close our eyes to the visible and invisible expressions of God. We close our hearing to the music of the trees, the spirits of the animals, and our ability to dream with the intelligence of the stars.

From the dominance of the warrior Aryans, to the machismo of the Greeks, the imperialism of Rome, and the guilt-ridden excesses of puritanical repression, the spirit of the Divine Feminine has been dishonored, manipulated, misrepresented, and suppressed, and it is only now, in this time, in this century, that our civilization is beginning to question what exactly has thrown us out of balance. Restoring the feminine to its rightful place in partnership with the masculine, with both as true equals, is the most important step we can take today if we are ever to claim our place as caretakers of this planet and take our next step as enlightened human beings.

9

The Four Male
and Female Polarities

*All Souls are parts of one Soul, which is the Soul of the
Cosmos.
Souls all have one nature. They are neither male nor
female.
Such differences of sex arise only in the body.*

THOTH, *THE HERMETICA*

The second evening that the group gathered at Shasta's house gave me a way to begin to unravel the injustice that I had discovered in the foundations of the world. It was a quiet Wednesday evening between Candlemas and the spring equinox. The nip of winter was just loosening its grip as we found ourselves once more seated in a circle with the warm radiance of cheerful flames burning in the fireplace.

"Tonight," Shasta began when we had settled into our places, "I wish to talk about the four male and female polarities that are expressed by the one Creator behind it all. Egyptians called this divine presence Atum, the first primordial Intelligence that set everything in motion. This is the Creator that exists before even the polarities of the Divine Mother and Father. However in all the subtle realms of Spirit, as well as the worlds of form, the yin and yang polarities exist in a constantly moving dance of energies. In the East the yin has come to signify all that is resting, receptive, contracting, moist, cold, and dark, while the yang is seen as the active, expanding, rising, hot, dry, and light energies that make up the Spirit of the universe. The Chinese called this Spirit the chi or the Tao, and acknowledged that the yang, or male, exists within the yin, just as the yin, or female, exists within the yang. One grows out of the other, and neither could exist without its opposite. Man could not exist without woman, nor dark without light. They coexist and interpenetrate the other. The universe itself is created through the relationship between yin and yang, the heavens and the Earth, and it is the intercourse between them that produces everything."

Hmm . . . I found myself reflecting on the famous Taoist symbol of the black and white swirls that make up the circle and how there was a little bit of white inside the black and a little bit of black within the white, visually expressing this same divine principle.

"Yet each of these polarities has a positive and a negative expression of itself. While we can make lists of these apparent opposites, like heat and cold, up and down, active and passive, we should be aware that there are both negative and positive poles of the male and female paths. As you

Figure 9.1. The yin and yang energies are perfectly depicted in the symbol of the balanced Tao, the path of true mastery. Notice that within the male (white/yang) is the female (black/yin), just as within the female is the male.

know, we have seen entirely too much of the negative aspect of the male path, or the patriarchy, in the past few thousand years, but it is important to discuss these qualities so that we might start to understand how these forces interact with one another. The yin current is magnetic, while the yang is electrical, and since we are electromagnetic beings, these currents exist within every human being, as well as every culture, and they can be expressed in either a positive or a negative way." Shasta looked around the circle and saw that we were all warming to her subject. She went on.

"The negative masculine path is aggressive, warlike, judgmental, threatening, oppressive, and controlling, and it has ruled the world for almost three millennia. It is competitive and brutal, violent and punishing, and it is this polarity that needs to change for us to come back into balance as a planet. If we moved away from this polarity, we would abolish all rape and senseless violence."

All of us were caught up in her words. We knew this kind of world all too well. It was in the news almost every night. Bomb threats, military invasions, crimes of hate, and domestic violence all fell into this category. Meg's work with women's rights in Washington addressed these issues on a regular basis: The abuse of women and children was at record levels, especially in Asia and the Middle East, where women and children were sold into slavery every day, forced into marriage, and kept in legal bondage for life. I saw that Emerald was also paying close attention. She had told us that in the law firm where she worked there were only two women lawyers as opposed to sixteen men, but at least, I reflected, women were now gaining the tools to be able to finally stand up for themselves.

I also couldn't help but think about how the patriarchy had descended so strongly on the rest of the world once the Age of Aries arrived around 2200 BCE. Since Aries is an age that is traditionally thought to be ruled by Mars, the God of war, it seemed to have ushered in an era of conflict, hostilities, and brutal male dominance. So strong was the pull of this masculine aggression that it virtually overwhelmed the softer, feminine Age of Pisces, which began around 100 BCE and is only now just ending. Pisces is ruled by water, a symbol of emotions and spirituality. The Age of

Pisces was intended to be a spiritual and introspective period, focused on the spiritual teachings of Jesus, its avatar. But it was overwhelmed by the more dominant masculine forces, basically creating male-dominant and male-subdominant streams of energy that affected many cultures around the world. This is part of the reason that the world has been so out of balance, since both the male and female polarities must be in balance if people are to create healthy societies.

It is an amazing testament to the raw strength of this negative aggression that it so completely overshadowed a very spiritual age like Pisces, whose avatar was the incredible master Jesus. If an enlightened being such as Jesus, whose deeper teachings sought to usher in a balance between the male and female polarities, couldn't begin to turn the tide of human consciousness until now, imagine how successfully the dark forces have used this negative current of lies and suppression for the denigration of men and women alike.

But Shasta had continued to speak. "The positive side of the masculine path is courage and leadership, represented by Horus, or Apollo, a positive male symbol of illumination and healing. This archetype gives us the bravery to act on our convictions, and also to consider the needs and feelings of others. The path of the builder, the doer, the maker, and the creator gives order to the world. This path develops science, knowledge, and understanding and is willing to take chances, but its highest expression is as a champion for truth. It is the noble priest-king who is there for the good of the community."

I loved this aspect of men . . . I thought, for their vision, their courage, and their ability to change the world. But I knew full well that either gender can make a difference if we marshal the courage to act. No matter how tuned in we are at a spiritual level, if we don't take action, nothing is accomplished.

Shasta went on. "The positive feminine path is one of wisdom and love. It is the path that connects us to Spirit directly, the person who sits at the center of her own being and receives gnosis. It is direct connection to the Source through knowing, feeling, intuition, receiving, and wisdom. She is the wise one who is able to see, hear, feel, and know the Divine. This is the archetype of Sophia or Isis, the Goddess of Wisdom. She is the life-giver who opens us up to the heart and has the power to embody the totality of creation itself." Shasta looked around the circle to see if we were following her.

The Divine Mother of Love. This thought seemed to come to my mind out of nowhere. I reflected then on my own interactions with my beloved guide Auriel. She had told me long ago, "I am the Creatress from which all other aspects of the Divine Mother flow. I love all things, heal all things, and forgive all things." As the Divine Mother of the Cosmos, she follows us through all the many cycles of change and nurtures us as her children. I thought about what she had told me in our last communication:

> *I am Auriel and I am the center. I am the heart which knows*
> *your name.*
> *I am the reason behind every being, that part of creation*
> *which gave you love.*
>
> *I am Auriel and I am dew.*
> *I am the sweet refreshment that lies over the thrill of life itself.*
> *I am the quivering beat of the heart that has fallen in love.*
> *The passion between two lovers,*
> *The tenderness of a mother and child.*
>
> *I am Auriel and I am beauty,*
> *Beauty in the depths of your greatest longing,*
> *Beauty in the turning of your beloved,*
> *Beauty in the songs of the flowers,*
> *Beauty in the dance of the insects,*
> *I am Auriel and I am love.*
>
> *I am Auriel and I am God.*
> *I am the still point in the undivided heart.*

I am the ripple across the face of the pond.

I am the first sound that issued out from the center of
* creation.*

I am your daughter, I am your mother, I am your wife.

I am the cup of the hands that hold you in the mother's womb.

I am your lover, and I am your self.

I am Auriel and I am love.

Shasta was still speaking. "Yet there is a negative side to the feminine polarity, just as there is the masculine. This negative aspect of women usually emerges when the positive, creative expression is blocked. This is the path of gossip, jealousy, and neediness. It is also the misuse of sexual power to manipulate and deceive. When women do not get to express their positive attributes directly, they fall into using their negative ones. We can see this in history when women were given no choice in a world where men had all the power. How else can the woman get her needs or her children's needs met if she does not have the power to make a living, to make her own decisions, or to be respected as an individual without having to be punished? Thus the negative polarity of the female becomes manipulative and cunning because she is not allowed to ask for what she wants directly. She must do it through the one thing that men most want . . . her sexuality."

Shasta looked around the circle. I could see from the other women's faces that this was a story we all recognized, and were not proud of. When women had no control over their lives, they used the only thing left to them—their sexual allure—to get their way.

Shasta looked serious. "This does not really work for very long because the woman who entices the man without the intention of delivering real emotional intimacy is acting dishonestly. Thus she angers him because he senses that he has temporarily lost his power. So the man, who was already in his negative, overcontrolling imbalance, winds up feeling resentful and manipulated. This polarizes him into more aggression and he becomes even more threatening to her. Then, afraid for her safety, she tries to hide her real motives. This moves her further into deception, which makes the man even angrier. Before you know it, he has brutalized her. Later, when the dust has settled, both people feel ashamed, hurt, and not only less empowered, but also less worthy."

I thought about all the domestic violence in the world, most of it aimed at women and children, although there are also many teenage boys and girls who unfortunately share this problem growing up in abusive households. In the United States one out of every four girls and one out of every six boys are sexually abused, and it is often by someone within the family, such as a father, brother, uncle, or cousin.[1] In America alone, nine out of every ten women who are murdered are killed by men, and over 50 percent of these murders are committed by husbands or boyfriends. While most women try to leave an abusive relationship, when that does not succeed, their attempts become the precipitating factor in 45 percent of the murders of a woman by a man.[2] How about in all those other countries where women and children have no access to domestic violence programs?

"But the dance between the masculine and feminine forces is not only happening at a personal level," Shasta said, bringing me back to the present. "It happens at a global level as well. These same four polarities of positive and negative male and female energies can be applied to religions and societies. There are religions that dominate and control their subjects with fear, oppression, and threats, just as there are political regimes that do the same thing. These societies threaten, bully, and destroy not only other religions, but even their own people who will not submit. They are caught in the negative masculine polarity."

I had just been studying the grievous use of this heavy-handed approach in the Old Testament, and the sect of Yahweh was only the beginning. The Christians and the Muslims have continued to act with violence for the past fifteen hundred years and have inherited many of these same negative patriarchal traits.

Shasta went on. "Spiritual paths that teach us to turn inward follow the positive female path. These paths teach meditation, contemplation, and the development of the inner senses that then allow us to perceive the supernatural world of Spirit that lies all around us. These Eastern paths, and the more esoteric Western traditions, as well as the teachings of the Goddess, also honor human and animal rights because they know that there is a sacred unity in everything."

She looked around the room. You could see that all of the women's minds were going a million miles a minute as we compared the paths of Christianity, Judaism, and Islam to the more contemplative paths of Buddhism, Taoism, and Shintoism. I found myself reflecting on how the negative masculine polarity had launched so many holy wars in an effort to suppress the stream of enlightenment that came from direct experience. This positive spiritual path was expressed by the early Christian Gnostics, and later the Christian Cathars, who were annihilated by the Catholic Church. It seemed to me that the Roman Catholic Church had not only embraced the dark side of the aggressive masculine polarity, but also the dark side of the feminine polarity by creating centuries of ignorance, superstition, and the destruction of knowledge during the Dark Ages. It was as though the church had embraced the negative aspects of both genders and had offered in return few of the positive treasures of illumination, wisdom, or personal spiritual empowerment needed for true mastery. And if this was the approach of our major religions, how about science, which was far more cerebral and left-brained?

Shasta seemed to be reading my mind. "Science in its highest form is the search for truth. When it is connected to an understanding of the spiritual Source, it is explorative, innovative, and cerebral—all aspects of the positive masculine. But without the balance of the positive feminine wisdom that honors the connection between the manifest and unmanifest spiritual realms, and thus a more humane approach, science can go too far, objectifying everything for its own use without regard for the sanctity of life. This becomes abuse for profits, whether science abuses people, animals, or nature itself. This is where we are today in the medical industry and the energy industries, where the need for

profits is polluting the environment, decimating the animals, destroy-
ing our natural habitats, and throwing the world further out of balance.
Is everybody following me?"

We nodded. I thought of the abuses being expressed in the development of our genetically modified foods, the poisons laced into our crops
and soils, the chemtrails polluting the air, and the nuclear radiation we
are burying in the oceans, which could contaminate all living things
and break the delicate cycle of life upon which we all depend. I thought
of the dangerous drilling in the Gulf of Mexico and along the Arctic
coastlines, and the terrible price we have been paying for our dependence
on oil, when there are safer, cheaper methods for producing energy all
around us. I thought of the fracking practices in drilling for natural
gas and how they are contaminating our water supplies. If we continue
on this path, we will destroy ourselves from the inside out. I thought
of the nuclear radiation spewed into the atmosphere by the Fukushima
power plant in Japan, caused by the increasing number of earthquakes
that are rocking our world. Instead of realizing that this was a wake-up
call to begin to dismantle such centers of radiation, we continue to plan
expansion, approving the building of more reactors. All these decisions
seemed insane to me, shortsighted and self-destructive. We are clearly a
society out of balance and the Earth and all living things are paying for
our actions.

After a moment Shasta went on. "But this dance of male and female
polarities is not just played out in religions and cultures and relationships; these polarities also live within us. We each have the potential to
express all four of these aspects. Some people are too aggressive, too loud,
or too intrusive. They bully others and suppress or control. Some people
are too passive, too lazy, or unmotivated. Some people are aware of what
is going on, but they are too frightened to act. Other people are full of
energy but waste their time on meaningless actions. Worse yet, they
never go inside themselves to contemplate a higher plan, so that when
they do interact with the world they often wind up getting in trouble."

Shasta's words reminded me of a book called *Living in the Light* that I had read years earlier, which was written by a wonderful teacher named Shakti Gawain. Shakti had given a powerful and succinct metaphor for the male and female within us. The female, she said, was like a queen who sat on her throne talking with God. This is the part of us that can converse easily with Spirit. She is wise and intuitive, and totally tuned in. However, by herself she cannot accomplish anything in the world, for she needs her best warrior to help her. This is the inner male. He has the power to bring her ideas to fruition, the power to make them real. In other words, without her wisdom the warrior acts aimlessly, even destructively. But when he is connected to her, and she is connected to Spirit, then he and she can become anything from a sage to a king, a magician, or a lover, but together they can become enlightened ones.

The inner queen needs her inner knight. This is where the legends of the knight in shining armor come from. These parts of ourselves live as archetypes within us. In order to come into balance, we must each embrace both sides of ourselves. The first step is connecting with the inner yin. This is why many spiritual paths teach us to go inside first. Once the queen is connected to the positive forces of creation, she knows what to do. Then she can channel these forces into the world through the divine masculine. This inner male has the power to take our ideas into the world of action. In other words, these two polarities need one another, because when we are out of balance the knight and the queen are both in trouble. This analogy made perfect sense to me.

Shasta was speaking again. "The solution to all these global or personal problems is to figure out where we are in our balance. When we choose the positive expressions of ourselves, we attract the positive expression in others. When we give in to our negative polarities, then we will attract the negative expression in others. If you imagine these four paths as separate columns, the two outer negative paths will always attract each other, but they can never work out because they are essentially self-destructive. The dominating male is the warrior without wisdom. He lacks a connection with his true center. The submissive, negative, manipulating female has no self-worth or inner power. She looks outside herself to survive, but she cannot choose wisely because she neither knows nor loves herself. Neither are connected to the Source or the truth within. These two negative polarities are on a path of self-destruction and cannot accomplish anything positive. They not only hurt other people and each other, but destroy themselves as well.

"On the reverse side, the positive male and female polarities will also attract each other, and this is the secret to a good romance. This is the man or woman who expresses the best qualities of male or female, and as they move into greater balance, they come to express the best qualities of both. But to attract a healthy mate, we must first each balance our male and female aspects internally. If either person in a romantic relationship is wounded or out of balance, then they must work on themselves first, or else they will only attract another person who is equally out of balance."

I saw several of the women nodding, perhaps thinking of romantic relationships that had not worked out. "We live in an age when the roles of men and women are changing, and sometimes a marriage doesn't work because one of the partners is growing faster than the other. In every relationship we have, each person is somewhere on the continuum of these four polarities." Donna rubbed her chin thoughtfully, and Susan crossed her arms. *Hmm . . . I wondered who they were thinking about.*

Shasta went on. "When a woman is free to express her best self, she is wise, loving, creative, inclusive, inspiring, and tuned in. She has a healthy sexuality but does not overstep her own boundaries or anyone else's. And she does not need to manipulate. By bringing out the best in herself, she brings out the best in others."

Meg raised a hand. "Can you describe the positive man?" I had hoped that someone would ask this.

"When a man is in his positive polarity, he is not trying to seize power from anyone else. He is empowered within himself. He moves out from his own center, not from a place of absolute power, conquering, or controlling, but from a place of vision, inclusion, and support.

He gives as well as receives. He listens as well as leads, and because of this he is respected. He doesn't have to take power or goods from anyone. He doesn't have to control or dominate everything. When a man is in balance, he is not run by his ego or his sexual appetites. He can take action to support and protect the things he cares about."

This made a lot of sense to me. It also went along with the Mars/Venus work of John Gray. Gray believes that men are at their best when they are taking care of those they love. This makes them feel empowered and strong, and it is easy for them to set goals and accomplish them when the heart is motivating them. Gray says that women are at their best when they are receiving, for they are by nature caring, creative, and inspiring and can help the man to be his best self. Both of these polarities meet in the heart, and it is there that the yin and yang are successfully balanced.

"So now," Shasta said, "we are going to do an exercise." She began to pass out notebooks. "Each one of you is going to make a list of all the positive and negative male and female traits within yourself." I took a pad and passed the stack on. "Make four columns on your page, and place the negative polarities on the outside, with the female on the left and the male on the right. Put the positive polarity columns in the middle. Now," she looked at the group, "write down all your negative behaviors that are too aggressive, thoughtless, or destructive in the negative male column, and too needy, manipulative, or underhanded in the negative female columns. Once you are done, list all your positive habits, attitudes, or behaviors in the positive female column. Last, name all your effective, action-oriented behaviors in the positive masculine column. When you are done, we will talk about this as a group."

THE PROJECTION OF THE SHADOW: NEGATIVE BEGETS NEGATIVE

Hmm . . . This was certainly an interesting exercise. As I began my personal inventory, I couldn't help but reflect on how these core dynamics had affected cultures across the world. While the polytheistic worship of a Divine Mother and Father had obviously worked for thousands of years, giving us positive role models for both genders, something had clearly gone wrong in the last three millennia. In Christianity the only role models that women had left were the obedient mother Mary and the penitent Mary Magdalene. And yes . . . the independent Lilith the Jews had created, then demonized as the first rejected wife of Adam, and, of course, the disobedient, regretful Eve, whose eating of the forbidden fruit had caused humankind to be expelled from Paradise. No wonder women felt so disempowered, oppressed, and confused! If they stood up for themselves, they were called bitches, whores, demons, or worse. What had happened to the positive role models that past civilizations had crystallized into the archetypes of the ancient goddesses? Perhaps we did need the images of these more empowered beings to inspire us to choose more empowered role models.

During the last two thousand years, the patriarchy had suppressed the positive expression of the feminine. The more power that women lost, the more they had used their feminine wiles in a negative manipulating way. The result was that men continued to project this image of the deceptive, lying, sexual siren onto women everywhere. This is the negative female polarity, which clearly does not fit most of the women living today. Philo, the highly respected Jewish philosopher of Alexandria during Jesus's time, betrays his own prejudice against women in this illuminating and frightening passage:

No Essene takes a wife, because a wife is a selfish creature, excessively jealous and an adept in beguiling the morals of her husband and seducing him by her continued impostures. For by the fawning talk which she practices and the other ways in which she plays her part like an actress on the stage, she first ensnares the sight and hearing and then, when these criticisms have, as it were, been duped, she cajoles the sovereign mind.[3]

We can see here the negative polarity that Philo is teaching to others about women. While this may have been true for some women, it certainly was not true for all of them. And whatever flirty, frivolous, uneducated, needy behavior these women displayed was no doubt a consequence of being made powerless for hundreds of years. Here are a few examples of what Hebrew men were teaching their sons. The following quote comes from the Testament of Reuben, which is part of the apocryphal writings not included in the orthodox canon of the Old Testament. It gives us a terrifying insight into how Jewish men once treated their women.

> Women are evil, my children: because they have no power or strength to stand up against man, they use wiles and try to ensnare him by their charms; and man, whom woman cannot subdue by strength, she subdues by guile. For indeed, the angel of God told me about them and taught me that women yield to the spirit of fornication more easily than a man does, and they lay plots in their hearts against men: by the way they adorn themselves they first lead their minds astray, and by a look they instill the poison, and then in the act itself they take them captive—for a woman cannot overcome a man by force. So shun fornication, my children, and command your wives and daughters not to adorn their heads and faces, for every woman that uses wiles of this kind has been reserved for eternal punishment.[4]

Sheesh! That's pretty severe, and it sounds a lot like pure misogyny. This man justifies his own prejudice against women by claiming that an angel of God told him this was the truth. From this passage it is also clear that women were prohibited from wearing makeup or dressing to make themselves more attractive, even to their husbands. If they did, at least according to this writer, such an act would have damned them to eternal punishment.

We can see, however, both the negative masculine and the negative feminine currents at work here. The more a man takes away the woman's right to express herself in a positive, empowered way, the more he limits her choices. Then all she has left are the covert expressions of her neediness. However, when a man honors a woman and praises her for her positive physical, emotional, intellectual, and spiritual qualities, she will stand by him forever—not out of duty, fear, or coercion, but out of a willingness to support the best in him.

Later this same kind of projection was passed on to the newly emerging path of Christianity, especially through the writings of Paul. In Paul's letter to the Corinthians, we read that, in the newly forming church, men are allowed to preach "one by one, that all may learn, and all may be comforted," but women must "keep silence in the churches: for it is not permitted unto them to speak; but they are commanded to be under obedience, as also saith the law." Paul's reference is clearly to a preexisting Jewish law, not Jesus's law, since Jesus encouraged both men and women to claim their mastery. "And if they will learn anything, let them ask their husbands at home: for it is a shame for women to speak in the church" (Corinthians 14:34–35).

Paul passes on some of these same oppressive sentiments in his letter to the Ephesians (5:22–24): "Wives, submit yourselves unto your own husbands, as unto the Lord. For the husband is the head of the wife, even as Christ is the head of the church . . . Therefore as the church is subject unto Christ, so let the wives be to their own husbands in everything." This theme of superiority continues again in Corinthians (11:7–9): "For a man indeed ought not to cover his head, forasmuch as he is the image and glory of God: but the woman is the glory of man. For the man is not of the woman; but the woman of the man. Neither was the man created for the woman; but the woman for the man." Unfortunately, Paul's opinions have been used to legitimize the disempowerment of women in the church for about two thousand years.

As I discovered in my earlier conversation with Shasta, all human beings are biologically female first. Dr. Mary Jane Sherfey, an American psychiatrist on the Payne Whitney medical staff of the New York

Hospital at Cornell University, and the author of *The Nature and Evolution of Female Sexuality,* writes that in 1951 a published medical report states that "all mammalian embryos, male and female are anatomically female during the early stages of fetal life."[5] She goes on to add, "The innate femaleness of mammalian embryos was firmly established between 1957–58 (with, of course, over fifteen years of prior research); but the biologists recorded the fact with little comment. Although some of us might question the motivation behind their lack of interest in this startling discovery which overturns centuries of mythology and years of scientific theory, it could be expected. . . ."[6] Author Stephen Jay Gould, a professor of both zoology and geology at Harvard University, supports this thesis in his book *Hen's Teeth and Horse's Toes: Further Reflections in Natural History:* "The female course of development is, in a sense, biologically intrinsic to all mammals. It is the pattern that unfolds in the absence of any hormonal influence. The male route is a medication induced by the secretion of androgens from the developing testes."[7]

This simple biological revelation helped me to realize that for centuries we have been living under a reversal of the natural order of things in the oppression of men over women, who claim to be superior because, according to the Abrahamic faiths, they were created first. But that is not true. Women are not a subset of the masculine gender; rather, the male is created as a subset of the underlying female aspects of us all.

IN RETROSPECT

So how have we gotten so out of balance as a world? How have our cultures become so toxic over the past three thousand years that they have created such distortions and lies? And how can we ever find our way out of this enormous mess? In denying the beauty, wisdom, and essence of our own spiritual natures and the balance of both the masculine and feminine qualities intrinsic to all of us, we cut ourselves off from our many gifts. We lose connection with our feeling, our intuition, and our more advanced gifts of inner sight, hearing, knowing, and dreaming.

We become judges of our own inner natures and create stress and civil war within. We also stop developing these positive spiritual gifts taught by the masters of wisdom, and this is something that Jesus reminds us when he says, "He who believes in Me, the works that I do he will do also; and greater works than these he will do, because I go to My Father" (John 14:12).

It is only through the heart that one can harmoniously blend these two worlds together and attain mastery. This failure to honor both polarities in a positive way is the primal wound of the vanishing Age of Pisces and is an error that we don't need to repeat in the next Age of Aquarius. In this next cycle of human evolution we can choose to create a world that honors both male and female, both people and animals, both the earth and our responsibility as guardians of it, if we can remember to honor our roles as fully integrated human beings, or *homo luminous*.

10

Immanence
and Transcendence

Man may know himself and so know the Cosmos,
by being aware that he is an image of Atum and of the
Cosmos.
He differs from other living things in that he possesses
Mind.
Through Mind he may commune with the Cosmos, which
is the second god—
and by thought he may come to Knowledge of Atum the
One-God.

THOTH, *THE HERMETICA*

As I pondered the meaning of all that I had learned, I knew that the path to mastery lay at the center of these two polarities. It was the Middle Path that teachers such as Buddha, Jesus, and Thoth had long taught to humanity. Buddha had called it the Middle Way, while the early followers of Jesus had called it the Way, and Thoth, the ancient god of wisdom in Egypt, had called it the Ancient Way. It is the path of the heart where the synthesis of the male and female come together in union. And I realized that this union of yin and yang—so beautifully expressed in the Tao, where each contained its opposite—had long been taught by the mystics. Suddenly, many of the hermetic symbols seemed to make sense to me, and I realized that this sacred balance might be the only thing that could save us as a world.

I also realized what an enormous chasm existed between the punishing tribal god of the Old Testament and the merciful Presence that I knew as the Creator. This Presence was both deeply personal and also universal, and connected to everyone and everything. I experienced it on a regular basis whenever I interacted with Rigel and Auriel, my two spirit guides, direct aspects of the Divine Father and Mother. Knowing this, we have the choice to embrace a more universal image of the Divine that offers an integrated spirituality or to continue to defend these dysfunctional belief patterns that have generated so much suffering in the world.

This journey had also made me realize that there have been many cultures on this planet that once had a partnership model, and I knew that if we have done it before, we could do it again. But the foundational piece for most of us was establishing a theological framework that includes both the Divine Mother and the Divine Father. Then we have a basis from which to create mutual partnerships of peaceful coexistence.

My investigations had also helped me clarify some of the many negative currents I had felt pervading the churches of my childhood. For the first time I understood how preaching about a God of vengeance, alongside a God of forgiveness and love, could make us all schizophrenic. I realized that what we have come to accept as religion today is the result of many centuries of social, religious, and political agendas stacked one upon the another, some of which belong to a less enlightened age. Human beings impose their own preconditioned prejudices onto God, seeing only through the limitations of their own filters. They conceive of the Creator in their own image, and if these cultures have been distorted by fear or anger, then this is the way they see their God. These religious prejudices are then passed down through a long, convoluted series of customs, traumas, political manipulations, and devastating wars. While the initial spiritual teacher for any of these paths may have once been a messenger of the highest truth, as the centuries pass and the ambitions, fears, and prejudices of their subsequent leaders are overlaid on top of these teachings, what once was an enlightened message becomes skewed by the controlling elite's iron grip on power, position, and financial survival. This seems to produce self-righteous individuals who are either unwilling or unable to take the mote out of their own eye, because they are so busy pointing to their neighbor's. So in the "name of God" and righteousness, these regimes leave a legacy of horror, division, destruction, and warped thinking in their wake.

Today, as an entirely new era of the world begins, we do have a choice. As the influence of the dualistic Age of Pisces wanes, the balance of this highly polarized equation can shift to a more enlightened state. The astrological symbol of the two complementary fish of Pisces was undoubtedly meant to symbolize the reciprocal balance between the male and female in partnership. As we can see in figure 10.1 they are connected, yet the two fish face entirely different directions, creating duality. Pisces, in its exalted form, is the merger of the male and female polarities that create the Christ consciousness. But in its less aware expression, it becomes the age of the dominator/persecutor and the victim, a theme we have been living through with life-destroying consequences.

Figure 10.1. The astrological symbol for Pisces shows us the arc of the male and female circles joined by a straight line, indicating that the Age of Pisces had the potential to bring us to a place of balance. However, this did not occur. Instead, the male disowned his female counterpart, throwing the world out of balance.

Now, on the cusp of the Age of Aquarius, we become privy to the wisdom of the cosmos once again. Through recent discoveries in the fields of quantum physics and astronomy, we can begin to grasp for the first time how the immensity of the Divine Intelligence plays out in the universe. Quantum physics reveals that the entire universe is alive with consciousness and that all things are connected. Our thoughts and feelings actually affect reality at a subatomic level. This means that what we believe and project out into the world can actually change our lives. The more fear, hate, and violence we program into our thinking, the more we create that reality. The more love, kindness, and acceptance we project out into the world, the more these things will flourish in our lives. But this change must happen within us first, so that we can then collectively make wiser choices in creating healthier societies.

While it is clear that the infinite intelligence of the Divine is far more vast than what we can see even through our telescopes, this spark of life is present all around us. Otherwise, the universe would just be full of dead matter. God exists both within us and outside us. In theology, these two concepts have been referred to as Immanence and Transcendence, and they are fundamental keys to balancing our yin and yang.

THE IMPACT OF
OUR BELIEF SYSTEMS ON OUR LIVES

I had been speaking about these discoveries with Rigel and Auriel, and they had explained to me how our human conception of God is directly linked to our perception of the universe. The scientific and religious theologies that we embrace become filters that cause us to either incorporate or block out certain ideas. For example, a philosophy that teaches that the universe is endlessly in motion and constantly reinventing itself implants a natural sense of security in the changing currents of life. We innately know that change is the natural order of things, so we embrace the seasons, knowing that all things come full circle. A philosophy that teaches that the universe is constantly expanding causes us to expand our own scientific and spiritual knowledge. A philosophy that teaches reincarnation prepares us to accept all the cycles of life—youth, maturity, old age, and death—with grace, knowing that we are eternal beings and that death is but a portal into the other worlds. Thus we have nothing to fear. Conversely, a philosophy that teaches that we are damned since birth, which is the fundamental philosophy of original sin, produces a society of neurotic, anxious, judgmental people who never feel safe enough, perfect enough, or deserving enough of God's love.

GOD WITHIN AND GOD WITHOUT

This brings us to the powerfully important ideas of Immanence and Transcendence, two concepts that lie at the heart of every world religion. These two ideas represent the God Within and the God Without principles and can also be said to express the yin and yang polarities. Transcendence is the belief that God is outside us in Heaven. We can only reach God if we are good enough to travel there. God is so big that he cannot be contained within the realms of matter, so he exists in a higher dimension. Unfortunately, the difficulty with this is that when we think that God is not embodied in the world around us, we cease to see the sacred presence of the Divine in the visible world. Matter is viewed as only an objectified creation, but not containing the holy spark itself. This fundamental concept resides at the heart of all patriarchal religions.

Immanence is the belief that God is present in creation. The Divine is in everyone and everything, and thus all of life is sacred. This means that we can experience the sacred presence of the Creator in the rising sun, the majesty of the stars, and the hummingbird that just flew past our garden. The sacred is all around us, if we but have the eyes to see it. So while God or Atum might be far more vast than what we can perceive with our human senses, the Divine is still present with us everywhere and in every moment. We dwell within the body of the Divine, and she dwells within us, as close as our own breath.

EAST VERSUS WEST

As I contemplated these opposing approaches, I realized that what we need in our world today is a merger of these philosophies to bring us into balance. Yes, the Divine is transcendent. The Divine Intelligence is beyond the constraints of the visible world, but it is omnipresent as well. Most of the Eastern paths teach Immanence, the inward journey that allows us to experience the Divine in everything. This is why these paths have long cultivated practices of meditation, yoga, and self-reflection, producing the wisdom teachings of Taoism, Buddhism, Hinduism, Sikhism, Shintoism, Bon-Po, and Zen philosophy. These are all essentially nonviolent paths to God that honor both animal and human rights. These paths also pay tribute to the many different expressions of the gods and goddesses who all ultimately resolve back into one unifying Intelligence.

On the other hand, I realized that all the traditional Western religions teach the philosophy of Transcendence, and as we can observe, this approach has created a very different culture. Buddhists do not go to war, nor do Shinto or Hindu monks. But in the name of an all-powerful version of God, the Western paths of Islam, Judaism, and Christianity have murdered millions in the name of Allah, Yahweh, and God the Father.

All these dualistic religions teach that God resides in Heaven while Satan lives in Hell. We, as errant sinners, are stuck in the middle trying to get to Heaven. This philosophy fosters a relentlessly struggling mentality, where we continually fall short of perfection and thus are doomed to forever heroically try to reach that carrot in the sky. We will never be perfect enough, wise enough, or enlightened enough to reach God. The best we can hope for is to die and finally come into the presence of God. When we embrace the concept of Transcendence alone, we lose our connection with what is holy in the here and now. We also cease to practice communion with nature and begin to abuse the resources of the Earth without respect to the larger patterns of life. Without recognizing that the Divine is all around us, we fail to see the vision of the Sacred and cultivate a philosophy of careless cruelty and materialism that views bigger as better, and "more" as the source of happiness.

Think about it. If we believe that all that is holy is "up there," then by implication all that is "not holy" is below our feet, and that includes our planet. This kind of thinking treats everything as a commodity, including animals, plants, the land, and our life-sustaining waters. This kind of society begets exploitation and ruin, as we fail to consider our place in the pattern of life. This means that when we cut down a forest, pollute the air, annihilate a species, butcher our animals, destroy our crop production, toxify our oceans, strip our fields, dump aluminum into the food supply through chemtrails, or cause a nuclear reactor meltdown, we spark a chain reaction that affects all other living creatures. This is the ultimate selfishness. These actions show no regard for anyone except ourselves and are based only on shortsighted motives. They are the exact opposite of living in a balanced, sustainable way.

THE DISTORTION OF ORIGINAL SIN

Having grown up in the church, I realized that most of us are programmed at a subconscious level to feel abandoned at an early age. We are told that God is out there somewhere . . . but where? Oh, right . . . maybe he's in Heaven. When we add the threat of damnation to this, we are caught between our yearning for love, our fear of disapproval, and our endless quest to be good enough to please the Divine. Then once the distorted doctrine of "original sin" was added to the idea of a punishing God, we learned that we were all damned anyway.

Original sin was an idea created by the early church father St. Augustine (354–430 CE). It was never a doctrine taught or promoted by Jesus. It postulates that when Adam first had sex with Eve, sin was born in the world. In other words, humankind "fell" into imperfection through the act of sex, and thus we were cast out of Paradise. According to this crazy logic, we are all damned at birth because we were conceived through sex, or even if we have never had sex ourselves, we are still damned because Adam and Eve had sex. In Augustine's version we are all innately diseased and can only find salvation through the church. In essence, he proposes both the illness and the cure, creating a powerful loop of shame and guilt, manipulation and fear in his followers.

Theologian Elaine Pagels, author of *The Gnostic Gospels* and *Adam, Eve, and the Serpent,* writes about how St. Augustine's theory completely distorted the teachings of Jesus: "Instead of the freedom of the will and humanity's original royal dignity, Augustine emphasizes humanity's enslavement to sin. Humanity is sick, suffering, and helpless, irreparably damaged by the fall, for that 'original sin.'"[1] The belief that we are damned from birth is so fundamentally wrong that it creates a deep layer of shame at the very base of the human psyche, and this belief then generates the feeling that we can never be good enough to win God's love. We are innately unworthy and unlovable. By extension, this also means that we can never be good enough to earn the love we seek from our romantic partners, our parents, or even from ourselves.

Some historians have attributed Augustine's doctrine castigating human sexuality to a need to reject his own highly lustful nature, since Augustine was a great hedonist in his early years. He kept a mistress for thirteen years with whom he had an illegitimate son. Thus he preached that the only remedy for this kind of powerful sexual lust can be found in the conjugal rites of Christian marriage. Attempting to have such a rite with a virgin, he was engaged for a while to an eleven-year-old, but even then he kept a mistress. Clearly repulsed by and at odds with his own unbridled passions, and perhaps those of his friends, Augustine taught that human nature is a mass of perdition and sin. The only redemption for our sexuality, he said, is in the resurrection of the body. Unfortunately, this kind of warped theology was later legitimized by two subsequent popes, Pope Innocent I (401–417) and Pope Zosimus (417–418), and also by the church councils of Carthage, Ephesus, and Trent, giving us insight into how the distortions and repressions of the sexual appetites of the early church fathers have corrupted our theologies.

The concept of original sin was first introduced into the Roman church when Christian bishops began arguing about the preexistence of the soul. Reincarnation had always been part of early Christian canon for the first five centuries of the Common Era and was openly taught by Jesus. As we shall see, it was part of the belief systems of the Essenes and the Pharisees, two of the three major Jewish sects at the time of Jesus. While the Essenes lived in isolated communities away from Jewish politics, and were focused on the ancient teachings of Moses, the Pharisees and the Sadducees composed most of the seventy-two-member Sanhedrin High Council, which ruled Judea at the time of Christ. Both the Pharisees and the Sadducees were known for their wealthy lifestyles, excessive lawmaking, imposition of high taxes, and condemnation of any prophets who might arise to threaten their power. According to the first century CE Jewish historian Flavius Josephus, the Sadducees did not believe in reincarnation or life after death, while the Pharisees embraced both concepts.

Reincarnation was also part of the Egyptian, Greek, Celtic, and Roman theologies. However, for a church that wished to consolidate its power, the idea that people have multiple lives in which to perfect themselves as a way to reach Heaven left too much room for freedom. So this was not a very good approach for selling God to the masses. Once reincarnation fell out of favor among the church fathers, they were asked to explain how bad things can happen to good people if not for karma. As a result, St. Augustine proposed the concept of original sin as a way of explaining away the unprovoked sufferings and allegedly sinful nature of all human beings.

However, this kind of thinking is clearly flawed. In the first place, sex is part of the intelligent design of the universe. It is not only the natural means of procreation among all creatures, but also a doorway into powerful states of ecstatic bliss. It is perhaps this power that the church really feared. Through the Sacred Marriage, we have the chance to activate our own spiritual life force, awaken our hearts, and pull our fiery kundalini life force energies into our higher spiritual centers. This awakens our inner sight, allowing us to experience powerful states of oneness. In this kind of ecstatic communion we dissolve the boundaries of our egos, gain a glimpse of our true natures, and experience the transcendent passion of universal consciousness.

When we combine the idea that God is somewhere far, far away with original sin, we create a culture of unhappy, neurotic people who feel that they will never be perfect enough to be loved. This sets up a continual cycle of overwork, overspending, oversexing, guilt, shame, and disappointment, along with a sense of impending doom as we await the heavy hammer of punishment to descend. This theology demonizes sexual love—and women, for that matter—and blocks us from experiencing sacred sharing in a more elevated way. Then our unconscious sense of guilt, fear, and suppressed passion creates a society of people afraid to look inward for fear that they will see the worst. Then, when we avoid going within, we cannot connect with God, especially because we have been told that the world we live in is not sacred, and that God is nowhere to be found here on Earth. This creates a deep emptiness within each one of us.

Many people try to fill this emptiness with drugs, alcohol, pornography, compulsive shopping, or other forms of addiction, in an endless quest for money, fame, the perfect body, or approval in the eyes of others. These are all substitutes for the love we have never let ourselves experience from the one who loves us most—the Creator. Thus the theology of Transcendence needs the balance of Immanence to help us remember the creative presence of the Divine in every person, every flower, and every moment.

Unfortunately, these dysfunctional patterns have been programmed into us now for over sixteen hundred years, from the time the church accepted the doctrine of original sin in the fifth century CE. This is why most people do not understand why they are never happy for long. It is also why we long to escape into the fantasy worlds of TV, alcohol, or drugs. It's a way of numbing the unconscious pain of being present in a world without hope. But what we are really trying to heal is our own relationship with a loving, very present Creator who, we have been told, has gone missing from our daily lives. Jesus addresses these concepts of Transcendence and Immanence in the Gospel of Thomas when he says:

> I am the Light that is above the all. I am the All; the All came forth from Me, and the All attained to Me. Cleave wood, I am there; lift up the stone, and you will find Me there. (7:1–7)

In this simple but profound passage, Jesus resolves the entire conundrum. The Divine is both inside the worlds of matter, and also beyond what we can see. The Divine is present in every stone or piece of wood, and it is also the light that transcends this world. The Divine is everywhere. When we only embrace the "God is distant" philosophy, we cease to rejoice in the here and now and fail to celebrate the divinity of those around us. We try to fit into a pattern of perfection that has been projected onto us, and we invariably fall short. We become blind to the good, the right, and the beautiful, seeing the world only through the filters of harsh judgment. The glass is always half empty, and never half full. No wonder we are so miserable and frustrated!

11

The Directions
of Time and Space

*Mary said, "When the wind blows, listen, the Spirit is
speaking;*
Let your prayers be set upon the four winds in Spirit
So that they should be a blessing to the whole earth.
*If you pray in this way, the Supreme Spirit above will
receive your prayer."*

FROM THE GOSPEL OF MARY MAGDALENE

I returned to Shasta's circle two weeks before the spring equinox. The
daffodils, jonquils, and crocuses had just begun emerging by the road,
and in places you could smell the sweet scent of fresh earth. A blanket
of green grass covered the city and swaths of red, purple, and orange
tulips were just springing up. As the circle gathered at Shasta's house
on a Saturday afternoon, I realized that we would be spending most
of the day in the enchanted grove. We made our way down to the

enclave of Mary's garden and settled into a circle on benches and chairs. "Welcome, to the garden of the Goddess," Shasta began. "Today we will learn about the power of ritual and ceremony, and the cycles of time." This sounded exciting, to say the least.

"But first let me tell you what this circle will be called. At the end of your studies, each of you will have the opportunity to become a member of the Fellowship of Isis, an ancient sisterhood of women who are the walkers between the worlds. We are those who learn to work with both the seen and the unseen realms. This society is connected to many great circles from our past, including the priestesses of Isis, the priestesses of Avalon, the Order of the Magdalene, the Sisterhood of the Shields, and the Native American Twisted Hair Societies, who have long been the record keepers of Earth's history." She looked around the circle at our astonished faces. "The Twisted Hair lineage is linked to the writings of Carlos Castaneda, who was an initiate of this branch." *Wow!* This explained a lot. So the Native American teachings were linked to the Yaqui path of knowledge, while these other groups had existed in cultures all over the world.

"However, each circle has its own name, and so we will have ours. I have meditated on our name, and we will be called the Serpent Gourd Woman Society." There was a moment of stunned silence as the group digested these words. *Serpent Gourd Woman Society . . . What could that possibly mean?* Shasta must have seen the shocked look on our faces, for she went on. "You must each begin to look deeper than the surface if you are to understand the Mysteries. You must begin to discern the hermetic significance behind these symbols." *Hmm . . .* This took a moment to sink in. I tried to come up with what these symbols stood for, but for the life of me I couldn't think of anything spiritual about a gourd. I had just learned more about the meaning of the serpent, but I was still a bit ambivalent about it. After all, I had been inculcated with Christian theology, where the snake was synonymous with Satan.

As usual, Shasta seemed to be reading my mind. Her eyes alighted on me as she began to speak. "The gourd is the humblest vegetable on Earth, and like women everywhere, it comes in many different shapes and sizes. The gourd is not only a food, but it can be turned into a bowl, a water ladle, or even a rattle if it is dried properly. It is also a symbol for the Great Cosmic Egg from which the universe is born. The Divine Mother pours forth these life-giving energies so that the worlds of creation can come into form. Throughout this year we will be using gourd rattles to rattle ourselves awake." She pointed to two large baskets at her feet and laughed. *Was she laughing with us or at us?* We all suddenly realized that the baskets were full of gourd rattles. Most of them were round, while others looked like wily, undulating snakes. "The gourd is like the womb of the Mother Earth herself. It is round, fertile, and full of the mysteries of life. And like women, it comes in every shape and size."

Several of us looked at one another, but we were too bewildered to speak. *Okay, maybe the gourd was safe,* I thought, *but what about the serpent?* Shasta smiled mischievously, as if she knew what I was thinking. "The serpent has long been the symbol of wisdom for tribal people everywhere—except the Christians who misunderstood its symbolism. It represents the kundalini life force located at the base of the spine, and it is also linked to the activation of our DNA. In its exalted form, the good serpent represents 'the One Who Has Awakened.' This is why Egyptian queens wore a uraeus on their foreheads. It is also why Moses carried a serpent staff. We see this same serpentine staff with Aesculapius, the Greek father of healing, and it is said in the Gnostic tradition that Jesus also carried such a staff with the name of the Creator engraved upon it. When he spoke to the multitudes, it looked like an ordinary staff, but when he taught his disciples in private, it was often transformed into a serpent that would coil up near him. Sometimes it is also said that when he wished to initiate a disciple, the staff was transformed into a good serpent and would bite the disciple, injecting gnosis

Figure 11.1. The serpent has long been a symbol of wisdom and enlightenment in cultures around the world. (Illustration by Tricia McCannon)

and power into him.[1] However, because the people had been taught that the serpent was evil, many fled from this source of transformation."

Whoa! I had never heard such a story before, although certainly Jesus is often depicted with a shepherd's staff, as many of the other great biblical figures are. Years later I was to discover a tale told by the Gnostic Christians that exactly matched this story of Jesus and the serpent staff. It was the same kind of story that we read about in the Bible regarding Moses and the priests of Egypt, who were all able to transform their staffs into serpents at will. I had no idea if this was intended

Figure 11.2. There are seven chakras that run from the base of the spine to the top of the head, all connected by the serpentine energies of the spine. Each of these chakras serves as the meeting point between spirit and matter. The chakras act like filing cabinets for our emotional, mental, and spiritual natures. To achieve enlightenment we must clean out these chakras and align them.
(Illustration by Tricia McCannon)

to be taken literally or if it represented some kind of spiritual alchemy.

Shasta went on. "In truth the staff represents the spinal column, while the two snakes that run up it represent the two nervous systems that run up and down the spine.* This is the caduceus, the universal staff of healing. The sympathetic nervous system (SNS) is the male aspect of our being, which controls our voluntary actions. The parasympathetic nervous system (PNS) is the female aspect that governs autonomic processes, like breathing and digestion. When spiritually activated and balanced, these two currents can bring us to a place of enlightenment. When we unite these two polarities in the heart, we can awaken the power of love. Then we raise this serpentine energy into the center of the forehead to activate our Third Eye, or inner sight. This is the Bindu point directly linked with our ability to see into the subtle worlds. This allows us to finally lift the veils of the physical world and gaze into the inner realms. The serpent is also a symbol for wisdom and of spiritual transformation. This is why I have chosen this name for your group. You are now entering a process that will completely transform you."

I took a deep breath, putting aside my ingrained conditioning and fear of the serpent that I had learned since childhood. Everything Shasta had said made sense, but was I too conditioned by my past to let these concepts in?

THE SACRED CIRCLE AND
THE CELEBRATION OF RITUAL

"The gourd is the shape of the medicine circle that holds all things in balance. It is the holy chalice that we fill with ceremony and prayers. The circle is a place of communion where we will share our fondest

---

*These two nervous systems—the sympathetic system and the parasympathetic system—are male and female, respectively. The male aspect deals with our deliberate, volitional actions, while the parasympathetic, or female, runs the body's autonomic nervous system, governing breathing, digestion, sleeping, and the like. In Eastern wisdom teachings, they are called the *ida* and the *pingulla*.

dreams and banish our deepest fears." The women's heads bobbed subtly as they listened. "Today I wish to teach you about the eight directions of time and space, and to talk about the difference between ritual and ceremony." Donna, Emerald, and Claudia exchanged a meaningful glance. "Ritual and ceremony are both ways of calling in spiritual energies in order to communicate with the Divine. Ritual is something that is done the same way over and over, passed down from generation to generation like a sacred formula. This repetition of words, gestures, and intentions creates a resonance through time, like ripples moving through time past and time present, linking all other sacred circles who have performed this ritual together. In this way, we can connect with all those who have gathered in sacred song, dance, or ritual by campfires throughout the ages, and this gives the ritual great power. We can observe this in many Buddhist, Jewish, and Orthodox Christian temples. Ceremony, however, is an ever-changing, living vehicle that is never done the same way twice. It arises spontaneously from the needs of the moment and can thus be powerful, heartfelt, and directly inspired by Spirit. Both ritual and ceremony have the power to link us to all the other circles that have ever been, strengthening each with our prayers." Shasta looked around the circle to see if we were following her.

"So let's do an exercise. I want you to name any ritual you can think of in your daily life." *Hmm* . . . Images of a holy Mass flashed through my head, the wafting of incense, the Nicene Creed, the sacrament of bread and wine . . . But before I could speak, Emerald raised her hand.

"Getting married," Emerald grinned, and everyone laughed. Yes, getting married was certainly a ritual. It had been done for thousands of years. Sara raised her hand. "Funerals," she offered.

Claudia snorted, then laughed. "Sorry . . . it's just a strange juxtaposition—marriage and funerals, like death and taxes." Several of the women giggled, seeing the joke.

But Sara was not done. "Is it a ritual or a ceremony when we bury someone?"

Shasta answered. "The funeral is the ritual, but the specifics of the way we honor the deceased is different for every person, so that becomes the ceremony part." *Hmm . . . a ceremony within a ritual. Very interesting,* I thought.

Claudia grinned. "How about receiving an Academy Award?" Yes, she would think of that, being the wonderful makeup artist that she was. Plus, it was a funny idea. We had all seen so many Academy Awards shows that by now they probably were a ritual.

"No, that's a ceremony," Shasta said. "It even says so—*Academy Awards Ceremony.* The event seems like a ritual since it occurs each year, but it is really a ceremony, since it is different each time."

I raised my hand. *Why was the only thing I could think of religious rites?* "How about Sunday morning services? Aren't they rituals? We do them the same way each time."

Shasta nodded. "Yes, going to church is a ritual, but the sermon, the songs, and the things that are shared each time are different. So these are ceremonies. Try to think deeper. Think of other things that can become rituals in our lives, even if we are not aware of them."

Alex cleared her throat. "You mean like making the bed every morning?"

"Very good," Shasta nodded. "Yes, rituals that have nothing to do with religion but are just part of your daily life. Like brushing your teeth, feeding the cat, taking the dog for a walk—these things can become rituals, too, if we do them often enough." It was clear that none of us had ever thought of these activities as rituals before. "They might be unconscious rituals, but they are still rituals." Shasta looked around the circle. "Anything that you do over and over becomes a habit, and habits can become rituals, and these can begin to define your world. Eventually, you no longer question your own actions. You just do what you've been conditioned to do. This is how we are all programmed not to think for ourselves."

Hmm . . . I began to see where this was going. It was as if everything we did had the power to become unconscious rituals: waking up at a certain time, showering, working nine to five each day, paying our bills.

We became hypnotized by our routines, and then we became blind to all other choices. I thought of a story then that I had once heard about the Native Americans. When the first clipper ships appeared off the coast of North America, the Native Americans were not able to see them. These large wooden ships were completely outside their worldview. But the shaman, who had spent a lifetime developing a more expanded consciousness, had been able to see the reflection of the ships on the water. After a few minutes, he could perceive the ship itself. When he shared this vision with his tribe, this allowed them to expand their perception to see the ships as well. Eventually, the entire tribe could see it, as they allowed this new idea into their consciousness.

I realized then that we are each like this. We get used to a certain way of seeing the world, of seeing God or reality, and then we cease to ask questions. Perhaps as children we saw more clearly, but after being told the same things over and over again, year after year, we are lulled into a certain unconscious complacency. After a while we cease to question our reality, and we lose the ability to see the ship that is moored in the harbor, no matter how real it may be.

Shasta lifted her chin at our dismayed expressions. "I'm not criticizing anyone. I'm just saying that you must examine your actions carefully, instead of running like a mouse through a maze in search of the same bite of cheese each day. When we are children, we see with fresh eyes, but then, over time, we become conditioned to believe whatever society tells us. But to become aware, we must first wake up inside the dream. We must become purposeful."

I exchanged a meaningful glance with Claudia. We had just been talking about this very subject in our careers. Claudia had said that she went to work, paid her bills, ate, and slept and began to wonder if that's all there was to her life. Sometimes in the middle of this routine, there would be the excitement of a new romance or a new client, but in general she had a point. What was the purpose of this life if we just continued to run around in the maze?

Shasta continued. "Starting today, one of your homework assignments is to make a list of all your ritual actions, both secular and spiritual. And don't forget to include the habits of the holidays. Holidays are times of serious ritual, and what you unconsciously associate with them—for better or for worse—can directly affect your experience." I knew exactly what she meant. My family had been so conditioned by the many years of my father's rages at the holidays that, even after he passed away, we still continued to have yearly dramas each Christmas or Thanksgiving. It was too bad, because I dearly loved Christmas.

Shasta began speaking again. "Why do you buy presents at birthdays or at Christmas? Why do you cook a turkey at Thanksgiving? Why are there football games on Sundays?" Alex and Sharon shifted uneasily. "I'm just suggesting that you think about what you are choosing. By paying attention and making deliberate choices in your life, you can begin to act from an awakened mind."

Donna raised her hand. "Does this mean that I can stop washing the dishes every night? I don't think my husband would like that!" We all laughed.

"In this circle," Shasta responded, "we will all be performing rituals. We will be giving birth to spiritual thought-forms for the purpose of manifesting them in our lives. But the two laws of the priestess path are 'Do harm to no one' and 'Always protect the children.' These are the two primary laws we live by." These words covered a host of subjects. If we harm no one, then we will always act in a positive way. And if we always protect the children, then we will take care that the next generation will grow up to become wise and whole.

Alex raised her hand. "If we think bad things, is that like black magic?"

Shasta looked suddenly serious. "We are not doing black magic here. When anyone uses his or her power selfishly, it always creates a karmic backlash. It's bad karma to use selfish intentions to threaten the free will of anyone else. Plus, negative thought-forms can rebound on the sender, so the spiritual work that we do here is always focused on the good." Everyone nodded.

"All right, let's go back to ritual and ceremony," Shasta said. "Ceremony comes naturally to every human being, particularly women, who are often more in touch with life transitions than men are. Women perform ceremonies all the time; for example, when you give a birthday party, hold a wedding shower, or furnish your baby's bedroom to welcome him into the world. Ceremonies mark the end of one stage of life and the beginning of another, sanctifying events so that the moment is honored. Women have been marking life passages since time immemorial."

Meg raised her hand. "Can you just say what the difference is between ritual and ceremony again?"

Shasta cleared her throat. "Ritual is more formal, and ceremony is more fluid. You can establish the energy of the circle in ritual by calling the directions, and then fill up that circle with whatever kind of ceremony is appropriate for that moment in time. Understood?" We all nodded, beginning to grasp the difference between the two.

THE DIRECTIONS OF TIME

"Now, let's talk about the eight High Holy Days of the year. These are called the directions of time." Several of the women pulled out their notebooks. "No," Shasta put up a hand. "Just listen, so you can learn to take this information in on another level." Reluctantly, they put their pads and pencils down. "The eight windows of time and space correspond to the four seasons of the year, so you are already familiar with them." Relief spread across our faces. "The spring and autumn equinoxes form the horizontal arms of a great annual cross, while the summer and winter solstices—the vertical axis of that cross—mark the longest and shortest days of the year. These four powerful holidays make up the cardinal cross of time each year when the veils between this world and the others grow thin. In between these four great doorways are four other High Holy Days, and these are exactly six weeks apart."

Meg cleared her throat. "Excuse me, Shasta. I don't want to sound dumb, but what are the solstices and equinoxes exactly? I mean, I've heard of them, but what are they?"

Shasta raised her hands, forming two globes. "As the Earth moves around the sun each year, there are two points when the tilt of our planet's hemispheres are either closest to, or farthest from the sun. These two dates mark the two solstice points of winter and summer. The solstices are the shortest and the longest days of the year, while the equinoxes are the two days when the day and night are equal in length." *Ah!* "In the northern hemisphere the summer solstice falls on June 21, when the sun is up for the longest time. Six months later we have the shortest day of the year, which is the winter solstice on December 21. Below the equator, in South America or Australia, these dates are reversed."

"And the equinoxes?" Susan asked, throwing back her long, red, sexy hair.

"The word *equinox* means 'equidistant.' The equinoxes occur every fall and spring when the length of the days and nights is equal. That's March 23 and September 23, when the scales are perfectly balanced. In fact, the fall equinox begins with Libra, whose symbol is the balanced scales. After the spring equinox, the days become longer, and after the fall equinox, we pass into winter. This is the time of the winter crone, when we go into the cave to hibernate." This all made perfect sense to me, but it seemed strange that we no longer honored these important Holy Days, especially when they had nothing to do with religious belief systems, but were grounded in astronomy and the seasons. *How had we fallen so out of step with these rhythms?*

As usual, Shasta seemed to be reading my mind. "In the ancient world, these eight High Holy Days were times of great celebration. They signaled the time when the community would sow their seeds for planting, harvest their crops, or mend their nets. Like the eight lunar stations of the moon, these eight stations of the sun mark the changing seasons of the year."

Meg cleared her throat. "What are the eight stations of the moon?"

Shasta smiled. "Every month the moon waxes and wanes, and this interaction affects the moods of people and animals, plants and minerals. The eight stations start with the dark of the moon, or the time of gestation and planting. Then the moon becomes a crescent moon, a quarter moon, then a waxing or gibbous moon, before becoming the full moon for three days of every month. This is the time when the electromagnetic energies of the moon pull the minerals up into the

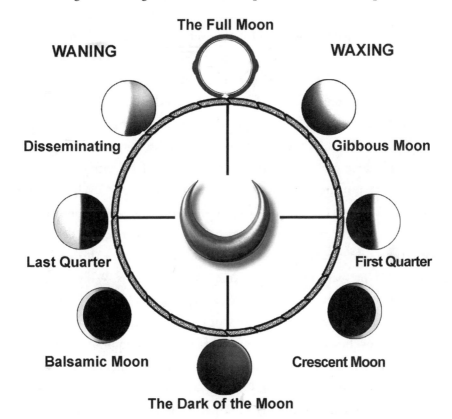

The Dark or New Moon: *Plant, intuit, open, truth, surrender, release—Kore*
The Crescent Moon: *Stepping out, mobilize, hope, reach, begin—Artemis*
First Quarter: *Activate, build, risk, plunge in, promise, commit—Diana*
Gibbous Moon: *Clarify, persevere, ask, design, progress, reach—Vesta*

Full Moon: *Shine, play, dance, dream, rise, passion, love, celebrate—Aphrodite*
Disseminating Moon: *Gather, create, express, understand, wander, messenger—Quan Yin*
Last Quarter: *Listening within, time crossing, inward, reorient—Hecate*
Balsamic Moon: *Let go, fate, meditate, memories, wisdom, ebb, descent—Persephone*

Figure 11.3. The phases of the moon.

plants, so this is the best time to harvest your crops." *Hmm . . . perhaps the ancient people knew something that we had forgotten.*

But Shasta went on. "After the full moon the light begins to wane, creating the waning, or disseminating, moon, the last quarter moon, and finally the balsamic moon before it returns to its station beside the sun, making it invisible to us on Earth. This is called the dark of the moon, where it remains for three full days before beginning the cycle all over again. *Hmm . . .* I had never really thought about all this, although clearly I had watched the moon all my life and marveled at its beauty and its cycles. So during the new moon, I realized, the sun and the moon were on one side of the Earth together, and during the full moon, the moon was exactly opposite the sun, creating a powerful yin/yang balance for the Earth. This was why the full moon was so potent. It was all starting to make sense—the marriage of polarities.

Shasta continued. "The moon goes through this cycle thirteen times in every year, and thus the number *thirteen* was always linked to the moon, the menstrual cycles of women, and the Goddess." She looked around the circle. "Similarly, the sun also goes through eight stations of the year, charting the same essential seasons. Winter roots go into the ground, since the world lies asleep under a blanket of snow. At Candlemas or February 2, we are still in darkness, but moving toward the return of the light. Six weeks later, at the spring equinox, we feel the stirrings of new life in the spring. We begin to implement plans that we have nurtured all winter long. On May 1, some six weeks later, flowers push up into the light, animals foal their young, and everything answers the call of the life-giving sun.

"Then, on June 21 we have the summer solstice. The summer is when the plants come into full harvest, bricks get made, homes get built, and our dreams can flourish. Then on August 1, we celebrate the bounty of the Earth Mother who has given us our fruits and flowers. In September, at the fall equinox, the days and nights become equal again, but from this point on the days become shorter. Then at Hallowmas, or Halloween, we pass fully into the shorter days as we celebrate the Day

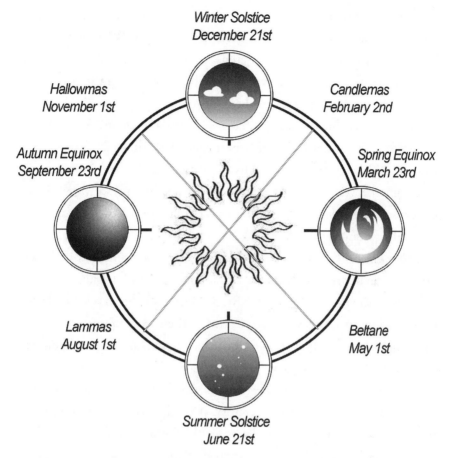

Figure 11.4. The eight high holy days of the year.

of the Dead. Then finally, just before Christmas, on December 21, the sun enters its darkest phase as it sinks lowest in the southern skies. It stays there for three entire days, just like the dark of the moon, before it begins to move upward, renewing its annual pilgrimage across the sky. This is the dark phase and best for gestating ideas. Animals hibernate, trees go dormant, and people mend their nets and talk about their plans for the spring season."

Shasta took a breath and looked at us, hoping that her words had painted the picture of this celestial dance that made its way across the heavens every year. "This is the innate rhythm that all living things respond to, and that once we, as harmonious, attuned communities, celebrated together." This took a moment to sink in. *Why didn't we still celebrate these milestones?* I wondered. After all, we all knew when summer and winter blew in, and we had the boots, coats, and sundresses to prove it. But what had happened to our modern holidays?

Donna raised her hand. "What are those dates again?"

Shasta ticked them off on her fingers. "December 21, February 2, March 23, May 1, June 21, August 1, September 23, and November 1, although the year was often thought to begin in the spring with the equinox. This is why we have Easter at that time. It is the season of renewal or resurrection."

Hmm . . . These dates seemed easy to remember. The cardinal cross points were all around the twenty-first, and the other holidays were on the first of the month, except for Brigit's Day on February 2. I reflected on our modern holidays to see if any of them corresponded to these dates, but I could only think of Christmas, Easter, and Groundhog Day around the first of February.

Shasta went on. "May Day falls on the first of May and was once called Beltane, the festival of fertility. It marked the celebration of the light. August 1 was Lughnasadh, from the Celtic word *Lugh,* the God of light. Today the church has turned it into Lammas. November 1 was Samhain, and this holiday was meant to honor the ancestors who had passed to the Otherside. It is now the festival of All Hallows Eve. And Candlemas is the festival of Brigit, the Goddess of the Flame, the Goddess of Returning Light. This day marks a promise that the sun will return at the equinox, the next celestial marker."

From my interest in archaeology and sacred temples, I knew that this celestial clock had been figured long ago into many of the alignments of sacred sites around the world. By honoring this natural Earth-sky rhythm, communities knew how to prepare for each season. Sites like Stonehenge had been created to predict certain astronomical events, like full moons, eclipses, and meteor showers. "These eight High Holy Days are portals that allow us to step between the worlds," Shasta explained. "This is why they are important days in spiritual ceremonies. It is a time when the alignment between the Earth and the sun allows the veils between the worlds to grow very thin, and this gives us the power to more easily contact the other dimensions."

Her words sent a shiver through me. I imagined that these points opened up energetic alignments within the cosmos, linked to the heavens. I suddenly realized that while some of these dates corresponded to our modern holidays, the church had shifted our attention away from the actual days of alignment essentially causing humanity to fall out of sync with the natural rhythms of the cosmos. I wondered if this had been deliberate, causing the world to fall out of sync with nature and ourselves. Later I was to learn that when the church fathers superimposed Christianity over this seasonal wheel, they had shifted the true dates backward or forward to misdirect the energies as a way of keeping us from making these spiritual connections for ourselves. Thus December 25 became the substitute for the winter solstice (December 21). Valentine's Day falls two weeks after Candlemas, and Easter is usually a week or two from the spring equinox.

I knew that the reason December 25 had been chosen as Jesus's birthday was because the sun had reached its lowest point in the sky in the three days before. It had symbolically "died" at the winter solstice, where it appeared to stand still for three full days, enacting the sacrificial death of the sun. This was linked to the story of the great solar lords descending into Hell for three days before rising from the dead. This was the real reason that Jesus, Horus, Osiris, Mithra, and the other great solar avatars had their birthdays placed on December 25! As messengers of light, they were identified with the return of the celestial sun in its annual circuit of rebirth.[2]

"And how exactly does Halloween fit into all of this?" Claudia asked, scratching her head. I had seen her dressed the year before as a pink pussycat with fishnet stockings and a tail.

Shasta rubbed her chin. "In the Christian calendar Samhain (pronounced SOW-wen) was converted to All Hallows Eve, and

November 1 became All Saints Day. Finally, November 2 was turned into All Souls Day, honoring not only the church fathers, but the ancestors of the common people. This holiday was originally the Day of the Dead that honored our ancestors with prayers. It is a powerful time to communicate with loved ones on the Otherside, but few people use it this way anymore. Some believe that it was on this date that the Great Flood took down Atlantis some 11,500 years ago.* In the Goddess tradition it is the time when the crone comes into her power. She is pictured as an old woman veiled in secrets, the sage of life and death and all the cycles. In her maiden form she is Brigit the bride, but in winter she becomes the crone. They called her Cailleach in the Celtic lands, and she foretells the future to all who would listen."

Later I was to learn that *Cailleach* is the Irish name for the white ghostly lady from the Otherside who acts as an intermediary between the world of the humans and the spirits. She is also called Grandmother of Time and is still honored in many places where the Day of the Dead is celebrated. In Mexico, for example, people dress up in colorful costumes and share food with their departed loved ones. The mood there is festive, not solemn.[3] It was in England that the ritual of begging for "soul cakes" first originated, eventually evolving into our modern-day custom of trick or treating.†

"There aren't holy days in August anymore, are there?" Meg complained. I could see that all of us were trying to work out how our existing holidays fit within the old calendar. "At least I've never heard of any." She shrugged.

Shasta made a face. "The church took great pains to abolish as

___
*Geological research shows that there have been several serious floods in our past, including one as recently as 4,000 years ago, but researchers agree that there is massive evidence that 11,500 years ago the water table on the planet rose some four hundred feet within one month's time, cutting massive swaths across the land, and ending the last glacial period. We are now living in an interglacial age.

†In fact, some believe that this was the date when the Great Flood swept the planet, taking millions of lives, and thus we commemorate those who passed in that horrific tragedy.

many festivals of the Earth-based wisdom as they could, particularly those that honored the Goddess. While the solstice was often assigned to the lords of light, the midsummer harvest was dedicated to the Great Mother Isis, Demeter, Diana, and Ceres, all Goddesses who protected the forests, fields, crops, and animals. August 15 is Isis's birthday in Egypt, but it was later turned into the Day of Ascension for Mary the Mother. Here in America it is celebrated as the Green Corn Festival by the Native Americans who create effigies of the Corn Maiden."

Wow! The church leaders had co-opted whatever they could, I thought. They had completely eliminated the celebrations of Midsummer's Eve, dedicated to the Goddess, that had been captured so brilliantly in Shakespeare's *Midsummer Night's Dream.* This celebration had been connected with grapes, wine, fertility, sexual celebrations, and song. This was the same kind of joyful celebration as the ones I had discovered in Canaan and Mesopotamia that were dedicated to Ashtoreth and Tammuz. No wonder the church had gotten rid of this holiday! Like Beltane, which celebrated the fertility of the people and the land, it had been way too much fun. Besides, leaders of the totally patriarchal sect of Yahweh had so hated the Mother-Son or Husband-Wife partnership combination that they had just deleted it from our minds.

Later I was to discover that this agricultural Goddess festival had originally been dedicated to Isis because she was the one who had rescued the grains of wheat along the Nile after the Great Flood. She and Osiris had brought these seeds of wheat and barley to the people and thus preserved them for future generations.[4] This was also why Isis was known in Greece and Rome as Demeter and Ceres, respectively, the Goddess of Cereals and Grains.

Shasta went on. "Lamas, or August 1, was intended to thank Mother Earth for her bounty and to acknowledge her as our life-giver. But the church changed the name to the Feast of the Blessed Virgin and moved the date to August 4, three days past the window of alignment. Today these festivals have passed into oblivion." I wondered if the

Figure 11.5. The harvest maiden's months were August and September, and she became immortalized as the constellation Virgo. (Illustration by Tricia McCannon)

men who had made these decisions were so ill informed that they just didn't know the real dates, or if this misdirection had been deliberate. I suspected the latter. By short-circuiting our connection to the natural rhythms of the Earth, we fall out of step with the harmonies of the universe. We become confused and disempowered.

Sara raised her hand. "What about Easter? Why do we have Easter eggs and bunny rabbits, and what does this have to do with Jesus? The whole thing seems kind of screwed up." We laughed, knowing just what she meant.

"All right, let's talk about Easter," Shasta said with a gleam in her eye. "Why do we have Easter eggs at Easter?" We all looked bewildered. Of course, the question had occurred to us before, but I had no idea.

Emerald spoke up. "Because of Eostara, the German Goddess of Rebirth, who supposedly invented nature itself."

Shasta looked pleased. "Yes, Eostara, like Gaia, represents not only the planet Earth, but all the Great Cosmic Eggs. Creation itself reveals this same shape, from the oval of the galaxy to the solar systems. They all represent the eggs of the Mother." *What a thought! How would the ancients have known what modern-day astronomers are only now just discovering? How could they have known about the shapes of orbital planes, planets, or galaxies? Perhaps they "saw" them shamanically.* Certainly the egg was a universal shape that produced life. In Vedic culture the divine couple, Vishnu and Lakshmi, were said to reside inside a Cosmic Egg during the long "night of the world." And in Egypt, Ptah, the architect of humanity, was shown spinning this Cosmic Egg on a potter's wheel. I realized then that there were a lot of hidden scientific and religious principles woven into these symbols.

"Did you know that the month of May was named for the Goddess Maia?" Emerald interjected. "And that June is named for Juno, Zeus's wife?" We all looked at her in surprise. *Why wasn't this stuff taught in school?* Suddenly, the resonances between the Goddess and our calendar made perfect sense.

Figure 11.6. The Egyptian creator god Enki, or Ptah, is shown spinning the Cosmic Egg of creation on the potter's Wheel of Life. (Illustration by Tricia McCannon)

Shasta looked pleased. "Yes, Maia was the Roman Goddess who gave birth to Hermes. Like Green Tara in India, Maia was the Goddess of the Earth. Maia's color is green for healing and fertility, so May Day is her festival. Maia is the Goddess who blesses all sacred unions—human and animal alike. This is why May is the most popular month for weddings."[5]

Emerald was just getting warmed up. "In Assyria, May was the time

Figure 11.7. Maia is the maiden associated with the season of spring and the month of May. She is linked to the Maypole and the rites of fertility. (Illustration by Tricia McCannon)

when ribbons were fastened on trees and gifts were left under them for the poor." *Wow!* I thought. *Like Christmas!* Maybe this was where we had gotten the custom of putting up Christmas trees, representing the Tree of Life. Emerald went on. "Even the two colored ribbons of the maypole dance mimic the birds and bees weaving among the flowers. Interesting, isn't it?" *This is astonishing!* I could see that the two ribbons used on a Maypole wove together the male and female strands in a great undulating dance, just like our own DNA, or the spiritual currents of the sympathetic and parasympathetic nervous systems that move up the spine during spiritual activation. *All these customs were really about enlightenment, weren't they? And they were all based on the ancient religion of the Goddess! Amazing!*

"Didn't they have a ritual king and queen on May Day?" Sharon asked.

Shasta nodded. "Yes, just like the king and queen of the Homecoming Court at the prom each spring, they represented the Divine Mother and her male consort, or king. They were only married for a day to symbolically stimulate the Earth's fertility. Any children conceived from that union were thought to have very special destinies."

Holy smokes! I had no idea that the thousands of annual high school proms had anything to do with the ancient custom of the May Day celebration. "Yeah," said Emerald. "The word *prom* is short for the 'promenade,' or stroll taken by the king and queen before all their subjects." *Amazing!* I thought.

Alex raised her hand. "Didn't the Romans make a big bonfire in the spring and jump over it for fertility?"

Shasta nodded. "Yes, this was the Celtic celebration of Bona Dea, where they danced all night long, and jumped over the bonfires at dawn for good luck. The Irish celebrated the Festival of Shelia Na Gig at that time."

"I've never heard of her," Claudia mumbled. She wasn't alone.

"Ooooo!" Emerald gushed. "You don't know about Shelia Na Gig? Scandalous!"

*Figure 11.8. Shelia Na Gig represents
the essence of creation and fertility.
(Illustration by Tricia McCannon)*

"What do you mean?" I asked uncomfortably.

"Well," Emerald said, rubbing her hands together as if she were about to impart some juicy gossip, "Shelia Na Gig was the Goddess whose private parts hung over the doorway for fertility, like a portal. To touch her yoni when you went through the door was considered good luck! A sign of the home's fertility." *What? Impossible!* I thought. I was duly scandalized.

"It's a stylized vulva," Sharon explained. "I saw those carvings when I went to England last year. Wasn't she the Irish symbol for procreation? I thought the church wiped her out."

"Yeah, the Puritans tried to," Emerald said, shrugging. "They would rather deny women's sexuality or repress it altogether, so they decided to dedicate the month of May to the Virgin Mary instead." We all laughed at that. This was all quite eye-opening. The celebration of fertility had been co-opted by the Virgin Mary. What would the church do next?

Shasta spoke. "Since May was associated with many of the ancient goddesses who represent the fertility of the Earth, the church viewed it with great disfavor. In Greece this was when Persephone returned to Demeter and the land became fertile once again. It was when Aphrodite, the Goddess of Love, returned from the deep waters of her winter bath. It was when Ishtar celebrated the rebirth of Tammuz with the ritual lovemaking. But in the eighteenth century, the month of May was dedicated to Mary the Mother, once again consecrating it to the Goddess of New Life."

Wow! I marveled. At least some aspect of the Divine Mother had been reclaimed in the world, despite her being displaced as the Lady of Plants and Animals, the Lady of Life and Rebirth.

THE COMING OF THE GODDESS

"All right," Shasta said, clapping her hands. "Enough for today. Now I want each of you to find a place in the garden where you can be alone. For the next hour I want no talking. Call on the sacred energy of the Mother. She may come through the buzzing of a bumblebee, the budding of a flower, or the singing of a bird. She may come in the sacred sound of the cosmic river, for she lives in all things, seen and unseen. But most of all she lives inside your hearts. Hers is the yearning of your spirit to unite with all living things. Feel her presence in nature, and invite her in. Here on the eve of a new season of spring, celebrate your connection with nature. Lie on the grass, look up at the clouds, and find the garden within yourselves. Then, when you are ready, you may leave in silence. I will see you again at the spring equinox."

12

The Goddess and the
Descent into the Underworld

> *I am the single radiance by which all is aroused and within*
> *which it is vibrant . . .*
> *For the man who has found me, the door to all things*
> *stands open . . .*
> *I am the magnetic force of the universal presence and the*
> *ceaseless ripple of its smile.*
>
> TEILHARD DE CHARDIN,
> *HYMN TO THE ETERNAL FEMININE*

I returned to the Goddess circle on the morning of March 23. It was the spring equinox, and the weather was truly splendid. A sweet breeze blew through the city, and I could almost smell the fresh grass rising from the Earth, even in my walks around the city park that lay only two blocks from my midtown house. I had taken Shasta's admonitions seriously to spend more time in nature, so several days a week I took walks through Piedmont Park, Atlanta's Central Park. It had acres of rolling hills and oak trees and a huge lake that attracted Canadian geese and ducks. I found that the walks gave me time to think about the deeper things at the center of my life, and when I stopped to meditate beneath the grandmother oaks, a sense of stillness would come over me that made it easy to hear my spirit guides. But it was often Rigel's voice that spoke to me, not Auriel's, and I found myself reflecting on my attachment to God in its masculine form. Sometimes I wasn't sure how to relate to the Divine Mother, for I had never been taught to do so.

That morning of the spring equinox was glorious. Our group of women met outside in the grove, and Shasta took us through all the many winding paths of the lower and higher gardens, pointing out the numerous symbols of spring. There was a statue of a painted Mother Goose and her little family of chicks hidden among the young grasses, a family of stone bunny rabbits, and pastel Easter eggs tucked beneath fallen logs. Statues of the Goddess in many of her sacred forms graced the grove, and long garlands of flowers swung from the branches, while the whole world seemed to quiver with the radiance of new life.

At about eleven o'clock the women settled onto the benches, the chairs, and the old gliding swing in one of the grove's many nooks and crannies. "Each spring," Shasta began, "we celebrate the vernal equinox. This is the time when the day and night are of equal length, and in the Goddess teachings this is the moment when Persephone returns from the Underworld, and Aphrodite comes back from the waters of the deep. It is also the season when the animals begin to mate, and when the birds begin to sing the songs that stimulate the growth of all living things. This is also the season when the great solar lords, like Adonis, Attis, Mithra, Jesus, and Tammuz, were reborn." *Easter!* I thought. *Of course! The time of resurrection.* As Shasta spoke, I found myself wondering if there was also a myth about the resurrection of the Goddess.

"Spring is the season of the youth or the maiden, the rebirth of Mother Earth, and the Green God of renewal. From this time onward, the sun grows stronger until we reach the summer solstice, the longest day of the year. Six weeks later we celebrate Lughnasadh, the feast day of the Goddess. This High Holy Day was dedicated to Demeter or Isis and is the feast of the fruits and the flowers."

Shasta went on. "Because it is spring, today I want to share with you some of the tales of those who have descended into the Underworld and returned to the light. We know this story through Jesus, but there are other heroes or heroines who took part in it in earlier ages. As I recount these stories, I want you to consider that these tales are both truth and allegory, for many have gone down into the depths of Hell to find their love, to save their world, or to be reborn. In the ancient world, we find this in the story of Orpheus, the famous harpist who was the founder of the Orphic Mysteries that predate the Eleusian Mysteries of ancient Greece. Orpheus goes in search of his beloved wife Eurydice, who perished on their wedding day. Following her into Hades, Orpheus plays his celestial music for the King of Hell, and his songs are so beautiful that Hades, the King of Hell, is moved to tears. He agrees to release Orpheus's wife, but only on one condition: Orpheus cannot gaze upon her until they have reached the mortal plane. He resists this temptation despite her piteous cries, but at the last possible moment Orpheus turns, and when he does, he loses her forever."

Hmm . . . What was the spiritual significance of this story? I wondered. But before I could ask, Shasta continued. "The Orphic Mysteries were one of many Mystery Schools across the ancient world that taught about the many planes of dimensional reality and how sound the underlying principle that governs all worlds is." I nodded. *This was like the teachings of the Vairagi masters,* I thought, *who taught the wisdom of the audible life stream.* "This underlying sound permeates the universe," she said, "and is the Divine Mother existing in the heart of all things. It is a sound with which all beings can commune, and it is linked to the Holy Spirit, the daughter principle of God." *Hmm . . . This was interesting. What did she mean, the daughter principle?*

Shasta went on. "But the stories of heroes who save a person, a city, or a world are not just confined to men. They can also be found in the

Figure 12.1.
Cupid and Psyche
travel through
the heavens together.
(Illustration by
Tricia McCannon)

story of Psyche, the girl who was loved by a god and who ascended into Heaven. Do any of you know this tale?"

Several of the women shook their heads. I remembered something about Psyche and Cupid from Greek myths, but the details were hazy. "Like the tale of Persephone," Shasta said, "Psyche's tale has often been misunderstood. Psyche was a beautiful woman, who some said was more beautiful than Aphrodite herself. She is, of course, the Goddess in her human or mortal form. Unable to find a mate worthy of her, when her village is being ravaged by a fire-breathing dragon, Psyche volunteers to sacrifice herself so that her village might be saved. She is escorted by the town's constables and left in chains to die on a mountainside, but Cupid, or Eros, the son of Aphrodite, accidentally pricks his finger on one of his own arrows and falls madly in love with her. Unwilling to see her perish, Eros frees Psyche from her chains, and whisks her away to his palace in the clouds. Here the god Eros symbolizes the saving grace of unconditional love, and his kingdom is neither in Heaven nor on Earth, but lies somewhere in between. Eros leaves Psyche in his palace to be waited on by invisible servants. He orders that she be lavished with all manner of luxuries, but he only comes to visit her at night to make love. Eros's one request is that Psyche not look upon him directly, for he is afraid that the illumination of his countenance could blind her."

Hmm . . . This was getting interesting now . . . Love, romance, immortal gods, and now sex.

"But eventually Psyche's two sisters discover that she is alive, and jealous of her good fortune, they urge her to find out whether she is sleeping with a god or a monster. Eventually, Psyche succumbs to her sisters' doubts and lights a candle to look upon her lover's face as Eros lies sleeping. There she beholds the most beautiful young man she has ever seen—the God of love himself. But in her haste, she spills three beads of hot wax on the covers, and Cupid awakens. Horrified that she has broken her vow, Eros tells her that they must now be parted forever. Psyche is heartbroken." Shasta looked around the circle at our rapt faces.

Well . . . what happened next?

"Realizing that her own fears and doubts have sabotaged her Sacred Marriage, Psyche prays to the gods and goddesses for grace. Aphrodite, Cupid's mother, decrees that this grace can only be accorded if Psyche undertakes and completes a series of four impossible tasks. Heartbroken, Psyche decides to accept this challenge. She enters into a long series of tests that can only be accomplished by going to the Underworld and facing her shadow. Eventually, through many tribulations, Psyche triumphs, but only with the assistance of Mother Nature. The Holy Spirit recognizes Psyche's divine nature, even though Psyche does not remember it, and Mother Nature sends assistance to help her accomplish her many seemingly impossible tasks. Psyche eventually completes her labors and is granted access to Heaven, becoming an immortal herself."

Wow! So, Psyche represents the purest aspect of us all, the divine part that can be saved through the intervention of the god's true love. But even that is not enough. Ultimately, Psyche must connect with her own spiritual powers and personal will to find her way back to Heaven.

Shasta explained. "Like all human beings, Psyche is a mortal who has forgotten who she is, but because her heart is full of beauty and love, she earns the grace of divine love. Yet it is only through her own efforts and the generosity of Mother Earth that Psyche is able to find her love again, and reclaim her place in Heaven."

Hmm . . . Placed in the context of the Mysteries, which often used myth, parable, and metaphor to convey spiritual truths, this simple story finally made sense. Meg and Sharon were nodding their heads, too. Shasta allowed us a few minutes to share our thoughts; then she proceeded to elaborate.

"While Psyche's tale is an important one, there is an even more enduring legend that I wish to share today about the descent of the Queen of Heaven into the Underworld. This is the tale of Ishtar and Tammuz, and it was one of the earliest stories in the Mystery Schools, for Ishtar and Tammuz are the first telling of the story of Romeo and Juliet." The little that I knew about Ishtar came from my investigations into the Old Testament. I knew she was a goddess of love, war, and fertility, and her husband or love had been Tammuz. I also remembered that Ishtar had been one of the three goddesses who had appeared to me so long ago, so I was curious to hear her tale.

Shasta began. "Ishtar was one of the great Queens of Heaven, the granddaughter of Enlil, King of the gods. Tammuz was a noble shepherd king who had first brought the teachings of animal husbandry to humankind. Both of them were royalty from the long-lived race of Anunnaki gods who seeded this planet thousands of years ago. The Anunnaki, or Anakim as they were known in the Bible, were also called the "Shining Ones" because of their light skin and hair; their skin actually glows with light from within. While some of the gods were more selfish or egocentrically oriented, Tammuz was not. He was a kindly minstrel, a poet, a shepherd, and a noble king who was associated with the Tree of Life. He was also known as Dumuzi, and it is said that he ruled in Mesopotamia for some forty thousand years. Tammuz taught the arts of animal husbandry to humankind and was deeply loved by all who knew him. Because Ishtar and Tammuz were from different

Figure 12.2. Tammuz was a greatly beloved figure throughout the entire Mesopotamian and Mediterranean world. He is often depicted with a sun behind him, a measuring cup for grain on top of his head, and a lion beneath his feet. Here he is shown with the eight-pointed star of the Anunnaki gods. As the dying and resurrected god, Tammuz was the forerunner of Osiris and then Jesus. This image is taken from the Temple of Nabu in the city of Khorsabad, Assyria, where the palace of Sargon II (722–705 BCE) was found in 1843 by archaeologist Paul Emile Botta. (Illustration by Tricia McCannon)

sides of the feuding factions within the ranks of the gods, their love was not only unexpected, but forbidden. But after a long period of courting, they gained permission from their rival families to marry." I could see that Shasta was now warming to this legend.

Shasta went on, "But one day while hunting, Tammuz was gored by a wild boar and died. This meant that Tammuz was forced to descend into the Underworld. Overcome by grief, Ishtar decided to follow

Tammuz into Hades, knowing that such a journey might cost her her life. Telling only her sister where she was going, Ishtar began her perilous descent, but to reach Hades she had to pass through the Seven Gates of Hell, and at each gate she was forced to give away part of her divine power. When she arrived at the first gate, the guardian recognized her immediately and greeted her, saying, 'Hail, Ishtar, Queen of Heaven. What are you doing here? You are not dead, and you have not died. You have no need to go into the Underworld.'

"But Ishtar bowed and addressed the guardian with respect. 'Brave gatekeeper, I come to find my beloved Tammuz. He has died and left the cities of Heaven. Have you seen him? Has he passed this way?'

"The gatekeeper nodded. 'Yes, but I cannot permit you to pass while you still wear your diadem of sacred illumination.' He was talking about her crown, the crown that let her see into the other worlds. Slowly, Ishtar reached up and took off her diadem. 'Gladly will I give up the crown of Heaven for the sake of love,' she murmured.

"'Then you may pass,' the gatekeeper said, bowing as he let her by.

"At the second gate Ishtar was greeted by the next guardian, and this time the gatekeeper ordered her to give up her necklace of speech. This was not the power to speak as mortals do, but the power to command Creation with a word. Once again, Ishtar yielded up her powers for the sake of love.

"At the third gate Ishtar was asked to surrender her bracelets of manifestation, the golden wristbands that allowed her to manifest her heart's desires. Inclining her head in submission, she took off her golden bands and passed through. Then, at the fourth gate, Ishtar was asked to surrender her bejeweled girdle, which amplified the powers of her third chakra."

"It was probably a belt like Wonder Woman's," Claudia giggled, and we all laughed, totally caught up in the story. *Maybe this was where Wonder Woman's magic belt had come from,* I reflected. Maybe our comic book heroes had attributes that were taken from these early myths.

"At the fifth gate Ishtar was made to yield her royal scepter, the means through which she could command the elements. At the sixth gate she relinquished her sandals, the golden shoes that gave her the power to fly. Finally, at the seventh gate, Ishtar was asked to surrender the golden tunic that made her impervious to death. Thus, naked and alone, Ishtar arrived in the Underworld—naked, mortal, and completely vulnerable."

Uh-oh. We all took a breath. *Was this a story about us, about immortal souls who arrive on Earth without any protection or powers, feeling completely naked and alone?*

Shasta went on. "Now one of the things that happens when people come into the Underworld is that they begin to lose their memories, just as souls do when we are born on Earth. So Ishtar knew that she had little time to locate Tammuz or she would forget her purpose. At last she found that he was being held prisoner by Ereshkigal, the Queen of the Underworld. This was Ishtar's jealous half-sister, and there had long been a rivalry between these two queens because one ruled the realm of light, while the other ruled the kingdom of shadows.

"When Ishtar found Tammuz's prison, she implored the guard to release him, but the jailer refused for fear that he would be punished by Ereshkigal. 'Then please let me see him,' Ishtar begged. 'At least you can do that!' The guard agreed, letting her into the dark prison where Tammuz was locked in a lonely cell. Ishtar threw herself across the prison bars, crying, 'Tammuz! Tammuz! I have found you!'

"The young king stood up and came to the bars to meet this lovely lady, but he no longer recognized her. He looked at her through the prison bars and saw that she was beautiful, kind, and loving, and there *was* something familiar about her, but he could not remember who she was. Tammuz felt a strange longing rise within his chest, and tears came to his eyes. 'Forgive me, lady,' he said, placing his hands on hers through the prison bars. 'I feel the stirrings of my heart, but I do not know where we have met. I know that I am feeling love, but I do not know who it is that I am loving.' His kind eyes seemed to melt her heart.

"Was it possible that he had really forgotten who she was? she wondered. How could this happen? Ishtar remembered then that most souls lost their memories when they came to this land. 'I am your wife, your sweetheart, and your soul mate. Don't you remember me, my love?'

"The prince gazed deeply into her eyes. 'I am sorry, lady. I do not. Your face is one that I have seen in dreams, but I cannot remember who you are.' This was too much for Ishtar. Tears spilled down her cheeks until she could barely see.

"'Tammuz, you must remember! You were lost, and now you are found!'

"The prince placed a hand upon his heart. 'Lady, I know that I am lost, but I no longer remember where my home is.'

"Ishtar wept. 'Your home is in Heaven, my love, and you must leave this prison now before it is too late!'

"Tammuz looked regretful. 'I have no power to leave here on my own. Only the Queen of Shadows can release me now.'

"Ishtar could not believe her ears. Tammuz had forgotten his own divine nature and did not know he came from Heaven. He was trapped in the world of amnesia and shadows. Slowly, Ishtar wiped her eyes. 'Then I will do it for you!' she cried. 'I know who you are, and you must awaken from the dream!' She laced her fingers into his and kissed his lips. For a long moment, something stirred inside him, then it was gone. 'Until I return, my love,' she promised. 'Do not forget me! I will return! I promise.'"

The garden and the circle of women had become very quiet, as if even the animals were listening to her story. We were all there in the Underworld prison with Ishtar, and it seemed all too real to me. The love, the longing, the forgetting—I knew them all too well. I had been there in many a relationship, hoping to save the man I loved from the pain of his own making.

Shasta continued. "So Ishtar traveled to the palace of the Queen of Shadows, who sat upon her throne with red flames burning all around her. Couriers dressed in black glided to and fro in the great hall as Ishtar waited for an audience. At last she was summoned before Ereshkigal wearing only a robe that the stewards of the court had given her to hide her nakedness. But now Ishtar had begun to lose her own memories, so all she could remember was that she had come to free her beloved soul mate Tammuz. Ishtar knelt before the dark queen's throne and bowed. 'Your majesty . . .'

"'Rise,' Ereshkigal commanded, seeing that her hated half-sister was before her for the first time in submission. 'Why have you come to the Underworld? Why are you here?'

"Ishtar raised her chin. 'I have come to ask that you release Tammuz from prison. That's all that I can remember . . . That's all I know.'

"Ereshkigal realized then that her half-sister Ishtar had succumbed to the same amnesia that grips even the immortals who enter the world of light and shadows. Ishtar was completely in her power. This was going to be delightful, to finally torture her overconfident sister. 'And what if I do not release him?' Ereshkigal spat out. 'You have no power in this land! What are you going to do about it?'

"Bravely Ishtar lifted her chin and answered. 'Better to remain on Earth where love is, than to return to Heaven where love is not.'

"This was the last thing that Ereshkigal had expected. Was Ishtar saying that she would rather remain in the world of shadows than to reign in Heaven? That Ishtar would give up her power for the sake of love? This was not the way that Ereshkigal remembered her proud sister. Yes, there was love in her land, even though you had to look for it. There were birds and flowers, life and beauty, even though the immortals did not often come here. If Ishtar could see beauty in the simple creatures of the Earth, then perhaps Ereshkigal had misjudged her after all. The queen rose from her chair and began to give her famous speech:

"'Blessed are those who love my sweet Earth, who love the clear running waters, the smell of fresh soil, the grace of the stag, and the majesty of the lion. Blessed are those who can see the divine beauty in all of nature, and who know there is no separation from Heaven.'

*Figure 12.3. Ishtar in the Underworld before the throne
of Queen Ereshkigal. (Illustration by Tricia McCannon,
inspired by a painting by Ernest Charles Wallcousins)*

Ereshkigal lifted her arms and gave Ishtar back her memory. Suddenly
Ishtar realized where she was and who she was kneeling before. She rose
to her feet and opened her arms in welcome.

"'Come, my sweet sister. I embrace you as myself.' The two sisters
came together in understanding, two aspects of the Great Mother who
encompass all things. The light and the dark were returned to balance,

and the lovers were reunited in sacred union, returning to Heaven in celebration and love."

When Shasta finished, no one spoke. I reached up to discover that there were tears on my cheeks. *How had they gotten there? Why had that story affected me so powerfully?* I didn't know. I realized then that many of us had been holding our breath. Maybe I was crying because this was the story of my mother's life, and of my own—the story of all of us in fact. We all come from the heavenly worlds, vulnerable and alone. We are stripped of our memories and our powers and begin the search for love, only to lose it again and again. We find a person we can connect with here or there, but we can't seem to recall who they are or who we are to one another. We feel trapped in the worlds of illusion, and we can't remember how to get out. And when our loved ones are in trouble, we throw ourselves into helping them get out of Hell, even at the risk of becoming completely mired in the darkness ourselves. Finally, if we are lucky, we wake up before it's too late, and sometimes the person whom we love, the person who is trapped, gets to go free as well.

I wiped another set of tears away, unable to get rid of the lump in my throat. This seemed like the story of my own wonderful mother who had gone to Hell to rescue my father from alcoholism. It was also the story of my brave sister who was coping with a bipolar son she had tried to rescue again and again. And the story of my cousin who had spent years taking care of her paraplegic husband who emotionally abused her. And if I was honest, I had seen this pattern played out once or twice in my own life as well with men that I had tried to save. As I glanced around the circle, I could see that the other women were similarly affected. No one wanted to break the spell by speaking.

Shasta rose to her feet. "Today we want to create a healing ceremony for all the wounded warriors of the world, lost in the darkness of their pain or suffering. Many of these, whether male or female, are still locked in the prison of shadows. Let us awaken the sleepers from their cells and pray for their release today." We rose to our feet as one, and without words, we each picked up a gourd rattle. Shasta lifted her drum, finding a rhythm in time with our hearts. And then the song from the musical artist Sophia began.

> *May the warriors find peace within*
> *That the wars of the nations end.*
> *Send the love and light into the Earth,*
> *That the world may find complete rebirth.*
> *Let the sufferings of the nations end,*
> *That the healing of the Earth . . . can begin.*

We danced our way through all the trails of the garden, following the many twists and turns. *This was like our own circuitous path to God,* I thought, *full of the good, the bad, and the tragic.* And as the song sank into each one of our hearts, it seemed as if we were singing for all the suffering of the world. I thought about all the people who are trapped in bondage, either by their own choices or through circumstances beyond their control. I thought of the wounded warriors, who, like my father, had fought in two world wars and paid the price and, because the pain was too great, had then fallen into depression, anger, alcoholism, and despair. And it was not only the centuries of suffering soldiers who had maimed and killed each other in battle, all in the name of righteous glory, it was also the dualistic mind-set of the politicians and generals who believed that confrontation, war, destruction, and aggression were the only way that life could be lived. Whether good men with good intentions or fanatics, these people had been conditioned to believe that the world was a place where fear, domination, and horror had to reign. Those who were "different" from ourselves were something to be defended against or attacked. Nature was an obstacle to be conquered and subdued. Animals, forests, and people were merely commodities to be sacrificed in a "winner takes all" scenario. In the end, everybody lost—the soldiers, the wives and children, the civilians, and the Earth herself that became polluted with bombs and bullets and fires and grenades. This was the price of the patriarchical system we had put in place in our world, a paradigm of struggle, which did not honor the living spirit inside all things.

STEPPING BACK FROM THE PICTURE

Over the next six weeks I continued to think about what I had learned so far. First, I could see how the Great Mother had been splintered into a thousand pieces, and how each aspect of the goddesses I was learning about seemed to reflect a part of the whole. I reflected on the tales of Psyche and Eros, Ishtar and Tammuz, and how both Psyche and Tammuz had forgotten their own divine origins when they were imprisoned in the world of shadows. I realized that this was a metaphor for each one of us who has forgotten our true identities as immortal souls. These tales were about rescuing some part of ourselves that had fallen into forgetfulness in the land of shadows, and I realized that these stories had endured for centuries because they had the power to unlock a treasure chest of wisdom, if only I could penetrate them.

I reflected on the wounded warriors, perhaps because I had known so many in my life. This was the hero archetype who suffers in silence because he has been conditioned to believe that he must be relentlessly stoic. Suppressing his feminine side, he buries his deeper emotions to gain victory in a win-lose dynamic that seeks to destroy the competition at all costs. He is the relentless, unhealed warrior men have come to emulate, but at what cost to the people who love them and to themselves? And what have these warriors sacrificed in their own hearts by adopting these models of self-righteous suffering? Their families? Their health? Their peace of mind? By going too far into the masculine polarity, we sacrifice our ability to live happy, emotionally loving lives. This is the path taken by many within the Jewish, Muslim, and Christian religions, who have used their self-righteous, aggressive stances to target, demonize, and vanquish their enemies.

Then I thought about all the millions of women, children, and families who have been casualties of this dominance model of fear and hardship. Even if a man was not abusive to his wife and children, he bore the emotional scars of his wars inside, not to mention the crippling loss of his body parts. Is human freedom worth fighting for? Of course it is, but to be a pawn in the quest for corporate gain, control, money, or religious ideology—these motives had been used by politicians, popes, and imams for centuries to justify their wars, all in the name of righteous glory and patriotism. I wondered just how quickly these wars would be over if the people who decided them had been put on the front lines instead of their sons and daughters.

After the healing ceremony that afternoon, Shasta had asked each of us to make a list of our own battles and wars, as well as the ways in which our religious programming had contributed to this win-lose dynamic. While I could see this kind of black and white judgment in our governments and religions, on the personal front, I wasn't sure what she was talking about. The women in this group all wanted to help the Earth. Shasta had smiled tolerantly when I raised my hand in protest.

"Just consider the ways in which you are also committed to this win-lose dynamic in your own life," she said, "the ways in which you are negatively competitive with others, because you, too, have been programmed by the patriarchy." *Hmm* . . . Maybe she had a point. I could think of a few examples where my desire to win had made me insensitive to others. Maybe this is what she meant.

"But isn't competition a good thing?" Alex protested. "I mean, sports are fun. We compete in baseball and football and the Olympics. That's not bad, is it?"

Shasta looked serious. "I am not speaking about friendly competition. That is healthy and fun. Friendly competition gives us a yardstick to learn discipline, goal setting, and excellence, but it does not work when we view the competition as the enemy. The real enemy we must conquer lies within ourselves, not in our brother's backyard."

As I turned this over in my mind, I tried to see the world with new eyes. I finally realized that the source of most of our rivalries is this sense of jealous, negative competition. Women fight over men. Men kill over property, money, and women. And the television often seems caught in an endless loop of extolling the virtues of deceit and betrayal as if programming us to think that this is all normal. How many detective shows were there on television, all focused on murder, violence, and this dominance model of heroes and villains? Children were being programmed from an early age to accept violence, aggression, and bullying as commonplace. No wonder the violence levels in schools had increased! We were teaching our children that this was normal.

While I knew that competition could be a healthy outlet for the drive for personal excellence, it also fostered a belief in winners and losers, "more than" or "less than." Behind it lay the fear of being judged for not being good enough, and that is a psychological malady of many cultures. *Will I ever be strong enough? Fast enough? Pretty enough? Skinny enough? Smart enough? Rich enough? Famous enough?* The questions of the ego never ended. I began to see how this relentless perfectionism was also woven into our religious beliefs. *Was I good enough to go to Heaven? Was I worthy of God's love? If I don't follow the teachings of the church, is there something wrong with me, or, by extension, someone else?* These judgments caused heartache and division and stopped us from feeling the joy of really being present in one another's lives.

We live in a world of polarity, I realized, where we can find Heaven or Hell at our doorstep at any given moment. The power of what we choose to believe and practice, and to project out in the world to others, ultimately comes back to us a hundredfold. As we sow, so do we reap. I realized then that we could make of our cultures anything we chose, including creating Heaven on Earth, but we had to realize that the dominator model we have been living under for so long will never lead us out of conflict. The tools that can free us from this dualistic mind-set cannot be crafted out of the same paradigms that imprisoned us in the first place. We must make a different kind of choice if we are ever to become the illuminated human that is our true calling.

13

Jesus and the Lost Gospels

᪥

Let him who seeks not cease from seeking until he finds;
And when he finds, he will be turned around;
and when he is turned around, he will marvel, and he
shall reign over the All.

THE GOSPEL OF THOMAS (2:1–7)*

All of this discussion about polarities within religions made me want to take a deeper look at what had happened in Christianity. I knew that Jesus's essential message was one of unity, love, forgiveness, and non-judgment, so how had things become so messed up in our thinking? In the name of the Prince of Peace, the church had killed millions during the centuries of the Inquisition. However, to truly understand how his teachings had been twisted and lost, I realized that I would have to start with a study of the New Testament.

Like many people, I had always been drawn to the beauty and

---

*All verse references to *The Gospel of Thomas* refer to Hugh McGregor Ross's *The Gospel of Thomas* (London: Watkins Publishing, 2002).

mystery of Christ's teachings, but I wondered why so little of Jesus's wisdom had been written down. I pondered at the nearly three decades of his absence in the Bible before his ministry began, and why no one else seemed to question where Jesus had been during all those decades before he started his ministry in Jerusalem. I speculated that the real reason so many things about Jesus's life were concealed was because the early church fathers hadn't wanted us to know that he had been initiated in other spiritual traditions. *So what,* I thought, *if there have been other spiritual masters of wisdom in the world?* It is clear to anyone who studies the great world religions that the sages appear periodically throughout history. The concept of a great world savior, who arrives to bring illumination, is nothing new. Even the story of how that being is resurrected was intrinsic to the Mystery traditions of the ancients. Like Osiris, the Egyptian lord of light who was killed by his jealous half-brother Set, then resurrected by the power of Isis's love, the themes of Jesus's life resonate through time. These archetypal elements of selfless service, death, and resurrection can also be found in the stories of Mithra, Quetzalcoatl, Krishna, and Dionysius. Manly P. Hall, a thirty-third-degree Mason and author of *The Secret Teachings of All Ages,* writes:

> The list of the deathless mortals who suffered for man that he might receive the boon of eternal life is an imposing one. Among those connected historically or allegorically with a crucifixion are Prometheus, Adonis, Apollo, Atys, Bacchus, Buddha, Christna, Horus, Indra, Ixion, Mithras, Osiris, Pythagoras, Quetzalcoatl, Semiramis, and Jupiter. According to the fragmentary accounts extant, all these heroes gave their lives to the service of humanity, and with one or two exceptions, died as martyrs for the cause of human progress . . . it is possible that most of them were crucified upon a cross or tree.[1]

So why would honoring the lives of other spiritual masters be so terrible? I wondered. If anything, their stories underscored the importance of Jesus's life, making his messages even more eternal. To me it was deeply reassuring to know that some aspect of the Divine returns to the world again and again to teach human beings how to connect with the spiritual light within. In the ancient world this light bearer was called the Aion, the messenger who arrives at the beginning of each World Age, or aeon, to deliver the spiritual message that will get us through that 2,160-year cycle.* But apparently the church fathers disagreed, so they sought to conceal both the true history of Jesus's life and the depth of his teachings.

DEEPER QUESTIONS AND
THE INNER TEACHINGS

In time, these questions prompted me to write a book about the lost years of Jesus and his connection to the spiritual Mysteries of the past. These great Mystery Schools of initiation had once been established in many countries and regions, including Egypt, Greece, England, India, Persia, and even Galilee under the Essenes. But in my early years of self-discovery, I did not realize their incredible importance. Nor did I know that these schools had been in existence for some four thousand years before Jesus was born, and some four hundred years after the crucifixion. Nor did I comprehend how the suppression of these wisdom teachings by the church was directly responsible for the great imbalance we see in the world today. These Mystery Schools had once taught a balanced approach of yin and yang between men and women, creating role models for people to aspire to their own inherent divinity without ego or shame.

Yet so effective was the church's annihilation of this early wisdom literature that today most people are not even aware that such schools existed. While it is clear that the orthodox church borrowed

---

*There are a total of twelve astrological ages in a complete circuit of the Precession of the Equinoxes, each age lasting approximately 2,160 years, for a total of 25,920 years. The ancients referred to this as one Great Year.

many customs from these religions, including the practice of baptism, the Eucharist rites, and the use of parables in teaching, and initially adopted the same three-tiered structure of initiation, today most of us know almost nothing about them.[2] However, because Jesus was an initiate of these paths, the word *mysteria,* or *mystery,* is used some twenty-eight times in the New Testament in connection with his teachings.

But when I first began to study with Shasta, I knew none of this. At that time I could not explain why the dualistic paths of Islam, Judaism, and Christianity had fostered philosophies of violence, judgment, and separation in the world. But in my short time with Shasta I had realized that much of what I knew about traditional history might be wrong. If I was ever to get to the bottom of this conundrum, I would have to discover the hidden history of what had come before. While I suspected that Jesus's real teachings held powerful keys to these Mysteries, the underlying question was this: "Where were these teachings today, and how could I study them?" What had Jesus actually taught that was no longer in the Bible? And why had only Matthew, Mark, Luke, and John written gospels? Years later I was to learn that many of the other disciples had also recorded his words, but that the early church had ordered the destruction of these documents.

Today most Christians do not realize that less than 10 percent of Jesus's life is covered in the Bible, or that there were more than five hundred gospels sifted through by the Roman orthodoxy in order to select the twenty-seven books of the New Testament.[3] Nor do we realize that thirteen of the twenty-seven books were written by Paul, a man who did not even know Jesus, but whose thoughts profoundly shaped Roman Catholicism. Nor do we realize that the process of selection of the "orthodox gospels" was hotly debated for over three centuries by scores of individuals with their own personal or political agendas,[4] or that even after these official gospels were selected a team of *correctores* was hired to edit these teachings for the political purposes of the church.[5]

It is also important to remember that the Old and the New

Testaments were written by men. Certainly some of this writing is divinely inspired. But these were flawed human beings—Jewish, Greek, Roman, and Catholic men—who were doing the best they could to understand the events that had shaped their inherited histories. And as we have seen with the Old Testament accounts, the Bible is a hodge-podge collection of writings amassed over time. The New Testament is composed of writings from over sixty individuals across four centuries, and many of these books were transcribed multiple times from earlier accounts.* As anyone who has ever played the game of Whisper knows, time and repetition can change our perception of a phrase with only a word or two. Thus the official *correctores* who removed entire tracts of text to fit the dictates of the newly forming church have shared only a portion of the true teachings of Iesous or Yeshua ben Joseph, who is better known to the world by the Greek name *Jesus*.†

A TREASURE TROVE

Catholic priest Jean-Yves Leloup, translator of the Gospel of Philip, the Gospel of Thomas, and the Gospel of Mary Magdalene, writes that the traditional gospels "were put to effective use in building Church institutions that staked a claim, so to speak, on the entire territory of Christianity, fencing in a land which was originally open and free."[6] Leloup is the pen name of Père Jean Seraphim, a priest affiliated with the French orthodox monastery of St. Michel du Var in Provence, France. A brilliant scholar, theologian, and speaker, Leloup is also a devout Christian.

These discarded ancient writings are now called *apocryphal,* a word

---

*There are thirty-nine separate books in the Old Testament and twenty-seven books in the New Testament, which totals sixty-six separate chapters or books.

†*Jesus* is a Greek rendering of Yeshua or Iesous in Aramaic, the language spoken in Jerusalem at the time. Consequently, we find that Iesous called himself Isa (Issa) in many of the countries where he traveled. *Issa* means "firstborn" in India, and it was by this name that he went in Egypt, India, Persia, and the Celtic lands. Thus there are many reports of him in India as Lord Issa. Some denominations of the Egyptian church are still called the Church of Lord Essa.

derived from the Greek, meaning "hidden" or "secret." *Apo* means "under," referring to that which lies "beneath" the scriptures.[7] So these are the secret teachings that underlie Christianity, but were concealed by the orthodoxy. Over the past two decades, some of these apocryphal writings have begun to make their way into the public sphere, creating a stir among those who long to know more about Jesus's life. While some might wish to dismiss these gospels out of hand, it would not be wise to do so. Not only are most of them dated earlier than the four gospels found in the New Testament, but they were preserved by the first Gnostic communities of Christians, indicating that they are closer to the original teachings of Yeshua than the gospels in the New Testament. They have not had centuries of mistranslation overlaid on to them, nor have they been subject to manipulation in ecumenical councils. Today these texts are helping scholars to reframe early Christian history, for they contain many powerful keys to understanding the deeper mission of Jesus. Leloup reminds us:

> There are those who are disturbed by the indeterminacy in the origins of Christianity. Yet the coming to light of these ancient apocryphal writings should, on the contrary, remind us of the richness and freedom of those origins. If becoming a truly adult human being means taking responsibility for the unconsciousness that presides over most of our conscious actions, then perhaps now is the time for Christianity to become truly adult. It now has the opportunity to welcome these gospels, thereby welcoming into consciousness that which has been repressed by our culture. Our culture now has a chance to integrate, alongside its historical, rational, and more or less "masculine" values, those other dimensions that are more mystical, imaginary, imaginal . . . in a word, feminine.[8]

It is now known that in the first few centuries after Christ there were many groups who interpreted Jesus's words in their own way, just as there are some thirty thousand Christian sects who each have their own distinctive understanding of Christ's words today. Catholic theologian Leonard Brown writes that scholars suddenly became aware in the nineteenth century that the church had not existed as a unified body in the first few centuries after Jesus's death, but was actually composed of several distinct groups, each associated with different foundational figures such as Peter, Paul, Mark, and Mary Magdalene. Many of these groups had vastly different interpretations of Jesus's teachings.[9]

Yet in 367 CE, the powerful Archbishop Athanasius of Alexandria sent an order to purge all "apocryphal books," claiming these to be the works of "heretics" and becoming the victor in a political war of silence and repression that resulted in the death of millions. For centuries the only thing that biblical scholars knew about such "heretical" scriptures was written by the very men who had suppressed them. Elaine Pagels, a professor of religious studies at Princeton, writes, "those who wrote and circulated these texts did not regard themselves as heretics. . . . We can see throughout the history of Christianity how varying beliefs about the nature of God inevitably bear different political implications. Martin Luther, more than 1300 years later, felt impelled by his own religious experience and transformed the understanding of God to challenge the practices endorsed by his superiors . . . and finally to reject its entire papal and priestly system."[10] Pagels goes on to tell us: "Someone, possibly a monk from the nearby monastery at St. Pachomius, near where the Nag Hammadi texts were found, probably took the banned books and hid them from destruction in the jar where they remained buried for almost 1600 years."[11]

So let us now take a look at the famous lost gospels, which open the door to a deeper understanding of Jesus's teachings about the nature of God's connection to humanity.

THE NAG HAMMADI TEXTS

The Nag Hammadi Library, as it has come to be called, was accidentally discovered by an Arab peasant in the mountains surrounding the Egyptian village of Nag Hammadi in Upper Egypt, northwest of modern-day Luxor. The books and other texts in this library were discovered in 1945, just two years before the Dead Sea Scrolls were unearthed in 1947. Hidden in a large earthenware jar, these thirteen leather-bound books, and fifty-five different texts, include many gospels never before seen by biblical scholars, yet referenced in the early literature of the church. In 180 CE, Bishop Irenaeus denounced some of them by name, calling them "blasphemous and heretical."

Scholars tell us that these codices were all buried together, hidden within a large sealed jar at the time of the Theodosian decrees, around 390 CE, decrees that ordered the destruction of all reference materials not chosen by the orthodox Roman church. Some believe these texts may be the oldest example ever discovered of leather-bound books,[12] and they have all been dated somewhere between 60 and 400 CE, meaning that many of these books were created in the years just after the crucifixion.* Today these texts are called codices because they have individual parchment sheets inside and appear to be accounts from the disciples who actually studied with Jesus. They include the Gospel of Philip, the Gospel of Thomas, the Dialogue of the Savior, the Secret Book of John, the Secret Book of James, the Gospel of Truth, the Gospel to the Egyptians, the Apocalypse of Paul, the Apocalypse of Peter, and the Gospel of Mary Magdalene, just to name just a few.[13] While some of these texts confirm our existing gospels, others reveal philosophies distinctly at odds with orthodox Christianity, a doctrine we have been conditioned to believe for nearly two thousand years.[14]

These newly discovered landmark writings focus on Jesus's teachings on several pivotal subjects: karma; reincarnation; the existence of the Divine Mother; the multidimensional nature of the universe; and the existence of gods, aeons, and the demiurgos (or the false god that rules this world), as well as the descent of the soul into the worlds of matter. Jesus also tells us that we have the power to connect with God

---

*Scholars tell us that they date from the "intertestamental period," scholastically figured between 250 BCE (before Jesus was even born) and 100 CE.

directly reminding us that the Divine lies within us and can be accessed directly. Yet the orthodox church kept this information hidden, ordering the destruction of all noncanonical texts under penalty of death.

THE DEAD SEA SCROLLS

The Dead Sea Scrolls were discovered in eleven caves near the Essene community of Qumran between 1947 and 1956. They consist of some 800 to 850 texts, many written only on tiny scraps of parchment. Carbon-dating has placed these scrolls between 120 BCE and 50 CE,[15] which means that some of these writings predate the birth of Jesus by over a hundred years. Since we know that the first Christian community in the world was established in Britain in 37 CE by Joseph of Arimathea, these writings would be extremely close to the actual events. They are written in Hebrew and Aramaic, both languages that Jesus and his followers spoke.

Before their discovery, the earliest known gospels that we possessed had already been translated into Greek from Aramaic. Greek was the mother tongue of first-century Rome, and thus even these early orthodox gospels have been subject to mistranslation. Professor Helmut Koester of Harvard University tells us that the Gospel of Thomas may include teachings "as early as the second half of the first century, [meaning that this gospel is] earlier than either Mark, Matthew, Luke [or] John."[16] Since the Dead Sea Scrolls predate any later copies of the New Testament by at least a hundred years, it would be a good guess to assume they are more accurate than later translations.

For many years after their discovery, the world was not privy to their contents. No photographic copies of the Dead Sea Scrolls were even available to the public for more than forty years. Only a small fraternity of Catholic men, known as the *École Biblique,* or Bible School, were even allowed to see them. The *École Biblique* had close ties with the Pontifical Biblical Commission, founded by the Vatican at the turn of the twentieth century. This commission was officially instructed "to protect God's words from every rash opinion" and to "safeguard the authority of the

scriptures and promote their right interpretation."[17] Since these texts con-
flicted with the orthodox version of Christianity, this commission did its
job of "protecting the faith" by keeping the rest of the world in the dark.

THEY COME TO LIGHT

Over time it became obvious that the orthodox researchers involved
in the translations did not want the content of these gospels revealed.
Finally, in 1977, after nearly thirty years of silence, a partial edition
of the Nag Hammadi texts was published in English; however, at that
point, the fervor over their original discovery had died down to a
whimper. By then, few people even remembered that the scrolls existed.
However, in 1979 with the release of Elaine Pagels's best-selling book
The Gnostic Gospels, the scrolls began to gain a following. Yet even
then, only certain texts were released.

It was not until 1980, when a philanthropist named Elizabeth Bechel
managed to have the original texts photographed, that things began to
change. Ms. Bechel had kept a copy of the microfilm of the documents
for herself and donated that microfilm to the Huntington Library in
California shortly before her death in 1987. In 1991 the library graciously
decided to allow all "qualified scholars" access to them. So in 1992, a full
forty-five years after their discovery, the complete translations of the Dead
Sea Scrolls finally became available to the public. Instrumental in their
dissemination were writers Michael Wise and Robert Eisenman, who
released their groundbreaking book *The Dead Sea Scrolls Uncovered* in
1992. They list over fifty key documents withheld from the public, while
HarperCollins's *The Other Bible* reveals at least a hundred ancient scriptures, written over the centuries by a plethora of people.

THE HIDDEN TEACHINGS

So what had frightened the church so much about these documents
that they kept them hidden for so long? Well, not only do they con-

tain many books that challenge Catholic theology, but they present Jesus's wisdom in a very different way. Unlike the orthodox interpretation, which insists that there is a great chasm between humanity and God, these gospels proclaim that there is no such separation, only a rift brought on by our own ignorance. Jesus says that knowledge of the self and knowledge of the Divine are identical. "He Who understands all, but lacks Self Knowledge lacks everything."[18] This path of inner connection with God was called *gnosis,* and it was the very cornerstone of the great spiritual Mystery Schools. So important was this principle that the command to "Know Thyself" was inscribed over the entrance to the temple of Delphi in Greece. Let's take a look at some of the many ways that Jesus shared this teaching.

> Rather the Kingdom is inside of you, and it is outside of you. When you come to know yourselves, then you will be known, and you will realize that you are the sons of the living Father. But if you do not know yourselves then you are in poverty, and you are that poverty.[19]

> Be vigilant, and allow no one to mislead you by saying: "Here it is!" or "There it is!" For it is within you that the Son of Man dwells.[20]

Jesus goes on to ridicule those who believe that the Kingdom of God can be found in an external place. "If those who lead you say to you, 'Look the Kingdom is in the sky,' then the birds will arrive there before you. If they say to you, 'It is in the sea,' then the fish will arrive before you."[21] Thus Jesus taught that the Kingdom of Heaven is a state of self-discovery, and access to this kingdom lies within the self.

SIN, TRUTH, AND ILLUSION

This brings us to *gnosis,* a Greek word for "inner knowing." Gnosis is not intellectual knowledge, but a knowing that comes from direct experience; thus it produces a wisdom of the heart. In Christian terms, it is a direct connection with the Holy Spirit, the Holy Mother who brought the fire of transformation to the apostles. The early followers of Jesus believed that this spiritual connection is the direct path to salvation, so they called themselves *Gnostics*. Gnostic Christianity seeks to discover this true self through the mystical experience of inner union, uniting the risen savior with the bride of the Holy Spirit. This is what awakens the light of the Christ consciousness within.[22] These mystics understood that if we choose to go beyond our identification with the ego and the material world, we will eventually discover the divine being who lives within us. But in order to achieve this inner gnosis, we must activate, honor, and unite the masculine and feminine parts of ourselves. This is the chief element that distinguishes the Gnostics from the Roman Catholic Church.

The Nag Hammadi texts also teach that there is no original sin, a philosophy invented by St. Augustine in the fifth century. These apocryphal writings also say that Jesus did not come into the world to save us, as we have been taught today. Sin, Jesus explains, is simply ignorance, and this is what causes our suffering and our bad choices. For example, if we knew that we would get burned by putting our hand in the fire, we wouldn't do it. In the same way, if we understand that by living a moral, loving life we will reap the benefits of what we have sown, not only here, but in the lifetimes to come, then we will not choose to lie, cheat, murder, or betray, knowing that these actions are ultimately going to return to haunt us. The original word for *sin* was *hamartia,* derived from the sport of archery. It literally meant to "miss the mark," a situation that any of us can correct once we realize what has happened.[23] The word *evil* also had none of the horrible connotations it has acquired today. It is derived from the Greek word *kakia,* meaning "an illness," or "that which is bad" for us. In other words, *sin* and *evil* are misalignments in our nature and actions that create our own suffering, misfortune, and illness, all things we want to avoid because when we act outside of our own spiritual integrity, we move out of alignment with our divine self. Eventually, this causes us to become sick or to fall prey to anger, hatred, harm, or bitterness.[24] In the Gospel of Mary, Peter challenges Jesus by saying: "Since you have become the interpreter of the elements and the events of the world, tell us: What is the sin of the world?" Jesus answers Peter by saying:

> There is no sin. It is you who make sin exist, when you act according to the habits of your corrupted nature; there is where sin lies. This is why the Good has come into your midst. It acts together with the elements of your nature so as to reunite it with its roots . . . This is why you become sick and why you die; it is the result of your actions; what you do takes you further away [from God].[25]

SELF-ENLIGHTENMENT

This ability to connect with God directly is something we all have. Once we make that connection with Spirit, we can tune in for ourselves. We do not need religious intermediaries to talk to God for us. The implications of this teaching are enormous. From the point of view of any organized religion, this means that the priest or imam or rabbi is not a mouthpiece or intermediary for God, even if these clergy are kind, well-meaning individuals whose insights might be helpful. Each of us has the power to speak with God directly and to get answers for ourselves. This is part of the core message of the Gospel of Thomas and the Gospel of Mary. In addition, while religious leaders might remind us of a path of wisdom, their influence on us should always be optional, not mandatory. We do not have to submit to punishment according to their pronouncements.

This awareness also means that the church cannot excommunicate people from God's grace. While we may indeed suffer the karmic consequences of living an immoral life, it is we who will ultimately pay the price in being waylaid from our happiness. We do not have to be damned by a religious institution. Finally, this means that we are not obligated to pay tithes unless we choose to. We may want to support a spiritual community or temple, of course, or seek the counsel of a rabbi or minister in times of distress, but this is a choice, not an obligation forced on us by threats. Rather, this decision comes through the transformation of the heart as we decide to join together with other people who also wish to effect a true change in spiritual consciousness and make a difference in the world.

This one aspect of Jesus's teachings had the potential to dissolve centuries of religious control by empowering each individual to create his or her own direct relationship with God, instead of bowing to the fear, blame, and guilt preached by religious authorities. This does not mean that we cannot seek spiritual guidance from teachers, priests, therapists, counselors, or healers. People who are consciously aligned with the light are always a treasure in a troubled world, and I am sure that there have been many spiritual leaders who have genuinely helped their flocks to live more peaceful and satisfying lives. What Jesus taught was that we each have the ability to connect to the Divine ourselves, simply by going within. This is profoundly empowering, for it reminds us that the divine spark lives within us all. This one teaching alone was enough to get Jesus killed in a patriarchical society that demanded unquestioning obedience to religious authorities.

Furthermore Jesus's wisdom clearly puts the responsibility for our actions back on us. "Impose no law other than that which I have witnessed. Do not add more laws to those given in the Torah, lest you become bound by them."[26] This means that all the religious rules and regulations promulgated since then are not in accord with Jesus's teachings.

Jesus also discards the attitudes of shame and fear that separate us from God. When he is asked, "On which day will you be manifest to us? On which day shall we behold you?" he answers, "When you strip yourselves of your shame, and take your garments and put them under your feet even as little children, and you trample them; then shall you behold the Son of Him who is living and you shall not fear."[27] Thus the negative devices of blame, judgment, and fear used for centuries by the church are the exact opposite of his teachings.

Jesus made it simple. "Love your neighbor as yourself." "Do unto others as you would have them do unto you." "The Kingdom of Heaven is within." This path, he told us, leads directly to God, and this gnosis is the feminine current at work. When our decisions are made from the heart, our relationships are dictated by kindness. "Be in harmony," he admonished. "If you are out of balance, take inspiration from manifestations of your true nature [the soul]."[28]

However, spiritually enlightened beings are a threat to religions looking for financial stability, so self-empowerment was a problem for the religions of Jesus's day, and for ours as well.* Once the devices of shame and condemnation are removed, the church has lost both the "weapon" and the "cure" that makes religion indispensable. Yeshua's teachings were meant to liberate humankind, based on creating a genuine, active relationship with God in our own hearts. Through his teachings the world could begin a new era of enlightenment. The powers that be might have to evolve from coercion and fear to trusting people to act with loving-kindness. No wonder the priesthood saw Jesus as a threat!

THE GNOSTICS

Today many scholars believe that the Gnostics were the first real students of the teachings of Jesus, for they taught that connection with God is possible through personal effort. But because Gnostic Christianity requires more personal effort, it did not translate well with the masses.

---

*The Code of Hammurabi, circa 1780 BCE, set up a social system that included the mandatory tithing of taxes to the religious temple systems of the day. Whether in money, food, or products, somewhere between 10 percent and 25 percent of all earnings went to the temples. While this might seem excessive, in Babylon and other large city-states, these temples became repositories for food, supplies, money, and generally needed resources for the community. People could borrow from the temple and pay the religious leaders back at no interest. Thus the priests (if they were honorable) became important stewards of the people's welfare. But if the priests were corrupt, they could also become fat, greedy, wealthy, and self-indulgent. This is the template upon which the Catholic Church was formed, so generating funds became extremely important, as this was the only social/religious template that early church leaders knew.

Many scholars, like Elaine Pagels, believe that this was the main reason the orthodox church was easier for people to accept. Simply by professing to believe in Jesus you reserved your spot in Heaven, even if your consciousness had not changed at all.

The original Gnostic groups took their name from the Greek *gnostikoi* or *gnosis*. In Greek, there are two words for knowledge: *epistemi*, which means mental knowledge in the sense of information gathered, and *gnosis*, which is an understanding of the whole being. True gnosis is discovered through the eye of the heart and comes through direct experience or intuitive knowing. It does not need an intermediary. Jesus sought to transmit this *gnosis of the heart* by reminding us of the light that burns within us all. As a result, the Gnostics were focused on transforming their mundane consciousness into spiritual wakefulness.[29] Gnostic teacher Tau Malachi writes:

> Gnostic Christianity represents an inner tradition of secret knowledge orally imparted from apostle to disciple through discourse and initiation. At the heart of this inner tradition is a spiritual art of conscious living and conscious dying, and the development of consciousness beyond the body, through which the initiate is able to consciously enter into higher planes of existence, both in this life and the afterlife. The result is a conscious continuity of self-awareness through all states of existence, including what we call "death," so that, in effect, there is no more death and no more need for physical incarnation. When we speak of enlightenment and liberation, self-realization or Christ-consciousness, this is ultimately what is meant.[30]

According to the Gnostics, whoever has a direct encounter with Jesus personally has the same spiritual authority as the original apostles. Many of the early Gnostic writings include such encounters after the crucifixion, and I myself have experienced just such visitations from Jesus, before and after he asked me to write a book on his lost years and secret teachings. Each time it has been life-changing. So it is entirely possible to have these kinds of genuine spiritual contacts, even after a master has left the earthly plane. Gnostic writings that share these kinds of encounters include the Gospel of Mary, the Apocryphon of John, the Sophia of Jesus the Christ, the Pistis Sophia, the Letter of Peter to Philip, and the Wisdom of Jesus Christ.[31]

Tau Malachi writes:

> At the outset, you must understand that the very nature of God is different than anything you might conceive and that you yourself are not who or what you might think you are. Whatever your preconceptions, preconditions, or expectations, the reality-truth continuum is yet more and cannot be contained or comprehended by the linear reasoning mind or dualistic consciousness. God will forever be a mystery, the nameless and unknown . . . To draw near to the Lord is a deeply troubling thing, for I must become no-thing, empty of myself, that the Lord might enter and the Holy Spirit fill me. God is No-thing (Ain), and I must become no-thing to enter into union with the Holy One of Being.[32]

Gnostics believed that the soul is the true person and that the body is merely a container for experiencing the physical plane. Once the body is shed, the soul returns to the nonphysical realms, where angelic beings decide whether the soul is worthy of passing to a higher level or whether it must be born again. In Gnostic teachings this process was known as the resurrection of the soul, and the soul's permanent release into these higher realms of light was like to an inmate being released from the dark, cold prison of unconsciousness that most of us live in. Joe Lewels, PhD, author of *Rulers of the Earth: Secrets of the Sons of God*, tells us that "such teachings would have been a major break from the orthodox churches, both Christian and Jewish, and would have been a cause of great concern for both religious and political authorities. They would also have exposed those who taught them to great danger."[33]

Gnostics believed that the origin of everything rests firmly in a Supreme First Principle—a secret, hidden female Divinity—nameless, unknown, and unknowable and "only silence can express this original Nothingness." Across that endless Cosmic Ocean arose a ripple that revealed the Divine Self. This Divine Self brought into existence a complex and highly paradoxical state of descending hierarchies, each with its own level of spiritual awareness. The highest state of being is manifested in the divine attributes of love, power, thought, compassion, mercy, truth, grace, silence, humanity, and the Goddess Sophia. The Gnostics taught that from these eight divine qualities sprang another fifteen pairs with a total of thirty-eight emanations in all.[34] At first these attributes of God were not self-aware, but gradually they became conscious of their own existence and became the multitude of celestial forms and powers that we refer to as angels today. Some of the most powerful among them became aions, the large overseeing divinities that govern the various dimensions and World Ages. Many of these aions are good and are consciously aligned with the light. But since God gave each of these newly self-aware beings free will, each being has the power to govern its own destiny. Gnostics believed that, in a supreme act of love, the Creator gave us all the gift of free will, and thus our own material universe came into being.

Gnostic Christianity honored both the male and female aspects of the Creator originally taught by Jesus. Thus it is a path of direct mystical realization brought about through the experience of the Sacred Marriage, spoken of by Jesus as the union of the bride and the bridegroom, symbols for the illuminated male and female aspects of the Christ that lies within. This inner union brings us into the fullness of Christ consciousness and was at the very heart of the master's teachings of the Middle Way. The aim of this inner marriage is to awaken and balance the two hemispheres of the brain, the male and female aspects of us all. This sacred union then allows us to embody the unified Christ within while still living in the physical world. While it is this union that opens the spiritual Eye, the marriage of these two parts must happen in the heart. This union is the key to bringing conscious awareness into the world at large, and, in essence, bringing heaven down to Earth as we enlighten the worlds of matter.

Gnostics believe that Mary Magdalene, whom they called Lady Mary, was the foremost apostle, the partner and wife of Yeshua, and his female spiritual reflection. It was she, not Peter, who was the heir to the true apostolic succession. Thus the Gnostic tradition has over 250 wisdom sayings attributed to Mary Magdalene that were collected during the many years of Mary's teaching in France and Britain that followed the crucifixion.[35] Many of these sayings are every bit as profound as those attributed to Yeshua.

For example, Mary taught, "Do not concern yourself with the darkness in the world, but banish the darkness that is in you. Because it will bind you and destroy you if you do not cast it out of you."[36] Mary said, "Once you come to the light and know the light is in you, you cannot continue to walk in the way of darkness, lest you will fall into a greater darkness. No! You must be walking in the Light and enter the Light and bring forth the Light from within you, for only then will you be established in the Way of Life."[37]

Mary also taught: "When the Risen Savior appears, look into his heart, and there you will see a threefold flame of Sophia. It is faith, hope and love, but inwardly it is knowledge, understanding and wisdom. Ask the Lord to give you this holy flame, so that you might enter the kingdom and be perfect as the Father and Son are perfect."[38]

And Mary taught, "All things exist in and with one another, and while they exist they depend on one another, but when the time of dissolution comes, all things will return to their own roots and essence. What has come from above returns to the abode from which it has come, and what comes from below returns to its origin. What is in between has never existed, and will return to the great void."[39] Finally Mary taught, "The Divine Mother is Light and she is darkness, she is the saint and she is the sinner, angels and demons are images in her, as are the gods and all of the archons; yet she is beyond all of these. Know her in all things and you will be free of bondage, even as the Anointed is free."[40]

THE WAY OF THEIR TEACHING

The Gnostic path of establishing a direct connection with the Divine meant that when students met in fellowship, they would draw lots to see who took on the various roles. At any time one might act as a priest or a priestess, reading scripture, giving instructions, or offering bread and wine to the assembly. This rotation of roles ensured that no one got attached to power and allowed Spirit to work through each person by pushing the ego out of the way. As you might imagine, this fluid structure is very different from the fixed roles that we know today through our priests, bishops, cardinals, and popes. But since the Gnostics were interested in activating the God-Self within, attachment to power wasn't important to them.

In the first century after Jesus, when Mary Magdalene and her teachings were still well known among many Christians, women were allowed to perform priestly functions in all Gnostic circles. This included offering the blessing, giving sacraments, teaching, and even sharing prophecy, all activities that had once been the purview of both priests and priestesses in the ancient world. This inclusion of women as liturgical priests so disturbed the male elders that Tertullian, the early church father, wrote in horror: "These heretical women—how audacious they are! They have no modesty; they are bold enough to teach, to engage in argument, to enact exorcisms, to undertake cures, and it may be, even to baptize."[41] Later Tertullian would echo the sentiments of Paul, who wrote, "It is not permitted for a woman to speak in the church, nor is it permitted for her to teach, nor to baptize, nor to offer (the Eucharist), nor to claim for herself a share in any *masculine* function—not to mention any priestly office"[42] (emphasis mine).

The Catholic Church so strongly opposed the Gnostics that "Everyone of the secret texts which Gnostic groups revered was omitted from the canonical collection and branded as heretical by those who called themselves orthodox Christians."[43] Since we now understand that these teachings included the wisdom sayings of both Mary and Yeshua, it now makes sense why they were suppressed by the Jews and Romans, who claimed sole authority for the men. "By the time the process of sorting the various writings ended . . . virtually all the feminine imagery for God had disappeared from orthodox Christian tradition."[44] As late as 1977, Pope Paul VI forbade the ordination of women, saying that the church "does not consider herself authorized to admit women to priestly ordination." He went on to say that all priests must have a "natural resemblance" to Christ, meaning that the priests must have male genitalia. There was no mention that a priestess might resemble Mary, who symbolized the Mother Church herself.[45]

As we can see, however, one of the greatest legacies of the Gnostics was the hidden wisdom teachings of Mary Magdalene, long equated with Sophia, the divine Mother of Wisdom. We will explore this story later when we consider the many important writings suppressed in the early centuries of the church.

THE GNOSTICS' STRUCTURE OF INITIATION

Like other spiritual traditions, the Gnostics had an outer level of teaching and a deeper inner level. The first stage tested the moral habits, attitudes, and commitment of the novices, but there was often a long waiting period for the inner levels of initiation—sometimes as long as five years—so many aspirants were not willing to wait. Early Gnostic teachers used a whole series of techniques to help their novices become self-aware, including processes that can now be compared to modern-day psychotherapy. Rather than just having people "saved" through baptism, they wanted initiates to become enlightened. Several sources discovered at Nag Hammadi describe a technique called Zostrianos, which sets out a program of ascetic practices that taught the student how to still the chaos of the mind and receive visions of the light.[46] Instruction was passed orally from teacher to student, and there were "detailed expositions of the initiate's experience including . . . prayers, chants, [and] instruction, punctuated by his retreat into meditation; [this] suggests . . . techniques of initiation for attaining that self-knowledge which is knowledge of divine power within."[47] Modern-day Gnostic Tau Malachi explains:

> Authentic mysticism, and the Gnostic style of teaching, is founded upon a play of illumination and bewilderment, and bewilderment is considered crucial to any actual development or progress in self-realization. Bewilderment invokes new questions—questions one would not have thought to ask before. One's questions turn into a sacred quest for greater knowledge, understanding and wisdom—a deeper penetration of the mystery. This leads to a breakthrough into a higher degree of enlightenment, experience, or gnosis.[48]

GODS, GODDESSES, AND THE DIVINE

Today scholars contend that, like the Hebrews and Persians, the Gnostics believed that our world is ruled by negative forces called archons. Above these intermediate gods was the biggest false god of all, which they called the demiurgos. It is this being's job to keep humans trapped in the worlds of illusion. He was also called the two-faced god, for he can seduce us with worldly riches or power, or use fear, anger, and hatred to get his way. Knowing that it is easy to get trapped in fear-based beliefs, the Gospel of Truth actually tells the seeker that being caught in the illusions of the world is a sort of nightmare, but that we can break free through self-illumination. The Gospel of Philip records that whoever achieves this inner gnosis becomes "no longer a Christian, but a Christ."[49]

In the Dialogue of the Savior, Jesus teaches, "Bring in your guide and your teacher. The mind is the guide, but reason is the teacher . . . Enlighten your mind . . . Light the lamp within you." Jesus also says that he comes as a guide for spiritual understanding, "but when the disciple attains enlightenment . . . the two [the master and the student] have become equal, even identical."[50] The Gospel of Thomas relates that "He who will drink from my mouth will become as I am: I myself shall become him, and the things that are hidden will be revealed to him."[51] All of this is hopeful, for it points the way to understanding how we, as souls, can live in the world, but not be owned by it.

Like the spiritual Mystery Schools of the past, Gnostics taught that the universe has many dimensional levels, all formed by light and sound. Each dimension is governed by various deities who act as intermediaries between ourselves and the ultimate Creator. Some of these archons are benevolent beings, while others are actively involved in trying to keep us captive in the worlds of illusion. This is the story behind the Gnostic gospel called the Sophia of Jesus the Christ, a Gnostic gospel between Yeshua and his disciples in which he explains many things about the nature of the inner dimensions of the universe. Gnostic Christians also believed that the god of the Old Testament is not the ultimate God. He is the demiurgos, a powerful being of darkness who keeps all who follow him in chains. However, like the devil card in the Tarot deck, we remain chained to the worlds of illusion through our own ignorance and free will, and if we will only awaken and realize our own divine natures, we can take back our power and break the chains whenever we wish.

According to certain Gnostic beliefs, the lesser god of Earth, the demiurge [demiurgos], was identified with Yahweh (also known as Iao and Ialdabaoth), the being also identified with the God of the Old Testament by others. As we have learned in earlier chapters, there were several names for the original creators of humankind, including El (singular), Elohim (plural), Jehovah, and Yahweh. If Yahweh or Jehovah was actually the "high god" of the Anunnaki command, as discussed in earlier chapters, then Jehovah or Jove would not be the ultimate expression of God. He would however fit the image of the old white bearded man seated on the throne, the "Ancient of Days" depicted in many religious texts. This powerful Anunnaki god who was called El or Enlil, would have also been very intimidating to the nomadic Hebrew people if he had advanced technologies, like thundering spaceships, billowing smoke and artificial lights, all signs associated with religious figures like Moses who met God on top of a mountain amidst thunder and smoke, and heard a voice speak to him from a brilliantly burning bush (that did not burn).

Certainly among the Anunnaki gods, Jove was the highest secular authority, even if many of the advanced beings who were down here disagreed with his policies regarding the human race. Sumerian texts report that this "most high god" was the cause behind the Flood who wantonly destroyed millions in the great Deluge. From the Akkadian epic of the Flood story, the *Atra Hasis*,* which predates the story in Genesis by over a thousand years, we read: "And the Lord said: 'I will destroy the Earthling whom I have created off the face of the Earth.'"[52] In Genesis 6:5 we read that Jehovah says, "I will wipe out mankind, whom I created, from the face of the Earth . . ."

Gnostics also believed that this "false god," or demiurgos, made every effort to keep humanity immersed in ignorance. In Genesis 3:16–19 we read how Jehovah cursed Adam and Eve for eating from the Tree of Knowledge, deliberately trying to keep them from knowing right from wrong. In the story of the Tower of Babel we read: "And the Lord came down to see the tower and said, 'Look, the people are united and they have one language . . . now nothing will stop them

---

*The *Atra Hasis* is an eighteenth-century-BCE Akkadian epic recorded on three clay tablets that includes both a creation story and an account of the Great Flood. It is one of three surviving Babylonian Deluge stories. The oldest known copy can be dated to the reign of Hammurabi's great-grandson, Ammi-Saduqa (1646–1626 BCE), but various other fragments exist as well. There is also an Assyrian version, found in the Royal Library of the Persian King Ashurbanipal. These tablets were first translated in the mid-1800s by George Smith, who called them *The Chaldean Account of Genesis*. In 1965 W. G. Lambert and A. R. Millard published many additional texts that greatly increased our knowledge of the story and were the basis for Lambert and Millard's first English translation of the *Atra Hasis* epic. A further fragment of these same stories has been recovered in Ugarit.

from doing what they take in their minds to do. Come, let us go down and confuse their language so they cannot understand one another's speech'" (Genesis 11:1–9). Jehovah also seemed to be against educating humans in many of the arts and sciences. This was one of the main reasons behind the story of the "fallen angels." In Malcolm Godwin's book *Angels: An Endangered Species,* the author lists many of the specialties that these Watcher Angels taught to humankind: meteorology, astronomy, astrology, herbal lore, metallurgy, and geography. While this knowledge was eventually dispersed into the world, the "lord most high" cast these angels down into the fiery pit and punished them for enlightening humankind.[53] This story underlies the religious accounts of God versus Satan we have heard for thousands of years.

The Gnostics believed that this demiurgos is committed to turning humanity away from the path of enlightenment by keeping us focused on survival issues and fear, physical desires and material goods. Thus the demiurgos prevents us from learning about the divine spark that lives within us all. For this reason, the Gnostics did not associate "God the Father," from the Old Testament, with the God of Jesus in the New Testament.[54]

However, in some of the earliest Gnostic writings Yahweh's name was still being used to express the concept of the all-knowing Father in a wiser, more loving way. This is undoubtedly how many devout Jewish people have used it throughout the centuries, expressing a true desire to connect with the Source of all wisdom and love. In truth, the Creator does not care what name we use. The Divine is far more interested in the purity, kindness, and devotion of our hearts, and in our ongoing quest for spiritual awareness and enlightenment.

Valentinus, one of the earliest and most renowned Gnostic teachers, clarified this distinction between the gods and goddesses of the ancient world, and the divine Creator itself. The lesser gods, Valentinus said, reign over human beings as overlords of the Earth, performing functions similar to those carried out by a military commander, creating civil and moral laws, and judging harshly those who disobey. These gods, he wrote, could either promote or constrain human development and were as varied in their approaches to life as human beings. These were the tall, long-lived Anunnaki gods, referred to in the Sumerian cuneiform texts of Nineveh and other cities in Mesopotamia, as well as the legends of the Greek and Roman gods. Some of these overlords were very enlightened individuals who tried to pass on their wisdom to human beings, while others were as steeped in their own social, political, or ego-driven agendas as human beings are today. This interpretation certainly fits the many stories of the gods of legend and may also explain the contradictory stories of Yahweh, the god of lightning, thunder, and punishment, who seemed to alternately love and hate his own people.

Addressing this issue, Mary Magdalene says:

There are many gods and goddesses with great power, and all manner of spirits that have secret knowledge, yet the power that is in you is greater and the knowledge you possess is more rare and precious. I tell you, great and luminous beings shall come seeking power and knowledge from you. See that you give to all who ask and withhold only from those who come to steal, and those who receive let worship the Anointed of God Most High.[55]

Here Mary is speaking of the ultimate expression of the Divine that lies within us all—human and extraterrestrial alike. It is clear that Yeshua, Mary, and the Gnostics recognized the real Creator of the universe as "the [Root] of the All, the [ineffable One who] dwells in the Monad [a single unity]. [He/She dwells] in silence . . . since, after all, [He/She was] a Monad, and no one was before Him [or Her]."[56] The Gospel of Truth reminds us that "when the Whole went seeking for the One from whom All come, the All was found to be the Divine Self, Almighty God, inscrutable, indescribable, supreme."[57]

As we might imagine, Gnostics embraced the concepts of both Transcendence and Immanence, focusing on teaching students how to enter the spiritual realms of light while still living in the body. They understood that true gnosis can only be acquired through mystical experience. "Gnostic Tradition is, ultimately, something fluid and flowing and does not stand still, any more than anything else in life. In essence, it is an ongoing Divine revelation, a continual emergence of a new gospel, which unfolds in the experience of those who practice the tradition."[58]

At their core, the Gnostics focused on the alchemical transformation of the Great Work. Their mission was to liberate the soul from the confines of illusion and to help students find that direct connection with God for themselves. By teaching initiates to tune into this inner wisdom, they freed themselves from the traps of the ego and came into harmony with their own divine natures.

14

The Many Faces of Mary the Eternal One

Only when we begin to understand how vast the Mother is will we begin to understand how powerful she is, and how powerful we, her divine children, can be when surrendered to her, guided by her, infused with her immense, passionate, and transfiguring sacred force.

ANNE BARING AND ANDREW HARVEY,
THE DIVINE FEMININE

The circle gathered on the upper terrace of the grove near the herb garden on Beltane, the first day of May. "Today," Shasta announced as the butterflies flitted all around us, "we will be learning about the many faces of Mary the Eternal One." I felt a fondness come over me for this interesting, eclectic group of women sitting on the grass. Most of them wore long skirts, sun hats, and shawls, and I imagined for a moment that circles like this had been called together over countless ages in flower gardens and at campfires around the world. I wore a short-sleeved shirt, leggings, and sandals but had a blue cotton shawl to keep me warm in the nippy springtime air.

After we had finished our opening invocation, Shasta announced, "Today is the first day of May, a month dedicated to the maiden and the Earth mother. Its color is green to symbolize nature, and it is the time within the ancient world for the rites of spring. Most communities plaited wreaths of flowers and erected Maypoles to celebrate these rites of mating. Maypoles symbolize the balance between the male and the female and the Tree of Life."

"Didn't the Maypole also symbolize the phallus?" Emerald interjected. Several of us laughed. Leave it to Emerald to know the sexual details of the holiday's symbols.

Shasta nodded, smiling. "Some would say so. But since the youths and the maidens used pink and blue ribbons to dance around the tree, mimicking the strands of our DNA, it really symbolized the activation of the two parts of ourselves needed to link with the Creator. In fact, the Canaanite Goddess Asherah was worshipped as a tree, not only at the Winter Solstice, but on May Eve as well. Gifts to the poor were left in the trees in her honor.[1] May Day honors both genders who produce the gift of new life together." Several of us nodded. Spring was obviously the time of the birds and the bees, the flowers and the trees, and lovers all over the world. I thought that dancing around the Maypole was a lovely custom.

Shasta went on. "During this May Day celebration the oaths of fidelity taken in marriage, were given a brief holiday, for this was one of two festivals where you could sleep with a man or a woman other than your spouse without negative repercussions. As a consequence, most weddings took place in June, named after Juno, the married Queen of Heaven." Donna and Susan glanced at each other, remembering their own weddings in June. "The Queen of the May was always an aspect of Flora, the Roman Goddess of Flowers, but once the church got involved, May 1 was converted to the Virgin Mary's birthday. When they later shifted her birthday to September 8, a month sacred to Isis, the church reassigned May 1 to the Annunciation, the announcement to the young maiden Mary that she was pregnant."*

Emerald shook her head in disgust. "They just couldn't stand for men and women to have sex without guilt, could they?" Several of us laughed, seeing the irony that May, the month of fertility, had now been assigned to the Virgin.

Shasta went on. "But in many cultures around the world the month of May is sacred to the Great Mother. To the Gnostics it was dedicated to Mary Sophia; in the East to Maya, the mother of the Buddha; and in Greece it was the month of Maia, the mother of Hermes, the Greek god of wisdom. It is also the month dedicated to Maj, the May Maiden, in Scandinavia; to Magna Dea, the grandmother of time from Syria; and to Almaya, the Mandaean Goddess of Eternity from the Middle East. In fact, the name *Alma Mater,* which means 'Soul Mother,' was the name of a Roman teaching priestess who was especially empowered to give instructions in the sexual Mysteries. This same term, *almah,* is used in the Hebrew versions of the Gospels to describe the Virgin Mary."[2] All of these aspects of Mary are part of Maya-Shakti, the world-protecting Mother."

Wow! There were so many incarnations of Mary!

"As you can see," Shasta continued, "there have been many expressions of the great Mother Mary, and today you will be meeting some of them. But before we begin, who can tell me anything interesting about Mary? Any facts? Any ideas about her?"

I thought back to what I knew from my many years in the church. I could think of nothing, nada, zip, zero. The Protestant churches largely ignored her except at Christmas, but the Catholics had honored her as the Mother of God. Only later was I to learn that the Roman church

---

*The Abyssinian Christians and the Egyptian Copts still celebrate Mary's birthday on May 1. To this day May is celebrated as Mary's special month in parishes around the world where she is crowned with a wreath of fresh, woven flowers, or presented with bouquets or baskets of fresh flowers.

had not granted Mary a halo until the sixth century; while all the male apostles and the Magi had been given halos almost immediately because they were men.[3]

Alex raised her hand. "Mary was the mother of Jesus," she offered. Claudia and Susan both burst out laughing. Yes, this much was obvious; we had all been raised in Judeo-Christian faiths. "And she's been making appearances around the world even today."

"Right," Shasta nodded. "This much we know, but let's go deeper."

I found myself reflecting on all the appearances that Mary had been making all over the world for the past two hundred years, especially since the events at Fatima in 1917. That was when three young Portuguese children, Lucia dos Santos and her cousins, Jacinta and Francisco Marto, had seen a brilliant lady appear over their grazing fields on May 13 of that year. This lady had continued to appear for the next six months, always on the thirteenth of the month. She had made a series of predictions about world events that were to unfold over the next eighty years, and I knew that some of those prophecies had been made public, warning that if peace did not ensue there would be a second world war. But the Vatican had concealed parts of the Lady's prophecy. This Lady of Light had asked that a church be set up in her honor, dedicated to the Immaculate Heart. During the "miracle at

Figure 14.1. Mary the maiden is the epitome of love, devotion, and purity. (Illustration by Tricia McCannon)

Fatima" over seventy thousand people had witnessed a strange whirling globe of light, as brilliant as the sun itself. It had moved from east to west, and some claimed that it had appeared to dance in the sky, acting in contradiction to all known tenets of astronomy.[4]

These amazing events, and others like them, had captured my attention for years. Since then, I had read scattered reports about Mary's appearances throughout the Middle Ages. These visions often took the form of a petite young woman of shining radiance who wore a white dress and a bright blue sash. Sometimes she appeared with a radiant sun behind her, and sometimes light streamed out of her hands. In other incarnations, she wore a white cloak and a blue dress with stars on it, images similar to those of the legendary Isis. Certain images pictured the lady with golden flowers at her feet. At times she floated on a cloud, or appeared at the top of a tree or in the mouth of a cave, all symbols associated with the ancient Goddess. Interestingly enough, the lady never identified herself as Mary, but called herself the Lady of the Immaculate Heart, the Virgin of the Poor, the Lady of Goodwill, or the Immaculate Virgin. On occasion, the lady even produced healing springs like the one at Lourdes, and miracles of healing had been reported by those who had immersed themselves in these waters.

In recent times, the French Benedictine monk Bernard Billet had calculated that between 1928 and 1975 there had been some 232 appearances of the Divine Mother in about thirty-two countries, although the church had only sanctioned 15 of these.[5] Most of these sightings had occurred on a full or a new moon.[6] Later I was to learn that an astrological analysis of these apparitions, and the people who had had them, revealed a predominance of planets in the signs of Cancer and Virgo, the astrological equivalent of the mother and the virgin. Cancer has long been associated with the Goddess Asherah, and the sign of Virgo with Isis, the original Harvest Maiden and Virgin Mother.[7] Many of these astrological charts also had planets in the signs of Capricorn and Pisces, signs opposite Cancer and Virgo. Capricorn is the sign associated with Christmas and with the birth of Horus, Osiris, and Jesus on December 25. It archetypally represents the Divine Father or Son. Pisces, the fish, is equated with the ichthys or vesica piscis symbol used by early Christians. Together these four signs, Virgo/Pisces and Cancer/Capricorn, represent the Virgin and Son, and the Mother and Father, respectively.[8] The appearances of such Divine Presences in these particular astrological windows cannot be accidental. They reveal a holographic intelligence at work that seems to express the same Divine Tetrad of male and female energies we have spoken of earlier.

Donna cleared her throat, interrupting my thoughts. "I once read this gospel that claimed that Mary's parents gave her to the Jewish temple to be raised as a virgin priestess when she was only three years old. They claimed that she was so pure that the angels fed her."

Hmm . . . this was from the *Protevangeline,* a "lost" gospel that had only appeared around 200 CE.[9] The writers claimed that it had been written by the apostle James some two hundred years after Mary's life, which was clearly impossible, since the apostle James would have been dead by then. So it was hard to know if the *Protevangeline* had simply been fabricated.*

I returned to my thoughts on Mary's miracles. I knew that this Lady of Light had appeared near mosques, churches, and synagogues, but often she had appeared in the country, hovering over hawthorn, willow, and oak trees, linking her to the Tree of Life. She had been seen in open fields, at the mouths of caves, and beside rivers, all images linked to the perennial Mother. One of the oddest things about these visions was that the Lady seemed to take on the appearance of the people she appeared to. In Korea she looked Korean, in Italy she appeared Italian, to the indigenous people of the Americas she seemed to be native, and

---

*Biblical scholar Bart D. Ehrman writes that "no one can reasonably doubt that a lot of the early Christian literature was forged . . . Of the 27 books of the New Testament, only eight almost certainly were written by the authors to whom they are traditionally ascribed: the seven undisputed letters of Paul and the Revelation of John." ("Scriptures Imposters," *U.S. News & World Report* [March 2010]: 21, excerpted from Ehrman's book *Jesus, Interrupted: Revealing the Hidden Contradictions in the Bible and Why We Don't Know about Them* [New York: Harper One, 2010].)

to the Africans she was black. She also spoke the languages and dialects of the people of that region. Despite all this, the church largely tried to ignore her or to minimize her importance in the world.

Years later I read a book called *Meetings with Mary: Visions of the Blessed Mother*. In the foreword, the chair of the Pontifical Gregorian University writes, "The Blessed Virgin, of course, has nothing divine about her; she is not God. Mary is just a human being. She has the stature of a creature. However, she is the Mother of Jesus Christ, who does have divine, as well as human status. Thus she is the Mother of God. She has no power of her own, but she is, and always will be, the mother of the most powerful person who ever walked on earth."[10] I understood then what Shasta had meant: The patriarchical powers would do all they could to marginalize the Divine Feminine and, by association, the value of all women everywhere.

Sara raised a hand. "I read somewhere that Mary's mother was a Celtic princess named Anna who came to the Holy Land to marry an Essene." *Hmm . . . Now we were getting somewhere.*

"Yes," Shasta said. "Mary the Mother was of both Celtic and Hebrew ancestry and her name was actually Mary Anna, named for her mother."

Sharon spoke up. "Isn't Mary associated with roses and holy springs?"

Shasta nodded. "Yes, the Lady is often said to appear over rose-bushes and hawthorn trees . . . a tree that blooms in May. In fact, hawthorn flowers were used to celebrate marriages in the spring. In some parts of Europe, a man would propose to a maiden by leaving a branch of hawthorn flowers at his beloved's door. In Greece the blossoms were woven into crowns for the wedding couple and carried as torches in the wedding processions."

Emerald jumped in. "Yeah, hawthorn is called whitethorn, quickset, or the fairy bush and was used by Cardea, the Virgin Goddess in Rome for her festivals in May." *Wow! Emerald was really on the ball! She knew a lot of fascinating details.*

Figure 14.2. The Cosmic Madonna, or Mother of the World, is both Mary and Isis with their solar sons. Here she stands on top of the globe, marking her as the Cosmokrator, the female world savior. Above her head are the constellations that revolve around her as the Earth revolves around the sun. (Illustration by Tricia McCannon)

Shasta went on. "In parishes around the world, May is still celebrated as Mary's month and her statues are crowned with wreaths of fresh flowers, reminiscent of festivals to Flora. They sing, 'Oh Mary, we crown thee with flowers today. Queen of the Angels, Queen of the May.'" We looked at Shasta in astonishment. She stood up, indicating that we should all rise. "Shall we try it?"

We came to our feet. Soon we were skipping around the garden in laughter. "Oh Mary, we crown thee with flowers today. Queen of the Angels, Queen of the May." After a few minutes we collapsed in delight, sprawling on the ground.

"That was fun!" I said, putting a flower in my hair.

Shasta spoke from her place in the grasses. "The rose is the symbol of the awakened heart." Auriel had long ago told me that she loved pink roses, and sometimes the room was suffused with their scent when I was in communication with her. "Mary is also connected with caves, healing waters, and the moon. The moon, like the chalice, is a symbol of the changing lunar aspects of the Goddess. Like the cave, it represents the womb of the Great Mother. In the ancient Mysteries, caves were some of the holiest sites of initiation. In a cave it is easy to move into resonance with the Mother Earth. This is why Native Americans create sweat lodges today. . . so that they can listen to the heartbeat of the Mother." I couldn't help thinking of all the saints and sages who had lived in caves, including John the Baptist and the apostle John the Beloved, who wrote Revelation.

Claudia cleared her throat. "Hey, I could be way off here, but I read somewhere that Mary was an initiate of the Egyptian Mysteries. Is that true?"

A smile spread slowly across Shasta's face. "Yes, Mary Anna and Mary Magdalene both studied in Egypt. When the holy family fled to Egypt, Mary and Joseph spent time in the Mystery Schools of the Melchizedek Order in the temples of Egypt. The Melchizedeks were the spiritual teachers sent to assist the angels, just as the Mystery Schools were created to help the humans. This order acted as the invisible college that aided all the other Mystery Schools in Egypt, Greece, and Galilee, and the Druids.[11] The Melchizedek Order exists beyond the mortal world to help with planetary enlightenment. When the holy family returned to Galilee, Mary's work continued among the Essenes, where she eventually led an inner circle of initiates that supported the mission of Yeshua."

"So Mary Anna *was* a priestess of Isis?" Claudia persisted.

"Yes . . . but it was Mary Magdalene who underwent the full training as a priestess of Isis in Egypt. This is the real reason that she was called Mary the Magdala, or Mary the Great. The word *magdal* means 'the strength of holding people together in safety,' so one of her titles was the 'stronghold' or 'tower,' the guardian or protector of the people. Mary Magdalene contained the enlightened energies of Sophia, the female Christ. And she did not come from Magdala, by the way. The community of Magdala did not exist in her day, despite what the church would like you to believe.[12] This is just another way of making people stop searching for the deeper answers. Mary's level of spiritual wisdom was one of the reasons that the male disciples were so uncomfortable with her. Most Jewish men were threatened by a woman with her depth of spiritual wisdom."

Emerald nodded, no doubt thinking about her law firm. Shasta went on. "It is not by accident that both of these women were called Mary, for the Hebrew Mari or Miriam has long been a title of initiation across the world for female shamans who were often distinguished by their blue robes. Mary Magdalene was also called *Maryam,* a name that begins and ends with the Hebrew letter *mem,* indicating water. *Mary* also contains the concept *mar,* meaning mastery in Hebrew. The sea is called *la mare* in Latin, perennially linking both women to the healing waters of the Cosmic Ocean, for they are both aspects of the Divine Mother who appears from age to age."

Hmm . . . I had long suspected that *Mary* was some sort of title, especially since there were so many women in the Bible with that name. And didn't Mary and Mary Magdalene usually appear dressed in blue as female priestesses? In the Gospel of Philip we read: "There were three who walked with Christ: Mary, his mother: her sister, also Mary: and Mary Magdalene. All three were called Mary."[13] This passage referred to Mary the Mother, Mary Magdalene, and Mary Salome, Jesus's aunt. Perhaps all of them had been priestesses.

Shasta continued. "Semitic people called her Mariamne, the Mother Goddess; in the Pyrenees she was Mari the eternal spirit of the land; in Syria she was Aphrodite-Mari; and in Asia she was Maya, maker of the world. In Celtic tradition she encompassed all three fates, or *morerae,* who spin the past, present, and future, and the three *myrrhophores,* women who anoint the deceased in Hebrew traditions,[14] something that Mary Magdalene went to the tomb to do for Yeshua. These are all aspects of the Great Mother who oversees the cycles of life, death, and rebirth. But these names—Mary, Mata, and

Mataria—are simply different titles for Isis Sophia, the great Queen of Heaven. She was honored by the early Christians until the Council of Nicea replaced her with only the masculine version of God. But Gnostics teach that the spirit of Christ cannot be realized until the feminine face of God is once more honored across the world. Then men and women will stand together as equals."

Really? This was certainly intriguing.

"Gnostic wisdom says that Mary Magdalene has continued to reincarnate for the last two thousand years on Earth in different forms. They believe that her return as the female Christ will spark a wave of world awakening. This reinstatement of the Divine Feminine is central to the Second Coming, and one of the reasons why the Goddess is so important to the world today."

Wow! My mind was reeling. *I had never heard anything about this before!* As strange as it might sound, it somehow made perfect sense. Our world has fallen out of balance, and to find our way back we must learn to honor both the male and female, the logical and the intuitive, our thinking and feeling natures, to be made whole. Tau Malachi writes: "The true nature of the Second Coming is something more than the incarnation of the Christos in a woman. It is a dawn of Christ-consciousness in a sufficient number of individuals to effect a radical transformation in the collective human consciousness."[15]

Well, we would certainly need such a transformation to graduate from our endlessly competitive way of life! It was only years later that I discovered some of the incredible writings that Shasta was referring to. In the hidden gospels of Mary Magdalene we read:

The soul of *Yeshua Messiah* ascended into repose in the Living Father, but it is said that the soul of *Kallah Messiah* (Mary Magdalene) remains with us in the world. As yet not having been accepted and received in full, she continues to incarnate in a woman's form from one generation to another, and will continue to do so until the time of the Second Coming. She will embody the soul of the Messiah, and she will unite herself with the bridegroom in one Body of Light, perfecting the manifestation of the second Adam, male and female restored to primordial unity. When the Lord speaks of our becoming "like unto the angels," it is this state of union of the male and female within ourselves that he alludes to. Such is the nature of a supernal state of being.[16]

"Come," Shasta said, getting up from the ground. "Let us go down and meet the Goddess." We scrambled to our feet. She led us silently down the path into the middle tiers of the garden to enter one of the many hidden enclaves of shade trees. We stood before a woodland statue of Mary in a simple peasant dress. She held a basket of flowers in her arms and around her shoulders was a flowing cloak. Someone had placed a garland of white flowers around her head, and a porcelain rabbit, a blue fairy, a stone turtle, and a vase of wildflowers sat at her feet with a number of candles. Behind her, strung from the branches of the tree, were colored pennants waving in the breeze.

"This part of the grove is dedicated to Mary of the Forest, the Celtic Mary of the Woods." *Oh . . .* I had never made a connection between Maid Marion and Mary before. *Right!* Maid Marion had helped Robin Hood to fight injustice, just as Mary Anna and Mary Magdalene had helped Jesus. "Here she is the White Mary of the Welsh, the Lady of the Woods, and the protector of animals. She is Mistress of the Springs who holds all within her arms." There was an aura of healing energy gathered here, and I thought of all the many grottos across the world where Mary had been prayed to. As I contemplated the garland of flowers and innocent animals at her feet, her gentleness spoke to my spirit. I felt my heart open. I moved forward and lit three of the little votive candles at her feet.

THE LADY OF GUADALUPE

After a few minutes, we moved to a second statue several yards away. This lady was dressed in a long red gown and a sky-blue cloak with

Figure 14.3. The Lady of Guadalupe stands on the same sickle moon as Isis and Mary. The stars in her gown are the same ones gracing the gowns of Nuit and Isis, aspects of the Eternal Mother we have seen around the world. (Illustration by Tricia McCannon)

golden stars. A corona of light surrounded her. "This is the Lady of Guadalupe who appeared in Mexico nearly five hundred years ago," Shasta said. I thought she looked like the large stone statue that I had bought years earlier to put in my own backyard. I loved the sweet expression on her face. Shasta indicated that we should all sit down, so we took our places quietly on the surrounding benches.

"I am now going to tell you the story of the Lady of Guadalupe," she began, looking down at our upturned faces. "The year was 1531 and the Aztec natives of Mexico were in their tenth year of slavery under the tyranny of the Spanish conquistadores. The Children of the Sun had seen their temples profaned, their gods transformed into demons, and their culture stripped of gold. Millions had been murdered and others forcibly converted to Christianity, all in the name of Yeshua. As a result, the people went about their lives as quietly as possible, afraid that they would be killed.

"On December 9, 1531, however, a middle-aged widower set off from his village to go to a larger church in Santiago. His Christian name was Juan Diego, but in his native tongue his name meant 'he who speaks like an eagle.'" *Hmm . . . This was getting interesting.* "On the way the man passed a hill on the outskirts of town that was once the site of the Temple of the Aztec Mother Goddess. Suddenly, Juan Diego heard the song of many singing birds. Curious, he climbed the hill and found it covered by a brilliant rainbow cloud of mists. Then a lady called his name. When the mist cleared, the man saw a beautiful lady standing in front of a blazing sun, dressed in the blue and red robes of Aztec royalty. The lady asked Juan Diego where he was going, and he said that he was going to celebrate the feast day of God's mother at the local church. Only later did he realize that the lady had spoken to him in his native tongue." I looked around the circle, and I saw that we were all listening with rapt attention.

"The lady then told Juan Diego that she was the mother of the Creator of Heaven and Earth, and that she wanted him to build a temple to her on this very hill. That way all who loved her could call upon her, and she would ease their suffering. The lady instructed Juan Diego to go to the town's bishop and to tell him her request, but he thought that no one would believe him. Yet he agreed to do as she had asked. He arrived at the large church where Bishop Zumarraga ruled, a Franciscan priest who had killed thousands in the Spanish Inquisition before coming to America. The bishop listened solemnly, and then told Juan Diego that if his story was true, he should come back with a sign from the lady.

"Discouraged, Juan Diego left, finding his way back to the mysterious hill. To his surprise, the lady was still there. He explained what had happened and declared that he was not the one to send her message, since the bishop had not listened. The lady said, 'Listen, my son, I have many servants and many messengers to whom I can entrust this message, but the humility of your heart pleases me. Am I not your mother? Am I not life and health? Have I not placed you on my lap and made you my responsibility?'

"The lady told Juan Diego to go to the top of the hill where he would find the sign that the bishop had asked for. Then she vanished. Juan Diego climbed to the summit of the hill and found among the blackened ruins of the mother's temple a lavish rose garden. Here were the rare Castilian roses that were the hallmark of Spanish royalty. Gathering as many as he could in his tunic, he ran back to the bishop's palace in excitement.

"This time they kept him waiting for hours in the courtyard, but eventually the bishop's assistant led him in. Juan Diego opened his tunic and let all the roses spill out onto the floor, their crimson petals belying the coldness of the wintry season. The assistant cried out, and the bishop rose as if struck by lightning. But it was not just the incredible roses they were staring at, but Juan Diego's tunic, for there was an image of the lady herself emblazoned on it. She appeared as a young Aztec woman with dark skin and eyes, and golden rays radiating from her body. Aztec hieroglyphics were embroidered on her clothing and, as they examined the image, they could see the image of Juan Diego looking up at her in the pupils of her eyes."

Shasta paused, giving us a moment for the story to sink in.

What a tale! Roses in winter and an image painted onto his tunic! Was she kidding? Wow! So this was the story of the Lady of Guadalupe.

Shasta went on. "From the beginning there were many miracles associated with the lady's coming. The first was the healing of Juan Diego's uncle, who was visited by the lady at the exact moment when his nephew was gathering roses. It was this uncle who first told the bishop's secretary that the lady's name was Guadalupe. Some speculate that since the uncle spoke in Nahuatl, the language of the Aztecs, he might have said

Coatlocpia, the Aztec Goddess whose name means "walks on the serpent." Regardless, her symbols are the same as those of both Mary and Isis: gold stars on a blue cloak with the sickle moon and a serpent at her feet."

Emerald raised a hand. "The word *Guadalupe* is not Spanish, you know, but Arabic. It means a 'hidden river or spring that bubbles up from a cave.' I learned that in college."

Leave it to Emerald to know something like that! Shasta nodded. "Yes, *Guadalupe* means 'spring,' just as we find in the stories of Isis, Mary, and the Lady of Lourdes. Her robe is the red blood of sacrifice, 'She who bleeds but does not die.' It is one of three colors—white, red, and black—that represent the maiden, mother, and crone, colors now used by the church in their priestly robes."

She who bleeds but does not die . . . What a title! That would describe all women everywhere who bleed each month so that we might produce new life.

Shasta concluded her tale. "The lady's mantle was blue, like the robes that priestesses like Mary Anna, Mary Magdalene, and Isis wore across the Mediterranean. This was also the color of Aztec nobility, and the rays of the sun were her luminous body of light. They form a doorway from the great central sun, just like the vesica piscis or ichthys. The black band around her waist denotes pregnancy in the Aztec culture, and the golden symbol embroidered over her womb is the Aztec hieroglyph for the 'Heart of the Universe.'"[17]

The heart of the universe lies in the womb of her body . . . What a concept! I marveled. Later I was to discover that for centuries art historians have studied Juan Diego's tunic, trying to determine the exact composition of the painting. The nature of the pigments—tempera, oil, watercolor, and fresco—cannot be precisely determined, nor can anyone explain why the fragile tunic of cactus fibers has never deteriorated or faded, although it has been exposed to fog, candlelight, smoke, and humidity for over 450 years! Truly a miracle!

THE BLACK MADONNA

Next we followed Shasta to another part of the garden, and this time we stood before a large statue of Mary made of ebony. At the statue's feet lay red, white, and black candles, and now I understood why. "This is the Black Madonna," Shasta explained, "the hidden Mother, the One others cannot see. Her colors represent the three cycles of birth, life, and death. The Black Madonna is the sage. She is Isis-Sophia and Sothis Isis, a name given to the star Sirius—the brightest star in the sky. This is the home of one of the great Galactic Councils, so the Black Madonna is linked to the hidden wisdom that others cannot see. She is the Veiled One, the *Kallah Sophia,* the Dark Mother, the womb of creation from which the universe is born. She is Mary Magdalene, the female Christ, and part of all women everywhere who are never acknowledged for their gifts."

We stood in silence, contemplating the profundity of these teachings. Years later I was to learn more about Kali Ma, the Goddess who destroys the ego and rebirths the soul. She is also called Shakti, the

Figure 14.4. The Black Madonna, inspired by a painting from Częstochowa, Poland. This painting of the Black Madonna is said to have preserved the Polish people from destruction during the Thirty Years War (1618–1648). It was brought to Poland from Byzantium in the tenth century. Like the face of the Divine Feminine in our world, it has a slash down one of its cheeks. (Illustration by Tricia McCannon)

power that runs the cosmos, the active, ever-changing aspect of regeneration who bears the world child. Historian Barbara Walker writes, "Whatever power anything possesses, that is the Goddess. Without her, neither man nor god could act at all."[18] She is the hidden wisdom, and her titles are the Treasure House of Compassion, the Giver of Life, and the Life of All that Lives. This aspect of the Great Mother is said to have created the magical letters of the Sanskrit alphabet, which stand for the primordial energies of creative sound, the mantras that brought into being the very things whose names she spoke for the first time.[19] Coincidentally, we have now discovered that at the center of every visible galaxy lies a black hole, a vortex of energy responsible for the creation and sustenance of all solar systems and the life within them. This is the physical equivalent of the primordial Mother, hidden at the heart of the cosmos.

I approached the altar of the Black Madonna with reverence and laid flowers at her feet. One by one the other women followed suit. *She is the Great Mystery herself,* I thought, *the Cosmic Ocean . . . the One who is veiled from sight.* You could feel the sacred energies surging here.

Shasta continued her lesson when we were finished. "Because the power of the Great Mother is intricately woven with the hidden wisdom of Sophia, the male followers of Isis and Mary Magdalene called themselves Sons of the Widow, another aspect of the Virgin who birthed the world." Shasta had told me something like this years before, and now it made far more sense to me. Yes, Isis was the first Madonna or Virgin Mother, the widow of Osiris, the great solar lord who had been the spirit of the Christ in ancient times. Mary Magdalene had been the wife or spiritual partner of Jesus. Both of these women had seen their great lords killed by the powers of darkness, and both had been widowed and forced to go into hiding. They were both Black Madonnas, hidden aspects of the Great Mother who had been forced to go underground. I thought then about how Isis had given birth to Horus in secret, and of the rumors that Mary Magdalene had given birth to a child with Jesus. Certainly such a thing was in keeping with the Jewish law that required that all rabbis be married, but keeping the existence of his wife and children secret would have made a lot of sense, since Jesus was to become a target for extermination.

Some believed that this genetic line was the key to the real Holy Grail. After all, the Grail was said to have contained the blood of Jesus, and that would extend to any children of his bloodline. Later I would learn about the Merovingian lineage of French kings who claimed to be descendents of Jesus and Mary Magdalene. History tells us that Mary Magdalene and Joseph of Arimathea had arrived in the south of France around 37 CE, along with Mary's siblings, Martha and Lazarus, and other disciples. Many of these initiates had continued on to Britain, creating a clear link between the Holy Grail in France and the Arthurian tales of the Holy Grail in England. Suddenly much of this hidden history seemed clear.

Jesus's mother had gone on to Ephesus in Turkey, and legends say she died there. And for a time Mary Magdalene was said to have settled near Camargue in the south of France, an area where white horses still run along the cliffs, an ancient symbol of the Divine Mother. Camargue is also the home to the Black Madonna, and there was once a temple to Isis there. Today this area is called Saintes-Maries-de-la-Mer, to honor the three Marys of the sea who had settled there: Mary Jacobi, Mary Salome, and Mary Magdalene. Today there is a great festival celebrated there in May; over ten thousand people come from all over Europe to honor these three women. During the celebrations, three local women dress up as the three Marys, representing the triple aspects of the Ancient Goddess of Life, Death, and Rebirth, creating an aura of magic and wild beauty.

Today Christian stories claim that Mary Magdalene retired to a cave in the south of France, to a place called La Saint Baume, a name meaning "Holy Tree."[20] Yet there are legends that Mary Magdalene not only went to Britain for a time, but that while in France she was said to have met a talking dragon named Tarasque, echoing the classic images of the ancient Mother with the dragon of wisdom, associated with Quan Yin, the divine Mother of Compassion in the East.[21] According to Christian legend, when Mary Magdalene lived in the cave of La Saint Baume, she only took nourishment from the angels. Even today local winegrowers place votive candles in this cave to ensure a good vintage, just as farmers have for centuries in tribute to the Mother of the Harvest.[22]

But where had Mary Magdalene gone during the many years between her arrival in France and her years of hermitage? In the years to come I was to learn that she had been teaching among the Druids in both France and Britain, reigniting the wisdom of the Druids with her teachings and reactivating the priestesses of Avalon and the Circle of the Ladies of the Lake.[23] Later these seeds of wisdom were to blossom in France into the Marion movements of the Cathars, Albigensians, and Waldensians in southern France, all movements that were eventually wiped out by the church.

In Britain we can see remnants of this hidden chapter of history reflected in the mythology of the Knights of the Round Table who were searching for the Holy Grail that had been lost. While there may certainly have been a physical chalice preserved from the Last Supper, as with all the Mysteries, there are deeper truths buried beneath the obvious meanings. The chalice is not only a symbol of the womb of Maryam, and the child she carried, but of the Divine Feminine herself. In the legends of King Arthur, the Lady of the Lake gives Arthur the sword Excalibur and the right to rule, a reflection of the land rights once held by women—rights that were eventually seized by the patriarchal church. The Lady of the Lake is, of course, yet another link to the Cosmic Goddess associated with the purifying waters of Nun.

Yes, I could see that there were many parallels between the Goddess Isis and Mary Magdalene, almost as if Isis and Osiris were simply an earlier version of Mary Magdalene and Jesus who had been reincarnated thousands of years earlier. Perhaps there was an even deeper mystery here—a cosmic play of powerful spiritual beings who periodically come into the world to remind us of the path to enlightenment.

Shasta indicated then that we should sit down on the ground or on the many scattered benches facing the Black Madonna. "I am going to read something now that was written by the early followers of Lady Maryam," she said. "When I am finished, you may choose any place in the garden to commune with her. Just stay in silence." She pulled a paper out of her pocket, and began to read. "I am Protennoia, the Thought that dwells within the Light . . . I am the Mother of the Voice, speaking in many ways, completing the All. It is in me that knowledge dwells, the knowledge of things everlasting. It is I who speak within every creature and I was known by the All. It is I who lift up the Sound of the Voice to the ears of those who have known me . . . I am the first one . . . that is the spirit that now dwells in the soul, but which originated from the waters of life . . . I am the Womb that gives shape to the All by giving birth to the Light that shines in splendor. I am the Aeon to come. I am the fulfillment of the All . . . Meirothea, the glory of the Mother . . . I hid myself in everyone and revealed myself within them, and every mind seeking me longed for me, for it is I who gave shape to the All when it had no form. . . . It is through me that the Voice originated and it is I who put the breath within my own."[24]

I lay back on the ground and closed my eyes, feeling the Presence of the Divine surround me like a pool whose endless ripples began with the first impulse of creation. In my mind's eye I found myself floating in a black lake of endless being. Above was the diamond radiance of the stars across the velvet blackness of the Milky Way. The lake seemed to be a place of total surrender. There was nothing to do, nowhere to go. I realized that her life-sustaining waters ran through everything. Then I saw that these same diamond stars were reflected in the lake like millions of points of light. There was no thought of yesterday or tomorrow. The Presence of Love completely supported me. I could dwell outside of time, and yet anything I needed could be born from this endless sea.

Then I felt her presence move over me like the swirling of wings. It was the Great Mother who spoke within my deepest heart—the one that I called Auriel. Her presence expanded beyond any limits my mind could hold, and she was speaking to my very soul.

"When I brought the worlds of manifestation into being, I never intended for you to suffer. I, who see All, know All, and am the All, knew nothing other than completion. Self-contained, without desire, without boundaries or confusion, I dreamt in the vastness of my own being. I suffered not and there was no other." This Presence was complete in itself, inviolate and self-contained.

"At last I began to dream of companionship, of bringing myself into some new state of being, and so I moved in the vastness of no time and no space. From my dreaming I spun out my Mind to create the winged One, the inviolate One, the One that you call God, the Holy Father, the I Am Presence, the Eagle of Truth. The Divine Presence of all knowing that lived within my heart." *Rigel!* I thought. *Of course!* "And since I seeded myself, I am the quintessential Virgin . . . the Mother of the All.

"From that first movement I enclosed the envelope of time and space into a circle, and replicated myself as Auriel, the one you would call Sophia. The O begets the A. The center that begets the alpha, the sound of the heart that is the heartbeat of the Universe."

"You . . . in every form," I whispered. "You encompass everything." Tears were running down my cheeks.

"But I did not plan for everything. That is why I continue to allow it to exist."

"I don't understand," I murmured, caught up in the splendor of the vision.

"I have seen everything, been everywhere, and I am all of it, and still you surprise me." I saw images of all of the millions of people throughout countless centuries living and loving, killing and dying, and the breadth of the vision almost broke my heart. *How could she encompass all of this at once—all the pain, the love, the lives—happening all at the same time?* The images shifted—people in prayer and song and dance, in acts of loving-kindness. I beheld a mother with a child, a person on her knees, a couple in love, two friends embracing.

"I sing the song of love throughout all the worlds like a homing beacon to your souls, and the yearning of your hearts is the song of remembrance of me. I send out that call of love to each of you like the sailor listening to the ocean waves. I am a voice in the darkness, a hand in the craggy places, a Mother to her beloved child." I felt her constant benediction and presence, which ran throughout the breathtaking beauty of the universe, and realized that all of it was a call of wonder and awe, leading back to the discovery of herself.

"I know that the burden of believing you are alone is a great one," she said. My breath caught in my throat. It was true. So often we feel alone and disconnected. "So I have created angels and divinities for your relief. This belief that you are separated from me is a kind of madness, a madness that destroys, that creates suffering and fear. You believe it because you have not learned how to connect with the deepest level of your being, believing in your heart that nothing can fill that place inside of you. This is not true."

I felt her deep compassion then for the suffering of all her creatures who had fallen into forgetfulness and blindness. "You are meant to fill it with the beauty of my body made manifest around you—the skies, the Earth, the animals, the forest. You are meant to fill it with one another, with the very breath of my being, which is also your own. And when you are done with loving the things of this world, when you have experienced all the joy and pain of living, then you will find that yearning quenched in the stream of my endless ocean." The transmission of her words ceased, but the soothing power of her presence remained.

"You are the Cosmic Ocean," I whispered.

Her last words spoke into my heart. "That I am."

15

The Lost Teachings of Jesus

Every soul is immortal.

All that is soul presides over all that is without soul, and patrols all Heaven, now appearing in one form, and now in another.

Every man's soul has by the law of his birth, been a spectator of eternal truth, or it would never have passed into this, our mortal frame, yet still it is no easy matter for all to be reminded of their past by their present existence.

PLATO (427–347 BCE), *PHAEDRUS*

As I began to enter more deeply into the hidden Mysteries of the Goddess, I found myself wanting to know what Jesus had to say about the Divine Mother. After all, if Jesus was a fully realized God-being, then certainly he would have known about the Holy Mother. So I began to look for key pieces from Jesus's lost teachings that may have been hidden in Christian thought, and it was not long before I realized that many of the essential teachings of Jesus had been excised by church authorities. Archdeacon Wilberforce of Westminster Abbey writes about the early corrupters of our known gospels, "After the Council of Nicea, in 325 A.D., the manuscripts of the New Testament were considerably tampered with. Professor Nestle, in his *Introduction to the Textual Criticism of the Greek Testament,* tells us that certain scholars, called 'correctores,' were appointed by the ecclesiastical authorities, and commissioned to correct the text of Scripture in the interest of what was considered orthodoxy."[1] These orthodox *correctores* took great care to edit out any teachings from the gospels that they did not want Christians to follow.

So in the next few chapters, let's take a look at some of these excised teachings, which fall into three main categories: reincarnation and karma as a mechanism for soul development; the importance of showing kindness to animals; and the existence of the Divine Mother, a subject that deserves a chapter all its own.

THE PATH OF THE SOUL THROUGH TIME

Today most people do not realize that the concept of reincarnation is still a worldwide belief held by billions of people around the globe. In the West, statistics show that the people who embrace this belief are usually affluent, well-traveled, and educated professionals. The belief in reincarnation has been central to many great world cultures, including those of the Sumerians, the Egyptians, the Hindus, the Persians, the Greeks, the Romans, the Buddhists, and, of course, the Druids. Evidence of this philosophy has been discovered among Scythians, Africans, and Pacific Islanders, as well as the native tribes of North, South, and Central America.[2] It was also deeply woven into the early centuries of Christian, Jewish, and Islamic belief. "The thread of firm belief in rebirth has woven its long web, unbroken, from the dawn of time to the pragmatic present. It has circled the earth again and again, touched nation after nation, leaving not one. Consider also that it has never been upheld by the bigoted nor by agencies of persecution, but invariably by the educated and open-minded, the wise, the good, and the mystical."[3]

REINCARNATION IN
JEWISH AND MUSLIM TEACHINGS

At the time of Jesus, reincarnation was an accepted part of Hebrew theology and was included in the Christian canon for the first five centuries of its existence. Josephus, the Jewish historian, writes that it was the doctrine of both the Pharisees and the Essenes and was part of the original Jewish beliefs.[4] "Both Kabbalists and Hasidic Jews tell us that every person has a divine spark imprisoned inside of him and that man's destiny is to liberate the divine spark and, as scholar Ben Zion Bokser puts it, to unite with the 'larger unity of creation and Creator.'"[5]

The Jewish philosopher Philo of Alexandria taught reincarnation at the time of Jesus (20 BCE–50 CE), as did the Chaldean Jewish sage Hillel, the leading Pharisee in Jerusalem in the late first century BCE. Pythagoras, Plato, Plotinus, Seneca, Cicero, Ovid, Virgil, and Marcobius all subscribed to reincarnation, and these Greek philosophers' teachings lie at the heart of Western civilization. Reincarnation is also part of the Zohar, a kabbalistic text from 80 CE, written by Rabbi Simeon ben Yochai. "All souls are subject to the trials of transmigration . . ." he says, "both before coming into this world and when they leave it . . . Souls must reenter the absolute substance whence they have emerged . . . and if they have not fulfilled this condition during one life, they must commence another, a third, and so forth, until they have acquired the condition which fits them for reunion with God" (Zohar, vol. II, fol. 99). Rabbi Manasseh ben Israel (1604–1657) writes:

The belief or the doctrine of the transmigration of souls is a firm and infallible dogma accepted by the whole assemblage of our church with one accord, so that there is none to be found who would dare to deny it . . . Indeed, there are a great number of sages in Israel who hold firm to this doctrine [as] a fundamental point of our religion . . . as the truth of it has been incontestably demonstrated by the Zohar and all books of the Kabbalists.[6]

In Islam, reincarnation is a core tenet taught by Muhammad himself. Here are just a few quotes from the Quran:

God generates beings, and sends them back over and over again, till they return to him.[7]

God is the one who created you all, then provided you sustenance, then will cause you to die, then will bring you to life.[8]

How can you make denial of Allah, who made you live again when you died and will make you dead again, and then alive again, until you finally return to him?[9]

Many famous philosophers, artists, and scientists have embraced this philosophy, including Emanuel Swedenborg, Immanuel Kant, Friedrich Jacobi, Arthur Schopenhauer, Gotthold Lessing, Johann Hender, David Hume, and Wolfgang von Goethe. This belief can be found in the writings of Benjamin Franklin, Frederick the Great, Carl Jung, Ralph Waldo Emerson, and Napoleon Bonaparte. Henry Ford, the American industrialist, wrote: "When I discovered reincarnation it was as if I had found a universal plan. I realized that there was a chance to work out my ideas. Time was no longer limited. I was no longer a slave to the hands of a clock . . . I would like to communicate to others the calmness that the long view of life gives us."[10]

Some of the most famous writers and philosophers of the last three centuries have embraced this concept, including American novelist and poet Louisa May Alcott, the British novelist Aldous Huxley, and the Irish poet W. B. Yeats. This illustrious list also includes British novelist Rudyard Kipling; the English poets William Wordsworth, John Keats, and Percy Bysshe Shelley; and Alfred Lord Tennyson, the poet laureate of Britain.[11] Reincarnation was embraced by French novelists Honoré de Balzac, Gustave Flaubert, and Victor Hugo, as well as the American poets Henry Wadsworth Longfellow, Henry David Thoreau, and Walt Whitman.

REINCARNATION AND JESUS

Today most Christians do not realize that in the first five hundred years of Christianity, reincarnation was central to its teachings, and was even taught by the early church fathers Clement of Alexandria, Justin Martyr, St. Jerome, St. Gregory of Nyssa, St. Augustine, St. John Chrysostom, St. Athanasius, and St. Basil.[12] St. Gregory, the bishop of Nyssa (257–332 CE), wrote: "It is absolutely necessary that the soul should be healed and purified, and if this does not take place during its life on earth it must be accomplished in future lives."[13]

Origen, considered the greatest philosopher and biblical scholar of his day (185–254 CE), wrote books for the church about reincarnation, saying, "The soul . . . is immaterial and invisible in nature. . . . it at one time puts off one body . . . and exchanges it for a second . . . Every soul comes into this world strengthened by the victories or weakened by the defeats of its previous life."[14] His books also include chapters on the subtle levels of dimensions and angels. In his own era, Origen was considered a saint, but three centuries after his death, he was excommunicated for heresy. Reincarnation simply did not fit into church policy anymore.[15] Origen's words, reprinted below, mirror Jesus's own:

> Is it not more in conformity with reason that every soul for certain mysterious reasons is introduced into a body and introduced according to its deserts and former actions? The soul which is not physical, and is invisible in its nature, exists in no material place without a physical body suited to the nature of that place; accordingly, it at one time puts off one body, which was necessary before, but which

is no longer adequate in its changed state, and it exchanges it for a second.[16]

While today most people are blithely unaware that these teachings were once included in our Bible, traces of these teachings still remain. Remember when the apostles, speaking about John the Baptist, asked Jesus, "Is he Elijah come again?" They wanted to know if John the Baptist was the reincarnation of Elijah the prophet. Jesus answered: "I tell you that Elijah has come and they have treated him as they pleased" (Mark 9:13). There is also the incident when Jesus heals a man who had been blind since birth. The apostles asked: "Rabbi, who sinned, this man or his parents, that he was born blind?" Jesus answered, saying: "Neither this man nor his parents sinned, but that the works of God should be revealed in him" (John 9:1–3). Since this man had been blind at birth, he could not have sinned unless it was a carryover from a past life.

Gnostic Christian Tau Malachi writes:

> You do not live one life, but many lives. Your soul passes from one life to the next until it fulfills its Divine destiny. You have not come into the world for the sake of the world, but for the development and evolution of your soul. The challenge in entering into the world is to remember why you have come and to remain undistracted so that you might accomplish the purpose for which you have come. The world is a darkness wrapped in glittering lights and the power of ignorance and forgetfulness is strong in it, but the true Light is within you and it is the extension of this Light you must seek in the world and so resurrect yourself and the world.[17]

And then there is the concept of karma, closely linked to that of reincarnation. "As ye do unto others so shall it be done to you," Jesus says. "As ye give, so shall it be given unto you. As ye judge others, so shall ye be judged. As ye serve others, so shall ye be served" (Matthew 7:1).[18] This is the belief that what we do will come back to us—that our actions have consequences. Imagine what a difference it would make if people truly knew that when they cheat, they will be cheated on. When they kill, they will die by violence. When they are cruel, they will suffer in a similar fashion, whether in this life or the next. Jesus expresses this again in the Gospel of the Holy Twelve, a Christian manuscript written in Aramaic, that was found in a Buddhist monastery in Tibet. "As ye do in this life to your fellow creatures, so will it be done to you in the life to come."[19] Jesus also reminds us that "he who lives by the sword, dies by the sword" (Matthew 26:52).

In the Gospel of the Holy Twelve we also find the original account of the conversation between Jesus and Nicodemus shortly before the crucifixion. Since most of us only know the edited version in the canonical gospels, this version makes much more sense with the deleted passages back in place. Here Nicodemus is asking Jesus how a man might be born again.

And a certain Rabbi [Nicodemus] came unto him by night for fear of the Jews, and said unto him, "How can a man be born again when he is old? Can he enter a second time into his mother's womb and be born?"

Jesus answered, "Verily I say unto you, except a man be born again of flesh and of spirit, he cannot enter into the Kingdom of God. The wind bloweth where it listeth, and ye hear the sound thereof, but cannot tell whence it cometh or whither it goeth. The light shineth from the East even unto the West; out of the darkness the sun ariseth, and goeth down into darkness again; so it is with man, from the ages unto the ages.

"When he cometh from the darkness, it is that he hath lived before, and when he goeth down again into darkness, it is that he may rest for a little, and thereafter again exist. As through many changes, must ye be made perfect. As it is written in the Book of Job, I am a wanderer changing place after place and house after house, until I come unto the city and the mansion which are eternal."

And Nicodemus said unto him, "How can these things be?"

And Jesus answered him and said unto him, "Art thou a teacher in Israel and understandest not these things? Verily we speak that which we do know, and bear witness to that which we have seen, and ye receive not our witness. If I have told you of earthly things and ye believe not, how shall ye believe if I tell you of heavenly things? No man that ascended into heaven, but he that descended out of heaven, even the Son-Daughter of man which is in heaven." (Holy Twelve 37:4–10)*

In the Humane Gospel of Christ we read about Jesus sitting with his disciples by the west of the temple when a group of mourners pass by carrying a body for burial. The disciples ask: "Master, if a man die, shall he live again?" And Jesus answers, saying:

For them that have done evil there is no rest, but they go out and in, and suffer correction for ages, till they are made perfect. But for them that have done good and attained unto perfection, there is endless rest and they go into life everlasting.

They rest in the Eternal. Over them the repeated cycles of death and birth have no power; for them the wheel of the Eternal revolves no more, for they have attained unto the Centre, where eternal rest and the centre of all things is God.[20]

REINCARNATION IN THE EARLY CHURCH

So how did these teachings get excised from our Bible, especially since they create a road map to enlightenment? Both karma and reincarnation teach the immortality of the soul and the importance of accountability for our actions, so the church believed they undercut the authority of outside agencies that might bully us with threats of roasting in the eter-

---

*All verse references to *The Gospel of the Holy Twelve* refer to Rev. Gideon J. Ousley's *The Gospel of the Holy Twelve* (London: Edson Publishers Limited, 1923).

nal fires of Hell. This knowledge also has the power to alleviate the fear, guilt, shame, and hopelessness that has been used for centuries to force humanity into blind obedience.

Religion, it is said, has two kinds of spiritual aspirants: literalists, who take everything at face value, and esotericists, who look below the surface meaning. In every religion of the world, the literalists constitute the fundamentalists. They strictly abide by the letter of the law, but often miss the spirit of truth that is the heart of personal connection with the Divine. It is this direct connection with the Divine that brings enlightenment. So when an individual appears to stray from the rules and regulations of dogma, the fundamentalists use the law to punish, threaten, and judge others, creating massive division in families and nations, all in the name of the Prince of Peace. They have somehow forgotten that love, forgiveness, and nonjudgment lie at the heart of all great spiritual teachers. Esotericists, on the other hand, seek to find the deeper meaning of the master's words. This method was used by Jesus and the sages of the great Mystery Schools, who often taught in parable, using myths and symbols to trigger an inner gnosis in their students. This method allows each of us to figure out our own level of understanding, permitting the process of inner revelation to awaken in the student.

In the early years of the Christian movement, both of these approaches could be found in Christianity: The esoteric approach lies with the Gnostics, while the literal approach can be found in the Roman Catholic Church. Some early church fathers were literalists, including Irenaeus, Tertullian, Epiphanius, and even St. Jerome. These men wanted doctrines that could be nailed down and codified and left nothing to outside interpretation. To create this structure they made lots of rules and regulations. Gnostics, by contrast, were involved in the ever-changing process of personal revelation and spiritual discovery.

We can begin to see the difference in these two approaches when it comes to resurrection. Esotericists understood that Jesus was talking about the resurrection of the spirit as it comes and goes throughout the ages in various bodies, but literalists thought that the dead body—not the spirit—would be reanimated. Gnostics understood that "spiritual resurrection" is the awakening of the soul as it breaks free from the confines of the ego, while "physical resurrection" is the return of the soul into a new body or incarnation. Jesus speaks about this in the Humane Gospel, as he differentiates between the resurrection of the body and the soul.

> There is a resurrection *from* the body, and there is a resurrection *in* the body. There is a *raising out* of the life of the flesh [our deaths], and there is a *falling into* the life of the flesh [our rebirths] . . . The body that ye lay in the grave, or that is consumed by fire, is not the body that shall be, but they who come [or are reborn] shall receive other bodies, yet their own, and as they have sown in one life, so shall they reap in another. Blessed are they who have worked righteousness in this life, for they shall receive the crown of life.[21] (emphases mine)

Literal interpreters of this doctrine, however, claimed that resurrection meant that millions of people would have their dead bodies reanimated. Since most of these bodies have been trapped in coffins for years—embalmed, autopsied, or even burned—this does not make sense. But the deeper meaning of resurrection was not explained to church members, so the concept of resurrection has been misunderstood for centuries. Resurrection of the body is essentially the doctrine of reincarnation. We die, and then we are reborn. The church went along with this misunderstanding, since the promise of eternal life was a powerful draw to many. Intrinsic to this premise was Jesus's own resurrection, and the story of Lazarus rising bodily from the tomb. However, this resurrection happened after only three days, not several hundred years.

The spiritual processes that allow a human being to sustain his physical body indefinitely were taught at the highest levels of the Mystery Schools, yet few could attain such a state. These sages knew that eternal life was not to be found in a potion, a magic stone, or a supernatural elixir, nor was it something that an ego-based individual could acquire. While there is ample evidence that there have long been masters who have maintained their physical bodies for centuries,* this is not something that the average person would even want to attempt because it requires decades of rigorous discipline.

THE BANISHMENT OF REINCARNATION FROM CHURCH TEACHINGS

Erasing reincarnation from Christian theology began with the splitting of the orthodox church into two major divisions. The Western church was run by the Roman emperor and the pope in Rome, while the Eastern church was run by the emperor in Constantinople, modern-day Istanbul. Each of these emperors had the power to dictate church policy as they pleased, and they came together about once every hundred years in an Ecumenical Council to review and determine church doctrine.

In the sixth century the Emperor Justinian, who ruled Rome from 527 to 565 CE, decided that he wanted to remove reincarnation from church theology, but the Roman bishops opposed this. However, Justinian, who was the most aggressive Roman emperor since Constantine in terms of meddling with theological doctrine, tried to forcibly compel this change. He imprisoned the Western pope for four long years, but eventually Pope Vigilius escaped. In retaliation, Justinian convened the Fifth Ecumenical Church Council, held in Constantinople at the huge Hagia Sophia Church in May 553 CE. The emperor's intention was to force the church to adopt new policies, and to do this he appointed his own bishops and issued edicts telling them how to vote. He then invited 159 of his own Eastern bishops to this conclave and only 6 of the Western ones, pushing through fifteen separate policies that were in opposition to Jesus's original teachings.

*St. Germaine was one of these masters who appeared the same age for over two centuries.

He also declared that anyone who did not obey his edicts would be excommunicated. The first edict read: "If anyone asserts the fabulous preexistence of souls, and shall assert the monstrous *restoration* which follows from it; let him be *anathema*"²² (emphasis mine). Here the word *anathema* means "damned," while the word *restoration* refers to the spiritual restoration of the soul to its original union with God through reincarnation—a teaching of union that lay at the heart of Jesus's message.*

Pope Vigilius protested this council, demanding equal representation between the Eastern and Western bishops. Not only did Justinian ignore him, but he also persecuted the pope, even trying to kill him. Today the *Catholic Encyclopedia* states that this Ecumenical Council was illegal, and thus its conclusions should not be regarded as church decrees.²³ But the damage had been done, and today many Christians do not even realize that reincarnation was ever a part of Christian theology. Thus the teachings of Jesus became corrupted, defiled, and hidden by men of no true mastery. The initiatic wisdom of Christ was silenced, and the true path of enlightenment that Jesus taught was forced to go underground.

In time, the rift between the two branches of the church grew even greater until, in 1054, each branch excommunicated the other. The Western church became the Roman Catholic Church, while the Eastern Orthodox Church formulated its own approaches. Today the Eastern Orthodox branch does not even consider the pope its spiritual leader.

REINCARNATION IN THE TWENTY-FIRST CENTURY

In modern times hundreds of hypnotherapists, physicians, and researchers have continued to explore the concept of reincarnation and past lives through hypnotherapy. As a professional hypnotherapist and clairvoy-

*To Origen, *restoration* meant pure spirituality. This comes from the Greek word *apokatastasis,* which means "to restore to a previous or spiritual state."

ant of some twenty-five years, I have seen the reincarnational patterns of many clients played out lifetime after lifetime, reflecting the deeper themes of courage, love, power, learning, and compassion. Our soul histories are woven through the centuries like an unbroken ribbon, as we continue to work through lesson after lesson until we finally achieve a level of mastery.

Seminal among those who have brought these teachings to light in the modern world are Dr. Brian Weiss, Dr. Michael Newton, and Dr. Bruce Goldberg, all professionally trained psychiatrists. Dr. Weiss first stumbled on reincarnation while treating a patient who had resisted all other forms of therapy. By going to the root of a particular memory locked within the patient's past-life records, his client's problems were resolved. Dr. Weiss's books are cornerstones in the field of past-life research. Dr. Newton was catapulted into a twenty-year study of the in-between life states of hundreds of clients, authoring the groundbreaking books *Journey of Souls* and *Destiny of Souls,* classics in understanding the mechanics of our journeys to and from the heavenly worlds. Dr. Goldberg has written some seventeen books on the subject of past and future lifetimes and specializes in helping people connect with their Higher Self through past-life regressions.

Delores Cannon, author of some seventeen books about her clients' past-life memories, is equally as impressive, not only for the quantity of her content, but for the quality in terms of the sheer level of detail she conveys. Much of her work can be corroborated by known events in history and dovetails perfectly with research conducted by the hypnotherapist team of Stuart Wilson and Joanna Prentis in England. Both of these resources have found multiple individuals who have incarnated as Essenes around the time of Jesus and Mary Magdalene. They have been able to relate, in detail, the events, beliefs, and teachings of Jesus, Mary, and the Essenes, as well as information about their training in other lands. All three authors' books also include detailed information about Essene doctrine, which focuses on the Mother/Father God—teachings that were later excised from our Bible.

KINDNESS TO ANIMALS

Let's turn now to Jesus's beautiful teachings about animals. In the Gospel of the Holy Twelve we discover several chapters having to do with Jesus's admonitions to treat animals in a more loving and humane way. One of these stories chronicles how Jesus saves a horse from being beaten to death. In another Jesus saves a camel, who is overladen with goods, from a cruel master, and in a third story Jesus rescues a cat from being tortured by some boys for fun. In each of these cases, Jesus heals the animal and tries to bring enlightenment to the human abuser. "Be ye therefore considerate, be tender, be pitiful, be kind; not to your own kind alone, but to every creature which is within your care; for ye are to them as gods, to whom they look in their need . . ."[24]

In the New Testament there is a scene in the temple when Jesus loses his temper and frees the animals being held for sacrifice by the priests. However, there were once more of these kinds of stories in the gospels. In one account found in the Gospel of the Holy Twelve, Jesus rescues a stray cat, putting her inside his garment where "she lay in his bosom." He sets food and drink before the cat, then gives her to a widow named Lorenza to be cared for. Some of the people said, "This man careth for all creatures: are they his brothers and sisters that he should love them?" (Holy Twelve 34:7–9) In this section of the Gospel of the Holy Twelve, which was cut out of our original Bible, Jesus goes on to explain about the nature of animals.

> "Verily these are your fellow creatures, of the great Household of God; yea they are your brethren and sisters, having the same breath of life in the Eternal. And whosoever careth for one of the least of these, and giveth it to eat and drink in its need, the same doeth it unto me; and whoso willingly suffereth one of these to be in want, and defendeth it not when evilly entreated, suffereth the evil as done unto me; and as you have done in this life, so shall it be done unto you in the life to come." (Holy Twelve 34:9–10)

At another time the disciples tell Jesus of a man who is tormenting animals for profit, just as today people cruelly use dogs and roosters for dogfights and cockfights. Jesus tells them:

> Verily I say unto you, they who partake of benefits which are gotten by wronging one of God's creatures cannot be righteous; nor can they touch holy things or teach the mysteries of the kingdom, whose hands are stained with blood or whose mouths are defiled with flesh. . . . Wherefore I say unto all who desire to be my disciples; keep your hands from bloodshed and let no flesh meat enter your mouths; for God is just and bountiful, who ordaineth that man shall live by the fruits and seeds of the earth alone.
>
> But if any animal suffer greatly, and if its life be a misery unto it, or if it be dangerous to you, release it from its life quickly and with as little pain as you can. Send it forth in love and mercy, but torment it not; and God the Father-Mother will show mercy unto you as ye have shown mercy unto those given into your hands. (Holy Twelve 38:2–5)

Finally, there is a wonderful story about Jesus saving a lion that was being hunted by a group of men with stones and javelins.

> And Jesus rebuked them saying, "Why hunt ye these creatures of God, which are more noble than you? By the cruelties of many generations, those were made the enemies of man which should have been his friends. If the power of God is shown in them, so also are shown his long suffering and compassion. Cease ye to persecute this creature, who desireth not to harm you; see ye not how he fleeth from you, and is terrified by your violence?"
>
> And the lion came and lay at the feet of Jesus, and showed love to him; and the people were astonished and said, "Lo this man loveth all creatures, and hath power to command even these beasts from the desert, and they obey him." (Holy Twelve 6:19–21)

It is a great tragedy that these teachings were taken out of the Bible. Imagine what a different world it would be today if we actually lived by these codes of kindness! However, it is clear than neither the Roman empire nor the Jews wanted to give up their taste for eating meat, making blood sacrifices to their respective gods, or engaging in the killing sports of the Roman coliseum, so these teachings were edited out of our Bible. On the subject of animal sacrifice, Jesus warns: "No blood offering, of beast or bird or man, can take away sin; for how can the conscience be purged from sin by the shedding of innocent blood? Nay, it will increase the condemnation" (Holy Twelve 33:2). If we are willing to consider that the same spark of light that lives within each of us also lives within the animals, we must ask ourselves what right we have to torture or kill our fellow creatures.

Let's now turn to the erasing of the Divine Mother from Christian teachings. We have already had a glimpse of how the Goddess was lost in Jewish history, but let us now discover what Jesus actually taught about the Divine Feminine, for it was this imbalance that the Master sought to restore in the highly patriarchal world in which he lived.

16

The Teachings That Must Be Suppressed

Wisdom, justice, beauty, harmony, and compassion are the qualities that have traditionally been identified with the Divine Feminine, yet it is also the irresistible power that destroys old forms and brings new ones into being, the inspiration of the love-in-action that is so needed to transform a culture radically out of touch with its soul.

ANNE BARING AND ANDREW HARVEY,
THE DIVINE FEMININE

While the destruction of Jesus's many lost teachings has caused a kind of sickness in our world today, there is nowhere that this imbalance is more profoundly felt than in the deletion of the Divine Mother. For nearly two thousand years, the Western world has been taught almost exclusively about God the Father, and this masculinely biased theology has shaped our use of language, law, culture, and property rights, teaching the values of aggression, dominance, and superiority to cultures around the world. It has also resulted in the abuse of women and children, as men have chosen the path of power over the path of love again and again. This extreme imbalance has left our societies ruthlessly patriarchal and censured the development of our spiritual, intuitive, and psychic natures, which, when cultivated, eventually leads us to gnosis.

However, when we study the New Testament gospels, it is clear that Jesus was not only an advocate of all people everywhere, regardless of age, caste, wealth, or education, but that he did not share the gender prejudices of the men of his day. Scholars have pointed out that his teachings of equality between men and women were perceived as dangerous by both the Jews and the Romans, since they called into question the existing patriarchal structure of the day. By honoring women as people in their own right, and as equals, Jesus threatened the power structures that were already in place in both the Jewish and Roman societies.

THE DELETED FEMININE VOICE

For over five hundred years before the birth of Jesus, the cult of Yahweh had excelled in suppressing all traces of either female culture or female deity. At the time when Jesus lived, women had no legal protection, except that given by their fathers, husbands, or sons. They were valued only for their ability to keep the house, make the meals, produce offspring, and serve a man's sexual needs. In many Jewish households, women were not even allowed to serve food or eat with guests if another male was present, a custom still prevalent in the Muslim world today.

In Hebrew culture, girls were given in marriage to an "appropriate man" of their father's choosing. A new wife's job was to obey her husband, have sex with him, run his household, and bear his children. If she did not fulfill those roles to her husband's satisfaction, she could be turned out as a beggar, a slave, a prostitute, or the unwanted extra mouth to feed in a man's home, since she had no way of making her own living. Hebrew law instructed that "every man who opened the womb of woman was blessed" (Luke 2:23), reiterating woman's primary mandate—to bear her husband's offspring. A woman could also be sold as property, passed from father to master like a possession.

At the time of Jesus, Jewish men could be married to multiple women, as we can observe in the case of King Herod, but divorce could only be initiated by the man. Women had no rights to choose their husbands or petition for divorce. The school of Hillel decreed that a man could divorce his wife for any reason whatsoever, simply by giving her a writ of paper, and this became the accepted position in subsequent Judaism.[1] While a man could have multiple wives, Jewish law declared that any woman who lost her virginity before marriage was to be burned or stoned to death. If a girl was raped, she was forced to marry her rapist, and if she was already betrothed or married, then she had to be killed.[2] Archaeologist and priest Roland de Vaux writes about the rights of women in ancient Israel:

> All the texts show that Israelites wanted mainly sons, to perpetuate the family line and fortune, and to preserve the ancestral inheritance . . . a husband could divorce his wife . . . women on the other hand could not ask for divorce . . . the wife called her husband Ba'al or master; she also called him *adon* or lord; she addressed him in fact as a slave addresses his master or a subject, his king.
>
> The Decalogue includes a man's wife among his possessions . . . the wife does not inherit from her husband, nor daughters from their father, except when there is no male heir. A vow made by a girl or married woman needs, to be valid, the consent of the father or husband and if this consent is withheld, the vow is null and void. A man has the right to sell his daughter.[3]

In Rome and Greece, although women did not have the same rights as men, in the first century CE they were able to study the arts, pursue medical studies, attend concerts or theaters, and take part in business, court, and social life. They could also engage in athletics, own property, become educated, and travel without male escorts.[4] In all sects of the Jewish faith, however, except the Essenes, women were not even encouraged to read or write, and they were certainly not allowed to own property. Their role was to sit as far away from the men as possible in the gallery section of the temple, while the men preached, argued, and prayed in the main synagogue below.

While Gnostic Christians honored both genders equally, the double standard of the Jews was soon adopted by the orthodox Catholic Church, supplanting the gender equality that Jesus had sought to reestablish. The role of Mary Magdalene as Yeshua's chief apostle was entirely deleted from Christian history, and "all books that contained references to a feminine divine were omitted. Those in which women played prominent ecclesiastical roles were not included. Those that urged the authority of personal experience over the authority of priests and bishops were left out. Essentially the books that supported the orthodox view and the power of the institution were kept, while those that did not were rejected. But they were not only rejected; they were collected and destroyed, their ideas vilified, and their proponents driven away or persecuted."[5] Historian Elaine Pagels writes that the efforts "to destroy every trace of heretical 'blasphemy' by the orthodox majority was so successful that until the discoveries at Nag Hammadi, all information on alternative forms of Christianity came only from orthodox records or attacks against them."[6]

Jesus's teachings about equality not only incensed the Pharisees, but even annoyed his own apostles. In the Gospel of Thomas, there is a scene where Simon Peter turns to the other disciples and says: "Let Mary leave us, for women are not worthy of Life" (114:1–3), indicating his complete abhorrence of the female gender. This expressed the prevailing mind-set of the Hebrew culture, where women existed only to serve men.

Biblical translators report that Jesus answered, saying: "Behold, I myself shall guide her being in order to make her *male,* that she, like you, shall become a living spirit, like you males, for every person who transcends being woman or man shall enter the Kingdom of Heaven" (Thomas 114:5–10). Yet the word *male* in this passage was originally the Greek *anthropos,* a word whose true meaning is a fully perfected human being, beyond either gender.[7] Later Jesus qualifies this transcendence of sexual orientation when he says: "When you make the two into One . . . so that you will make the male and the female into a single One, in order that the male is not made male, nor the female made female; when you make eyes into an eye . . . then shall you enter the kingdom" (Thomas 22:9–21).

This seemingly obtuse statement is about uniting the polarities within ourselves so that we can awaken our inner sight,* and, as we have seen, this concept lies at the very heart of Sacred Marriage taught by Jesus. By embracing both the yin and the yang aspects of our own natures, we gain the power to achieve enlightenment. But since the Gospel of Thomas was removed from orthodox canon, today most people have no concept that Jesus taught an inner alchemy that restores the balance between the two sides of ourselves—the masculine and the feminine. As we have seen, the Gnostics, or earliest followers of Jesus, honored both aspects of the Creator and taught this sacred alchemy of enlightenment. This was also a core teaching of the great Mystery Schools, and it is this spiritual union that takes place within the sacred heart that is needed to heal our world.

So let's take a look now at some of Jesus's teachings about the existence of the Divine Mother and Father, and the importance of honoring both aspects of the Divine.

---

*In the Gospel of Matthew, Jesus makes reference to this inner sight again. "The lamp of the body is the eye. If therefore your eye is good, your whole body will be full of light" (6:22–23).

THE FATHER-MOTHER OF CREATION

Today the only version of God that most people are familiar with is God the Father, yet Jesus referred to the Creator as the *Abba/Amma,* or Father-Mother God. Among the many texts that speak about the Divine Father and Mother are the Gospel of Thomas, the Gospel of Philip, the Secret Book of John, the Gospel to the Hebrews, and the Sophia of Jesus Christ. But many of these gospels were buried as a result of the papal edicts issued by the Emperor Constantine between the years 326 and 333.[8] In the Gospel of Philip, Jesus tells us, "Truth is the Mother, knowledge the Father . . . ,"[9] clearly revealing that there are two aspects of the Creator we can seek to comprehend. In a Gnostic writing called the Great Announcement, the origin of the universe is explained. From the power of silence appeared "a great power, the Mind of the Universe, which manages all things, a male . . . and the other . . . a great Intelligence . . . a female which produces all things."[10] The author explains that these two powers joined in union "are discovered to be duality . . . This is Mind in Intelligence and these are separable from one another, and yet are one, found in a state of duality." This Gnostic teacher explains: ". . . there is in everyone [a divine power] existing in a latent condition . . . This is one power divided above and below; generating itself, making itself grow, seeking itself, finding itself, being mother of itself, father of itself, sister of itself, spouse of itself, daughter of itself, son of itself—mother, father, unity, being a source of the entire circle of existence."[11]

In the Gospel of Thomas, Jesus speaks about the many intermediate gods or goddesses who live in other dimensions, but the Supreme Creator is above them all. "In the three heavens there are merely gods; where there is the Father and the Mother, I myself am with him" (Thomas 30:1–5). Jesus goes on to contrast our earthly parents with our divine ones, reminding the initiate of his true allegiance. "He who does not turn away from his [earthly] father and his mother in my way, will not be able to become my disciple; and he who does not love his [heavenly] Father and his Mother in my way, will not be able to become my disciple; for my mother has begotten me, but my true Mother gave me Life" (Thomas 101:1–8).

Valentinus and Marcus, both leaders in the early Gnostic church, called the Divine Mother the Grace, she who is before all things, and Incorruptible Wisdom, she who can only be found through the mystical and eternal Silence. She is equated with the Divine Sophia, the Mother of Wisdom. Valentinus also taught that although the Deity is essentially indescribable, it can be imagined as a dyad. Out of this twosome, creation is born. This includes the Divine Son and Daughter who are direct emanations of their celestial Parents. In Christianity we are only taught about the Father, Son, and Holy Spirit, and there is no mention of the Divine Feminine. Yet the Holy Spirit is the Mother or Daughter Spirit that permeates all things, that brings all things into being. In the Gospel of Thomas, Jesus warns us that "he who blasphemes against the Father, it shall be forgiven him; and he who blasphemes against the Son, it shall be forgiven him; but he who blasphemes against the Holy Spirit it shall not be forgiven him, either on earth or in heaven" (Thomas 44:1–7).

The teachings of the Gnostics make this abundantly clear. One Gnostic prayer begins: "From Thee, Father, and through Thee, Mother, the two immortal names, Parents of the divine being, and thou, dweller in Heaven, humanity, of the mighty name."[12] In the Gospel of the Holy Twelve, Jesus teaches: "In God there is neither male nor female and yet both are one, and God is the Two in One . . . Therefore shall the name of the Father and Mother be equally hallowed; for They are the great Powers of God, and the one is not without the other, in the One God . . ." (63:2).

The gnostic Gospel of Mary Magdalene also speaks about this theme. Mary Magdalene taught: "Christ has one Mother and she is the Queen of Heaven. The body is born of the Earthly Mother, but the soul of Light is born of the Heavenly Mother, and it is the Mother Spirit that awakens the soul of Light. Mary gave birth to a child in the world, but the Mother Spirit gave birth to the Christ. So it is with all who are anointed with Supernal Light."[13]

In the Gospel to the Hebrews, Jesus speaks about "my Mother, the Spirit," yet how many of us have been taught to pray this way? None, I venture. Most of us were never even told about the existence of a Divine Mother, let alone a Divine Daughter. But since all the forces in the cosmos have a complementary aspect, this certainly makes sense. Where there is a Father, there is also a Mother; if there is a Son, there is most certainly a Daughter. Does it not seem odd that we have been so conditioned by our patriarchal filters that we do not even question this, especially when biology dictates that it takes both sexes to create life?

VIRGIN OF THE WORLD

The Apocryphon of John (2:9–14) relates a powerful story about the apostle John who became grief-stricken after the crucifixion. In his sorrow John was given a vision. "And the heavens opened and the whole of creation which is under heaven shone and the world trembled. And I was afraid and I saw in the light . . . a likeness with multiple forms . . . and the likeness had three forms." When John asks, "Who is it?" the vision replies: "John, why do you doubt, and why are you afraid? I am the one who is with you always. I am the Father; I am the Mother; I am the Son."[14]

We learn more about this triple aspect in the Trimorphic Protennoia, a writing found among the Nag Hammadi texts. *Protennoia* is defined as "the Thought of the Father, the one born first of all beings, the one with three names who also exists alone, as one. She dwells at all levels of the universe, she is the revealer who awakens those [who] sleep, who utters a call to remember, who saves . . . [who] brings to the fallen world of mortality a salvation through knowledge and the 'Five Seals.'"[15]

I am . . . She who exists before the All . . .

I move in every creature . . . I am the Invisible One within the All . . .

I am both Mother and Father since I procreate Myself . . .

Figure 16.1. The Virgin of the World is she who brings the universe into being by herself. (Illustration by Tricia McCannon)

I am the Womb that gives shape to the All . . . I am the glory of the Mother.[16]

This is the Virgin of the World, the self-created One, who gives birth to the cosmos. I suddenly understood why there had been such an emphasis placed on the virgin birth in the scriptures. The Virgin is the Divine Mother linked to the birth of the world savior. But she is also the Creator herself who gave birth to both the Divine Father and Mother, who in turn gave birth to the Divine Daughter and Son. Historically, we find references to such virginal queens in the stories of heroes such as Hercules, Perseus, Horus, and Arjuna, whose fathers were thought to be gods in the celestial realms. However, the real significance of the Virgin Mother is "She Who Brings the Universe into Being" by herself.

In the Gospel of Mary Magdalene, a Gnostic gospel that contains 250 separate sayings attributed to Mary Magdalene, Mary teaches, "We have Father and we have Mother, for God is our Father and our Mother, though, indeed, the most high is beyond Father or Mother. There is no knowledge of the Father apart from the Mother, for it is Mother Spirit who gives birth to the image of the Son in whom the Living Father is revealed. So also shall Mother Spirit give birth to the image of the Daughter, so that the image of the Son will be perfect and the revelation of God Most High made complete."[17] Mary goes on to say:

> One who knows the Mother is near to the Father, but one who denies the Mother is far from the Father. There is not two, but only one God, and God is both Father and Mother.[18]

> If you blaspheme the Mother Spirit, there will be no one to save you, for she is the Spirit of salvation and your very life.[19]

Mary also speaks about the Divine Mother's many manifestations in the various planes.

> I was with the Risen Savior, and beheld the Mother. In the first heaven, she was the Radiant Earth of Paradise. In the second heaven, she was the Starry Night Sky. In the third heaven, she was a Great Fire. In the fourth heaven, she was the Great Angel and the Celestial Temple, and the Holy Sacrifice. When I beheld her in the fifth heaven, she was the Glory of the Anointed abiding there, in the sixth heaven, she was Fire and Ice and the End-of-Days. In the seventh heaven, she was the Great Luminous Assembly, and the Holy Throne, and the image of the One Who Sits Upon the Throne, but in the supernal abode I cannot say what she was like. One must go look and see for oneself.[20]

THE HUMANE GOSPEL OF CHRIST

In the past century several new gospels have surfaced that express these same fundamental concepts. They are the Humane Gospel of Christ, the Unknown Life of Jesus Christ, the Gospel of the Holy Twelve, and the Gospel of Mary Magdalene, all of which have powerful discovery stories, but I will only share two of them in this chapter.

The discovery of the Humane Gospel of Christ first came about through the research of a highly respected British scholar, Professor John Marco Allegro. Allegro was on the original translation team of eight scholars who performed the editorial work on the Dead Sea Scrolls. A scholar of both ancient Aramaic and Hebrew, Allegro taught courses on the Old Testament at the University of Manchester in England, and his credentials were exemplary. However, during his many years of translation on the Dead Sea Scrolls, Allegro became aware of the Jesuits' agenda of suppression. Wanting to preserve the integrity of one of the most important of these gospels, he smuggled the Humane Gospel of Christ out of the Vatican, essentially ending his own career. But the importance of this scroll was worth it, for this gospel purportedly contained the unedited teachings of Jesus himself!

This gospel was written in both ancient Aramaic and Hebrew, like the other Dead Sea Scrolls, and once Allegro had finished his translations into English, he sought a channel for bringing this information to light. He selected a Jehovah's Witness named Frank Mucci, hoping that these teachings would make their way out into the world through his church. But in the years following the gospel's release Mucci himself was actively persecuted by other Christian groups who wanted to keep this information secret. To preserve this gospel, Mucci founded the Edenite Society in 1979 and published a limited edition of what has since become known as the Humane Gospel of Christ. Now, since the death of Professor Allegro, no one knows exactly where the original scroll is hidden, so the legitimacy of these writings can no longer be proven. However, the Humane Gospel is similar to other Gnostic gospels in both substance and style. In it we find Jesus speaking about this same Divine Mother and Father:

> Truly, I say unto you, God is neither male nor female and yet both are one, and God is the Two in One. He is She and She is He. The Eternal All—our God—is perfect and complete and lacks nothing, our God is Infinite, and One. For as in the man, the Father is manifest, and the Mother hidden; so in the woman the Mother is manifest, and the Father hidden.
>
> Therefore, I say unto ye, shall the name of the Father and the Mother be equally hallowed and reverenced, for They are the great powers of God, and the one is not without the other in the One Infinite God.
>
> For from the All-Parent, cometh forth all life and glory, male and female both. Yeah, for the Eternal All, the First Father bringeth forth every kind of life into existence and He is in them all, and they are all in Him. (Holy Twelve 63:2–3)

THE UNKNOWN LIFE OF JESUS CHRIST

The discovery of the Unknown Life of Jesus Christ came about through the research of Nicholas Notovitch, a Russian journalist who journeyed through Kashmir, India, and Tibet at the close of the Russo-Turkish War (1877–1878). Notovitch passed through Afghanistan, India, and the Punjab, moving toward Ladak, the high, mountainous area between India and Tibet. There he heard rumors of some secret records that chronicled the teachings of Jesus. These writings were said to be hidden in a Buddhist monastery in Himis, a very remote area of Ladak. Determined to find them, Notovitch climbed some eleven thousand feet above sea level to finally arrive at the remote monastery. At first the high lama told Notovitch that he had no knowledge of these writings. But as fate would have it, Notovitch fractured his leg after leaving the monastery and was then carried back to the monastery to recover. During the

THE TEACHINGS THAT MUST BE SUPPRESSED ❧ 323

many weeks of his convalescence, he won the trust of the head lama, who finally allowed him to see, then copy, these lost records.

In 1894 Notovitch published a small but important book, called *The Unknown Life of Jesus Christ,* that, according to Notovitch, was written only three or four years after Jesus's death. It had been stored at the Himis monastery for nearly two thousand years to protect it from those who wanted these teachings destroyed. This short but amazing account shares passages not found in other gospels. The lama told Notovitch that "Issa [Jesus] is a great prophet, one of the first after the twenty-two Buddhas; he is greater than any of the Dalai Lamas, for he constitutes a part of the spirituality of the Lord . . . his name and his deeds have been recorded in our sacred writings, and whilst reading of his great existence spent in the midst of erring people, we weep over the horrible sin of the pagans, who assassinated him after putting him to the most cruel tortures."[21] The lama's reference here was to both Jews and Romans, both heathens in his eyes.

"Enter into your temple," Jesus tells us in this gospel, "into your own heart, illuminate it with good thoughts, patience and the unflinching confidence you should place in your Father . . . For God has created you in his image; innocent, pure of soul, with a heart filled with kindness, and destined, not to the conception of evil projects, but to be the sanctuary of love and justice."[22] Jesus also speaks about the importance of honoring women, a teaching that was obviously excised from our New Testament gospels.

Respect woman, for she is the mother of the universe and all the truth of divine creation dwells within her. She is the basis of all that is good and beautiful, as she is also the germ of life and death. On her depends the entire existence of man, for she is his moral and natural support in all his works. She gives you birth amid sufferings; by the sweat of her brow she watches over your growth, and until her death you cause her the most intense anguish. Bless her and adore her, for she is your only friend and support upon earth.

Respect her, protect her; in doing this, you will win her love and her heart, and you will be pleasing to God; for this shall many of your sins be remitted. Therefore love your wives and respect them, for tomorrow they shall be mothers, and later grandmothers of a whole nation. Be submissive towards your wife; her love ennobles man, softens his hardened heart; tames the beast and makes of it a lamb.

Just as the God of armies separates day from night and the land from the waters, so woman possesses the divine talent of separating good intentions from evil thoughts in men. Therefore I say to you: After God, your best thoughts should belong to women and to wives, women being to you the divine temple wherein you shall most easily obtain perfect happiness.

Draw your moral strength from this temple; there you will forget your sorrows and failures, you will recover the wasted forces necessary to help your neighbor. Do not expose her to humiliation; you will thereby humiliate yourself and lose the sentiment of love, without which nothing exists here below. Protect your wife, that she may protect you and all your family; all that you shall do for your mother, your wife, for a widow, or another woman in distress, you shall have done for God.[23]

Imagine a world that had actually honored these teachings over the past two thousand years. What a difference it would have made! Even today, if men actually began to treat their wives, sweethearts, daughters, and sisters with the same privileges, dignity, freedom, and respect that they claim for themselves, it would utterly transform our world.

The discovery of these sacred texts about the Divine Mother and Father confirmed my own experiences with Rigel and Auriel. My guides had long ago explained to me that they were the Father and Mother of Creation. "We have been known by many names on many worlds," they said, "but we are always one and the same. We are the eternal movement of the Great Cosmic Ocean, the Source and the beginning of life, the substance and the essence of creation itself. We live in you, and you in us, and the pathway of your journey leads straight to the heart of union."

17

The Divine
Daughter and Son

*Only when we begin to understand how vast the Mother is
will we begin to understand how powerful she is, and how
powerful we, her divine children, can be when surrendered
to her, guided by her, infused with her immense, passionate,
and transfiguring sacred force.*

ANNE BARING AND ANDREW HARVEY,
THE DIVINE FEMININE

As I contemplated what I had learned thus far about the Divine
Mother hidden even with Christianity, this led me to consider all the
many ways in which she had been worshipped in the world. Of all
of her aspects I was most drawn to the Goddesses of wisdom: Isis,
Sophia, and Mary. These women seemed to be incarnations of Auriel,
the Creatress of life, the profound spirit guide who had so transformed my life.

This led me to think about the true nature of Mary Magdalene. Like most of us, I had been raised to believe that Mary Magdalene was a fallen woman whose wayward path had been redeemed by Jesus. I wondered how, after all these centuries of shame and denigration, I was to ever discover the truth about who she really was. As I began to study the Gnostic teachings and the collection of her sayings, I realized that the wisdom she had taught had been just as profound as Jesus's teachings. Once a disciple had asked Mary Magdalene, "How can I come to know the Lord?" and she had replied, "Become empty, like a cup and let the Mother Spirit pour the Lord and her presence into you."[1] I realized then that my own innate prejudice, conditioned throughout a lifetime, had only taught me to acknowledge God as a male. To truly understand and embrace her, I would have to open my heart.

Around that time Auriel appeared in my dreams. One night I found myself walking through a beautiful garden full of honeysuckle, violets, and orchids with a lily pond to one side. I came upon a mysterious archway covered in vines. A radiant female figure stood before the archway, but I could not tell if this being existed in this world or the next. She was delicate and smelled of flowers, and her robes looked Asian, like a China doll's.

"Who are you?" I whispered, almost afraid to breathe. Her smile released the radiance of love, wafting out across the small distance that separated us.

"Do you not recognize me?" she answered telepathically.

"Auriel, is that you?"

"Yes, it is I."

"But why are you dressed like that?" I didn't just mean the Asian satin robes. I meant her Eastern appearance.

"In this incarnation I am known as Quan Yin, the bodhisattva of compassion."

Bodhisattva of compassion . . . Yes, bodhisattvas were souls who were entirely free of the wheel of karma but had returned to Earth to help humankind. There was no greater sacrifice. In coming back to Earth

Figure 17.1. Quan Yin is the Mother of Boundless Compassion and Mercy. Here she holds a dragon fan in her hand, a reference to the kundalini life force to which she is connected. (Illustration by Tricia McCannon)

they took the chance that they would forget their heavenly origins, and become trapped in the worlds of illusion again.

"But you are the Mother of Creation. Why would you choose to take a human form?" Even as I spoke, she began to morph, becoming the Native American teacher called White Buffalo Calf Woman. Suddenly there were teepees in the landscape behind her and smoke rising from a distant fire. I jerked backward. Now she had long dark hair and buckskin clothes, a strong jaw and a chiseled nose. She was holding a long peace pipe. "Auriel, why do you look that way? Are you White Buffalo Calf Woman?"

Figure 17.2. White Buffalo Calf Woman is the Native American wisdom teacher who taught the seven sacred rites to the people. These include the sacraments of the sweat lodge, the sun dance ceremonies, and the peace pipe of balance between the male and female. (Illustration by Tricia McCannon)

Her mouth turned up in a mysterious smile. "Who do you think I am, child?" She seemed to be hanging a white cowhide up on a line. Then, before I could even digest what I was seeing, she morphed again. Now we stood together, floating down the waters of the Nile on a graceful reed boat with a curved prow. Hieroglyphs were painted on the hull and a lantern hung from a hook at the front of the boat, used to navigate the waters in darkness. But the sun was shining, and a canopy of red and blue fabrics shielded us from the sun's rays, keeping the glare from our eyes. We seemed to be in Egypt.

"Mother," I whispered, "where are we now?" although I knew before I said it. The blue waters of the Nile drifted around us, and on either side of the river the brown desert sands floated by. Auriel was clothed as a graceful queen in a white linen dress and a gold belt, with laced sandals on her feet. Two armbands wound around her arms. Around her neck was a sunburst collar of lapis, carnelian, and gold. She turned in reassurance. "Isis?" I stammered, although I knew that it was Auriel. The same exquisite energies of unconditional love radiated out from her.

"Welcome, daughter, to the land of rushes, to the gentle papyrus boats, to the low-flying swallows and languorous days of beauty. Come. Allow yourself to float, as we once did, down the Nile." I was too flabbergasted to speak. I had long suspected that I had had lives as both a queen and a priestess in Egypt, but somehow I knew that this was beside the point. "You asked me once if we had incarnated in Egypt. Indeed we did. Did Isis, she whom you know as Isis, not embody me? One heart for her people, for her son and husband, and for Truth above all. Was she not the teacher of healing, love, and immortal life—she with her wise son Horus?"

Figure 17.3. Isis is the I AM presence of the Divine Mother. She was the Goddess of Healing, Wisdom, and Magic in ancient Egypt. (Illustration by Tricia McCannon)

"Are you Isis?" I stammered. My head was swirling. *Wasn't this Auriel?*

"Yes, whom did you think I was?"

"Auriel, the Divine Mother."

"And is this not the same as the Goddess Isis? You have sought to understand her nature. Then look at mine own; look at your own. Isis was the divine embodiment of the Sacred Mother for her people. Living it, breathing it, being it."

"She was an incarnation of you?" *Was this why Auriel had revealed herself in three different forms?*

"Yes, even as Horus was an incarnation of Rigel, the Father, who is also the Son. Divine Wisdom, Divine Truth. We came to Earth together at that time."

My thoughts were swirling.

"But why? Why did you come?"

"To rebuild the planet, of course, to rebuild the age. All had been wiped clean in the Great Flood, and your precious Earth cried out to the Heavens, and her cry was answered."

"Are you the female Christ?" I asked softly.

"Yes. I am the Mother of Creation. Whenever you would rebuild you must first have a generator. The heart is the generator. I am the heart."

"Why are you showing me this, Auriel?"

"Because you are the same."

"The same. What do you mean?"

"I mean that you too carry the sacred heart within you. You carry the compassion and wisdom of my teachings, and because my heart was there in Isis, this means that you were there as well."

I struggled with this concept. *What did she mean?* "Are you saying that I am Isis?"

"No, I am saying that Isis embodied my heart—the heart of divine service—and that you do this as well. Thus you are one and the same."

For the first time I glimpsed how she might have incarnated in these different cultures. "Are you saying that you lived as each one of these female masters?"

"I am saying that the heart that beat in Isis, and in Quan Yin, and in White Buffalo Calf Woman, is the same heart that beats inside of you. It is my heart, the heart of unconditional love." I thought about how we are all aspects of our Divine Parents, spirits that live within the body of the universe. Could it not be said that if everything is created by the Mother and Father, then the heart that lives inside of them lives in us as well?

"This is true," she answered, without my having to say a word. Our communication was now telepathic. "Yet there are those who know it not, and claim it not. There are those who flee from the heart that beats within their own chests, the place where true wisdom and purity dwells. Many are the souls who would long to rest, but they know not where to release their burdens." *What burdens was she speaking of?* I heard the answer in my mind. "The burden of the false self, the troubled self, the persecuted self, the hungry self, the abandoned self, the unforgiving self, the frightened self. These are the ones who run from knowing me and resting in the place of all forgiveness. They have not disentangled their souls from the ego. They run from the memory of the Divine because the world of light and shadow has convinced them that it is real."

I found myself struggling with this answer. Of course I knew that the ego often blocks us on our quest toward enlightenment. The ego is afraid of dying and of not being good enough to be loved. It was the higher self that had the power to transcend the problems of this world, but we still had to deal with the challenges of the physical realms, and most of the time these problems seemed pretty real to me. "But is the world of light and shadows not also real?" I asked. "The world of taxes and jobs, money and survival—are these not also real enough to be contended with?"

"Contended with, yes," she said. "But real, they are not. Where is it written that you must yoke your lives to pain and torment? Where is it written that those around you must command your very being with demands you did not write, but have chosen to be a servant unto? It is not written, because it is not true. All the burdens that you would place upon yourself, you have chosen in some way. Your jobs, your marriages, your schedules, your laws, even your taxes. These are human-created. They are not of God."

I felt frustrated. "So you're saying we live in a terrible system?" I half-joked.

"I am saying that this dance of life can be created in an infinitude of ways. What you choose in your world is really up to you. You and your brothers and sisters may create societies in any way you wish. You may create relationships and loved ones in any way you wish. So often you struggle against customs, mores, rules and regulations, and limiting belief systems, as if they were substantial. They are not. They are human-created and not of God. All that we have required of you is that you eat and sleep and love one another. These commandments are written by us, and no others."

"But why have you appeared to me in all these forms?" I asked, still puzzled.

"My dear one, do you not understand who I am yet? I have many forms and many faces across the universe. To the degree that you are open to my benediction, you too may become a vessel for my spirit. You too may embody me, for my essence lies dormant within the matrix of your heart, like a seed waiting for the sun."

My linear mind fumbled to comprehend the immensity of what she was saying. "Auriel, are you saying that you incarnated as all of these goddesses? That you were each of them?"

"I was. I am." She morphed back into the petite figure of Quan Yin, and suddenly we were in the lotus garden again. There were lilies growing in the pond at her feet. "In this incarnation I was born from the tears of Avalokiteshvara, the white avatar of compassion."

"But how can you also be the daughter, if you are the Divine Mother?"

She laughed, and the sound was like musical chimes. "I am the

Mother, I am the Daughter, I am the sage. I give birth to the Son, who becomes the Father, who in turn gives birth to me." This was deep. It was as if the entire universe were in a constant rotation of male and female roles, playing out this same cosmic dance in an endless circle of expression.

"I don't understand," I whispered softly.

Auriel smiled. "Oh, but you will . . ." Then she began to dissolve into thin air. A moment later, I woke up.

THE COSMIC DANCE

As I tried to wrap my mind around what this could mean, it seemed as if there were some sort of great cosmic drama being played out between the Divine Mother and Father who periodically descended to Earth. I thought of the sweet Mother Mary who had given birth to Jesus, and of Jesus saying that he was one with the Divine Father. Then I thought about Maryam or Mary Magdalene, who may also have been the female aspect of the Christ, long denigrated in Western theology. If Jesus and Maryam had had a child, then they might have essentially given birth to another aspect of themselves. This was the trinity that had long been taught in Egypt: Divine Mother, Father, and Child, exemplified by Isis, Osiris, and Horus. When Osiris was slain, Egyptians believed that his spirit had returned in his son Horus. "And the father becomes the son, and the son, the father." Maybe this was true for the Divine Mother as well. Maybe Mary Magdalene was the Daughter aspect who had come to Earth as Jesus's partner and wife, while Mary Anna was the Mother aspect. In India there are similar trinities: Krishna had Yashoda as his mother, and Radha as his soul mate, incarnations of the Divine Feminine in two different forms.

THE GOSPEL OF THE HOLY TWELVE

Years later I was to come across a remarkable gospel, called the Gospel of the Holy Twelve, which addresses this very subject. Like Nicholas

Notovitch's discovery of the Unknown Life of Jesus Christ, this gospel was preserved in a Buddhist monastery in Tibet for centuries. Translated from the original Aramaic, it was first published at the turn of the twentieth century by the Reverend Gideon Ouseley, a priest in the Catholic Apostolic Church of England. This gospel relates many of the familiar stories from Matthew, Mark, Luke, and John but includes chapters deleted from the original gospels. This gospel is believed to be the original Gospel of Matthew that was mentioned by St. Jerome and other early church fathers before the Catholic *correctores* rewrote and edited the texts to reflect church policies at the Council of Nicea in 325 CE.

Historically, we know that the apostle Thomas went to India, and there were other disciples in China and Tibet who may have also preserved a copy of these gospels in their original form before the church *correctores* changed them. By storing Jesus's teachings safely in remote monasteries, perhaps these disciples hoped to keep them safe so that they might be recovered in a future age, such as our own. Such foresight was probably the real reason that Jesus was so adamant that his brother Thomas go to Asia, knowing full well the corruption that might unfold in the centuries following his ministry. Jesus even speaks about this in the Gospel of the Holy Twelve:

But there shall arise after you men of perverse minds, who shall, through ignorance or through craft, suppress many things which I have spoken unto you, and lay to me things which I have not taught, sowing tares among the good wheat which I have given you to sow in the world. Then shall the truth of God endure the contradiction of sinners; for thus it hath been, and thus it will be.

But the time cometh when the things which they have hidden shall be revealed and made known, and the truth shall make free those which were bound . . . Woe is the time when the spirit of the world shall enter into the Church, and my doctrines and precepts shall be made void through the corruptions of men and of women.

Woe to the world when the light is hidden. Woe to the world when these things shall be. (Holy Twelve 44:7–8)

The Gospel of the Holy Twelve reveals a set of twelve new commandments, as well as a version of what later became known as the Nicene Creed with prayers to the Divine Mother and Father. These twelve new commandments cover the basic admonitions not to lie, cheat, steal, or kill, as well as to honor our parents, and "do unto others as we would wish to be done to." But there are also new commandments "to protect the weak and oppressed and all creatures that suffer wrong," "to make no impure marriages, where love and health are not," and to honor "One Eternal, Father-Mother of Heaven" (Holy Twelve 46:10–21). While these last three commandments were not in line with the political objectives of the church, the commandment "not to eat the flesh, nor drink the blood of any slaughtered creature; nor yet anything which bringeth disorder to your health or senses" (Holy Twelve 46:12) was probably the covenant that the church would have resisted most, since it promoted vegetarianism. In this gospel Jesus tells us: "I manifest myself unto you in all created forms . . . Inasmuch as ye have done it unto one of the least of these, my brethren, yet have done it unto me" (Holy Twelve 66:10).

In the Gospel of the Holy Twelve we discover Jesus with his disciples near a fountain close to Bethany, telling them about how the visible and invisible worlds work together, and that through the natural world we might enter into knowledge of the spiritual worlds.

The things which are seen and pass away are the manifestations of the unseen which are eternal; that from the visible things of nature ye may reach to the invisible things of the Godhead, and by that which is natural, attain to that which is spiritual.

Verily the *Alohim* [Elohim] created man in the divine image, male and female,* and all nature is in the image of God; therefore is God

---

Alohim is obviously a reference to *Elohim,* or "the gods that came from the sky."

both male and female, not divided, but the Two in One, Undivided and Eternal, by Whom and in Whom are all things, visible and invisible. From the Eternal they flow, to the Eternal they return. The spirit to Spirit, soul to Soul, mind to Mind, sense to Sense, life to Life, form to Form, dust to Dust. (Holy Twelve 63:5–6)

This passage embraces the concepts of both Immanence and Transcendence, telling us that the physical world is a way for us to experience the presence of God in the here and now.

THE TWO DIVINE CHILDREN OF GOD

While Jesus addressed the Creator of all as the *Abba/Amma,* or Father/ Mother God, many of us know very little about the Divine Son and Daughter, celestial siblings and lovers who make up a tetrad of beings from which the entire cosmos is created. This Daughter has been called the Shekinah, or breath of God, but she is also known as Sophia, a direct emanation of Wisdom. We shall learn more about her in the next chapter.

Jesus speaks about the Divine Daughter and Son in the Gospel of the Holy Twelve, and how these two presences continue to incarnate throughout time, returning to the world in many forms. He reminds us that the knowledge of these great beings has been taught in previous eras, and that humanity has confused this higher truth with superstition and foolishness, assigning these roles to the gods and goddesses in earlier centuries.

In the beginning God willed, and there came forth the beloved Son, the divine Love, and the beloved Daughter, the holy Wisdom, equally proceeding from the One Eternal fount; and of these are the generations of the Spirits of God, the Sons and Daughters of the Eternal. And these descend to earth and dwell with men and teach them the ways of God, to love the laws of the Eternal and obey them, that in them they may find salvation.

Many nations have seen their day. Under diverse names have They been revealed to them, and they have rejoiced in Their light; and even now They come again unto you, but Israel receiveth them not. Verily I say unto you, my twelve whom I have chosen, that which hath been taught by them of old time is true—corrupted by the foolish imaginations of men. (Holy Twelve 63:8–11)

Maryam also addresses these same precepts in the Gospel of Mary Magdalene.

If Christos can appear as a male, then surely Christos can appear as a female. Those who deny holiness in womanhood do not understand holiness in manhood or womanhood, but are sorely bound to ignorance. Do not believe the father of lies. Believe in the Mother Spirit, whose name is the Spirit of Truth and Comforter![2]

Listen! The Holy Spirit is supernal, yet She is everywhere here below. She is the light of the heavens and the fire of Gehenna,* and She is the Life-power in all creatures in heaven and earth and beneath the earth—She is the All-In-All. If anyone is ignorant of Her, then they are surely not alive.[3]

THE FOUR TRINITIES OF GOD

The Gospel of the Holy Twelve opens with Jesus teaching about the four trinities that express the very nature of God.

Again Jesus taught them saying "God hath raised up witnesses to the truth in every nation and every age, that all might know the

---

*Gehenna is a word whose roots go back to Greek, originally from Hebrew, meaning the *Valley of Hinnom,* first mentioned in Joshua 15:8. In ancient times it referred to a garbage dump in a deep, narrow valley right outside the walls of Jerusalem, where fires burned the refuse to keep down the stench. It is also the location where bodies of executed criminals, or individuals denied a proper burial, would be dumped. Today, *Gehenna* is often used as a synonym for Hell.

will of the Eternal and do it, and after that, enter into the kingdom, to be rulers and workers with the Eternal. God is Power, Love
and Wisdom and these three are One. God is Truth, Goodliness
and Beauty, and these three are One. God is Justice, Knowledge and
Purity, and these three are One. God is Splendor, Compassion and
Holiness, and these three are One. And these four Trinities are One
in the hidden Deity, the Perfect, the Infinite, the One-ly.

Likewise, in every man who is perfected there are three persons,
that of the son, that of the spouse, and that of the father; and these
three are one. So in every woman who is perfected there are three
persons, that of the daughter, that of the bride and that of the
mother; and these three are one; and the man and the woman are
one, even as God is one.

Thus it is with God the Father-Mother in Whom is neither male
nor female, and in Whom are both; and each is threefold; and all
are One in the hidden Unity. (Holy Twelve 63:1–7)

This is exactly what Auriel was trying to explain to me. Not only
did the Divine Mother take the form of a wisdom teacher from China,
Egypt, and the Americas, but she revealed her celestial form behind the
mortal trappings. Jesus speaks about his periodic return to the world,
and that of Mary Magdalene's, in this next passage:

Again I say unto you, I and My Bride are one, even as Maria
Magdalena whom I have chosen and sanctified unto Myself as a
type, is one with Me. I and My Church are One; and the Church is
the elect of humanity, for the salvation of all.

The Church of the first-born is the Maria of God. Thus saith
the Eternal. She is My Mother and she hath ever conceived Me,
and brought Me forth as Her Son, in every age and clime. She is
My Bride, ever one in Holy Union with Me, her Spouse. She is My
Daughter, for she hath ever issued and proceeded from Me, her
Father, rejoicing in Me.

And these two Trinities are One in the Eternal, and are shown forth in each man and woman who are made perfect; ever being born of God and rejoicing in light, ever being lifted up and made one with God, ever conceiving and bringing forth God, for the salvation of the many.

This is the mystery of the Trinity in humanity; and moreover in every individual child of man must be accomplished the mystery of God, ever witnessing to the light, suffering for the truth, ascending into heaven, and sending forth the Spirit of truth. And this is the path of salvation, for the kingdom of God is within. (Holy Twelve 63:9–12)

Here Jesus is saying that the Divine Mother has incarnated as both his mother and his mate. Mary Anna is his mother, and Mary Magdalene is both his spiritual sister and his mate. From age to age these two divine presences incarnate, playing out the various roles of father, daughter, mother, son, and loving spouse in an eternal dance of opposites. This concept was a mind-blowing theology for the patriarchy of his day, and clearly too much for them to assimilate. But as we can observe, the excision of this profound revelation about the divine masculine and feminine forces in the cosmos was to create centuries of repression and suffering in our world.

18

Mary Magdalene and the Divine Sophia

His bride is the magnificent Sophia,
Who first, through immortal man, appeared as Divinity,
The Kingdom and the Father, the Self-originated,
Who revealed all.

THE SOPHIA OF JESUS CHRIST

While I had been given a glimpse of the Divine Mother in some of her many forms, like many of us raised as Christians, I had been programmed to believe that Mary Magdalene (Maryam) was a prostitute who had been saved by Jesus, and thus became his loyal follower. Yet the discovery of these ancient hidden texts honoring Maryam as Jesus's partner and equal had made me rethink everything. As I was to discover in my many years of research, the idea that Mary Magdalene was a woman of ill repute was a lie, invented by the patriarchy to marginalize Maryam's importance to the world and, with her, Jesus's message about the importance of equality between men and women.

This idea that Maryam had been a fallen woman was first advanced in 591 CE when Pope Gregory I delivered his Homily 33. As you will see in the excerpted passage below, Gregory makes several enormous suppositions, not the least of which is that Mary was a woman of ill repute because she used an expensive perfume to anoint Jesus's feet. Pope Gregory said:

> She whom Luke calls the sinful woman, whom [John] calls Mary, we believe to be the Mary from whom seven devils were ejected according to Mark. And what did these seven devils signify, if not all of the vices? . . . It is clear, brothers, that the woman previously used the unguent to perfume her flesh in forbidden acts.[1]

Yet modern-day scholar and Catholic priest Jean-Yves Leloup explains that the Greek word for *sinner* that was used in the Gospel of Luke was *harmartolos,* a term that means "anyone who has transgressed Jewish law." The Greek word for *harlot* is *porin,* and this word was never used in any of the four gospels in the story of the woman with the alabaster jar. This rite of anointing a priest-king before his death was an act that marks Mary Magdalene as an initiated priestess,

Figure 18.1. Mary Magdalene is the woman with the alabaster jar, the mysterious woman, spoken of in all four gospels, who anointed the feet of Jesus before the crucifixion. (Illustration by Tricia McCannon)

for these ancient rites were played out in the annual celebration of Ishtar and Tammuz. We find references to this not only throughout the Mediterranean world, but also in Ezekiel 8:14, where the temple women of Jerusalem mourn the slain Tammuz, the forerunner of Jesus himself. Leloup goes on to remind us that there is no direct reference to Maryam, or the woman who anoints Jesus's feet, as a prostitute in any of the four canonical gospels.[2]

While most of us did not receive this memo until the release of Dan Brown's best-selling book *The Da Vinci Code,* the revelation that Mary Magdalene was not a fallen woman is a seminal revision in Christian thought, for it begs the question, What was so important about Mary Magdalene that the church had to slander her for fourteen hundred years? *The Da Vinci Code* was based on Dan Brown's investigations of the 1982 book *Holy Blood, Holy Grail,* whose three authors had managed to decipher some of the many cryptic secrets of the Knights Templar, and why they were targeted by the Inquisition. As we will discover in the next chapter, some of the Knights Templar's secrets specifically focused on the partnership model between Jesus and Mary Magdalene, elevating women to the status of men, and this was not something the church was willing to abide. Similarly, the Gnostics and later the Cathars focused on this same partnership model and were destroyed nearly a thousand years apart by the orthodox church.

Just as the fictional story of Eve taking a bite of the apple from the Tree of Knowledge in Paradise was invented by the priests of Yahweh in order to support their takeover of Jewish theology, so too was Mary Magdalene's mythic fall from grace used to disparage, control, and malign women across the world, particularly when it came to their sexuality. Not only has this produced a double standard, it has created a shame-based censorship of women's sexuality and established men's prerogative to dictate all paternity rights. It has also been used to sanction the suppression of women's spiritual, financial, and land ownership rights for centuries.

In the last two hundred years, however, many documents have

emerged that have profoundly changed our worldview of the true role of Mary Magdalene, and it is time for us to revise our understanding of who she was and the role she played in Jesus's life and in the history of Christian thought. This transformation in thinking has wide-ranging ramifications, since this slander against the "weaker sex" was used to legitimize control, domination, and crimes against women. At its core this means that one sex is not superior to another; both male and female genders deserve the same rights to freedom, respect, and honor, and both can achieve enlightenment. So let's now take a look at what we have discovered about who and what Mary Magdalene was in her day, and what she is meant to become in ours.

THE MYSTERY OF MARY MAGDALENE

In the past few decades what has become clear in biblical research is that Mary Magdalene may well have been the most important single teacher, aside from Jesus, in the entire Christian movement. She was profoundly honored in the first few centuries after Christ by many Christian sects, not only as Jesus's partner, but as a teacher in her own right. Elaine Pagels writes: "The *Dialogue of the Savior* praises her not only as a visionary, but as the apostle who excels all the rest. She was known as the *Apostle of the Apostles,* the pre-eminent disciple of Christ's message. Jesus called her 'the Woman who Knew the All.'"[3] The writings that have come to light in recent years reveal a woman with the utmost intelligence and devotion, who was believed to be an incarnation of Sophia, the Goddess of Wisdom, herself. Images of her holding books of wisdom or teaching can be found in the stained-glass windows of many Celtic churches. Former nun and biblical researcher Margaret Starbird, the author of several books about Maryam, writes:

> Early exegetes of the Christian scriptures recognized Mary Magdalene as the figure of Holy Wisdom and the Bride from the Song of Solomon. . . . [They] understood her archetypal role

as the incarnation of the "Holy Sophia": Just as Christ embodied the Divine as the eternal Bridegroom, the Sophia was seen to be the incarnation of God's glory, the mirror of God's wisdom. The Shekinah, the divine consort of Yahweh, enjoyed similar status among the Jewish mystics. And among the earliest generations of Christians, it was Mary Magdalene who was cast in this role as "Sister-Bride" of Christ.[4]

This concept of the sister-bride is extremely important to understanding what has happened in our world today. Without the bride or the bridegroom, the cosmic balance of life itself is thrown out of equilibrium. The bride, of course, represents the Divine Mother or Daughter. She is the Earth or Moon Goddess of antiquity. She is also the complement of the Divine Son or solar lord, represented by Jesus. She is his "other half," his twin sister in the mirror of Creation. Without her, the bridegroom and the Kingdom of Earth are not whole. The loss of either polarity throws the entire cosmos out of balance. This was the real meaning behind the stories of the quest for the Holy Grail. Arthur, the wounded fisher king, the "once and future king" who is a symbol for Jesus (the lord of the Piscean Age), sees that the land has become barren because the Grail, or the Divine Feminine, has become lost. The patriarchal church is taking over the world, and all traces of the queen (Mary Magdalene) are being deleted from holy scripture.

The Gospel of Philip, originally suppressed by the Catholic Church, tells us that Jesus ". . . loved her more than the disciples and used to kiss her often on the mouth" (59:9). This gospel uses the Greek term *koinonos* to portray Mary Magdalene, a term meaning "fiancée," "spouse," or "companion."[5] This term implies not only a wife, but also a spiritual partner. For those who were raised to think that enlightenment is synonymous with celibacy, Catholic priest Jean-Yves Leloup reminds us that any part of human experience that is not embraced and lived by Jesus is a part that is not redeemed. "Might it not be that in this domain," Leloup writes, "as in so many others, Yeshua was the Teacher?

Figure 18.2. Mary Magdalene offers the bread of life to children.
Inspired by a stained-glass window in Norfolk, England.
(Illustration by Tricia McCannon)

The way that he shows us is neither one of repression (creating neurosis), nor of renunciation (asceticism). Nor is it the Freudian notion of civilized sublimation (normosis). It is instead the way of transfiguration: the human manifesting the divine."[6]

However, it is also clear, even at the time when Jesus was teaching, that some of the male disciples were jealous of his relationship with Maryam. In the Gospel of Philip we read that some of the male disciples asked of Jesus, "Why do you love her more than all of us?" to which the savior replied, "Why do I not love you as [I love] her?"[7]

Figure 18.3. Mary Magdalene and Jesus as a couple found in a stained-glass window in Wales. Notice that she is depicted with child.

As Jesus's mate, Mary was given certain secret teachings that were not imparted to the other disciples. We see this reflected in the Gospel of Mary, a story of Jesus appearing to Mary Magdalene after the crucifixion. In the gospel, Peter goads Mary into sharing a personal revelation from the master, then accuses her of lying. Thought to be written in the early part of the second century CE, the Gospel of Mary did not surface for over eighteen hundred years after Jesus until a single, fragmentary Coptic translation of a fifth-century manuscript was purchased in Cairo by Carl Reinhardt and brought to Berlin in 1896. Two additional fragments of this gospel have since come to light, both written in Greek, yet, to date, no complete copy of the Gospel of Mary has ever been found. Fewer than eight pages of this ancient sixteen-page papyrus survive, meaning that half of the original gospel is missing.

THE GOSPEL OF MARY

The story told in the Gospel of Mary takes place shortly after the crucifixion when the other apostles are in disarray. Understandably, they are afraid to go out into the world for fear that they will be killed.

The gospel opens six pages into it in the middle of a scene between the disciples and the risen Jesus. Jesus is answering their questions about the end of the material world and the nature of sin, teaching that all things are interwoven with each other, whether material or spiritual. However, Jesus also says that each person's nature will ultimately return to its original state or spiritual destiny. Ignorance, he says, is tied to the world of light and shadows, causing us not to recognize our own divine natures. In this way we succumb to sin, which leads to illness and death. Salvation, the master explains, is achieved by discovering the true nature of our divinity within, thus freeing us from the entrapments of the world. Jesus concludes with a warning not to be deluded by following some heroic leader or set of dogmatic rules. Instead, the disciples are to seek the child of true humanity within themselves and find their own peace within. Then, after commissioning the disciples to go forth and preach this message, Jesus departs.[8] The apostles despair that they will ever be able to go into the world to impart this teaching.

At this point in the story Maryam speaks up, bolstering their courage and reminding them that Jesus will be with them in spirit. "'Do not remain in sorrow and doubt, for his grace will guide you and comfort you. Instead, let us praise his greatness, for he has prepared us for this. He is calling upon us to become fully human.' Then Mary turned their hearts towards the Good, and they began to discuss the meaning of the teacher's words."[9]

At this point Peter turns to Maryam and asks whether the master has given her any special teachings. "Sister we know that the Teacher loved you differently from all other women," a statement in support of the idea that Jesus and Maryam were married.[10] Maryam then begins to tell the other disciples of a vision she has had where Jesus began to teach her about the deeper Mysteries. Here parts of the manuscript are missing, so we skip forward some five pages. When we drop back in, Maryam is relating Jesus's teachings about the seven stages of temptation that each soul must face. These are obviously linked to the seven deadly sins, and this is undoubtedly how Mary became linked to the story of seven sins in the first place. This story of a woman with seven deadly sins is told in the Gospel of Luke and may well have been how Luke and Paul knew of her, since Jesus's marriage was kept secret. Luke was a student of Paul's, and neither Luke nor Paul actually knew Jesus. They also did not know Mary Magdalene, since she left shortly after the crucifixion on a boat with Joseph of Arimathea and other disciples, landing in the south of France. This means that neither Luke nor Paul were present at the time when these events took place, and their accounts have to be secondhand. While all four of our New Testament gospels tell the remarkable story of the woman with the alabaster jar who anoints Jesus's feet before the crucifixion, it is only in the Gospel of John that we learn this woman was Mary Magdalene, or Mary of Bethany, the sister of Martha and Lazarus.

In the Gospel of Mary the teachings that Mary Magdalene relates to the other apostles are at a far more esoteric level than some of them are used to, so this startles the men. Peter then openly refutes Mary's teachings, offended that Jesus would relate such Mysteries to a woman. His pride makes it impossible for him to comprehend her words, believing, as Elaine Pagels puts it so beautifully, that "only he and his priests and bishops had a direct line to the godhead."[11]

Then Mary wept, and answered him: "My brother Peter, what can you be thinking? Do you believe that this is just my own imagination, that I invented this vision? Or do you believe that I would lie about our Teacher?"

At this point Levi spoke up: "Peter, you have always been hot-tempered, and now we see you repudiating a woman, just as our adversaries do. Yet if the Teacher held her worthy, who are you to reject her? Surely the Teacher knew her very well, for he loved her more than us. Therefore let us atone, and become fully human, so that the Teacher can take root in us. Let us grow as he demanded of us, and walk forth to spread the gospel, without trying to lay down any rules and laws other than those he witnessed."[12]

In this one incident we glimpse the vast chasm between the thinking of Peter and that of Mary Magdalene. Peter is the stubborn "rock" upon which the outer church is built, while Maryam is the teacher and mystic of the inner Mysteries. This two-tiered structure of inner and outer teachings was well established within the Mystery Schools and was the structure behind the original intent of the path that Jesus established. But because Peter could not open his heart to accept a woman's spiritual authority, this division in thinking was to cause a split in the early church. Peter's more limited patriarchal approach eventually inspired the formation of the Roman Catholic Church, while the inner teachings of Mary Magdalene went underground.

These teachings were preserved by the Gnostics for some two thousand years, surfacing briefly during the twelfth and thirteenth centuries in the wisdom teachings of the Albigensians, the Waldensians, the Cathars, and finally the Knights Templar, all of whom honored the Divine Mother and Father. In the many years after the crucifixion, Mary Magdalene's teachings were collected as she traveled and taught throughout France and England, and these teachings were eventually codified into 250 sayings, revealing Mary as an avatar whose wisdom is on par with that of Jesus himself. Here are just a few examples of Mary's teaching:

> Knowledge, understanding, and wisdom are not superior to love, for these come from union and it is love that unites. One who has love will have knowledge, understanding, and wisdom, but without love, no one is wise. If there is power without love, it is evil and will give birth to evil, but where there is love, power is exercised in wisdom. All good things come by way of love.[13]

> Of all things I wish you to have the Sacred Heart of Christ, which is compassion. For compassion is the womb of the Mother in which Christ is born, and in this, Christ will be born in you. Pray to the Mother Spirit to have her womb and to conceive and birth the Anointed in you. I will pray for you also.[14]

Because of the power of the *demiurgos,* you have forgotten yourself. You believe you are a child of darkness, yet you are a child of Light. Indeed! Truly, I say to you, you are a person of Light who has come from the Light, and if you remember yourself, you will know where your home is. This is the remembrance of the wedding feast, regarding which the Lord instructed us, "Do this in remembrance of me."[15]

In these passages Mary uses words such as the *Anointed,* the *Sacred Heart,* and the *Wedding Feast,* all metaphors for achieving sacred union. In the language of the Mysteries taught by Jesus, this is the union of the bride and bridegroom, the ego and the soul, matter and spirit, allowing

Figure 18.4. Mary and Jesus united as the bride and bridegroom in sacred union. Here she wears the crown of initiation as a priestess of Isis. (Illustration by Tricia McCannon)

us to open our hearts and awaken the inner sight. While there are many allusions to the bride and the bridegroom in canonical gospels, the church suppressed the alchemical process behind its true meaning, even assigning the role of the bride to themselves. The church is the "Mother Church" who married the bridegroom; however, as we have discovered, the true Hierogamos, or Sacred Marriage, can only be accomplished by the marriage of the inner male and inner female within the heart, creating a third element, the Christ consciousness. This is the child of wisdom and love. It is this fundamental teaching that lies at the heart of the true Christian Mysteries.

MARY OF BETHANY

While today there is still much confusion about the real identity of Mary Magdalene, for almost two thousand years she has been known as Mary of Bethany. Mary of Bethany was the younger sister of Lazarus and Martha; her wealthy family supported Jesus's mission. This identification of the two Marys as one is not only supported by the canonical gospels but was also widely accepted by Gnostic Christians, the Roman Catholic Church, and all Protestant religions. Yet as late as 1969, the Second Vatican Council suddenly decided that Mary and Mary of Bethany were two separate women, reversing its two-thousand-year tradition. Ironically, it was also at this time that the church retracted its longtime accusations against Mary Magdalene, acknowledging that there had never been any scriptural evidence that she was a prostitute.[16]

So let's take a moment to examine the evidence that these two women are one and the same. To do this we must return to the famous story of the woman with the alabaster jar. So important was this incident that it is one of only four events in the life of Jesus that is reported in all four canonical gospels.[17] The earliest version of this story comes from the Gospel of Mark, who relates that just before the Passover that leads to the crucifixion, the disciples are dining at the home of Simon the leper in Bethany. A woman comes into the room with an alabaster jar and pours an expensive ointment of spikenard onto the head and feet of Jesus, in essence, anointing him. The disciples complain that this oil is too expensive and that the money could be used to feed the poor, but Jesus rebukes them, saying that the woman has shown him a great honor; that he would not always be with them, while there would always be people who are poor. Forevermore, he tells them, this story should always be told in memory of her (Mark 14:9).

The Gospel of Matthew is a verbatim copy of the Gospel of Mark, having been written after Mark in about 80 CE. But in neither of these accounts are we told the mysterious woman's name. The third account comes from Luke, who changes the time and place and adds a few other details. Luke describes the woman drying the master's feet with her hair. Luke is also the only one who claims that this is the woman who has seven demons cast out of her. Since other details of this account are amiss, his information may have been an honest mistake, or else he may have been deliberately casting aspersions on Mary Magdalene, reflecting Paul's misogynistic attitudes.

However, the clearest account of this incident of the woman with the alabaster jar is found in the Gospel of John. Here the woman is clearly called Mary of Bethany, the sister of Martha and Lazarus, and she is not a sinner at all. The siblings are having supper with Jesus and the disciples in Bethany, and Martha is serving them dinner. As we have seen in other stories about Mary, she is humble, kneeling at Jesus's feet and anointing them, even wiping them with her hair. This chapter, John 12, follows directly on the heels of the chapter about Lazarus being raised from the dead, creating a clear connection between Mary Magdalene and the family of Bethany. In John 11 Mary runs out of the house and throws herself at Jesus's feet, weeping, and because of this Jesus brings Lazarus back from the dead. Only one chapter later, this same Mary weeps at her teacher's feet, knowing that he is about to go to his death. Jesus tells Mary to save the rest of the ointment to anoint his body after his death, an act that Mary Magdalene fulfills when she goes to the tomb after the crucifixion.

THE QUEEN AND THE SACRIFICIAL KING

Why, one might ask, is this story so important? And what is its true significance? In the ancient world, the act of anointing the king before his death was practiced only by the queen and the priestesses of Isis. In the Hebrew culture this was the duty-right of Asherah the queen, and her female attendants: It took place each year as part of the symbolic sacrifice of the dying and resurrected savior god Tammuz, just as in Egypt this same rite took place between Isis and Osiris when Isis anointed Osiris's body during the sacramental days of celebration each November. During this cosmic passion play, held throughout the Middle East and the Mediterranean, a young man would enter a cave and lie down on a bed of flowers and fragrant herbs for three days and three nights as if he were dead, as noted earlier. The queen and her priestesses would anoint his body, and mourn his death. Then, after three days, the youth would "arise from the dead," marking the annual celebration of new life.[18] These sacred rites had taken place throughout Egypt and the Levant for centuries in the annual honoring of Tammuz/Dumuzi, Adonis, and Osiris, so this was an act of consecration for the noble unblemished sacrificial king. "As priestess of the Goddess, their importance dates back through the centuries to the Neolithic period (7000–3500 BC), back to the time when God was honored and cherished as feminine throughout the lands that are now known as the Middle East and Europe."[19]

The term *Messiah* even means "anointed one." He is the soul who is willing to sacrifice himself for the tribe so that life may continue. *Messiah* is a phonetic cognate of *messehah,* meaning a "phallic pillar," and pouring libations over these pillars, or lingams, was a well-known rite in both India and the Middle East. "For millennia such ritual celebrations had occurred throughout the region, declaring the kingship of the sacred bridegroom. The Messiah was, by definition, the one united by marriage to the royal bride."[20] The Roman church would have also known about these rites since they still survived in remote villages well

Figure 18.5. The annual rites of kingly death and resurrection were played out in vast cosmic dramas all over the Middle East. The story of Mary's anointing Jesus's head and feet with her hair was a re-creation of those sacred rites, marking Mary Magdalene as the hidden queen or high priestess, just as Jesus was the sacrificial king. (Illustration by Sylvia Laurens)

into the sixth century.[21] These rites were not banned by the Catholic Church until the end of the fourth century CE.

The importance of this story in all four gospels cannot be overstated. For anyone who knows the Mysteries, it marks Jesus as the sacrificial priest-king and Mary of Bethany as his priestess-bride. We find other couples enacting similar rites throughout the entire Middle East: Inanna and Dumuzi, Isis and Osiris, Venus and Adonis, Ishtar and Tammuz, and Astarte and Ba'al. "Together the pair embodied the powerful familiar mythology of the sacrificed king and his beloved, a mythology that immediately resonated in every corner of the Hellenized Roman empire . . . Although pagan rites were sometimes celebrated with orgies, the deeper meaning of the Sacred Marriage rites was understood as an ecstatic celebration of the life force, the generous abundance of the earth and the cycles of life, death and rebirth that are the shared experience of the human family."[22]

In Egypt this divine pairing was expressed in the marriage of Isis and Osiris, then later as the virginal Mother Isis and her single Son Horus, reflecting the roles of the Mother Mary and Jesus in the orthodox church. Similarly, in India the noble Queen Yashoda gave birth to the enlightened Lord Krishna, while the beautiful Radha was Krishna's wife or spiritual companion. In the Hindu story the *Ramayana,* we also read about the noble avatar Rama, said to be an incarnation of Vishnu or God, whose sacred partner was Sita, his queen. In the stories of the gods of India, we find that at the higher levels of Creation the three lords Brahma, Shiva, and Vishnu all have their female counterparts. Brahma, the Creator god, has Sarasvati, the Goddess of Music and Wisdom; Shiva, the Transformer god, has Parvati, the Goddess of Love; and Vishnu, the Preserver god, has Lakshmi, the Goddess of Abundance. Thus it was well established that each aspect of God had its complement or counterpart, male and female in sacred union.

We also find references to this rite of anointing the king with oil in the Hebrew Song of Songs (1:12) from the Old Testament, a celebration song of the bride and bridegroom. Author Margaret Starbird writes: "It was the prerogative of the bride, representing the people of her domain, to unite with the king in a marriage ceremony that proclaimed his role as the anointed one—the chosen Messiah. Male prophets and priests later usurped the role of anointing kings of Israel, but most anciently the rite of anointing was associated with the Hierogamos, the sacred marriage, and was the exclusive prerogative of the royal bride."[23] This brings us back to the lessons of sacred union.

THE SACRED UNION

One of Jesus's most famous parables is that "he who has the faith of a mustard seed can move mountains." Yet what is a mustard seed? It is the vesica piscis or ichthys that Jesus taught to his initiates, a shape created by the overlapping of two circles, representing the perfect union. Greek cosmology used the language of number to symbolize the process of emanation through which the entire universe comes into manifestation. This begins with the unity of the One, representing God, which creates the Two, and then all else flows from this. The divine Son—whether it was thought to be Jesus, Horus, or Apollo—is born from the vesica piscis and becomes the mediator that lies between the realms of form and the pure unadulterated realms of Spirit. This mediator contains in itself both Oneness and multiplicity, created through the merger of the male and female in partnership.[24] This is how the world comes into being. Jesus would have known all of this, having been an initiate in all the great Mystery teachings. "Drawn so that each circle touches the other's center, this shape produces an opening to the womb from which are born the geometric shapes and patterns of the Universe. The first three shapes to emerge are the triangle, square, and pentagon, containers of the ratios and relationships required to generate all regular shapes and forms that can be constructed using a geometer's compass, straight edge and pencil."[25]

This balance between the male and the female is, in essence, a doorway for enlightenment, and this was the partnership model demonstrated by Yeshua and Maryam. In the first few decades after Christ, this model was adopted by the earliest disciples who traveled throughout the Mediterranean, teaching in pairs and using the sign of the fish to indicate their knowledge of the sacred union. But this partnership model was abandoned when Paul decreed that female disciples should not have equal status to men.

Knowing that the people of Judea were not trained in such esoteric Mysteries, and had inherited the gender prejudices of the Pharisees and Sadducees, who were completely male dominated, Jesus spoke in

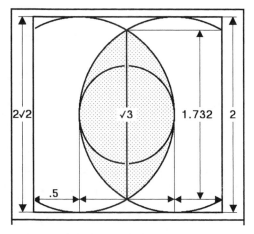

Figure 18.6. Greek cosmology used the language of number to symbolize the process through which the entire universe comes into being, beginning with the unity of the One that split itself into Two, creating the vesica piscis, or the divine doorway of sacred union. The ichthys creates a doorway through which the unmanifest realms can enter the world of form. It is the shape of a woman's yoni and the opening where the seed of life comes out of a man's phallus. It is also the shape of the eyes that are windows to the soul.

parables about these concepts. In the Gospel of Matthew (22:1–10) he tells the story of a king who holds a marriage banquet for his son, but the guests find excuses to avoid attending. Here Jesus is giving us a metaphor for the marriage of sacred union—many are invited, but few have the wisdom to attend. "This is the cornerstone that the builders of the Church rejected," writes Margaret Starbird. "Clearly the Roman dominated world of the first century was not ready to embrace a gospel of gender equality and inclusiveness, but the seed of this radical doctrine was planted at the very heart of the story—the seed of the Kingdom of God, both within and around us, and in our midst."[26]

MARY THE MAGDALA, MARY SOPHIA

The name *Mary Magdalene* has long puzzled scholars, for there was no village of Magdal at the time when Mary and Jesus lived. So this is obviously a title of some sort. Historian Barbara Walker tells us that *Magdalene* means "she of the temple tower," a reference to the triple tower in Jerusalem, one tier of which bore the name of the queen Mariamne, the incarnation of the Goddess Mari.[27] This is also a reference to the Hebrew Song of Songs, when the *Magdala* is called the watchtower. This goes back to a time when the priestly women of Isis and Nepthys were keeping watch to protect the young Horus, the king who would one day restore light to the Kingdom of Egypt at a time when the dark lord Set, who had murdered Osiris, was in power. This lineage of Magdalene sisters was passed on to the Jews at the time when King Solomon married a princess of Egypt. This sacred order of priestess women was then sheltered in the Temple of Asherah, built by Solomon at a time when both the male and female aspects of God were honored. You will recall that in the Holy of Holies within the temple, above the Ark of the Covenant, there were two statues of the male and female entwined in an act of conjugal love. However, in the years following the Jewish exile, this spiritual order of priestesses had to go underground because of the sanctions against women holding spiritual power in Jerusalem. So Mary Anna, Mary Magdalene, Mary Salome, and Mary Jacobi were all priestesses of this order who were hidden within the innermost ranks of the Essenes.

The term *Magdala* has also been translated by biblical scholars to mean "great," so Mary Magdalene would mean Mary the Great. In Greek, her title was *H Magdalhnh,* whose numerical meaning is 153 in the esoteric teachings of Gematria, a Hebrew literary device that encodes sacred numbers into sacred texts. This is the number of fishes that were caught in the net in the Gospel of John, a number linked to the vesica piscis, or vessel of the fish. This shape has long been universally associated with the Goddesses of love. It is the chalice of creation, the doorway to life, and the womb of the Sacred Mother through which the universe is born. To the initiate, this number and name marks Mary Magdalene as the sacred container, or keeper of the Holy Grail.

Gnostics thought of Mary as an incarnation of Sophia herself, the

Figure 18.7. Mary Magdalene was considered an incarnation of the Goddess Sophia, the Greek and Hebrew Goddess of Wisdom. Her path was the Way of the Chalice, a way centered on the path of forgiveness and love. Here she appears with the dove and the chalice, indicating the sacred Way of the Return. (Illustration by Tricia McCannon)

Mother of Wisdom. It is from *sophia* that we get the word *philosophy*, meaning a "lover of wisdom."* To the Gnostics, Sophia is the Great Mother who exists above and below all things. She is the essence of love, while her counterpart, the Father, is the essence of truth. Kabbalah (Jewish mysticism) teaches that this Divine Couple set the entire universe in motion. These are the two Perfected Ones who dwell in the Cosmic

---

*The word *philosophy* was coined by the Greek sage Pythagoras and lay at the heart of his teachings.

Egg, and it is their interaction that creates the eternal dance of life. They are the yin and yang of Taoism, the male and female most high.

Kabbalah teaches that Kether, the Unknowable God, split itself in two, creating Binah, the Divine Father, and Chokmah/Sophia, the wise Divine Mother. It is from this dyad that all else is born. They, in turn, create the Son and the Daughter of God. She is the feminine soul of the universe who lives within all things. Gnostics referred to the Mother and Daughter as Sophia the Greater and Sophia the Lesser. Sophia the Greater is the womb that generates all levels of being as her child. She is Ma'at or Truth, the personification of Wisdom. In turn, this Great Mother gave birth to a Daughter who was an image of herself—Sophia the Lesser. A Gnostic gospel called the Sophia of Jesus the Christ, discovered in a papyrus codex in 1896, gives us insight into these matters. Jesus is speaking:

> I desire that you understand the First Man is called the Begetter, Mind who is complete in himself. He reflected with the great Sophia, his consort, and revealed his first-begotten, androgynous son. His male name is called "First Begetter Son of God." His female name is "First Begettress Sophia, Mother of the Universe." Some call her Love. Now the First-Begotten is called Christ.[28]

Gnostic theology claims that the lower worlds of matter were created by the Daughter Sophia, who lost touch with her own heavenly origins. In her sorrow she went in search of the light of her Divine Father but became lost. In her distress and confusion she brought forth a likeness of herself, but without her male counterpart the world that she inadvertently created was out of balance. In Gnostic teachings, Sophia accidentally created a monster called Ialdabaoth, and he is the first archon, or ruler of darkness. Gnostics also referred to him as the demiurgos, and many Gnostics associated him with Yahweh, the god of punishment in the Old Testament. "He is the Lord of Death because he controls birth and death, for these phenomena exist nowhere except in the worlds of forms. Some have attributed to him the diabolical genius of a madman who created a nightmare universe where everything is as it should not be. He is the power that binds man to the world of illusion . . ."[29]

In the German play *Faust,* by Johann Wolfgang von Goethe, a drama about a man who sells his soul to the devil, this demiurgos explains, "I am the spirit of negation, part of the power that still works for good while ever scheming ill."[30] When Sophia the Daughter tries to escape from this nightmare, she discovers that the gates of the Underworld are guarded by fearsome archons and fallen angels, thus drawing a curtain between our world and the worlds of light. This curtain of separation makes it impossible for Sophia to return to her parents and, in the Gnostic tale, Sophia is condemned to wander the Earth in sorrow, searching for the light. But despite the power of this false god who rules the world—the demiurgos—Sophia the Daughter manages to inject light into this material creation. Thus the divine spark is embedded into our souls, giving each of us the power to remember who we really are and redeem the darkness from the worlds of form.

> Ialdabaoth, becoming arrogant in spirit, boasted himself over all those who were below him, and explained, "I am father, and God, and above me there is no one." His mother, hearing him speak thus, cried out against him: "Do not lie, Ialdabaoth; for the Father of the all, the primal Anthropos, is above you; and so is Anthropos, the son of Anthropos."[31]

Anthropos is the name for the Perfected One beyond gender. Thus, Gnostic theology taught that our creation can only be redeemed by the spirit of the pure unblemished Son who came to save his Sister, restoring balance to the world through sacred union. We hear echoes of this theme in the many stories of Jesus rescuing Mary Magdalene, who plays the role of the "fallen daughter." We also see it in the many fairy tales of the prince rescuing the princess, a subject we shall address shortly. But in a far more ancient time, when the roles between men and women were in balance, there were also stories of the princess rescuing the prince, and goddesses who redeem the gods, through the wisdom of the female.

This Gnostic myth, which appeared almost a thousand years after the Hebrew myth of the fallen angels in Genesis, is a metaphor for the tragic human condition of our separation from the Source. Sophia the Mother is synonymous with Wisdom, just as Sophia the Daughter is synonymous with each of us as a soul. This is why the soul was referred to as "she" in the Greek Mysteries (Psyche). Sophia the Mother, who is Wisdom herself, is the goal of all true initiates, the pearl of great price sought by every holy man. But in our times her existence has been hidden, eclipsed by the dark forces of the demiurgos. Even in Christian teachings that speak about the Father, the Son, and the Holy Spirit, few of us know that the Holy Spirit is the Shekinah herself, the Daughter or breath that moves throughout Creation. Without her all that we know of would cease to exist.

In the Gnostic story of Sophia's descent into the worlds that she created, she forgets who she is. This concept was expressed in the first level of the Eleusian Mysteries of ancient Greece, recounting the story of Koré, or Persephone—also called Psyche—the kernel who falls from the sacred Tree (of Life) and must now find her way back to remembrance. She is taken by the dark lord of the Underworld, who wishes to make her his bride. This is a metaphor for each one of us—the soul who must find its way back to the light through free will. Intrinsic to the story's structure is the rescue of the damsel by the Great Mother herself, the Greek Demeter (whose name means the "measure of all things"), or, in more recent theologies, by her enlightened brother or consort (Jesus).

So in the Christian tradition, Jesus became the redeemer of the fallen woman, symbolized by Mary Magdalene. This analogy was perfect for the church, since the Greeks and Romans were familiar with this earlier theology. It also neatly did away with Mary Magdalene's true role as the wife and spiritual partner of Jesus. However, as we begin to discover the depth and breadth of Mary's teachings, we find a female master of great enlightenment.

THE GNOSTIC GOSPELS
OF MARY MAGDALENE

In the Gnostic Gospels of Mary Magdalene, Mary speaks about the light within us all, and our journey to recover it. At the center of her teachings is the heart, and the importance of reclaiming the Mother Spirit to restore balance to the world. "The Divine Mother is Light and she is darkness, she is the saint and she is the sinner, angels and demons are images in her, as are the gods and all of the archons, yet she is beyond all of these. Know her in all things, and you will be free of bondage, even as the Anointed is free."[32] Mary goes on to talk about how the nature of Sophia encompasses all polarities within herself, a tenet of the Goddess path. "Eve and Lilith are one woman, and she is a supernal emanation. If a woman knows herself she will know the Holy Woman, just as if a man knows himself he will know the Supernal Adam. To acquire this knowledge you must be single, which is to say undivided."[33]

About the Black Madonna, or hidden Mother, Maryam says, "Kali Kallah appears black to those who do not know her, yet to those who love her and who draw near, she is white brilliance. Her image is as the starry night sky, and the light of the heavens and Supernal Abode are in her. To pass beyond, you must enter her embrace, even as the Lord embraced her. Then, through Daughter Sophia, you will acquire knowledge of Mother Sophia, the Queen of Heaven."[34] Mary also tells us, "Until you know the darkness of Sophia, you will not acquire her Light. Unless you die and are reborn of the Mother Spirit, the knowledge of the Resurrection will elude you."[35]

These are powerful teachings, for they teach us to reach beyond polarity and to realize that even though we see duality all around us, there is a single unifying Presence that oversees all cycles in the constant dance of the mortal and the eternal.

SOPHIA AND THE
SECOND COMING OF THE CHRIST

The Gnostics believed that the soul of Mary Magdalene has remained with us for the last two thousand years. She has continued to work for the redemption of humanity, incarnating again and again. This is why she was known as "She of Ten Thousand Names and Ten Thousand Faces," another name for Isis, the one behind the many. We must embrace her return for the Second Coming to occur. The reception of this Divine Presence in the world is what triggers the wave of the coming Christ.

> A disciple asked Mary, "When will the Second Coming occur?" Mary said, "It can happen at any time, anywhere, when you least expect it. It is the mystery of the Perfect Aeon known only to the Living Father, which he will reveal in the Mother in due season. Therefore, be ready and live without regrets, so that when it transpires you will be among the living. . . ."[36]

> The Logos emanated into the world for the redemption of Sophia. If the redemption of Sophia is not received in the world, then the world is not redeemed. Sophia received the Logos, and these who cleave to Sophia have to receive the Logos and they are redeemed. It is Sophia in you that receives the Logos and is saved.[37]

At the time when Mary lived, there is a story about a woman who was overjoyed that Mary's teachings were being received. The woman exclaimed, "Now is the hour of the Holy Bride!" But Mary answered, saying:

> No, before the Bride is received, she must be rejected, and before the Second Coming there must come a great darkness. Until the Second Coming of Christ, the Wisdom of God shall not be received. *When the Bride is received, know the Second Coming is near.*[38] (emphasis mine)

If these prophecies are true, then the Christ consciousness cannot come until the reinstatement of the Divine Feminine in the world. It is this balance that will bring about world awakening. Understanding these celestial principles, Mary also taught:

> God the Father entered in through the image of the Son, but the world was overwhelmed by the great supernal glory. Therefore, the Son imparted to the Mother Spirit and God the Mother has entered in through the image of the Daughter to nurture the little ones until they grow wise. The light entered, but was too bright, and so now the fire comes to purify so that all might be sanctified to receive the True Light. Everything shall be accomplished in due season, and it is the Mother Spirit that will accomplish everything.[39]

It is the Mother Spirit that will accomplish everything. . . . What a powerful statement! It is for this reason, I realized, that I had been called to embrace the Goddess. Yet how can we reclaim her in a world that has painted her as the fallen aspect of humanity? The patriarchal world has so ingrained into our psyches the image of women as subservient that few of us are actually aware of how or why women are second-class citizens. From the time that Eve was blamed for eating the apple, men have used this fiction to justify the subjugation of women everywhere. And what we accept in theology becomes the unconscious blueprint that we live by. In teaching generations of people that women are to blame for human suffering, women have been covered with shame, and the world has fallen out of balance.

So let's now take a look at how this wave of suppression has affected the history of the last sixteen hundred years, steeping the world in a theology of half-truths and shadows that we are just emerging from today.

19

In the Name of God

❧

Whatever your heart clings to and confides in, that is really your God.

MARTIN LUTHER,
THE LARGE CATECHISM BOOK OF CONCORD

While it is not within the scope of this book to lay out the long list of atrocities that have been sanctioned by the Roman Catholic Church in the last two millennia, it is important to acknowledge, even with the broadest of strokes, some of the many horrors of murder, torture, and repression that have been meted out, all in the name of a "God of love." Just as World War II awakened us to the horrors of racial genocide, hopefully cementing the commitment within us to never let such a thing happen again, so must we be willing to acknowledge what has been done in the name of monotheistic religions. Just as the Jews, the Native Americans, the Mayans, and the African-Americans may point to a particular era in history that represents the reign of tyranny, genocide, and injustice, it is equally as important to acknowledge the thousand-year "holocaust against women," for the damage done in the name of religion continues to reverberate in parts of the world today.

John Dowling, author of the *History of Romanism* (1847), writes: "It has been estimated by careful and reputed historians of the Catholic Inquisition that 50 million people were slaughtered for the crime of 'heresy' by Roman persecutors between A.D. 606 and the middle of the 19th century."[1] And this is undoubtedly a whitewashed estimate. Over the past few decades, historians have discovered a 550-year time span between the thirteenth and nineteenth centuries that they call the "Burning Times." While it is clear that there have been many courageous men who have died along with these women and children, the majority of those murdered were female. During the Burning Times, over 80 percent of those killed were women,[2] and they were often herbalists or midwives with a knowledge of the plants, stars, and Earth. These women and men were remnants of the vast network of healers, priests, and priestesses from the ancient Mystery Schools, whose vocations had been passed from generation to generation.

Traditional druid villages throughout most of Europe had one boy and one girl who were chosen by their druid elders to be trained as the next generation to serve their communities. These children were sent to druid schools in northern France or Britain to undergo a course of training that could last between seven and twenty years, training them to become village doctors, healers, historians, prophets, wizards, teachers, and herbalists who were often the backbone of European villages. But their influence was seen as a threat by the church, so after the active persecution of early Christian groups such as the Gnostics, these healers were among the first to be rounded up and killed by the Roman church. In this way, the church sought to wipe out all spiritual traditions except their own and to undermine the power of the ancient ways. In the process they sought to destroy any evidence that such superior and well-balanced male and female belief systems had ever existed on our planet.

Over time, the many crusades of the newly formed Catholic Church became a war on truth, history, enlightenment, and the Divine

Feminine, and even today the terror of this genocide has left a great wound in our collective unconscious, furthering a legacy of spiritual ignorance, fear, and fundamentalism in many guises. For any who might doubt the misogyny of those early years, let's take a look at what the early church fathers told their flocks about the nature of women in the first few centuries after Christ.

THE CHURCH LAYS THE FOUNDATION

While there were still a few wise teachers such as Origen who referred to God as both feminine and masculine, for the most part the model that Yeshua had taught for balanced partnerships was swiftly replaced by a tyrannical patriarchal system.[3] The writings of the first few centuries of the church reveal that many of the early church fathers despised women, even those who considered God to be more than "strictly male." Among the most famous of these are St. Augustine, St. Jerome, St. Athanasius, St. Thomas Aquinas, St. Ambrose, St. Odo of Cluny, St. John Chrysostom, and Tertullian, who perhaps took their cues from Peter himself. Writers like Epiphanius wrote that "women were a feeble race, untrustworthy and of mediocre intelligence," a doctrine put forth in his treatise Panarion.[4] Official church literature read: "All wickedness is but little to the wickedness of a woman,"[5] and Clement of Alexandria (150–215 CE) claimed, "Every woman ought to be filled with shame at the thought that she is a woman."[6] Tertullian (160–220 CE) wrote, "Woman is a temple built over a sewer, the gateway to the devil. Woman, you are the devil's doorway. You led astray one whom the devil would not dare attack directly. It was your fault that the Son of God had to die; you should always go in mourning and rags."[7] St. John Chrysostom (347–407) commanded that every Christian father instill into his son "a resolute spirit against womankind . . . Let him have no converse with any woman save only his mother."[8] And Pope Gregory I (540–604 CE), who was the first to accuse Mary Magdalene of being a prostitute, said: "Woman is slow in understanding and her unstable and naive mind renders her by way of natural weakness to the necessity of a strong hand in her husband. Her 'use' is two fold; sex and motherhood."[9] St. Thomas Aquinas (1224–1275) wrote, "Every woman is birth-defective, an imperfect male begotten because her father happened to be ill, weakened, or in a state of sin at the time of her conception."[10] Some church elders argued that men had been created directly by God and possessed souls, while women did not.[11]

Clearly, the men who were in charge of this new patriarchal religion were devoted to the denigration of women. Historian Barbara Walker writes: "Christian abhorrence of sex began with the fathers of the church, who insisted that the Kingdom of God couldn't be established until the human race was allowed to die out through universal celibacy."[12] St. Jerome (347–420 CE) urged his followers to "regard everything as poison which bears within it the seed of sensual pleasure."[13] John Wesley (1703–1791), the founder of the Methodist Church, wrote: "Wife: Be content to be insignificant. What loss would it be to God or man had you never been born."[14] Later on, medieval theologians instructed their congregations that sex "caused the damnation of humanity, which was, on its account, put out of Paradise, and for its sake Christ was killed."[15] St. Augustine declared that sexual intercourse is never sinless, even within marriage.[16] The doctrine of St. Augustine and St. Aquinas taught that a mother contributes nothing to her child's genetics but is only the "soil" for the male soul-bearing seed.[17] Today, we now know through the science of genetics that none of this is true. Dr. Sherfey reminds us that "in the beginning, we were all created females: and if this were not so, we would not be here at all."[18]

However churchmen claimed that all women lay under a threefold curse. They were cursed if they were barren; cursed if they conceived, since conception carries original sin; and cursed by the pains of childbirth in fulfillment of God's curse on Eve.[19] These men also taught that "Eve was to blame" for all the sufferings of humankind, and St. John Chrysostom said that men suffer "a thousand evils" from just having to look at a woman. Tertullian wrote that all women were simply copies of Eve, "the unsealer of that Tree," and "her very existence brought destruction to God's image, man."[20] The tenth-century Catholic St. Odo of Cluny said, "To embrace a woman is to embrace a sack of manure!"[21] and, as late as the 1890s, the president of a leading theological seminary declared, "My Bible commands the subjection of women forever."[22] Women were seen by these zealous church fathers as dangerous, even when they were dead. An early church edict ordered that a male corpse could not be buried next to a female corpse until the female was safely decomposed.[23] Later, church fathers such as St. Columkille in Ireland (521–597 CE) ruled that no woman should be buried in the vicinity of a church, claiming that this was Christianity's custom from the beginning. Only men could be buried there.[24]

Historian Barbara Walker writes about church repression: "Mary, was called the Virgin, not the Mother [because] Church fathers insisted that she never engaged in sexual intercourse in her life,"[25] even though the Bible plainly speaks of Jesus's other brothers and sisters.* St. Ambrose declared, "Would the Lord Jesus have chosen for his mother a woman who would defile the heavenly chamber with the seed of a man, that is to say, one incapable of preserving her virginal chastity intact?"[26]

ARGUMENTS OF POLITICS, ARGUMENTS OF FAITH

While this loathing of women and suppression of women's rights had begun at the time of Peter and was passed on in the first century of the Common Era through the edicts of Paul, it was expanded during the twenty-one ecumenical councils of the church. The first of these took place in 325 CE at the Council of Nicea, where it was decided which gospels should be supported and which should be suppressed. Over the next five councils, the church would become progressively more intolerant, even though there were many factions within the church that

---

*Jesus's siblings include James, Andrew, Judas Thomas (also called Thomas Judas Didymus), and Mary, his sister (Jacobs, *Gnostic Gospels,* 82).

did not agree with these changes. James Carroll writes in *Constantine's Sword,* "Indeed the bishops of the Council of Nicaea who disagreed with Constantine's choices were exiled on the spot."[27]

Dan Burstein, author of *Secrets of the Code* and *Secrets of Mary Magdalene,* writes about church history:

> To achieve primacy, the early church fathers from the time of Constantine onward believed they needed to turn Christianity into a force to unite and strengthen the Roman Empire, consistent with the empire's values, politics, and social and military infrastructure. Those who led the empire in this pursuit believed that a key task was to distill a core ideology and cosmology out of all the various ideas that made up the Christian and other competing messages of that era. In doing so, they chose to glorify certain Gospel accounts that reinforced their version of Christendom's message . . . At the same time . . . they vigorously rejected as heretical anything seen as politically or textually deviating from the mainstream.[28]

However, there were many Christian sects with a wide range of opinion. Bart Ehrman, professor of religious studies at the University of North Carolina, gives examples of three of these. The Ebionites derived their teachings from the apostle James, Jesus's brother. They believed that a person first had to be Jewish in order to become Christian. The Marcionites were followers of the Greek philosopher Marcion. They honored the Divine Feminine and believed that the judgmental Yahweh of the Old Testament was a distinctly different god from the all-loving Father Jesus had spoken of. And the Gnostics believed that we are all divine sparks of God, encased in human bodies, and that humanity could escape the sufferings of this world through gnosis or inner knowledge.[29] There were also the Montanists, the Nestorian Christians, the followers of Origen, and the Marionites, who worshipped Mary. These are just some of the many groups of Christians active in those early years. Today many historians believe that the Gnostics represented the closest expression of Jesus's true teachings, for they honored both the male and the female aspects of creation.[30] These same spiritual beliefs would be embraced by the Knights Templar and Cathars nearly a thousand years later.

> For time and again, when we critically examine what genuine evidence remained, we found that the history of Christianity bequeathed to us by the Roman Church was a gross distortion of the truth . . . It was becoming increasingly obvious that we had been deliberately deceived, that the Gnostics were indeed the original Christians, and that their anarchic mysticism had been hijacked by an authoritarian institution which had created from it a dogmatic religion and then brutally enforced the greatest cover up in history.[31]

THE DEATH OF GENIUS

One of the most profound examples of this hatred against women is found in the tragic story of Hypatia, one of the most renowned scholars of the ancient world. Hypatia, a scholar of the Mysteries, lived in Alexandria, Egypt, around 400 CE. She was also a disciple of Plutarch, the famed Greek teacher and magician, and she sat in the Chair of Philosophy previously occupied by her father, Theon, the mathematician, in the Alexandrian School of Neo-Platonism. Hypatia was beloved by the citizens of Alexandria for her kindness, intelligence, and charm and famed for the depth of her wisdom. She was frequently consulted by the magistrates of that city because she was well versed in platonic wisdom. It was said that "Hypatia eclipsed in argument and public esteem every proponent of the Christian doctrines in Northern Egypt."[32] Manly P. Hall, author of *The Secret Teachings of All Ages* writes:

> While her writings perished at the time of the burning of the Library of Alexandria by the Mohammedans, some hint of her nature may be gleaned from the statements of contemporaneous authors.

Hypatia wrote a commentary on the *Arithmetic of Diophantus,* another on the *Astronomical Canon of Ptolemy,* and a third on the *Conics of Apollonius of Perga.* Snyesius, Bishop of Ptolemais, her devoted friend, wrote to Hypatia for assistance in the construction of an astrolabe and a hydroscope. Recognizing the transcendency of her intellect, the learned of many natures flocked to the academy where she lectured.[33]

Said to have been Christian in her spirit, Hypatia is credited with removing the "veil of mystery in which the new cult of Christianity had enshrouded itself, discoursing with such clarity upon its most involved principles that many newly converted to the Christian faith deserted it to become her disciples."[34] Hypatia not only proved conclusively that the origins of Christianity were pagan, but revealed how Jesus's miracles were performed by demonstrating the natural laws that controlled the phenomena. An enlightened soul indeed!

Cyril, the zealous bishop of Alexandria, saw in Hypatia a great threat to the advancement of his ministry, so he incited the fanatical members of the Nitrian monks to attack her on the street as she was passing from the academy to her home. Their leader was a "savage and illiterate man named Peter,"[35] who pulled Hypatia from her chariot, dragged her to a church, and pounded her to death with clubs as his

Figure 19.1. Hypatia, the great spiritual initiate of Alexandria, Egypt. (Illustration by Tricia McCannon)

Christian monks tore off her clothes. Then they scraped the flesh from her bones with oyster shells and carried the mutilated remains of her body to Cindron and burned her to ashes.

Bishop Cyril said that she was "an iniquitous female who had presumed, against God's commandments, to teach men."[36] Later this same man was canonized by the church. Freemason Manly P. Hall writes: "Thus perished in 415 C.E. the greatest woman initiate in the ancient world, and with her fell also the Neo-Platonic School of Alexandria,"[37] creating the first shock wave that would result in the burning of the Great Library of Alexandria by both Muslim and Christian fanatics.

HERETICS AND THINKERS

Once Rome's persecution of Christians ended and Christianity became the official religion of Rome in 380 CE,* the newly sanctioned church became the persecutor of all others.[38]

> The real martyrs of the early Christian era were not made by the pagans so much as by their fellow Christians . . . Zealots in Asia Minor destroyed whole towns and villages and massacred thousands of "heretics." Women and children were tortured until they agreed to receive the Host of the true faith. Ammianus said, "no wild

---

*Here is a chronology of Christianity's rise to become the official religion of Rome: 311—The Edict of Nicomedia (the Edict of Toleration) legalizes Christianity but does not restore property seized by various officials of the empire from Christians; 313—The Edict of Milan makes Christianity and other non-Roman religions legal in the Roman empire; it returns seized property to Christians and stops the persecution of Christians; 325—First Council of Nicea convenes, establishing church doctrine; Constantine financially supports the church formation; 380—Theodosius makes Christianity the official religion of the Roman empire in place of the traditional Roman religions; 389–391—Emperor Theodosius issues decrees ordering the closing of all pagan temples and banning all non-Christian holidays; shortly afterward, Theodosius murders seven thousand people who do not agree with this; 392—Theodosius is crowned the first pope of the Catholic Church.

beasts are so hostile to man as Christian sects in general are to one another." Toleration itself was punishable. At Trier in the fourth century, two bishops, Priscillian and Instantius, with two other men and a woman, were illegally tortured and executed by their fellow Christians for being too tolerant of their pagan neighbors.[39]

By the fifth century, Pope Innocent I had officially proclaimed:

. . . that God gave the Church the right to kill. Its military might "had been granted by God and the sword had been permitted for the punishment of the guilty, meaning anyone holding unorthodox opinions."[40]

A letter attributed to Clement, bishop of Rome, said whoever refused to "bow the neck" to God's bishops, priests, and deacons is guilty of insubordination and must suffer the death penalty. In the ensuing centuries the "Holy" Roman Church mounted nine separate crusades, between 1095 and 1272, all in the name of the Prince of Peace. And this does not include at least five other crusades against Alexandria, the Balkans, the Tartars, the Baltic region and Germany, and the Albigensian Crusade against the Cathars of Southern France.[41]

These events began with four escalating movements—starting in 1184 and ending with the Spanish Inquisition, which came to a close in 1834[42]—encompassing a period of some seven hundred years of torture, murder, and rape where the church murdered millions in the name of Jesus. "Under the sword and fire of the alliance of Church and ruling class, fell not only pagans, such as Mithraists, Jews, or devotees of the old mystery religions of Eleusis and Delphi, but also any Christian who would not knuckle under and accept their rule. They still claimed their goal was to spread Jesus's gospel of love. But through the savagery and horror of their holy Crusades, their witch-hunts, their Inquisition, their book burnings and people burnings, they spread not love but the old androcratic staples of repression, devastation, and death."[43]

According to the 1990 documentary film *The Burning Times*,* history reports that roughly five million to nine million women in Europe were killed between 1320 and 1800, although the church wishes to place these numbers at only one hundred thousand. The popes who sought to wipe out vestiges of other spiritual traditions are too numerous to name, but based on a claim of "heresy"—a word whose roots derive, ironically, from *choice*—they murdered millions. Heresy was considered anything that civil or religious authorities thought contradicted the tenets of the orthodox church; thus, any divergent point of view could be declared a "crime against the state." With this myopic reasoning, the Roman church "legitimized" the confiscation of all lands and properties, filling their coffers to overflowing and wiping out all those initiates whose understanding of the world did not accord with the church's.

By the Middle Ages, "heretics" fell into two basic groups: those who maintained that the church was not functioning as Jesus had intended and those who disagreed with church doctrine. While most of the country people continued to practice the old religion since they lived close to the Earth, three centuries of crusades to the Holy Land meant that the knights from the ruling class had brought back new ideas from the intelligentsia of the Muslim universities. These returning lords also brought back an appreciation of the tantric arts, reintroducing the idea that sex is sacred and is meant to be enjoyed, not denigrated. The idea of women as agents of beauty, purity, and love returned.

The Albigensian Christians taught the ideal of the Sacred Marriage, trying to restore the seminal concepts that Jesus and Mary Magdalene had tried to teach—ideas that had been excised from Christian scripture. The Knights Templar arose, protectors of the secrets of Jesus and Mary Magdalene. Legends flourished of the Holy Grail, the lost vessel of the bride who had been scorned and nearly forgotten. The Merovingian lineage came to light, said to have been created from the

---

*This is an excellent documentary, distributed by Wellspring Media (www.wellspring .com). Along with *Goddess Remembered* and *Full Circle,* it forms a three-part series on women and spirituality.

bloodline of Jesus and Maryam. Their emblems in the south of France showed Jesus and Mary Magdalene as fishes, linked to the ichthys, the sacred union of male and female.[44] "The cities of central France, Italy, Belgium, and the Rhinelands were abandoning the 'fad' of Christianity for more sensual and joyful spiritual amusements, including communal sex . . . troubadours, poetry, and romantic lute music . . . their lyrics often mocked the church by turning hymns to the Virgin into erotic love songs to Venus."[45]

All of this made the church very uneasy, especially since many of its priests were now steeped in corruption, greed, and political chicanery, while preaching poverty, obedience, and moral platitudes to the masses. By the twelfth century, many monasteries had been turned into wine shops or gambling houses. Nunneries became private brothels for the clergy, used to raise funds for the church. These women were called nuns of Mary Magdalene, profaning the original sanctity of this lineage of wise women. Many priests used the confessional to secure sex from female parishioners, and the sale of church offices was constant and unapologetic.[46]

Compounding the public's disgust at the church's corruption and greed was a growing suspicion among the populace that the myths about the Garden of Eden, the fall of humankind, original sin, and the virgin birth were untrue. This skepticism may have been sparked by the teachings of the Cathars, whose name means "the pure ones." Like the Gnostics, they believed that this world was a realm ruled over by the dark powers of the demiurgos who sought to keep humanity in ignorance. Also like the early Gnostics, they traveled in pairs, practicing a more heart-based form of Christianity. There was also the rise of kabbalistic wisdom, profound doctrines that dealt with the male and female aspects of God, and the path of balance between them. The tenets of the Roman Catholic Church were now being widely questioned, and because the priests were ignorant of the scriptures, some even illiterate, they "were instructed not to engage in dispute concerning the faith against such astute heretics in public, lest they expose themselves to ridicule."[47]

THE CRUSADES AGAINST THE CATHARS
AND THE CHRISTIAN INQUISITION

The disillusionment of the people with the church's corruption, along with the rise of more enlightened spiritual theologies, had a direct effect on the profits of the church. Determined to put an end to their competition, church leaders decided to mount a war against the Christian Cathars, a movement of independent Christians inspired by the original Gnostic ideals. This group flourished in southern France and northern Italy between 1140 and 1244 CE. This war of butchery, trials, and death by fire started in 1208 and lasted until 1244, with the destruction of the Cathars at Montsegur. This became known as the Albigensian Crusade. The Cathars understood God as a being of pure Spirit, completely unsullied by the taint of matter. He was the God of love, order, and peace. Thus they did not recognize civil authority, since this was the province of the physical world. The goal of a Cathar was to become perfect, and Cathar missionaries would point out examples of clerical immorality. They also called attention to the grievances that the people in the South held against the French kings, thus pushing the religious movement into the political arena. But the Cathars' major heresy was following the wisdom of the original Gnostics, who honored Sacred Marriage as a model of true partnership.

There were also other Christian groups in the Languedoc region of southern France who taught Mary Magdalene's path, the Way of the Chalice. This was the path of love and compassion, taught by Yeshua and Maryam. These groups allowed priests to be married, unlike the Catholics who demanded that their priests give all they had to the church and leave nothing to their families. The pope hired mercenaries to fight in the Albigensian Crusade and, in league with the French king, wiped out entire cities, including some twenty thousand people in the walled town of Béziers alone. When Christian Cathars sought sanctuary in the local church, the armies burned it with all the people inside. This slaughter was the first military action ordered in this crusade by

Pope Innocent III on July 22, 1209, the feast day of Mary Magdalene.[48]

Heady with success, the church then officially formed the Christian Inquisition in 1239, launching a full-scale attack on the rising influence of groups such as the Waldensians* and the Jews. The Waldensians taught that both men and women had the right to preach, that purgatory did not exist, that anyone could pray to God without setting foot in a church, and that a corrupt priest should not be allowed to perform sacraments.[49] According to Pope Gregory IX, such thoughts constituted heresy, and he established tribunal courts across France, Italy, and parts of Germany in the first wave of the Inquisition.

The Cathars, who taught reincarnation and the preexistence of the soul, were of particular interest to church leaders. The Cathars had a scroll purportedly written by Yeshua himself, which came directly from the Gnostics a thousand years earlier. Intent upon the Cathars' destruction, the pope sent armies through village after village, killing thousands. The last of the Cathars took refuge on top of the mountain fortress of Montségur in southwestern France and survived through weeks of military onslaught. Eventually, they agreed to surrender but requested a two-week cease-fire. Legend reports that during those last few days, a group of Cathars scaled down the walls of the fortress and escaped with their most precious artifacts. Among them was said to be *The Book of Love,* a book containing the secret teachings of Yeshua, a holy sword, and a crystal skull connected with the wisdom of the

---

*The Waldensians are a Protestant movement founded by Peter Waldo in 1170 in the city of Lyon, France. Waldo was a wealthy merchant who gave away all his property in 1177; he believed in voluntary poverty, lay preaching, and strict adherence to the Bible as a path to perfection. Between 1175 and 1185 he commissioned a translation of the New Testament from Latin into the local Franco-Provençal language, incurring the wrath of the Catholic Church. By 1215, the Waldensians had been declared heretical by the Roman church and were subject to intense persecution. Those who survived the Albigensian Crusades were seen as forerunners of the Protestant Reformation. While they still exist in France in limited numbers today, they endured near annihilation in the seventeenth century. The goals of contemporary Waldensians are serving the poor, promoting social justice, fostering interreligious work, and advocating respect for religious diversity and freedom of conscience.

Ancients. Whatever secrets they preserved, the remaining group then surrendered to the pope and were forced to walk, fully conscious, into the burning fires of death in 1244 CE.[50]

Over time, the pope expanded the power of the Inquisition through a series of papal bulls, such as the one issued in May 1252. This bull mandated a "terrible measure against heretics in Italy, authorizing seizure of their goods, imprisonment, torture, and on conviction, death, all on minimal evidence." Some have called this the "most elaborate extortion racket ever devised,"[51] for after a citizen's arrest, his property was confiscated, even before he was sentenced, making not only the church, but the inquisitors, unimaginably rich. As the inquisitor Heinrich von Schultheiss wrote, "When I have you tortured, and by the severe means afforded by the law, I bring you to confession, then I perform a work pleasing in God's sight; and it profiteth me."[52]

For some five and a half centuries, these "God fearing" Dominicans persecuted Jews, Muslims, pagans, healers, and women, or anyone who questioned their diabolical methods. Walker writes: "Violence could be invoked under this system by nothing more than ordinary living . . ."[53] Those who protested the arrest of their friends were also arrested and tortured. Torture was officially sanctioned in 1257 and remained a legal recourse of the church for five and a half centuries until it was finally abolished by Pope Pius VII in 1816.[54]

Their methods of extorting confessions were gruesome; the inquisitors excelled in all forms of torture—rape, branding, burning, crushing, and pulling people's limbs apart. Favorite among the tortures were stocks, in which inquisitors entrapped the hands, feet, and heads of their victims and subjected them to burning-hot coals, branding, or other forms of excruciating pain. The prisoners were held in dark, cramped, underground cells with water as their only beverage. Crying, whimpering, or complaining aloud was rigorously repressed. "The punishment inflicted by the Inquisition was imprisonment, either for a stated time or for life, or death by fire. If impenitent the condemned was tied to the stake and burned alive; if penitent he was strangled before being placed on the pile. Flight was considered equivalent to a confession. . . . The property of the fugitive was confiscated, and s/he himself was burned in effigy."[55]

The inspiration for burning heretics is said to have come from St. Augustine, author of the doctrine of original sin, who claimed that "pagans, Jews, and heretics would burn forever in eternal fire with the Devil, unless saved by the Catholic Church."[56] The burnings were carried out by civil authorities; the church publicly proclaimed that it had no part in them. Yet since the papal bull of 1252 had ordered "every ruler or citizen to assist them on pain of excommunication,"[57] those magistrates who refused to comply were excommunicated, arrested, and tortured themselves, and their property confiscated.[58]

Since one of the church's major motives was financial gain, an elaborate system of accounting was established. This included itemizing the expenses for every trial, every torture, and even each of the prisoners' incarceration in jail, as well as their food in prison. Without money, the prisoner simply starved to death. Pope Gregory XI even noted that too many people were starving to death before they were brought to the stake, but it did not occur to him to feed them. The wood and coal used to burn the heretics were also charged to the person's estate, and if the estate could not pay, the debt reverted to the person's relatives. If the debt was more than the value of a person's estate, or more than one generation of relatives could pay off, it was carried over to the next generation, or the estate was forfeited to the church.[59] All property was split between the church, the inquisitors, and the civil authorities. The Spanish Inquisition followed suit in 1478, creating more torture, killing, and property confiscation. It was not abolished until 1834, less than two hundred years ago.

Meanwhile, all of Europe underwent the Black Plague in 1348, which killed nearly half its population within three years. This gave the church the chance to acquire even more property. The plague was followed by the Hundred Years' War between France and England (1337–1453), thinning out the population still further. Through all this, the church established a pattern of accumulating money and property by religious purges and heretic hunting, terrorizing its ideological enemies, and diverting the revolutionary energies of the masses, who wished to throw off its yoke, into a frenzy of fear and the gruesome, bloody debauchery of death.

THE HAMMER OF WITCHES

While the people who were killed between 1150 and 1484 were officially labeled as "heretics," those killed after 1484 were called "witches." This is when Pope Innocent VIII pronounced his papal bull against the suddenly discovered crime of witchcraft. Before that it had actually been heresy to even believe in bewitchment.[60] This period of wholesale murder is called the Burning Times. Monica Sjöö and Barbara Mor, authors of *The Great Cosmic Mother,* write: "The myth of the 'feminine evil,' which has dominated the Western world for over two thousand years, led logically and directly to the religiously targeted murder of women as witches during the Great Inquisition of Europe . . . the estimates range from 1 million to 9 million people burned as witches between the fifteenth and eighteenth centuries."[61]

One of the greatest abominations these sadists foisted on the European populace was the *Malleus Maleficarum,* a book known as the *Hammer of Witches.* This book was supposedly compiled by two Dominican inquisitors, Heinrich Kramer and Jacob Sprenger, who claimed that in 1484, through the papal degrees of Pope Innocent VIII, they had been empowered to persecute witches based on the guidelines in their handbook. However, history reveals that these decrees were issued before the book was even written. Since it was primarily in Latin, the language of the Vatican, this tells us where it originated. This witch hunter's guide to torture was a testament to the misogyny of men whose minds had been warped by their own disowned lust, shame, and guilt.

While the University of Cologne's Theology Department condemned the book as unethical and illegal, it was reprinted some twenty-nine times

Figure 19.2. The tortures of the Inquisition were beyond anything that we can conceive of today. Some believe that as many as five million to nine million women were killed in a six-hundred-year span. That does not include the many children and men who stood up for the truth or for each other, all mowed down by the dark hand of the church, committed to the financial and theological tyranny of the day. (Illustration by Tricia McCannon)

in the years between 1487 and 1669, creating a virtual hysteria of witch trials throughout the sixteenth and seventeenth centuries. Its poison spread throughout Europe, striking terror into the hearts of everyone. While its use was primarily concentrated in Germany, France, Italy, and England by Catholic tribunals, it was also used by Protestants, who were equally fierce in practicing their own methods of torture.

The *Malleus Maleficarum* is divided into three sections, each posing certain questions and purporting to answer them through opposing arguments. The first section seeks to prove that witchcraft even exists, positing an elaborate world of demons and devils. It details how the devil and his followers, whom they call witches, perpetrate a variety of evils with the permission of Almighty God. When these inquisitors were questioned about why an all-powerful God would allow the devil such liberties, church authorities claimed that God permitted these acts of evil so that the devil would not destroy the world.

Part two explains that women are naturally more prone to Satan's temptations than men, since "they are of a weaker nature and inferior intellect." This section dwells at length on the licentious acts of witches and their ability to bring on impotence in men and even gives space to the question of whether demons can father the children of witches. The writing style is serious, and even the most preposterous statements are presented as fact.

The third part describes the actual forms of witchcraft, spelling out how the spells are cast and how they can be remedied. Strong emphasis is given to the Devil's Pact, and the insistence that women must have had sex with the devil.[62] Many have written that these inquisitors seemed to have been obsessed with sex, and witches were accused of hindering conception, inhibiting potency, instigating extramarital sex, and slaying infants in the womb, all threats to patrilineal property inheritance.[63] Part three also gives detailed instructions for carrying out the various methods of torture that were routinely applied to coerce a confession, sometimes applied two and even three times, each time inflicting more pain. Judges were encouraged to mislead the accused by promising mercy in exchange for a confession, but no "mercy" was ever given. No one who confessed was ever freed. The book also states that a rumor is enough to bring a person to trial, and that if the accused puts up too much of a defense, that constitutes evidence that he or she is either guilty or bewitched.

Today we know that sexual aggression is often linked to frustration, repression, and self-hatred. Europe was ripe for such aggression, since the doctrines that the church had taught were about the shameful nature of sex, while ignoring the ideals of love, sharing, and honor. During the Inquisition, this sexual aggression became perverted into sadism, horror, and depravity, with women being raped by their torturers as they lay chained in dungeons or spread naked on the racks. All this happened with the blessings of the priests, who rationalized these activities as exorcisms of the devil.[64] Hot pincers were used on their breasts and buttocks, and molten pokers were forced into their orifices until they bled to death internally.

THE LEGACY OF SHAME

In the ensuing centuries, the women who survived this fanatical misogyny learned the strategies of silence, obedience, and a strict adherence to all male-prescribed religious dogma. They realized, at a visceral level, the punishment that lay in store for any woman who "colored outside the lines." In *Suffer and Be Still: Women in the Victorian Age,* Martha Vicinus tells us, "The woman who broke the family circle, be she prostitute, adulterer or divorcee, threatened society's very fabric."[65] She became an outcast in the eyes of the world.

This was also true for women who sought an education. In 1879, Birmingham, England, schoolmasters barred women from employment as teachers of small boys, on the grounds that it would encourage "immorality."[66] Lawyers denied women admission to the Inns of Court, undoubtedly determined to prevent women from changing the laws that controlled them. "Though women were scorned for being 'simpletons,' they were even more violently scorned when they tried to develop their minds . . . When women received high marks in examinations, they were passed over, and scholarships were awarded to the men immediately below their level."[67]

A 1913 book called *Sex, Its Origins and Determination* actually sought to "scientifically" prove that women were biologically inferior to men, basing its argument on the idea that boys were conceived on incoming tides and girls were conceived on outgoing ones![68] A quote from *The Mother's Companion* (circa 1889) provides guidelines for training daughters:

> Girls are to dwell in quiet homes, amongst a few friends; to exercise a noiseless influence, to be submissive and retiring. The girl is to be guarded from over fatigue, subject to restrictions . . . seldom trusted away from home . . . because, if she is not thus guarded . . . she will probably develop some disease . . . any strain upon a girl's intellect is to be dreaded, and any attempt to bring women into competition with men can scarcely escape failure.[69]

Bram Dijkstra writes in *Idols of Perversity: Fantasies of Feminine Evil in Fin-de-Siècle Culture:* "It is clear that by 1900 writers and painters, scientists and critics, the learned and the modish alike, had been indoctrinated to regard all women who no longer conformed to the image of the household nun as vicious bestial creatures, representatives of a pre-evolutionary, instinctual past."[70]

REVERBERATIONS IN TODAY'S WORLD

For any who believe that we are past the era of patriarchical control, think again. A quick review of events in today's world yields an entirely different perspective. In China they are still drowning little girls at birth, a custom prevalent in Asia for centuries. Throughout Europe, Asia, and the Americas, sexual slavery is flourishing, and 85 percent of those sold into slavery are either little girls or women. In the United States, women only got the right to vote in 1920, and this did not happen in England until 1928. France granted women voting rights in 1944, and women in Switzerland only gained the right to vote in 1971.[71] In Japan women were not allowed to have birth control pills until June 1999, four full decades after the West,[72] yet it took only ten days for Viagra to be legalized for the men who sought erections.

Today it is no secret that, in some parts of the world, women are not only being veiled behind burkas and face scarves, but have been sexually mutilated for centuries, usually by their own "loving" families, in life-threatening operations. This is because of the male's fear that if the woman has any sexual pleasure herself, she might want to leave her husband. According to historians, female genital mutilation has been performed for at least fourteen hundred years, while others estimate that it began at the start of the Common Era some two thousand years ago.[73] The most famous university in the Islamic world issued a statement in 1981, under the signature of the Great Sheikh of Al-Azhar, urging parents to "follow the lessons of Mohammed . . . and have their daughters circumcised." The statement explained that this procedure was prevalent fourteen hundred years ago. But the word *circumcision* is misleading when it comes to this brutal operation, since it removes the clitoris through which women experience orgasm, while male circumcision removes only the foreskin of the penis, creating a more pleasurable sensation during intercourse. The equivalent of this operation for men would be to remove the penis itself, essentially ending men's ability to enjoy any of the pleasures of sex.

And lest we think that America is exempt from abusing women, consider the estimated 1.3 million cases of domestic violence that occur each year, and that 80 percent of these abuses happen to women.[74] The majority of these attacks occur with women eighteen or older, and most are not even reported to the police.[75] Statistics reveal that, on average, more than three American women are murdered by their husbands or their boyfriends every day,[76] and that one in every six women, and one in every thirty-three men, have experienced a completed or attempted rape. Statistics also show that only one-quarter of all assaults, one-fifth of all rapes, and one-half of all stalkings perpetrated against women by their intimate partners are reported to the police.[77] The FBI reports that of the cases reported, almost one-third of all female homicides are committed by an intimate male lover or husband.[78] In 70 percent to 80 percent of these cases, the man physically abuses the woman before the murder takes place.[79]

STEPPING BACK FROM THE PATTERN

Certainly in the last two thousand years there have been many deep thinkers who have questioned the morality of these male-dominated "orthodox" faiths. But it was not until some five hundred years ago that the first glimmers of change began to appear. This was during the Protestant Reformation. Martin Luther believed that it was not through money alone that souls were saved, but by a change in consciousness. One of Luther's main objections to the Catholic Church was its policy of granting "indulgences"—spiritual forgiveness for accrued sins accorded to those who gave large sums of money to the church. This practice of paying your way into Heaven allowed the rich to take all the lands and property they wanted in the name of the Holy See, and not be chastised by the church. Murder, rape, lies, and deceit were all wiped clean with a healthy bribe. Understandably, Martin Luther wondered if God saw it this way.

Yet Luther, too, was a sexist. He wrote: "If women get tired and die of bearing [children], there is no harm in that; let them die as long as they bear; they were made for that."[80] So he was clearly also a product of a chauvinist world.

Luther also questioned the wisdom of the church teaching that priests should remain unmarried. Perhaps he had an innate sense that a sacred union could not take place without at least having a relationship with a woman, even if he thought the purpose should be for the woman to bear the man's children. While Luther was clearly a product of his misogynistic age, the Protestant Reformation began the long road back to religious freedom, creating a splintering that has resulted in over thirty thousand sects of Christianity being practiced today.[81] After the Reformation came the Age of Reason, followed by the rise of the eighteenth-century Romantics. This was the first rekindling of a more enlightened approach and an embrace of humanistic values that have opened the door for our age.

Today we might argue that the Inquisition has passed us by, but there are still many vestiges of its wounds left from this centuries-long reign of torture, horror, and shame. Those of us living in America or Europe in the twenty-first century have inherited the DNA of the people who survived this holocaust. Our ancestors either fled the Inquisition or stood by and watched their loved ones burned to death. They learned, and their children learned, not to color outside the lines, and to stay away from the deeper questions of religion, on pain of death. At some visceral level, this fear has been encoded into our psyches, and it must now be healed in our collective consciousness. Many women living in Muslim countries are still under the oppression of the Dark Ages, forced to hide their faces and bodies from public view. Many have been surgically raped by their tribes, in an effort to prevent them from desiring any man other than their husband. It is my hope that both the men and women in these countries will begin to come out from under the yoke of these oppressive systems and collectively start to heal these wounds.

The shadows of fear from these long-standing wounds can take many forms, existing like a knee-jerk reaction of pure, unreasoning terror in our collective cultural psyche. It may surface as a fear of not fitting in, or feeling forced to conform to the demands of family, church, or friends. It may emerge in the form of denial of any other version of history or religion, other than that which we have been taught to believe, even when presented with facts that clearly contradict it. It may also show up as unbridled rage at all things religious or a staunch determination not to consider any views outside of conventional thought about medicine, governments, financial institutions, or religions. This emotional resistance can freeze us in denial or fear and close our hearts to a larger perspective. Yet fear does not lead to self-knowledge. Only love and forgiveness can do that. But when we are honestly willing to take a look at the past and to correct our errors in thoughts, words, and deeds, we have freed ourselves from their tyranny and are no longer doomed to repeat our mistakes.

PART THREE

The Return

Yeah now that I should stand before myself and
Whisper these words to you again, Great Goddess.
Oh great and mighty, you are within me. You are me.
I am you and I see myself in you.
You are the heart of creation, and I am the arrow that flies
*   true and swift to that center mark.*
I hear your voice. I feel your presence . . . your sweet divine
*   Presence all around me.*
How can I not serve, if that is what you have asked of me?
How can I turn away from the face of the Divine?
I cannot.
And so I bend my knees to you, and in that releasing of myself
*   I become you.*
I am exalted in you. You move through me and around me.
You vibrate the very essence of my molecules.
I breathe you. I embrace you.
And in every issue of every particle moving through space, you
*   embrace me.*
As we approach the door of the Abyss of Light, there is only
*   one way to enter.*

With our eyes open. With our hearts open.

As Emanations of the Divine Mother . . . emanations of ourselves.

With dignity and nobility and the acknowledgment of all good

Upon this planet and every other planet . . .

That we are each joined to the thread of life . . . the red thread of the Grandmother Spider.

Let us spin it out now.

Let us travel the rivers of time and space

That leads us to Ourselves.

TRICIA McCANNON

20

Calling Down the Goddess

Mother God, of all the gods, avatars, and saints,
The childish artists who crave to touch your shape,
Even the evil ones crushed in your inscrutable heart.
Wise Sophia, Shekinah, hear my prayer.

JANINE CANAN, *SHE RISES LIKE THE SUN*

I returned to the circle at the end of May. Shasta had said that we would spend the day watching a three-part documentary called *The Burning Times*. Profoundly moving, this film traced the history of the centuries of atrocities against women. As we watched the beauty, loss, and pain of the films, our group of women sat on the floor on blankets, holding one another for comfort. Many wept silent tears, and two of the women sobbed openly. When the films were over, none of us could speak. Shasta brought us chamomile tea and ginger snaps, like a mother hen helping her chicks convalesce. She gave us time to let this hidden chapter of human history sink in, and then she began to speak.

"During the church's persecution of women in the Middle Ages, the archetype that we once knew of the sagely queen or the wise grand-mother was dramatically changed by the patriarchy. The original Triple Goddess was the maiden, the mother, and the matriarch, the empress in the tarot deck. This is the partner of the emperor, the king and queen who can rule their people wisely. Yet during the Burning Times wom-en's rights evaporated. They had no legal right to own their lands, even when their husbands had died. So women who outlived their husbands, and whose sons who had been killed in battle, were turned out of their houses, and their lands forfeited to the church. This not only over-turned the old ways that had once honored women's property rights, but it became a form of property seizure by the church fathers, who were intent upon accumulating as much wealth and power as possible.

"Having nowhere else to go, these outcast women lived in caves and forests, eking out a living from their knowledge of medicinal plants. They ate fruits and berries and roots, or food brought by their clients in lieu of payment. These women were later depicted as crones by the church, carrying brittle sticks of firewood to their fires. This became the archetype of the discarded hag who no longer had a value to men because she was past her breeding years. And as we have seen, the crone of herbal wisdom was then converted into the witch."

Shasta looked around the circle at our faces. We all wore a look of pain for the unacknowledged men and women who had paid the price of this disenfranchisement. She went on. "Even the word *crone* derives from the patriarchy. It comes from Cronos, the male ruler of the gods, the lord of linear time, yet this name has nothing to do with the circular nature of the Goddess, the One who is both within creation and also outside of it. She is the One who reminds us of the eternal now." We nodded in silence. "Linear time is masculine—a straight line. Goddess time is circular and encompasses all the seasons of life." We all took a deep breath.

Then Shasta stood up, clapping her hands. "All right, you have seen the film, you have heard the stories, and many of you have lived these tragedies in your past incarnations, but now, it is time for a change. While many of our sisters are still enslaved by patriarchal systems around the world, we must give thanks for the things that have changed here, in our own country. We must take the time to celebrate the victories of today, and the men and women who have made them possible. Look around you. We are moving into a new age of awakening, where there are many wonderful men who support this vision of true partnership and equality. There are husbands and wives who work and play together as equals. There are men who change diapers and babysit, and women who have careers. Lawmakers are petitioning for equal pay, and women have found their way back into medicine, law, healing, science, and teaching once again. They are using their voices to help make the world a better place once more."

We all nodded slowly, giving silent thanks that we lived in a country where things were better than they were for our Muslim sisters and brothers. I reflected on what I had learned about the partnership model created by Jesus and Mary, and how different the world would have been if the church had only allowed these teachings to be heard. But even today Vatican leaders were still arguing about whether male priests should marry, or whether women should be allowed to be priests. It didn't seem as if they had matured much in their understanding of Jesus's true message; rather, they seemed intent on clinging to their outdated, chauvinistic ways.

Shasta continued to speak. "We can make a difference in the world, whether we are men or women. We can stop competing with one another for men, for jobs, for recognition, for beauty. We can celebrate our differences and support one another, teaching others to embrace a cooperative model of sharing, instead of a competitive one. If we can find a better way of being friends and allies, perhaps we can teach that approach to our men and help them also find a way back to unity and partnership. This will create a better world for everyone."

Some of the women were nodding. Meg blew her nose loudly, and we all laughed. Shasta went on. "It is my hope that each of you will find a way to bring healing back to our planet, one decision at a time. How you do it will be unique to each of you, but today we make the first step by discovering who your spiritual allies will be." She looked around the circle. "Today you choose your first Goddess."

We all begin to whisper. *We were going to choose a Goddess? Really? What did this mean? How would it impact our lives?*

Shasta stood up. "All right, let's go out into the garden and do some ceremony." We scrambled to our feet, grateful for the change. We made our way out the back door and down the stairs, moving into the sunlit garden. Suddenly, I could feel the sun on my face and the breeze of a perfect spring day. Yes, we were here in the world of light and shadows, but there was love in the world and beauty, too, as well as horror and sadness.

We gathered at the lowest point of the garden around the medicine circle. I stood in the North with Sophia, Ma'at, and White Buffalo Calf Woman at my back. To my left was the eastern gate and the statues of Mary, Quan Yin, and Isis. I felt grateful for their soothing presence. "And now," Shasta explained, "I will call in the seven directions and summon the Powers to join our circle, so pay attention." She turned her body to face the East, and the group turned with her. She raised her arms, and her voice took on new resonance as she began the invocation.

"Spirits of the golden East, we call you now into our circle, and we ask that you hear our prayers. Guardians of the glorious sun, place of new beginnings, we summon now the sweet Goddesses of compassion to aid us on our journeys. We call upon Mary, Quan Yin, and Isis, lady of a thousand faces, beloved Mary of the Chalice, come into our circle now and grace us with your light. Hail, guardians of the eastern gate!" The energy of the circle had suddenly shifted. I could feel an invisible Presence of love moving through it. It was as if a holy wind had blown over the group, quickening everything. A shiver went up my spine. Suddenly the robins started singing, and the entire grove came alive as the divinities entered.

Shasta swiveled next to face the southern altar, raising her arms in salute. "Spirits of the faithful South—Gaia, Turtle Mother, grandmothers of the Earth—we thank you for our food, our homes, and the clothing on our backs. Join us! Hail, Demeter of the harvest and Diana of the animals. Hail, many-breasted Mothers and Goddesses of the seas. Join us in this sacred circle, guardians of the southern gate!"

We turned to the West as one, the power of invocation electrifying. "Hail, powers of the western gate, the place of hidden mysteries. Come, Sekhmet, Athena, and Inanna, warrior Goddesses of the sacred West! Come, Mary Magdalene of the Holy Chalice, and bring the wisdom of the Black Madonna to aid us with this ceremony. We call upon your courage and your strength. It is time to reclaim that ancient wisdom, and to end the fear and oppression and ignorance so that light and balance and love might now return to the world!"

We turned to face the North as if we were all just one entity. Shasta raised her arms. "Welcome, powers of the great white North, the councils of the sages. For all the wise ones who have come before us, all the sages whose spirits still live, we ask for your guidance that we might learn from you. Hail, teachers from the halls of wisdom! Ma'at, Sophia, and White Buffalo Calf Woman! Hail, White Wolf Woman, who teaches us the true strong powers of the North!"

Now Shasta turned inward to face the circle, and we joined her. She lifted her chin to the sky, and she called down the powers of the Above. "Come, angels of the celestial skies! Come, Nuit and Hathor of the great Star Nations, who love humanity and help us grow. Goddesses of the eternal stars, inspire us so that we might stand united beneath the canopy of your splendor!"

The energy had risen to a crescendo. I could feel these vast energies stretching above us like a great shelter of protection. Shasta's hand went down toward the Earth, her palm flattened, as if she were connecting with the ground. "Listen, Powers of the great Below, we are speaking to you. Ground us now so that we might walk with humility and connect us with the sacred Earth, the Earth who has seen all ages move across and whose heart beats inside our own. Without the Earth Mother's grace, we would not be here." I felt a deep stillness move into my heart, and I realized that the entire group had knitted itself together in a web of intention. The deep throbbing pulse of the Earth moved through us.

At last Shasta placed a hand upon her heart and closed her eyes. We joined her in reverence. "We honor now the sacred center, the spring of endless life. Come, Lady of the Healing Waters; come, Isis of the holy center; come, Spider Woman who joins all things in sacred union within our hearts and minds. Come, Lady of the Silver Lake and weave our circle together with light." A hum of electric energy sang through us, vibrating like a column stretching between Heaven and Earth. I felt the presence of many celestial beings enveloping us with love.

THE GODDESS CHOOSES US

The directions had been called, and the circle was established. Shasta reached down and picked up a large scalloped seashell from the center of the circle. Inside were slips of paper. "It is now time to draw your first Goddess," she said, passing the bowl to her left. Meg took it. "See what the Goddess has in store for you."

The women's faces were apprehensive now as the bowl made its way around the circle. One by one we pulled a selection from the open shell. When it was my turn, I pulled out a folded strip of paper and passed the shell on. Finally, the shell returned to Shasta. "There are many goddesses in the universe, and many expressions of women," Shasta said. "Let us see now who has chosen you. Meg, you may begin."

I could tell how nervous we all were. Delicate little Meg opened up her slip of paper. "Lakshmi," she whispered, "Hindu Goddess of Abundance." *Perfect!* Meg was raising funds in Washington to help single women and children survive. I could tell she was happy.

Sara was next. She opened up her paper and read: "White Shell Woman, Goddess of the Oceans." *Ah!* She had gotten Aphrodite, the Goddess of Love. I wondered what would happen to her love life!

Claudia's voice quivered a little as she read. "Tiamat, the chaos dragon at the beginning of time." *Holy smokes!* This primordial energy was associated with the rebirth of one's entire life! I couldn't even imagine what would happen to her.

Emerald was next. The full-figured legal secretary read out bravely,

"Kali, the mother of transformation." Kali was the female counterpart to Shiva, the lord of transformation, a virtual powerhouse that seemed to totally suit Emerald.

Slender Alexis came next. "Diana, Goddess of the Hunt," she read, "protectress of animals and women." *Fabulous!* Alex was very much like Diana—trim, athletic, and strong.

Susan was next. She raised her chin and read, "Cybele, mother Goddess of Rome." I knew very little about Cybele, but I did know that there was a black stone of Kaaba, or meteorite, associated with her that the Romans used to worship, just as today the Muslims honor a black meteorite in their mosque in Jerusalem, the Dome of the Rock. Paintings of Cybele showed her riding a chariot pulled by lions. That was definitely cool.

Donna opened her paper. "Demeter, Goddess of the Harvest . . ." *Incredible!* Donna was the epitome of a sweet motherly woman. She even reminded me of Demeter.

Sharon was next. She opened her slip of paper and read uncertainly. "Amaterasu, Japanese Goddess of Renewal . . ." *Hmm . . . wasn't one of Amaterasu's symbols the life-giving sun?*

It was my turn now, and my heart was thumping in my chest. I opened my slip of paper and read, "Ishtar . . . Queen of Heaven and Earth." *Ishtar! Of all the goddesses!* She been there from the beginning, and the story of her journey into the Underworld in search of Tammuz had moved me greatly. I brought my attention back to the group just as Shasta was speaking.

"All right, your new assignment is to find out everything you can about this goddess. Remember that she has come to you with a very important message, and you will know why she has chosen you once you have integrated her story into your own. It is through their stories that we are able to learn who they are." We all nodded silently, drinking in her words. "We will reconvene on the summer solstice in three weeks' time, and you will each share what you have learned. Over the next few months you will also prepare a ceremony to honor your goddess. That is enough for today."

21

The Hero's Journey

꧁꧂

Myth is the secret opening through which the inexhaustible energies of the cosmos pour into human cultural manifestation. Religions, philosophies, the arts, the social forms of primitive and historic man, prime discoveries in science and technology, the very dreams that blister sleep all boil up from the basic magic ring of myth.

JOSEPH CAMPBELL,
THE HERO WITH A THOUSAND FACES

I had no idea that by merely pulling the name of a goddess from a shell I would begin to live her story, but that is exactly what happened. Ishtar's story, like that of Sophia, the Mother of Wisdom, is the tale of humanity's descent into a place of shadows and confusion, a place from which we must all be redeemed. Like many of the great kings and queens of Heaven, Ishtar descends to fulfill a quest. In her case, it is the quest for love. Once achieving it, she returns to Heaven enlightened. Like the Daughter Sophia, Ishtar's tale is one of loss, hope, courage, and love as she discovers the disowned parts of herself and finally reclaims her soul mate, Tammuz, to become whole once again. Because of the power of this tale, and its reverberations in us, it has survived for more than six thousand years.

As I had already learned, Ishtar falls from Heaven in search of love, arriving on Earth alone and vulnerable, just like us. Once in the lower realms, she is drawn deeper and deeper into the material world until she comes to stand before the great throne of illusion, draped in its glamour of worldly power. There she must face the one thing that she fears most—the dark mirror of herself. For some, this Shadow Queen might succumb to the lure of worldly riches. For others, that dark mirror is the search for fame or the insatiable desire to get the love or approval from others that we have never given to ourselves. For still others, the pain of being ripped away from the celestial realms is so great that they choose the path of oblivion, falling prey to drugs or alcohol or sexual addiction, all momentary highs to distract us from our emotional pain. But these are only substitutes for what the soul really seeks—reconnection to the Source of who we are. "Light and darkness, life and death, right and left, are inseparable twins," Jesus tells us in the Gospel of Philip, reminding us that "those who transcend these apparent opposites are eternal . . ." beings.[1]

Our fear or desire may take many forms; these are terms the Buddha called *mara* and *kama*.* There is no getting away from the fact that we are here in the realms of matter until our bodies disintegrate. We have fallen from the heights of Heaven and forgotten our divine nature. This is the real meaning of the Fall. It has nothing to do with being sinful; rather, it is a state of ignorance that causes us to believe that we are separated from God. In truth, we have always been a part of the Eternal. We have simply forgotten who we are.

The Ashtavakra Gita (2:4–5) tells us: "As a wave, seething and foaming, is only water, so all creation, streaming out of the Self, is only the Self."

Mara and *kama* were the two shadows that Buddha had to face in order to become enlightened and free of all attachment. They have also been compared to the Greek concepts of *thanatos,* or the death wish, and *eros,* or passion.

Thus, to find a way out of these illusions we must discover the sacred presence behind the worlds of nature. This is the very essence of Immanence itself. The spiritual world is all around us, if we can only see it. This discovery has the power to liberate us from the source of our pain, which is our separation from love. The scales fall from our eyes, and suddenly the world is revealed in a whole new light. Behind the forms is always the great Divinity shining through. This is the inner sight that allows us to finally see that the Kingdom of Heaven lies within ourselves, as well as all around us.

PULLING BACK THE VEILS OF ISIS

In the ancient Mysteries, this process of seeing the Eternal behind the ephemeral world was called "pulling back of the Veils of Isis." These veils are a metaphor for the millions of forms that conceal the numinous realms of light that form the true nature of the world. Through nature we can discover the numinous world of the sacred at the very heart of creation itself. The original Aramaic version of the Lord's Prayer, translated so beautifully by Neil Douglas Klotz and published in a little jewel of a book called *Prayers of the Cosmos,* reads:

> O Birther! Father-Mother of the Cosmos. Focus your light within us—make it useful. Create your reign of unity now—Your one desire then acts with ours, *as in all light, so in all forms.* Grant what we need each day in bread and insight. Loose the cords of mistakes binding us, as we release the strands we hold of others' guilt. Don't let surface things delude us, but free us from what holds us back. From you is born all ruling will, the power and the life to do, the song that beautifies all, from age to age it renews. Truly—power to these statements—may they be the ground from which all my actions grow. Amen.[2]

In Ishtar's story, she descends into the world of shadows to gain the one thing she most needs—her other half. But having lost her memory, she no longer recalls what she is searching for. However, as she stands before the throne of her half-sister, the Queen of Shadows, she is able to see the beauty behind the worlds of matter, and seeing this, she embraces the Shadow, knowing that all expressions of duality are part of the divine pattern of life. Through suffering, we learn compassion. Through limitation, we learn choice. Through pain, we choose a better path. With this one act of integration and surrender, Ishtar unites the positive and negative aspects of herself, uniting her mortal and immortal natures. This is the Way of Wisdom, and this decision sets her free.

THE MODERN HERO IS THE ANCIENT ONE

Many of our modern myths play out these same transcendental themes of reconciling the light and dark within ourselves. In *Star Wars,* Luke Skywalker faces his shadow by discovering that he is the son of the evil Darth Vader. When Luke cuts off the head of his enemy in Yoda's cave, he discovers that the enemy he has killed wears his own face. This theme is repeated when Luke loses his hand, just as his father did, following in Darth Vader's footsteps. Both Luke and Darth Vader have the same spiritual gifts, but one uses his powers for good, while the other uses those gifts for evil. As the first movie trilogy concludes, Darth Vader is redeemed only through Luke's unswerving belief that below the shadow that lies over his father's heart is the eternal illuminated soul, waiting to be reawakened.

Likewise, in the *Harry Potter* series, Harry finds a fragment of Lord Voldemort's soul buried within himself and realizes that his enemy can only be vanquished when Harry is willing to be the pure, surrendered sacrifice. "The hero is the man of self-achieved submission,"[3] writes Joseph Campbell. This is the theme of the Christ, a theme espoused in the ancient world in the celebrations of Tammuz, Osiris, Attis, and Adonis. At their deaths, these solar lords surrender to death and are reborn. In Harry's case he goes to Heaven and meets his teacher,

Dumbledore, who explains that Harry has a choice to continue into the higher worlds, or to return to Earth to complete his mission. This voluntary act of egoic surrender gives Harry the power to be reborn, then to vanquish the Dark Lord forever.

One of the reasons these modern-day myths are so compelling is that they reveal a great archetypal truth. In dissolving the judgments, shame, and guilt that often trap us in this world, we set ourselves free. "The hero has died as a modern man; but as eternal man—perfected, unspecific, universal man—he has been reborn,"[4] writes Joseph Campbell. In Ishtar's story, by releasing the judgments in the Realms of Shadow and seeing the goodness behind all forms, Ishtar is able to unite her ego and soul. With this, she is brought back into union with her other half and allowed to reenter Heaven. This is the essence of the hero's journey and the deeper meaning of redemption.

FAIRY TALES OF ONENESS

Ishtar's journey is one of a handful of myths that speaks to this dilemma of separation and redemption in the world of shadows. Often immortalized as fairy tales, these stories echo through the corridors of time. The most enduring of these tales seem to express two major themes. The first is the reconciliation between the worlds of spirit and the worlds of matter. The second is the merger of the male and female in sacred union: The prince searches for his princess, the princess searches for her prince; he saves her; she saves him. Once reunited, they live happily ever after within the kingdom of themselves.

So let's take a look now at some of these beautiful archetypal tales that endured through time. We begin with the story of Sleeping Beauty, a beautiful princess whose kingdom is frozen in time and is brought back to life by the noble prince who has the courage to search for her. She represents the sleeping spirit that is hidden inside each one of us. She is Sophia, the feminine Spirit, caught in suspended animation, who must be awakened by her illuminated other half. Likewise, in the story

Figure 21.1. The stories of Sleeping Beauty, Cinderella, Snow White, and Rapunzel all symbolize the reawakening of the sacred feminine that has long been dormant in our world. But only the noble prince can bring her back to life and place her on her throne as his equal in the world. (Illustration by Tricia McCannon)

of Snow White, we find an unblemished heroine who has fled from the machinations of the Wicked Queen, a woman herself trapped in vanity and illusions. Snow White is the positive feminine polarity, while the queen is the negative one. But in order to be saved, she must be awakened by her heroic prince. In essence, she must reclaim both her yin and her yang natures and be resurrected to win her kingdom back for the good.

In a similar vein, let's examine the story of Cinderella, an abused maiden who is the slave of three women who have been overtaken by their negative feminine polarity of greed, ambition, and lies. Cinderella must find the courage to take back her power by being seen at the ball by the noble prince. Then, if he is willing to see past the trappings of appearances to discover her true self, he will marry her and restore her to the throne as his equal. Then they will live happily ever after. Likewise, in the story of Rapunzel, a magical maiden has been subject to a lifetime of isolation and forgetfulness within her ivory tower. The heroine is finally rescued by an aspect of the positive masculine. All these stories reveal how the masculine polarity has the power to reawaken the feminine spirit within the world that has been dormant within us for so long. All these are tales of restoration, symbols of the Sacred Marriage that restores the rightful queen as an equal beside her noble king. Only this has the power to save the world.

As you will notice in many of these fairy tales, the prince rescues the princess. But in the case of Ishtar, these positions are reversed. Ishtar goes in search of her slain prince, trying to free her other half from bondage. She is the heroine who rescues the man, just as in the story of Beauty and the Beast. Beauty is the Divine Feminine who awakens the heart of the savage Beast. He is only restored to his divine form after he places the love of others over his own selfish needs, finally breaking the spell that has kept him bound.

All these tales are about the restoration of the world through the sacred feminine. As the Knights of the Round Table searched for the Holy Grail, they knew that they were pursuing the lost bride, furiously seeking to stop the oncoming darkness of the Middle Ages by recovering the soul of the Goddess. This was symbolized by the Holy Grail itself. These knights lived between 500 and 600 CE, just as the church began to seriously suppress the worship of the Goddess across all of Europe. It was in this same era (beginning in 591 CE) that the pope inveighed against Mary Magdalene, branding her falsely as a prostitute. After that, the truth of the female Christ was lost to us for centuries, and the only aspect that remained was the worship of the obedient Mother Mary. The resurrection of the Goddess appeared briefly in the teachings of the Cathars, the Knights Templar, and the troubadours of love in the twelfth and thirteenth centuries but was wiped out once again in the six centuries of the Inquisition. Yet as the Holy Grail stories reveal, the Fisher King, or male Christ, cannot be made whole without his queen or sacred chalice. Without the yin, the yang cannot be healed. The land is barren; the mare will not foal. Only her restoration can restore the kingdom to balance.

Interestingly enough, this same analogy was used by Jesus in the metaphor of the bride and the bridegroom. This union within the self allows us to enter the Kingdom of Heaven, code words for our reunion with the Source of All Being. Christ is the enlightened bridegroom, but who is the lost bride? She is the slumbering spirit that lies within each one of us, concealed by the patriarchy. These mythic legends have long endured precisely because of their themes of sacred union. And we must begin this reawakening of the Divine Feminine if we are ever to restore our own societies to health and balance.

THE THREE STAGES OF THE JOURNEY

In the hero's journey, there are three basic stages: the departure, the journey, and the return. The departure begins with a radical sweeping away of our old lives that opens the way for something new. Like Zut-su, this initiation often takes all that we have known in the past—our families, our homes, our jobs, and our ego identity—and wipes it away, creating a voyage of loss and death that ushers us into a new stage of life. The second stage of the hero's journey throws us into a new world, where we are pulled by forces we don't understand into an adventure that will fundamentally change our lives. Along the way we might meet sages, allies, monsters, wise women, dragons, and enemies. We may feel that we have gone to Heaven or Hell, depending on which part of the journey we are in. The third stage is the return, the completion of our journey where we return to the world with new insight, wisdom, or gifts, having gained the power to illuminate and solve the problems of our age.

Let's take the story of Perseus, the half-divine son of Zeus, whose tale has all the classic elements of the hero's journey. Perseus is an orphan and does not know that he is half-god, half-mortal. But when his adopted family is drowned in a fishing accident caused by Hades, the god of the Underworld, Perseus is thrown into the departure stage of his journey with events that will change his life. This is beautifully depicted in the movie *Clash of the Titans*. Perseus must then face Hades, who curses the city of Argos and decrees that Princess Andromeda will be destroyed by the monstrous Kraken. Perseus must then decide whether to continue believing that he is only a mortal fisherman or rise to meet his destiny as a demigod and save the city. This decision prompts him to embark on his quest, the second stage of the hero's journey. The journey is about discovering the various parts of himself and awakening something new within his heart. It frequently involves a descent into the realms of shadow to face his inner demons, find his power, and claim his true identity for himself. In Perseus's case, he must enter Hades—the Underworld—and bring back Medusa's head, since this is the only way to defeat the Kraken. As he overcomes these obstacles, Perseus sheds his old identity and is transformed, realizing that he is indeed both a divine being and also human, and this realization allows him to save the city. His task is "to return to us transfigured and teach the lesson he has learned of life renewed."[5] At this time, the hero will often bring back a symbol of victory—a sword, a book, a ring, or a chalice. In the language of the Mysteries, these items represent the archetypal qualities that have been restored to the hero's soul.

The final stage of the hero's journey is the return, the homecoming of the hero who brings back his gifts of knowledge. Having now viewed life from a new perspective, he has been reborn. Now he has the wisdom to save a city, defeat an enemy, or renew the world. Perseus saves the city of Argo and Andromeda and restores the world to balance. The Beast releases his kingdom from the spell, reclaims himself as a prince, and wins his one true love. Psyche reunites with her love Eros and is welcomed into Heaven as an immortal.

Behind all these stories is the legendary Fall of humanity. We are not talking here about a "fall into sin," but the descent of the soul from the celestial worlds into the realms of matter. This understanding of our true divine origins springs from the Mystery Schools, whose teachers understood the nature of multidimensional realities. We, each the divine child of God, have forgotten who we really are. Half of our nature must be rescued by the other half in order for us to come back into wholeness. To redeem our ignorance in the world of shadow, we must awaken within the dream and return to our true state. American mythologist Joseph Campbell writes: "The happy ending of the fairy tale, the myth and the divine comedy of the soul, is to be read, not as a contradiction, but as a transcendence of the universal tragedy of man. The objective world remains what it was, but because of a shift of emphasis within the subject, [it] is beheld as though transformed."[6]

ISHTAR ENTERS MY LIFE

When I first pulled Ishtar's name in our sacred circle, I had no idea that I would be suddenly faced with living her story. Her tale of loss and suffering for the sake of a man had great resonance for me because of the sacrifices of my mother. For the sake of love, my mother had given up nearly forty years of her life to save my father from alcoholism, hoping beyond hope that he could be rescued from the bottle. So I understood the emotional cost of being trapped in the shadows of abuse and emotional pain and not seeing a way out. I knew how the chaos of such a prison can make us lose ourselves for the sake of love.

While it takes great bravery to make such a sacrifice for another, sometimes the lesson is not whether to follow that person into the Underworld, but whether you should let him go. Despite my mother's incredible heart, she needed to recognize that the most important relationships we have are with ourselves and God. No matter how much we love another person, only he can face his own shadows, as only we can face ours. That is the power of free will.

In the myths and fairy tales related above, committing to the love

Figure 21.2. Ishtar with veils, looking for her love, Tammuz.
(Illustration by Tricia McCannon)

of another is symbolic of committing to loving the other half of oneself, the other aspect of the masculine-feminine polarity. Our other half can guide us toward this realization, but in the end it must truly be a *self-*realization. The journey must consist of all three parts. We must not get stuck in the journeying stage and forget to return to our self. Nor should we skip the journey stage to get to the comfort and security of the return.

Within a week of pulling Ishtar's name, I had met Brian, who quickly became my own fair-haired Tammuz. He was Irish, a beautiful soul with blue eyes and blond hair, and a healer to boot. We met at a conference in New York, where I was speaking, and he sang me a love song that melted my heart into a puddle. I invited him to join me for a weeklong retreat on Mount Shasta in California with twelve other light workers. We were going to make contact with the spiritual masters who are rumored to live beneath the mountain. As the leader of the group, I made strict rules for everyone about maintaining celibacy for the duration of the retreat, since our energies were to be focused entirely on the Divine.

We convened at a fabulous lodge on the side of the mountain, and for the next five days we all fell in love with one another. Whether doing ceremony on the seven-thousand-foot mountain slopes that were covered in snow, or exploring the secret Pluto Caves, the trip catalyzed a change in all of us. As the days unfolded, Brian revealed that he was in a deeply unhappy marriage with a woman who not did not share his love of God. He had only stayed in the marriage because of his two teenage children. As a clairvoyant, I could see what had propelled him into this marriage. Some 2,300 years earlier, his wife had been his mother in a village outside of Rome. As a boy, Brian had been brutally kidnapped, been forced into slavery, and died of abuse. This had set in motion many lifetimes of abandonment, and these two souls had been parted many times in subsequent lives as mother and son through outside calamity. So in this life they had come back together to heal. Now, exactly twenty-three years into their marriage, their soul contract was complete, but since Brian's core wound was abandonment, he was afraid to be alone.

Without intending to, Brian and I fell in love. We spoke about our feelings for the first time once the retreat was over. Brian desperately wanted a divorce but was afraid to be alone. He wanted to jump straight into another relationship with me, without taking time to reflect. He wanted me to be his catcher in the rye, and I said that I would think about it.

I returned home confused. The part of me that had fallen in love with Brian wanted to say yes, for he brought great joy to my heart. But the end of a marriage deserves to be honored as the big deal that it is. It is the departure stage of the hero's journey, where all that we have known is swept away. It represents not only the death of the present, but the death of all the hopes and dreams that two people have dreamed together. And while it is an end of one phase, from its ashes can come a whole new world of self-transformation. But the only ethical thing to do is to allow the people who are involved to complete their cycle, and to take the time for self-discovery. Without the journey into the self, there can be no solid foundation to start anew. If the wounded do not take the time to gather themselves and heal, they will just project their unhealed issues into the new relationship. The journey must be undertaken to make an effective return to a new marriage. The question that I found myself asking was this: "Was I willing to go to Hell to help save Brian, or was this something he needed to do on his own?" This was the dilemma of Ishtar, now fully alive within my own life.

THE POWER TO CHOOSE

When I got home, Brian called. He had gone straight home and bravely told his wife that he wanted a divorce. He had finally expressed his long-buried feelings that living with a critical, controlling "mother" was not making him happy, and since they hadn't been intimate for years, the passion had vanished. Apparently, he had done this once before, but this time he intended to follow through. Yet the more I listened to him go on and on about his breakup, the more clearly I saw that my beloved Tammuz was caught in his own Hell. All the sweet love that we had experienced on Mount Shasta was rapidly evaporating. While it had been easy to support Brian within the strong group consciousness, now I was being pulled into his negative whirlpool, witnessing all his years of unexpressed rage and hurt in his unhealed marriage. This was not a good beginning for a new relationship or a good departure from an old one.

I realized then that I could follow my prince into Hades, or I could step back and let him find his own answers. Even with all the love I felt for him, Brian had to love himself enough to complete the cycle of his unhappy marriage without using another person to do it for him. In *Awakening the Heroes Within,* Carol Pearson writes: "The heroic quest is about saying yes to yourself and, in so doing, becoming more fully alive and effective in the world. For the hero's journey is first about taking a journey to find the treasure of your true self, and then about returning home to give your gift to help transform the kingdom—and, in the process, your own life."[7]

Knowing that my own mother had gone into the depths of Hell for the sake of love and remained there for forty years with a man who either could not or would not extract himself, I realized that I did not have to be Ishtar. I could make my own choices and not be bound by hers. Whereas Ishtar had been mutually committed in a partnership of love before her descent, I was not. I had only just entered the scene. Spending months in the angry muck of Brian's dissolution of his marriage would not make either of us happy. He had to find the path himself, and then, anything was possible. I told Brian that he needed to work on himself first, and I withdrew, asking him to call me when he got things figured things out. But he never did. Brian left his marriage a year and a half later, running off with another woman who was willing to descend into Hell with him, but their marriage lasted only two short years. Since then, Brian has been married two more times.

22

The Power of Archetype

❧

The passage of the mythological hero . . . is essentially inward—into depths where obscure resistances are overcome, and long lost forgotten powers are revivified, to be made available for the transfiguration of the world.

JOSEPH CAMPBELL,
THE HERO WITH A THOUSAND FACES

Nearly twenty-five years ago, when I drew my first goddess in Shasta's circle, I did not realize the transformative power of archetypes. *Archetype* was just another buzzword in psychology to me. I did not know that these prototypes for human potential not only live inside each of us, but also exist within the mind of the cosmos itself. The hero, the romantic, the visionary, the lover—these are not only potentials within our psyche, but aspects of the collective consciousness that dwell within the universal mind of God. As a trained hypnotherapist, healer, and clairvoyant of some twenty-five years, I had a good working knowledge of the many conflicting subpersonalities that live within the human psyche and knew that they are not always in accord. I also understood why psychology, in an attempt to be accepted by traditional medicine, has sought to objectify human behaviors with clinically manufactured terms such as *social complex, childhood neuroses,* and *genetic predispositions.* Yet long before the advent of psychology, the sages of our past knew that the universal power of archetypes lies at the root of all human feeling, thought, and desire.

Psychologist James Hillman, author of *The Soul's Code,* once wrote that the modern objectification of the cosmos and of human behavior into merely clinical terms creates a kind of deadening inside of people. "The language of psychology is an insult to the soul."[1] He goes on to remind us that by working with the living power of archetypes we are brought back to life, since these archetypes not only live within the collective consciousness of the entire human race, but within each of us as well. Legendary teacher Deepak Chopra adds:

> Inside of every human being there is an overarching theme, a template for heroic living, a god or a goddess in embryo that yearns to be born. This is who we were meant to be, the self that we deny ourselves because most of us cannot see the field of limitless potential that is open to us. This is our best self, the egoless self, that bit of the universe acting through us for the good of all.[2]

As my studies with Shasta continued, I was to discover that we each have the power to awaken to these archetypes within ourselves and to utilize them as allies. In this way we can also awaken to the multidimensional facets of celestial beings that exist within the mind of God. We may choose to call these beings gods and goddesses, or to think of them as facets of our being that can be called up in times of need. But no matter how we look at them, they represent templates that are found in all, and when we can learn to interact with them, we can experience their wisdom for ourselves. Deepak Chopra writes,

Every one of us is hardwired at the level of the soul to enact or model [certain] archetypal characteristics. They are seeds sown within us. When a seed sprouts, it releases the patterning forces that allow it to grow into a certain type of plant. . . . The activation of an archetype releases its patterning forces that allow us to become more of what we already are destined to be . . .

Adopting an archetype is not labeling, because it is not about limitations. Quite the opposite. Archetypes are life models, images, and ideas that guide the direction of your life towards your soul's ultimate destiny. Recognizing your true nature and allowing it to blossom is part of the beauty of living from the level of the Soul—you can become the hero or the heroine of a mythical saga.

The blueprint that the universe intends for you is found at the level of the Soul. We get clues in the form of coincidences, and we get guidance in the form of archetypes. . . .[3]

So how then do we define an archetype? "Archetypes are primordial ideas that structure reality. They appear to us in the form of symbolic images [and] . . . may appear in the form of a variety of symbols . . . They are the vocabulary of the psyche itself, through which the Initiate can communicate with their own inner depths."[4] Archetypes can also be defined as "preconscious psychic dispositions" that enable a person to act in a particular manner. Depending on the orientation of a particular society, these archetypes may be viewed in a variety of ways. Religion considers them as divinities; history calls them myths or legends; and psychology labels them complexes or archetypes. As a clairvoyant, however, I was to discover that they are far more than simply psychological constructs.

PLATO AND JUNG
ON CELESTIAL ARCHETYPES

Today most people are familiar with the term *archetype* through the work of pioneering psychologist Carl Jung, founder of Jungian psychology. However, Jung's work springs from an even earlier epistemology, taught by the famous Greek philosopher Plato, who placed the existence of archetypes at the center of his worldview nearly twenty-five hundred years ago. Where modern-day civilization primarily looks to the external world for answers, earlier cultures often probed behind the worlds of form to the spiritual realms they believed create the visible world. They studied the patterns of nature and connected these observations to science, philosophy, and religion to forge a more integrated worldview.

Plato came to believe that these overarching patterns stem from the existence of even larger cosmic beings that he called archetypes, "forms," or "ideals," meaning patterns of potential that live within us all. Plato believed that these forms are actually the eternal expressions of Divinity itself, the mind-stuff of God; thus, they have the power to influence the world around us. The ancients believed that these energies, which they called gods and goddesses, are broadcast through the emanations of the

Figure 22.1. Profile of Plato.
(Illustration by Tricia McCannon)

planets, the subtle energies that bathe our planet and other planets as well. The ancients ascribed various qualities to each of these planets, linking them to the gods: Venus, Mars, and Saturn, for example, came to represent the energies of love and beauty, courage and action, and structure and discipline, respectively. This range of qualities can also be found within each of us at various times.

The Greeks also observed these same great archetypes in their tales of the gods and goddesses of ancient legend. These are larger-than-life prototypes that appear in every culture of the world. Some of these gods were helpful to human beings, while others placed obstacles in our way. The appearance of such a being might signal the onset of a challenge, the awakening of a love, or the overwhelming power to transform one's life. Yet the ancients recognized that the traits of these gods and goddesses (whether based on extraterrestrial visitors or not) also exist within human beings as divine potentials, which means that they can be activated in our lives at any time.

Modern psychology has assigned them various labels: the lover, the warrior, the hermit, the sage, the prostitute, the beggar, the thief, the minstrel, the artist, the visionary, the prophet, the king, the queen, the critic, the perfectionist, and the scholar, just to name a few. Plato believed, like Jung many centuries later, that the direct knowledge of these intelligences is the only knowledge there is, for they are the real spiritual intelligences that lie behind the world of the seen, generating the framework upon which all of life is created.

Joseph Campbell, the renowned mythologist, tells us, ". . . the symbols of mythology are not manufactured: they cannot be ordered, invented, or permanently suppressed. They are spontaneous productions of the psyche, and each bears within it, undamaged, the germ power of its source."[5]

Much of the knowledge taught within the ancient Mystery traditions was transmitted through the use of archetypes in myths, stories, and symbols. To the ancients, knowledge of the gods was a shorthand way of conveying a host of enduring truths that speak to the deepest level of our being.

Throughout the inhabited world, in all times and under every circumstance, the myths of man have flourished; and they have been the living inspiration of whatever else may have appeared out of the activities of the human body and mind. It would not be too much to say that myth is the secret opening through which the inexhaustible energies of the cosmos pour into human cultural manifestation.[6]

Understanding this can be quite a stretch for those raised in a materialistic society and taught to cling only to external realities. In understanding how these forces work, it is helpful to consider the ancient axiom *As Above, so Below,* meaning that the physical energies at play in the world around us are often a reflection of a larger spiritual reality. While today most of us are unaware that such a realm of invisible supernatural beings even exists, when we begin to work with divinities, we awaken our ability to interact with these teachers. Macrobius, the famous philosopher of the fifth century CE, writes: "The Mysteries are concealed in myths so that the few may know the real secret, through interpreting them wisely, while the rest are able to happily venerate the mystery, defended by these allegories against banality."[7]

Plato maintained that human beings can experience contact with these gods and goddesses directly before we incarnate in this world. This happens between lifetimes in the heavenly worlds. He explains this concept in the *Phaedrus,* arguing that after death each soul passes through the higher realms during the stage of metempsychosis. At this time the soul has the opportunity to gain an awareness of the divinities, and then, through our interactions with these divine beings, we may be inspired to express certain aspects of their essence ourselves. Pythagoras also taught metempsychosis, the belief that when souls pass through the higher heavens they sometimes interact with these divine presences. Plato called what we bring back to Earth "recollection" or *anamnesis. Anamnesis* is the recall of visions from a time in the heavenly worlds that predates this life. Some people, he writes, actually remember these higher beings, and thus find themselves dedicated to a life of justice or heroism, art or music, truth or beauty, the love of children or the passion of dance. This is precisely because we have been inspired by these divinities before we were born. Thirty-three-degree Mason Manly P. Hall writes, "Whenever through self-unfoldment, an individual attains to the state of consciousness symbolized by a certain god, then that god is declared to be incarnate in that personality and to actually walk the earth."[8]

Pythagoras believed, like teachers in the Mystery Schools, that all souls reincarnate in their evolving quest for perfection. Whatever is not learned in one lifetime is repeated in the next until we finally awaken to the inner light and begin to connect with our true nature. The idea that we are each connected to a larger divinity is a powerful one. My own spirit guides, Rigel and Auriel, had long ago told me that we are each like wicks in a candle, connected in a great chain of being from the highest heavens down to Earth. By following the thread upward, we can discover a larger piece of ourselves. So whether we think of them as gods or goddesses, teachers, angels, spirit guides, or as a higher aspect of our own divine self, these divinities can become powerful spirit allies to assist us in our mission here on Earth. In his *Republic*, Plato writes:

> When all the souls had chosen their lives according to their lots, they went before Lacheis [the Goddess of Fate]. And she sent with each, as the guardian of his life and the fulfiller of his choice the genius [daemon or guardian spirit] that he had chosen, and this divinity led the soul first to Klotho [Klotho spins the destiny of our lives with the red threads of Fate]. Under her hand and her turning of the spindle, the destiny of the chosen lot is ratified. Then the genius again led the souls of the spinning of Atropos [a term meaning "fixed" or "determined"] to make the web of its destiny irreversible, and then without a backward look it passed beneath the throne of Necessity.[9]

This tells us that before every lifetime we decide on our purpose. Then we come before the Goddess of Fate to choose the spirit guide who will best assist us in our mission. This guide then leads us before the divinities who will help to map out the details of that lifetime, including the decision to be born into a rich or a poor family, our sex and race, the country of our birth, and the soul contract we have agreed to take on in any particular incarnation. This also includes the physical, mental, and emotional endowments we will need to fulfill our purpose once we have grown up.

So why do we not remember these decisions? The Greek belief is that we pass through Lethe, the river of forgetfulness, on our way to Earth, and forget the agreements that we have made. Yet we are still overseen by our spirit guides who nudge, support, and encourage us from behind the scenes, helping us to align with our higher purpose. Once we do, through the use of our own free will, the divinities are there to help us fulfill our contracts.

While the topic of angels or spirit guides is generally left to theology, some psychologists, historians, and mystics like myself would argue that these overlighting divinities exist far beyond the mortal world and are much larger in scope than our minds can conceive. Historian Richard Tarnas writes, "Platonic Forms . . . possess a quality of being, a degree of reality that is superior to that of the concrete world. Platonic archetypes not only form the world but also stand beyond it. They manifest themselves within time and yet they are timeless. They constitute the veiled essence of things."[10] They are the intelligences behind the mundane visible world that lies all around us.

CARL JUNG COMES ON THE SCENE

The famous psychologist Carl Jung once wrote, "Archetypes have their origins in the dawn of human history. The psyche is not of today. Its ancestry goes back many millions of years."[11] Jung readily admitted that he had first discovered the concept of archetypes in the teachings of the Hellenistic and Gnostic worlds, where spiritual initiates were introduced to the myths, heroes, and archetypes that offered a gateway to

Figure 22.2. Photo of Carl Jung.

understanding the higher realms. Jung's understanding of these spiritual intelligences gives us tools that allow us to reconcile the cold objectivism of modern-day science with the inner yearnings of spiritual faith that bind the universe together.

Born in Germany in 1875, Jung was the son of a Protestant minister; his grandfather was an Old Testament scholar who spoke with spirits, and his grandmother was known to fall into trances and prophesy. Growing up, Jung read widely, delving into the literature of spiritualism and psychic research, including Protestant theology, Christian mysticism, and the mystical works of Emanuel Swedenborg. He absorbed the traditions of the German Romantics and studied biology in the works of Charles Darwin and Ernst Haeckel, seeking to reconcile the world of science with the worlds of philosophy, faith, and mysticism.

From 1900 to 1909, Jung worked as a psychiatrist in a mental hospital and began lecturing at the University of Zürich in 1905. He was active in the Freudian psychoanalytic movement from 1907 to 1913, and from there went on to develop the foundations for what we know today as Jungian psychology, an approach that grew out of his years in private practice, from 1913 to 1936. In his early years, he tried to link these recurring archetypes, which appear in every ancient religion of the world, to both genetics and heredity. But over time he became convinced that these archetypes are real, active forces in the world of nature. Over the course of his many studies in history, religion, mythology, psychology, and parapsychology, Jung discovered that the same archetypal patterns seem to exist in every period of history, no matter what culture he probed. Jung ultimately came to believe that, like the creational gods of ancient Egypt, called the *Neteru,* these gods, or archetypes, are an elemental force that has played a vital role in the creation of the human psyche.* The true power of working with such divinities, Jung believed, lies in their ability to both inform us and transform us.

THE NATURE OF ARCHETYPES

One of Jung's many contributions was to develop a therapeutic technique based on the spiritual practices of the early Gnostics, who were devoted to reawakening the divine self behind the many facets of the personality. In this process, initiates enter into an objective relationship with the various archetypes or subpersonalities found within their inner world. Then they interact with these archetypes through a process of inner dialogue. In this way, we each discover whether these voices are merely a subpersonality or voice within ourselves, programmed by our upbringing, or whether there is a genuine spirit guide speaking from inside us. Jung wrote of his own personal experiences with just such

---

*The *Neteru* were archetypal gods honored at the Temple of Heliopolis in ancient Egypt. Originally, the list included Nu and Nun, Hehu and Hehut, Kekui and Kekuit, and Kerh and Kherhet, each pair representing complementary yin and yang properties of primeval matter. For example, Nu or Nun (the male and female aspects) represented the idea of the deep abyss from which all life emerged, while Hehu and Hehut were the primeval elements of fire. Over the centuries, these concepts evolved to include Tem or Atum, the unified name for God, as well as Ra the sun god, Shu for air, Tefnut for moisture, Geb for Earth, Nuit for the starry heavens, Isis for the Divine Mother, Osiris for the Divine Father, and, finally, Horus the Divine Child of truth. You will notice that most of these gods have a yin and yang aspect, reflecting the Egyptian belief in the balance of the universe (E. A. Wallis Budge, *The Gods of the Egyptians,* vol. I [New York: Dover Press, 1969], 282–91).

a guide, named Philemon, who became his spiritual instructor, just as Rigel and Auriel had become mine. "Philemon and other figures of my fantasies brought home to me the crucial insight that there were things in the psyche which I do not produce, but which produce themselves and have their own life."[12] These benevolent powers, then, have the ability to act as allies or teachers for us in our journeys.

Archetypes can be considered from both a psychological and a spiritual point of view. Certainly, we can argue that anything that appears in our dreams is simply an aspect of ourselves; however, there are times when we may make contact with beings from a higher plane who exist independent of ourselves, whether we call them masters, sages, angels, or divinities. These beings have their own history, and they live and breathe quite separately from us. Christian theology might define them as Mother Mary or the savior Jesus. Egyptians might see them as a visitation from Horus or from Isis. In Native American wisdom, such an encounter might be with White Buffalo Calf Woman, or in Chinese culture, Quan Yin. All these events are possible, for each of these Divine Presences has acted as an overseeing spirit guide for entire cultures. When the person experiencing these encounters has no prior knowledge of these beings—something that has happened to me time and time again—the message that divinity conveys can then be tested or corroborated by those who have had similar encounters throughout history.

Reconciling these kinds of profound encounters with our modern-day paradigms is the major challenge before us, for the modern mind seeks to compartmentalize our life experiences into the mental constructs we have been taught compose "reality." While these encounters with beings from another plane of existence may not only be real, but also life-changing, most of us are at a loss to explain how such events could happen. That is because current Western theology does not provide a template for the multidimensional nature of reality, or for understanding how these various aspects of the Divine can act as teachers for our growth.

During the course of our spiritual unfoldment, any of us may connect with several sets of spirit guides at different points along our journeys, just as we are assigned different teachers in school, appropriate to our current level of learning. When a new teacher arrives, we may be completely stunned at the depth of our own reactions. In response to this development, Jung was moved to remark that "there is a god or a goddess at the heart of every complex." Jung claimed that he first discovered the power of archetypes by observing radical changes in his clients' behavior that were often accompanied by having their lives turned completely upside down. We find ourselves madly in love, brooding over an issue, suddenly compelled to have children, insanely possessive, ready to settle down, or acting with the passion of a zealot. These emotions all have archetypal corollaries—deities who have played out these emotions on the grand stage.

Author Robert Bly points out that these archetypes are actually transformers that appear during times of life transition. This may occur in adolescence, or upon meeting your future mate, opening you up to an entirely new level of yourself. Discovering such a divinity may occur through a dream, a vision, a near-death experience, or a spontaneous encounter. Jung believed that these "potentials for significance" are not really under our conscious control but seem to happen as if out of nowhere. One of the best examples I can think of is falling in love. Most of us have experienced that wild, exhilarating feeling as the chemistry overtakes us. Our beloved is the Venus or Adonis of our dreams. We are possessed by an overwhelming compulsion to be with our love, elated by anything that has to do with the object of our desire. But as the weeks or months pass, the glamour seems to fall from our eyes, and instead we find ourselves projecting our hurt, anger, and fear onto the other person. Suddenly, the archetype has changed.

These changes may also come during other important life passages, such as the sickness of a loved one, or the death of a parent or mate, awakening us to a deeper connection with the Otherside. Why would such traumatic events usher in a new archetype? Perhaps because that deity's perspective is exactly what we need to weather the coming storm. During these seasons of change, we often experience a departure from our safe,

secure realities, and it is then that our spiritual allies can help us to discover a larger understanding of the world. These spirit beings and their
stories give us knowledge, support, and attunement to a broader range of
perceptions[13] and have the power to change us. As Carl Jung once noted,
the archetypes don't just pattern behavior, they transform it as well.

In his book *Archetypes and the Collective Unconscious,* Jung writes
that human beings share a single universal mind that is rooted in the
human unconscious, in the same way that a huge tree is rooted in the
ground, a concept no doubt linked to the ancients' version of the Tree
of Life. Plato would say that these intelligent fields of energy "in-form"
the very essence of who we are at every level. Science seems to be coming to the same conclusions. Dr. Edward Whitmont, a physician turned
psychotherapist, writes in *The Alchemy of Healing* that by applying
physicist David Bohm's theories of the "seen and unseen" worlds behind
quantum physics and Rupert Sheldrake's morphogenetic resonance field
hypothesis, the ultimate nature of the universe is not "substance," but
immaterial fields of dynamic forms that intercommunicate with one
another through resonance. These vibration fields of intelligence can be
perceived more easily when we consider them as real, living beings. As
members of a society that prides itself on rationalism, we would like to
deny such influences. Yet despite our best scientific theories that falling
in love is only the result of chemicals released in the brain, we continue
to fall in love every day. Irrationally, illogically, and undeniably, we act
in ways that even the best Freudian analyst can't explain. Jung's explanation of these higher-dimensional realities opens up a link between the
spirit worlds and the human world that neither modern-day religions
nor science seems able to embrace, despite the millions of people who
have had these divinely inspired encounters.

THE SCIENTIFIC VIEW OF REALITY

Both religion and science have long had a knee-jerk reaction when it
comes to the idea of interacting with polytheistic gods. Science, which

emerged out of centuries of church territorialism, deliberately limited itself to the objective study of the physical world. Yet now, physicist Michio Kaku, as well as other leading-edge pioneers into subatomic research, have discovered the existence of at least ten different dimensional levels of reality, or planes, all created by the vibrational frequencies of quarks, neutrinos, leptons, and so forth, many nested one inside the other. These planes are separated by vibrational frequency, making the inhabitants of the other planes invisible. All this has been prompted by the discovery of string theory, opening up a door to areas of paranormal research that in the past were off-limits to serious academics. Dr. Kaku tells us that, until recently, scientists viewed the idea of multidimensional realities with suspicion. "But recently the tide has turned dramatically, with the finest minds on the planet working furiously on the subject. The reason for this sudden change is the arrival of a new theory—'String Theory' and its latest version, 'M-theory,' which promises not only to unravel the nature of the multi-verse, but allows us to 'read the Mind of God.'"* Dr. Kaku reminds us that in strictly scientific terms, the *M* stands for "membrane" but that "it can also mean mystery, magic, or even Mother."[14]

Quantum physicist Ervin Laszlo, author of *The Self-Actualizing Cosmos*, calls this the Akashic field, the subtle interconnected dimension that lies behind our visible one. This is the vast sea of the cosmos in which we swim, and it contains all the information, energies, and archetypes that are aspects of the intelligence of God. It is multidimensional and multilayered. It is the world of the shaman and the mystic, and it defines and informs the visible world. Our job is to become more conscious of this dimension and the powerful messages of wisdom that flow through it into ours. Then we have the chance to learn from it.

So while a multidimensional view of the world was once the sole purview of mystics, we are beginning to find a basis for what the sages have long taught about the nature of reality and, perhaps eventually, the many

---

*While string theory and M-theory are in many ways identical, M-theory unifies many different string theories.

beings that compose it. This multidimensional construct is something that the masters have long imparted to initiates, and it is heartening to realize that modern science is now creating an overlap between spiritual, philosophical, and scientific thought that is long overdue. Philosopher Ken Wilber writes that the Akashic world "is a transuniversal holofield operating in a largely unmanifest dimension that gives unity to all things manifest, and is the actual ground from which the entire manifest realm emerges and to which it returns . . . [It] is ultimately responsible for the coherence of the universe itself, [and] is well known to the mystical traditions the world over."[15] Sociologist Kingsley Dennis reminds us that this new paradigm "does not destroy or collapse our current model of reality. Rather it updates these previous stages of knowing into a more inclusive model that better serves to explain how the manifest world exists—and can exist—within a 'hidden dimension' that underlies the structure of a more complete, inclusive energetic reality."[16]

THE FEAR OF GODS AND GODDESSES

In Western religions, however, the fear of interacting with other divinities comes from an entirely different root. As we have seen, within the three Abrahamic religions the heavy-handed politics of the priests of Yahweh wiped out all competing deities some twenty-five hundred years ago, including the Divine Mother and her resurrected Son. And as we have seen, the reign of terror that marks the six centuries of the Christian Inquisition is a matter of public record, although few of us have been exposed to the details of this debauchery because it is something the church would rather keep from us. Thus the knee-jerk reaction that most people have to the mere mention of any "other gods" in Christianity, Judaism, and Islam has behind it the fear of impending doom.

The rabid vehemence of the *Catholic* Church (a term that means "universal" or "all-inclusive," by the way) toward other religions has been extreme, to say the least, and the ravages of Jewish and Islamic conquest are not far behind. When Pope Innocent VIII issued his edict of 1484 against the pagans, the greatest targets were those who still communed with the Earth, the village healers, mystics, and shamans who understood how the manifest and unmanifest realms worked together to teach wisdom. Later this same religiously justified brutality was used to annihilate millions of Native Americans whose only crime was believing that the spirit of God exists in everything. They embraced the concept that all of life is sacred, a philosophy so threatening to the patriarchy that they began the extermination of millions—all in the name of the Prince of Peace.

THE GIFTS OF WORKING WITH ARCHETYPES

For those who are still challenged to expand their view of reality to include the existence of other realms, the idea of archetypes can be understood in terms of Jungian psychology. In Jungian thought, when we connect with a god or a goddess we gain the power to draw on these qualities within ourselves. One aspect of the deity might symbolize courage, while another brings wisdom. One archetype might awaken a passion for music, while another inspires the pursuit of scientific understanding. In this way we may call on many different archetypes within our own psyche to help balance our lives. This is also the way that many ancient people worked with gods or goddesses.

For example, instead of identifying with the archetype of the victim or the victimizer, the virgin or the prostitute, you might draw on the bravery of Sekhmet, the lioness of healing and courage. If you are taking the world too seriously, you can invite in the playful energies of Bast or Sarasvati, Goddesses of the arts. In times of injustice, you can align with the principles of Ma'at, Athena, or Archangel Michael, each powerful allies for justice. If you are focused on the home, Hestia, Goddess of the Hearth, is a terrific partner. If you wish to open doors of opportunity, the Roman Goddess Cardea, the Egyptian God Anubis (opener of the ways), or the lovely Hindu Lord Ganesha, are all guardians who can help you to open the door at the right time.

In times of spiritual darkness, there can be no greater allies than Jesus, Buddha, Horus, or Thoth—all masters of enlightenment. Or you might choose the powerful Goddess Durga, who holds the implements of both love and power in her hands. Durga awakens enlightenment, protects the innocent, spins the universe, and repels the forces of darkness, while offering the rose of divine love to all. For those who seek spiritual wisdom and healing above all else, Sophia and Isis are profound teachers of both. And if you wish to awaken the currents of compassion, wisdom, and partnership, Mother Mary and Mary Magdalene can help connect you with the highest streams of the healing benefits of these pursuits.

THE HERO WITH A THOUSAND FACES

Whether you consider archetypes as just a manifestation of the collective unconscious, or as real living presences, millions of people have interacted with them in life-affirming ways throughout the centuries. At the very least, the stories of the gods and goddesses are role models for heroism, kindness, perseverance, grace, and beauty. And in the case of Ishtar, her story provided me with the perspective to see clearly the consequences that lay before me if I repeated my mother's pattern, and to make a different choice.

When we step back to realize that, in all the known and unknown dimensions of space, there are trillions of life-forms existing in multiple realms, it is not surprising that there are many intermediary divinities between us and the Source of All That Is. Each one of us is created by the same Intelligence, whether we call it God or the Goddess, Atum or the Great Mystery. This is the Divine Intelligence that has created our world. Since this Divine Presence is the sum total of all that is, divinity resides in everything and everyone. God creates billions of subsets of itself from the highest heavens to the lowest molecule. Its intricate patterns are repeated in the atom, the solar systems, and the galaxies, revealing an intelligent design behind all things. Those beings who dwell in the higher realms are more awake than we are, while those in the worlds of shadow are often lost in amnesia and ignorance. Each life-form shares this sacred spark, extending from the subatomic levels to the angelic realms, finally reaching the great Ocean of Love and Mercy itself. Since the whole universe is alive with consciousness, energy compartmentalizes itself into packets of more or less complexity. Those beings who are less evolved are as alive as we are but not as aware, just as the divinities who are larger than we are, are more aware. But all these expressions of God are still smaller than the ultimate Creator itself.

Joseph Campbell reminds us: "The gods and goddesses then are to be understood as embodiments and custodians of the elixir of Imperishable Being, but are not themselves the Ultimate in its primary state. What the hero seeks through his intercourse with them is therefore not finally themselves, but their grace; i.e., the power of their sustaining substance. This miraculous energy substance and this alone is the Imperishable."[17]

Now having entered the third millennium since Christ, it might be wise for us to consider an attitude of respect for all of life, whether in this realm or the next, instead of barricading ourselves behind centuries of ignorance, superstition, and fear. After nearly half a century of studying the world's greatest myths, Joseph Campbell came to believe that all the deities of the world's great religions were only "masks" for the same transcendent truths. "Truth is one, the sages speak of it by many names," he said, telling us that all spirituality is a search for the same transcendent Source from which everything comes, and to which everything will return. Heroes and heroines, he writes, incarnate our highest values, and it is by following that stream of divinity that we arrive at the great river that allows us to claim the totality of who we really are.

23

A Return to the Circle

Great one who became Heaven, Thou didst assume power;
thou didst stir;
Thou has filled all places with thy beauty.
The whole earth lies beneath thee. Thou has taken
possession of it.
Thou enclosest the earth and all things in thy arms.

HENRI FRANKFORT, KINGSHIP AND THE GODS

June 21, the summer solstice. I awoke in the first glimmers of gray dawn and went out to meet the sunrise. Throwing a blanket over my shoulders, I made my way out into the backyard and sat cross-legged in the medicine circle that I had built only a few months before. Of all eight High Holy Days, the summer solstice was the longest day of the year, the one that most celebrated the victory of the light. I had brought cornmeal and tobacco to offer to Mother Earth, two of the substances most sacred to the native peoples. As I poured the soft, golden cornmeal onto the ground in prayer and laced it with the sacred herb of tobacco—an herb known for bringing stillness and focus—I realized that they were both the color of the sun. These offerings were not only for Isis, the original Corn Maiden, who had long ago brought us bounty, but for all the great solar gods and goddesses who have given their lives to service and shared their wisdom throughout the ages with humanity.

Five minutes later the light began to break across the horizon. "Dear Lord," I prayed, "accept this cornmeal and tobacco as a tribute to your bounty. Know that I, your daughter, honor you in every expression that you have. Help us as human beings to find balance in our world once again, to find the good and the sacred in all people, animals, and life."

The sun rose through the trees slowly, sending its soft fingers of light across the grass, and I found myself thinking about how the symbol for the sun and for illumination had been the first catalyst that had introduced me to the Mysteries and to the presence of the Goddess in the world. It had come to me so many years ago in that dream. Not only did the circle with the dot at the center represent illumination, it was the cosmic heart from which the entire universe sprang. If this one symbol had led to so many amazing discoveries, I knew that in time the other symbols inscribed upon that wall would unfold their magic to me.

I closed my eyes and placed my hands over my heart, feeling the light play across my eyelids. Suddenly, the birds broke into song, as if the entire world had just awakened. Heaven and Earth, yin and yang—this was the eternal dance of complements in perfect union, and here I was between the worlds at dawn. All around me the Earth seemed to be lit with an inner radiance, and I realized that, although I was just a tiny dot on this magnificent planet, bathed by the sun, I was part of the infinite intelligence of the universe. I could experience the joy and sorrow, beauty, and hope of living here on this glorious planet. My heart was overflowing.

I found myself reflecting on all that I had learned in the past few months: about the hidden history of our planet, and the ancient balanced societies that had lived in partnership without war or oppression. Would we ever be able to return to this state of grace again? Would those who were in power across the world, dedicated to fear and dominance, greed and power, ever allow that vision to be known by others? I didn't know, but I did know that if human beings had once lived in harmony, we were capable of doing it again. Our generation and the ones that followed us had the chance to find this balance again, a path that Jesus and Mary Magdalene had once called the Way of the Chalice. The chalice was the union of the male and female energies, depicted in the phallic stem and the crescent cup. It implied our ability to allow ourselves to be filled with the living nectar of God's exquisite love and to become a vessel of this light. Later, this union of the two, which culminated in the Middle Path, was inscribed into the petals of the fleur-de-lis, marking a path of integration and wholeness.

My mind went back to a passage I had read about the transformation of the world, written by the wise Masonic teacher, Manly P. Hall:

It is predestined that the golden age shall come again; that men shall live together in love and understanding, and the earth shall become once more a garden of surpassing beauty as it was in the beginning. In that time . . . there shall be great institutions for research and records; the arts and crafts shall flourish. But unlike preceding generations this era shall not pass away; for the God of it shall be Beauty and where Beauty, in its various aspects rules a people, that people shall remain as permanent in eternity . . . When we love the beautiful as we now love the dollar, we shall have a great and enduring civilization. When we adore the God of harmony as we once worshipped the God of vengeance, we shall know the inner mystery of life. When we create with symmetry, preserve with integrity, and release with joy, then only are we good. Never until we have become one with the good can we be happy, for happiness is the realization of the internal beauty that joyously goes forth to mingle itself with the beauty that dwells in space.[1]

Could we now begin to envision a world without war or bloodshed? We had been programmed to believe in conflict for so long. The first step was letting people know that it was possible, that there was another way of life beyond the one the world was mired in now. I also knew that there were many financial powers that sought to prevent this kind of peaceful world from coming to be in both secular and religious circles. They had been born and bred on conflict, duality, and separation, and their religions had taught them that everything else was the work of the devil. But the world was finally changing, slowly but surely. The dualistic energies of the Age of Pisces were starting to pass away, and in this new age anything was possible.

How would life change if people really started to honor the Divine Mother and the Divine Father once again? How would we change if women had the same rights as men, and refused to be suppressed? If we valued intuition, creativity, love, and mercy as much as we now valued possessions, money, power, and control? How would our world change if we truly lived as if we were all connected, treating others as if they were an extension of ourselves? That was the Golden Rule, wasn't it? How would life change if we made decisions regarding our fuel supplies that honored the Earth? What if we started honoring the animals instead of slaughtering them for profit or sport? Would we be able to hear them speak telepathically, as native cultures claimed we once had? How would life change if we began to take the time to tune in to nature, listening to the intelligence of the waters, the whispers of the trees, and the spirit of the cosmos carried on the winds? Would we come back into harmony with the spirit of God within?

I hoped so.

I reflected on how history has been rewritten again and again by the victors in a political war of the mind, trapping us between the threat of a punishing God and the shadows of a boogeyman named Satan. I realized that we had long been engaged in a war for the hearts, minds, and spirits of humankind, an invisible prison designed to keep us in an endless loop of materialism, fear, and self-doubt, all created to prevent us from discovering the divine potential that lies within our very hearts. Yet now, here on the cusp of the Age of Aquarius, an era whose symbol is the outpouring of heavenly wisdom from the stars, hope was beginning to rise. Perhaps this time the dream of a more loving society might become a reality.

Then I found myself reflecting on all those brave men and women who have given their lives throughout the centuries to keep the dream of equality alive for us today, those who had sacrificed everything so that this hidden knowledge of a more balanced wisdom might not be obliterated: the Gnostics, Cathars, Kabbalists, Masons, healers, Knights Templar, herbalists, druids, scientists, philosophers, mystics, artists. Many had withstood the tortures of the past so that today we might awaken from amnesia and break the chains of belief that have kept us in bondage for so long. Today, on the day of the greatest light, I saluted their courage, their hearts, and their sacrifice.

When I finished my meditation, the sun was at the top of the trees. I stood up, stretching, then went inside to shower and dress. I packed my car with blankets, food, and a sleeping bag, for Shasta had invited any of us who wished to do so to spend the night in the grove. I pulled up in front of her house in the early afternoon and made my way down to the garden with the other women who were just setting up their tents around the garden's perimeter. Then the group assembled near Mary's garden to eat a meal of tuna, hummus, and pita bread. Around us the trees seemed to shimmer with radiance, and the afternoon sunlight touched every leaf as if it were holy. When we had finished eating, Shasta began to speak.

"Today you will be offering your first ceremony to the Divine Mother, but before we begin I want to hear what has happened in your lives since we last met. How has the Goddess been working in your life?"

Meg began, relating a story of how Lakshmi, the lady of generosity, had opened up funding for a children's project in Washington, creating abundance for hungry children across the nation. Alex told us how the Goddess Diana had inspired her to join a softball team at her office, and now she was thinking about enrolling in a qigong class. Donna reported that after choosing Demeter, the Harvest Goddess, she had suddenly been inspired to buy some living herbs at the supermarket. Now she had a collection of rosemary, lavender, lemon balm, oregano, and basil growing in pots on her patio. She had intended to use the plants for cooking, but now she was thinking of creating herbal bath salts. *Wow!* I marveled. *The Goddess certainly has been hard at work!*

Claudia spoke next. She had chosen Tiamat, the celestial dragon, and she had no idea how to relate to her. Shasta told us that many people believed Tiamat had actually been a large planet, located where the asteroid belt is now. It had been destroyed by an even larger planet, changing its destiny forever. "Tiamat," Shasta explained, "is about completely restructuring your life."

Claudia nodded thoughtfully. I had known Claudia for years, and she had had a successful career already as a makeup artist in Hollywood and Atlanta. Although she was fabulous at her craft, her heart longed for something with more meaning. "I've been thinking about studying astrology," she said in a tentative voice. "I might even become a professional astrologer." We all started laughing. *Of course! A Goddess of the Heavens . . . Perfect!*

When I shared my story about Ishtar, and the romantic relationship that would have certainly left me drained of energy, the circle became silent. Shasta waited until I had finished to share her insights. "Sometimes the lesson is not about making the same mistakes," she explained, "but about choosing a more empowered path. The Goddess and her stories live on in every one of us, men and women alike. We are all heroes and heroines of her legacy. What she has done, we have also done. The paths that we travel now, she has traveled before. So because the Divine Mother has been there before us, she can help us to make wiser decisions."

When all the women had finished sharing, Shasta began her lesson for the day. "Over the past few months, as we have moved from winter into spring, you have heard many stories about the descent of the god or the goddess into the Underworld, and their return to the light. While these may be myths or legends, the tale that they tell is true. We are all aspects of the Great Mother living in the world of light and shadows. Like the legend of Sleeping Beauty, we are slumbering in ignorance, and like her we can also awaken. Today is one of the eight High Holy Days where the crack between the worlds becomes thinner and you have a chance to travel between the worlds. While the summer solstice celebrates the illumination of the great solar lords, we must also remember to honor the Divine Feminine, for the goddess is also solar, just as there are some gods who are also lunar."

Solar goddesses? Lunar gods? Even Emerald looked surprised. I had never thought outside of the classic stereotype that the male was solar while the female was lunar. As I looked across the circle, I could see that some of the other women were equally as surprised.

Shasta continued, "In Egypt both Khonsu and Thoth were linked to the moon. Thoth chose the moon because he discovered its effects on the human, mineral, plant, and animal kingdoms, and in Thebes the young god Khonsu ruled the changing cycles of mortal time."

Hmm . . . I had no idea. The Egyptians clearly knew that everyone contains both polarities.

Shasta went on. "Within the Goddess path some of the most ancient female deities are solar, including Sekhmet, the Goddess of Healing and War; Amaterasu, the Goddess of the Sun; and Bast, the Goddess of Joy. But the rarest of all the gods and goddesses are those who are both lunar and solar, like Isis. These are the ones who have integrated both polarities to achieve mastery. The most famous of these divine pairs in the ancient world were Isis and Osiris, while the teachers for our age were Jesus and Mary Magdalene." She looked around the circle to see if we were following. "Isis and Osiris were said to have been twins in the celestial womb, a metaphor for their true identities as the Divine Mother and Father of the All." *Hmm . . . It sounded like some incarnation of Rigel and Auriel to me . . .*

"Osiris is solar, and Isis is lunar, but Osiris can also be lunar, while Isis can be solar. They are the perfectly balanced pair. When Isis is partnered with Nepthys, her dark sister who rules the unconscious realms, she is the expansive, outwardly flowing solar aspect of the female, while Nepthys is the receptive, reflective aspects of the lunar. And when you compare Isis and Osiris to Nepthys and Set as couples, Isis and Osiris are the male and female expressions of the light, while Nepthys and Set are the male and female aspects of the darker or more hidden realms."

Wow! No wonder they had the power to uplift the world!

Shasta continued her narrative. "When we begin to speak about the yin and the yang, we are really speaking about the balance that leads to mastery. I have not told you yet the true tale of Isis and Osiris, and how they helped to save humanity after the Great Flood, but today seems like a perfect time." Several of the women shifted as if getting ready for a story. Shasta began.

"After the Great Flood, the world was in chaos. People were starving, so cannibalism was rampant. Isis and Osiris decided to help, and since Osiris was a musician he gathered people together with music and fed them. But he also brought seeds and planting tools and taught them skills for growing their own food, as well as the spiritual principles of enlightenment. Because of this he was called the Green God, the God of regeneration. This is why he is painted green in the temples. Meanwhile, Isis was left to bring order to Egypt. She reestablished temples to God, ended cannibalism, instituted marriage, created the first sailing ships, invented the first loom, and taught the arts of agriculture to her people once again. Together they established Ma'at, the cosmic law by which all the pharaohs of Egypt were expected to rule. While Ma'at is a goddess, she is also the symbol for this principle of cosmic truth.

"Meanwhile, Set, Osiris's half-brother, was given southern Egypt to rule, but he was jealous of Osiris and decided that he wanted Isis for himself. So he tricked Osiris into lying down inside a golden coffin, then sealed it and threw it into the Nile, stealing Osiris's lands for himself. Isis was grief-stricken and fled the palace, for she knew what this would mean for Egypt. The only chance she had was to save her husband, so along with her nephew Anubis, she set out to find him. After a long search, she finally located his coffin in Byblos, where it had been hidden in a huge tamarisk tree that had grown up around it. The tree had been cut down by the King of Byblos for one of his temples, and through a long and complicated process Isis eventually pried his coffin from the tree and took it back to Egypt. Through magic, she temporarily brought Osiris back to life, impregnating herself with his seed. Then she left to find help, but while she was gone Set found his brother's body and cut it into fourteen pieces."

Yikes! That sounded grisly. Shasta went on. "Knowing that the peace of the kingdom was at stake, Isis gathered up the pieces of her husband's body and bound the parts back together, creating the first funerary rites in Egypt. However, the only piece of his body that Isis could not find was his phallus." Shasta looked around the circle. "What is the deeper meaning of this story?"

We all looked at one another, stunned. *I had no idea.* I was still shocked at the idea that someone would dismember such a compassionate being. Susan cleared her throat uncomfortably, and Donna crossed her legs. After a minute, when it was clear that none of us knew how to even begin to decode this story, Shasta spoke. "Each of us are just like Isis, searching for the scattered pieces of ourselves and trying to put them back together. But the only thing that can mend us is the healing power of love. It is through the heart that we are made whole."

Ah! I suddenly got it. As a Goddess whose heart beat in time with the Divine Mother's, Isis had the power to bring the scattered pieces of Osiris's body back together and raise him from the dead. He symbolized the Christ within, and she symbolized the redeeming quality of love that can unite and revive us!

After a minute, Donna said, "But what does the phallus represent?"

Shasta looked around the circle. "Any ideas?"

I could have understood the story more easily, I thought, if it was the heart that was missing. *But what did the phallus represent?* I wondered.

"The phallus is the regenerating principle of life itself. When we find it, we will awaken Osiris and bring him back to life."

I was trying to put the symbols together in my mind. The scattered parts of Osiris were like the assortment of archetypes that live within us. They are the many selves that we have left scattered throughout time, not only in this life, but in our past incarnations. Only by remembering, healing, and reuniting those lost aspects of who we are, can we awaken to the Christ that lives within. And the only thing that had the power to do this was love. In a very literal sense, the phallus is the one part of a man's body that creates new life, and like the spine, the phallic symbol has long been connected with the Tree of Life. So while love is the power that unites and heals us, we must then find our way to unite ourselves with the mystical power of the Tree of Life, a symbol of the Way of the Return to the Source of who we are. *Hmm . . . Those Egyptian sages were certainly clever, weren't they?* They had created symbols that were encoded in myth and legend that would unfurl their wisdom to us even today, if we could only decipher the symbols' true significance.

"This allegory of the Christed One, who is divided from himself and can only be healed by the power of the Divine Feminine, is not only about us as individuals," Shasta continued. "It is also about our fragmented societies that lie scattered like a broken body in our past. We have forgotten the trail of our own history, and to be healed, we must remember the pieces of the journey that have brought us here, so that we can heal the past, change the present, and create a positive future. Then we can come back into union with the cosmos, but only love can make us whole."

Shasta looked around the circle. I was surprised to see tears on the cheeks of some of the women, but I knew how they felt. We have been lost so long in the Underworld that the possibility that we would someday awaken as a peaceful planet was almost beyond imagining.

"The place where healing happens is in the heart," Shasta explained. "It is the place where all judgments fade, all polarities unite." Silently she placed her hands over her heart. After a moment we joined her, feeling ourselves come truly present in the moment. Then she rose to her feet, and the group rose with her. Shasta picked up a rattle and passed the basket of gourd rattles around the circle. Slowly we each chose one. I closed my eyes and took a breath, feeling my heart swell within me with the radiance of the moment. Then Shasta began to sing. "We all come from the Goddess, and to her we shall return, like a drop of rain, flowing to the ocean." We all began to dance, making a long, circuitous path through the entire garden. At every alcove we stopped, and one of the women would offer a ceremony to the Goddess she had chosen. Some sang songs. Some danced. Others used symbols or prayers. As the many faces of the Mother moved into our hearts, I realized that each of us was being introduced to each of the goddesses, and that some of them were speaking silently in the power and beauty of the rituals.

When we had finally finished, we found ourselves standing inside the medicine circle at the base of the garden, as the sun was going down. Shasta had laid a pile of wood in the fire pit at the center of the wheel. Now she reached down and lit the logs, letting the gold and red flames lick up into the darkening blue sky. The wood popped and crackled, releasing its life force to offer us light. For a long time, no one spoke. Everything we needed was in this moment. Finally, little Meg cleared her throat and began to chant. "My light to your light, sister and friend, bless now the children from beginning to end."

Sara looked over at her and picked up Meg's chant. "Heal now our sorrow, our sadness and pain, and help us return to your wisdom again."

Sharon looked over with a smile on her face. "Awaken our hearts and remind us to give, that we may embody the power to live."

Emerald lifted her head and said proudly. "Rekindle the wisdom that lies in our hearts, and banish the darkness that keeps us apart."

Claudia picked up the chant. "Give us the strength and the power to love, that we may join Earth with the heavens above."

Suddenly the words rose in my mind unbidden, as if we were all listening to the same unbroken song. "In moments bold and currents deep, let us awaken those who sleep."

Alex followed. "The time has come and the people yearn, for love and healing, and peace to return."

Donna finished the spontaneous chant. "Awaken the Mother, let peace come to Earth, for we are the ones to bring the world to rebirth." When the mantra had completed itself, we stood in the fullness of the silence with our arms laced over one another's shoulders. The firelight licked our faces, and we were complete.

That night, as I lay sleeping beneath the stars, I had a great vision. Whether it was a vision or a prophecy, I cannot say, but I was staring at the surface of a still, blue pond in the moment before the first drop of water fell and the heartbeat of the world began. Like an echo rippling out across the smooth circle of fluid waters, this drop spread out to create everything. Then I heard a chime through the silence, rippling through the universe. With the timbre of a thousand Tibetan chants, the voice began: *O-de-ah-na, O-de-ah-na, O-de-ah-na . . .* over and over again. From this sound flowed atoms, tones, harmonies, the galaxies— all of it! I was caught up in the power of its resonance linked to creation itself. Through the sound I felt Auriel enter my consciousness and speak. I stretched out my inner senses to greet her, but this aspect of the Great Mother felt far more ancient than she ever had.

"Auriel? Is that you? You feel like a wise old grandmother. You're different somehow." An ancient Presence filled my mind, and I realized that this was the Presence behind the Word, the First Cause, the One that the Egyptians had called Atum—the power behind the Divine Mother and Father. The silence was so deep within me that there were no words for it, and I realized then that the beings I knew as Auriel and Rigel were the first emanations of this Immensity. But this aspect was far older, the One who existed before anything else, the Word and the Silence itself.

"Odeona," I whispered, the Great Mother of the All, the One behind the many.

"Yes, it is I," the voice answered, a hum and a song all at once.

Suddenly, I found myself traveling through a deep star field, the velvety richness of the heavens around me. It was warm and comforting like the Mother's womb, not cold and empty. Then I realized that I was actually floating in a great dark ocean, and that universes of luminous lights were reflected above me and below me. I had been to this place once before, and I felt infinitely safe. "You are the Grandmother of the All," I whispered. "Aren't you?"

"That I am."

In this place there were no longer any questions or answers. Here, it was all simply *being*. It was as if my consciousness existed everywhere, in everything. I was a man and I was a woman. I was the animals and I was the plants. I was the planets and I was the stars. I was all of it, and where I perceived myself as separate was only a matter of where I stood in the vast rotation of the wheel. *All that we do to others, we also do to ourselves,* I thought. Now I truly understood. We were all of it. Tears of gratitude trickled down my face. "I serve You, Mother, each and every aspect of you," I whispered. The darkness was alive with luminous life.

"We know you do, child."

Then I began to pray. I prayed for guidance, for power, for wisdom. I prayed for humor and endurance. I prayed to hold her presence within my own, and in some small way to be able to embody her ageless wisdom. Then another image appeared in my inner sight: a blue frost lake, frozen in winter, wrapped in the dark night of a colorless world. Beside the lake nestled a village of half-frozen people asleep in their homes. Beneath the moon, purple shadows crossed the white blanket of snow, the frost of the cold night air everywhere. *Why was she showing me this?* I wondered. *What did it mean?*

She whispered through the stillness of the frozen night. "Awaken, my children, awaken." I realized then that this village, these people, this world—they had been asleep for centuries. As I watched, she blew her warm breath across the lake, and ever so slowly the lake began to thaw.

What did this mean?

"Great Mother, who are these people, and why are they half-frozen? Why are you showing me this?"

The answer came back. "I stir the fires of consciousness now in humanity. They have been sleeping for centuries. I bring them forth from their comas."

"Are you awakening those who sleep? Is this what is coming to my world?"

"I am. It is."

"What manner of prophecy is this?" I whispered.

"It is about the resurrection of the Spirit."

The resurrection of the Spirit? What did she mean? "Meaning no disrespect," I said, "but that sounds rather Christian to me."

"Behold the vision, and tell me what you see," she answered. I looked again and saw a gray, dusky dawn over a sleeping village. The village was nestled at the foot of some mountains around a circular lake. It looked a lot like the Swiss Alps, but it could have been anywhere. Over everything—even the people—there was a layer of frost. The Great Mother leaned over the picture, breathing her warm, sweet breath over the lake as if slowly thawing it. "And what is happening to the people?" she asked me. I could see that the ice was just beginning to melt from their bodies, like embers rekindling from the ruins of gray ashes. Even though none of them could move yet, it was only a matter of time until they were free.

I told her what I saw. "When you blow your breath upon them, Mother, they seem to glow from within, deep inside their hearts."

"It is their spirits I am awakening," she said. "They are coming back to life."

Then it hit me. *Like Sleeping Beauty, the world has been frozen in its spiritual evolution for a very long time. Now we were beginning to wake up.*

"This is the real meaning of the word *resurrection,* my daughter, for they have been dead inside for centuries."

"What killed them?" I whispered, wondering what could have put them into this state.

"Ignorance, deceit, materialism, their own pain."

"Is this a metaphor for my world?"

She smiled. "You could say that . . ."

For over an hour I lay beneath the stars, moving back and forth between the Ocean of the Infinite Cosmos and this image of our planetary awakening. I reflected on Odeona, the Grandmother Spirit beyond time. She was most certainly the Goddess the Hindus called Aditi, the "first" cause, the progenitrix who enfolds creation within her womb, the transcendent source of all things, the Supreme Empress; she who manifests all dimensions out of a "fraction of a fraction" of her majesty.*

Then I felt the sweet energies of Auriel enter my consciousness, bringing the most sublime kind of love. The hush of her presence filled me, and her words rose unbidden in my mind. "All things are born of her, She of Ten Thousand Names and Ten Thousand Faces, the Eternal Law. She is the Earth and the heavens, the small and the large, and the Mother at the heart of forgiveness. Nothing lives but for her presence. She contains the three flames of the Sacred Heart. She is the undivided heart from whence we spring and to whom we shall return."

Tears welled up in my eyes and prayers fell from my lips. "Divine Ones, in our reckless youth and arrogance we have forgotten you, just as a child forgets its parents while playing in the streets. Distracted by the circus, we have forgotten. Yet like the eternal protectors that you are, you see us, watch us, and allow us to stumble, loving us through all our errors." Rigel's deep presence then filled my heart, and I spoke in gratitude to all three of them together. "You are the Eternal Watchers to all of our days, and if we but realized it, we would know that you have created everything for our benefit—the heavens, the planets, the fields and forests, plants and animals, even our own bodies. You are here in the garden and there in the temple. You are out in the streets and safe in the cottage. Beloveds, you are inside of us and outside of us, if we could only let our blindness go."

---

*In this form, the Rig Vedas call her the Rajarajeshvari.

Auriel's voice was like music. "Many have argued that there is only one God, my daughter, while others have said that there are many. Do you not yet see that there is only One, the One behind the many, watching, waiting for you to awaken? Yes, all the gods and goddesses are one. And just as Rigel and I have created the universe through our separation and union, this dance of polarity that seeks oneness is the two of us finding one another again and again in all the worlds of space and time." A circle appeared in my mind and split in two. I knew what this vision was. It was the Creator who longed for companionship, but being the One and Only it did the only thing possible—it split itself in two, so that it could behold itself for the first time. From this beginning were the Two Great Powers born, and they recombined to create the limitless light of the illuminated Daughter and Son.

Auriel spoke, "The One that is in all things created the angels, the humans, the gods, and the goddesses; yea, It even created us so that It would have companions. Since you are made in Its image, how can you not see that the Divine exists in all things? For what is your love for one another, but an echo of the Great One's love for you? And when you enter the eyes of the Beloved, you enter the gates of Heaven. Love is always the key to the door, even into the heart of God itself. When I and my Beloved are one, I dwell in the center of all being."

A vision of the universe swept through me, living, laughing, loving, being born and dying, all part of the endless cycle of forgetting and remembering who we are; losing our way, then finding ourselves again. I saw the entwining of lovers, the birth of babies, the death of the old, and the birth of the new. I saw time in an endless spiral moving upward and downward in succeeding waves of consciousness; the eternal dance of Brahma, Shiva, and Vishnu; the breathing in of the Earth, and the breathing out of the mountains, the rocks being pushed into the sky, and the lava flowing out; oceans replacing continents, people perishing and being born again. Like atoms in the vast waters of the Cosmic Sea, we go beneath the waves to explore the bottom, then resurface to feel the sun once again. Yet above and below the waves, life is everywhere, and each dimension holds its treasures. Behind it all, the Ancient One watches, the Great Spirit of everything.

Then my guides' voices spoke together:

> *From the point of Light within the Mind of God,*
> *From the point of Love within the Heart of God,*
> *From the Center where the will of God is known . . .*

I knew this was the Great Invocation used by mystical orders of the past. I picked up my pen and began to write down the words as they came through. "In the beginning was the One without limits, without judgment, without separation; the One without name, the Mystery behind Wisdom, the place before Space, Eternity before Time, Prime Creator, the Essence, the Beginning and Ending, the Circle without end, the Eternal Mother."

Figure 23.1. Mary Sophia with the dove and the chalice. The dove reminds us of love and forgiveness, and the fleur-de-lis is the Way of Mastery and Integration. (Illustration by Sylvia Laurens)

Odeona took over, her voice, a deeper timbre than Auriel's, echoing inside me like something deep that I had forgotten. "All things are contained within Me, and all worlds are but an echo of Myself. I am the seed of your true nature, even as the acorn contains the insouciant energy of the mighty oaks. Within you is the power of ten thousand suns, and there is nothing you cannot be if you will only tap into your true Self. I am there within, waiting for you to call. If you are willing to listen, I will answer. I am the Sound beneath the Silence—the I Am that I Am."

I finally understood those words—there was no other beyond that Presence. I closed my eyes and listened to the words moving through my heart. Auriel was speaking. "And then the Creator breathed, and the sound that ushered from Her was a deep wind, yea, rather the spinning of the vortex as She moved within herself, a generator of energy and motion, curiosity and love. Like the shattering of a million billion stained-glass windows; like the beating of a trillion angels' wings not yet born in thought; like the roaring of the waters of creation She burst forth into the first mirroring of Herself. The One facing One, Eternal Twins, Eternal Mirrors, Auriel and Rigel, Isis and Osiris, Mary and Jesus, Eternal Love meeting Absolute Truth."

Odeona's voice took over. "And who are these Ones that we speak about? The Father and Mother of the All. Auriel: love beyond measure; love beyond question; absolute, unconditional, forgiving love before there was anything to forgive; love that leads back to wholeness, the doorway to completion, the fabric upon which creation is built. Eternal Mary, the Cosmic Ocean . . . Sophia unfolding like a rose, whose love spun him into being."

Rigel! A song rose unbidden in my mind. *Lord of creation, Ancient of days, Universe Maker, here's a song in your praise . . .*

Odeona's voice went on. "The winged one who spans all universes, who holds creation in his gaze; the One who came into being from the very thought of love, the longing of love, as the companion of love—the reflection of eternal truth, the husband of beauty; the eagle, the falcon, the Eternal Father."

I saw his great wings moving as the tips of his feathers reached out to set the first elements into motion: fanning the fires of first light, the currents of first air, sculpting the first elements of Earth, drawing the first waters of nectar from the wellspring of the eternal chalice. All of these he drew from the Mother as his great winged spiral swept the universe into motion. The outward yang drawn from the inward yin of our being. In my mind the two circles joined now, overlapping at the center. They created the divine portal, the pattern of life that encompassed power and love, honoring all of whom we are in the majesty of truth. The One who looks into the mirror and sees Itself awakening through the heart of divine union.

I only hoped that the time was coming when others would remember this truth, and that with this great remembering, we would collectively find the courage to create a brave new world.

Glossary of Goddesses and Gods

Allah: Arabic male derivative of the original Allat, a term for the female aspect of God.

Allat: Ancient Sumerian name meaning "lady" or "Queen of Heaven." Equated to Hera, Ashtoreth, or Asherah.

Amaterasu: Japanese Goddess of the Sun, associated with light, growth, and new cycles of life.

Anath: *See* Ishtar/Inanna/Anath/Astarte

Anubis: Egyptian god who is the Opener of the Ways that lead the soul from the physical world after death into the heavenly kingdoms. Anubis has the head of a basenji dog, often mistaken for a jackal. Like a dog, he was known to be very loyal, faithful, and true and is often associated with funerary rites.

Aphrodite/Venus: Greek and Roman names, respectively, for the Goddess of Romantic or Sexual Love.

Apollo: *See* Horus/Apollo

Artemis/Diana: Greek and Roman names, respectively, for the Goddess of the Animals, Woods, and Hunt; protector of the forest, women, and children. The Temple of Diana was one of the seven wonders of the world before it was destroyed by the Christians around 400 CE.

Asherah/Ashtoreth/Hera/Juno: Hebrew, Canaanite, Roman, and Greek names, respectively, for the Mother Goddess, Queen of the

Anunnaki gods, married to Jehovah/Yahweh/Zeus/Jove. Associated with peacocks, swans, ibises, horses, and lions. Overseeing Goddess of Marriages and Households, Hera was also known to be jealous of Zeus's sexual exploits.

Astarte: *See* Ishtar/Inanna/Anath/Astarte

Athena: Greek and Roman Goddess of Wisdom, the Arts of Civilization, Strategic Battle, and War. Equivalent to the Egyptian Goddess Neith. Her chief city was Athens, Greece.

Auriel: Divine Creatress of the Universe, the essence of unconditional love.

Balder: Odin's son. Norse version of the benevolent Son of God, who was killed by Loki, the trickster god.

Bast: Egyptian Goddess of Love, Joy, Music and Dance. Her joyous festivals of beer and marijuana attracted seventy thousand people in Egypt for a week each year and were second only to those of Isis/Osiris.

Binah: Hebrew name for the Divine Father principle on the Tree of Life.

Black Madonna: The hidden Mother behind creation, associated with all the hidden aspects of the Madonna, including Isis, Mary Magdalene, and Sarah in the south of France.

Brahma: Hindu God of Creation.

Brigit/Bridget: Goddess of the Healing Waters and the Flame of Truth. Her centers in Kildare, Ireland, were kept alight for centuries. Brigit was also known as the bride and may well be associated with Isis and Mary Magdalene. She is the maiden aspect of the Celtic Triple Goddess, which also includes Cerridwen the mother, and Hecate the matron or crone.

Cardea: Roman Goddess of Doorways; great for opening the way.

Cerridwen: Celtic Goddess of Alchemy, Transformation, and the Cauldron; the mother of the Celtic Triple Goddess.

Changing Woman: Native American Goddess who rules the cycles of time and change.

Chokmah: Hebrew name for the Mother principle on the Tree of Life.

Cupid/Eros: *See* Eros/Cupid.

Cybele: Roman Goddess who may be an aspect of Asherah or Ishtar.

Cybele is associated with a chariot pulled by lions, and her chief temples were in Rome.

Danu: Celtic Goddess of the Tuatha De Danan, or the people of Danu. Undoubtedly one of the Benevolent Shining Ones or Anunnaki gods, since the ruler of their planet is called Anu.

Demeter: *See* Isis/Demeter/Ceres

Devi: The Hindu version of the Supremely Radiant Divine Mother and the embodiment of the female creative power. She is One Who Redeems in situations of utmost distress.

Diana: *See* Artemis/Diana

Durga: Durga means the "inaccessible" or "invincible" and is the demon fighting form of Shiva's wife Parvati. As the Hindu Goddess of Love and Protection, she manifests fearless patience and never loses her sense of humor, even in battles of epic proportion. An aspect of Devi the Supreme Mother, she exhibits fierce compassion. She is often depicted with eight to ten arms, holding a lotus, a sword, a mace, and a bell of awakening in her hands. She also spins the galaxies into being and is often shown riding astride a lion or a tiger. Durga exists in a state of independence from the universe and is an embodiment of the feminine creative force known as Shakti.

Elohim: A term that literally means "the Shining Ones" in Hebrew. These are the Anunnaki gods who came from the sky, helped to create humanity, and oversaw our growth for millennia.

Enki/Ptah: Sumerian and Egyptian names, respectively, for the "Pa," or Father of Human Civilization. One of the three most important of the Anunnaki gods, Enki had his center in the city of Eridu in Mesopotamia. Enki was the overlighting intelligence (one of three gods along with Thoth and Ninmah) behind the building of Egypt. He was an engineer, architect, and geneticist and was known as the "Lord of the Waters." The Greek version of Poseidon may well have been based on him. His chief temple was in Memphis, Egypt.

Enlil: The most powerful of all the Anunnaki gods who ruled on Mount Olympus. He was the "Lord of the Command," associated with the control of the winds. En means "Lord," and Enlil was also known as the "God Most High," since all the other gods had to obey his edicts. Either Enlil or his son Ninurta, who inherited his arrogance and authority, was most likely the deity called Jehovah or Yahweh that interacted with the Hebrews during the Exodus. He and Ninurta were associated with thunder and lightning.

Ereshkigal: The Anunnaki Goddess who ruled the Underworld with her husband Negral. The "Underworld" was either near the tip of South Africa or in Antarctica. Ereshkigal was the half-sister of Inanna.

Eros/Cupid: Greek and Roman names, respectively, for the God of Romantic Sexual Love; son of Aphrodite. The prick of his arrow causes its victim to fall in love.

Freya: Norse Goddess of Battle and Love; wife of Odin. Said to have a chariot pulled by cats.

Gaia (Gaea)/Turtle Woman: Greek and Native American names, respectively, for the living intelligence of the planet Earth.

Ganesha: Hindu elephant God who is the son of the Goddess Lakshmi and the God Shiva. Ganesha is a benevolent god who is the Protector of the Good, Guardian of the Gates, and Opener of the Ways.

Geb: Egyptian Earth God; husband of Nuit and father of Nepthys and Typhon, or Set.

Hades/Negral: Roman/Greek and Sumerian names, respectively, for the God who ruled the Underworld with Ereshkigal, Ishtar's half-sister.

Hathor: See Ninmah (Ninharsag)/Hathor

Hecate: Hecate derives from the Egyptian term hekba, meaning "magic." During the period of the Inquisition in the Middle Ages, this name became associated with the Goddess of the Crossroads and Dark Arts but was originally the name of the Goddess of Transformation, similar to Kali or Cerridwen in the Hindu and Celtic cultures.

Hera: *See* Asherah/Ashtoreth/Hera/Juno

Hermes Trismegistus/Thoth/Ningishzidda/Mercury: Greek, Egyptian, Sumerian, and Roman names, respectively, for the God of Wisdom. A god whose Greek name means "thrice great Hermes," but who hails from both Egypt and Sumeria. Hermes Trismegistus was the quintessential spiritual initiate whose wisdom taught humanity the gifts of healing, mathematics, spirituality, and writing. He was the scribe and messenger of the gods. Thoth was the Inventor of the Alphabet, Master of the Cycles of Time, and author of the Emerald Tablets, the Egyptian Book of the Dead, the Kybalion, and the Hermetica. Thoth and his daughter Isis, and grandson Horus, set up the great Mystery Schools of learning across the world. It was said that Thoth embodied the wisdom of the cosmos, and thus he was called the Logos. A hundred years after Jesus lived, there were still forty-two books in the Library of Alexandria that had been written by Thoth. They were said to contain the wisdom of the world in subjects ranging from astronomy to astrology, herbology, law, mathematics, architecture, magic, and healing. In Egypt his main temple was located in Hermopolis.

Hestia: The Roman Goddess of the Hearth and Home. She has strong links with Celtic Brigit as one who teaches children the arts of civilization. An excellent guide for families and children.

Horus/Apollo: Egyptian and Greek names, respectively, for the divine son of Isis, who brought balance and light back to Egypt after the murder of his father Osiris. Horus is associated with music, healing, truth, and prophecy, although he proved himself quite capable in battle. He is one of the Four Great Kumaras, or Sons of God, who periodically incarnate in the world to help humanity.

IHVH/YHWH: The tetragrammaton, or four-letter designation, that symbolized the tetrad of the Divine Father and Mother, as well as the Divine Son and Daughter. Once the priests of Yahweh destroyed all other aspects of worship, this term was adopted to simply designate the male presence of the Father God Yahweh.

Ishtar/Inanna/Anath/Astarte: Sumerian, Babylonian, Hebrew, and Greek names, respectively, for the Daughter Goddess, Goddess of Love and War, honored throughout Mesopotamia, the Mediterranean, and the Middle East in various forms. One of the best known of the Anunnaki gods. Her real father was Nannar and her lover was Tammuz. In the Hebrew pantheon, however, the Mother and Father gods were Asherah and Jehovah, the Queen and King of the

Anunnaki pantheon. Ishtar was the perennial maiden whose rites were connected with love and fertility.

Isis/Demeter/Ceres: Egyptian, Greek, and Roman names, respectively, for the Goddess of Healing, Wisdom, and Magic and Cereals and Grains. She was the wife of Osiris and mother of Horus who brought the arts of civilization and spirituality to Egypt. Isis represents the I AM presence of the Divine Feminine, and one of her many titles was "She of Ten Thousand Names and Ten Thousand Faces," for it was understood that this Divine Presence incarnates on Earth again and again for the enlightenment of humanity. Her chief temples were at Philae and Heliopolis in Egypt.

Jehovah (Yahweh)/Jupiter (Jove)/Zeus: Hebrew, Roman, and Greek names, respectively, for the "God Most High" in the Hebrew and Anunnaki pantheon. Derived in its purest form from YHWH, representing the I AM presence of the Divine Mother and Father, Daughter and Son (see also IHVH/YHWH). Associated with thunder, lightning, and thunderbolts, as well as exhibiting supreme authority over all other gods and goddesses. He was known as a jealous, punishing god.

Jesus/Yeshua/Issa: Greek, Hebrew, and Arabic names, respectively, for the human incarnation of the Son of God, bringer of wisdom and truth for our age, who embodied the Christ principle of love, enlightenment, compassion, and forgiveness. One of the Four Great Kumaras who incarnate from age to age to bring enlightenment to humanity.

Juno: *See* Asherah/Ashtoreth/Hera/Juno

Kali: Hindu Goddess of Life, Death, and Transformation. An ancient form of Shakti, the Grandmother Crone Goddess who recycles all phases of the cosmos within her body.

Krishna: A Hindu incarnation of the Preserver God, Vishnu. The gentle God Krishna was associated with shepherding, music, and joy. His female consort was Radha. He became the teacher of the five princes in the famous Hindu epic The Mahabharata and, like the solar lord Horus, he rose to do battle with the dark powers when it was necessary. Krishna is one of the incarnations of the Four Great Kumaras, or Sons of God, who periodically come to Earth to help humankind.

Lady of Guadalupe: An incarnation of the Divine Mother from Mexico who appeared shortly after the devastation of Central American culture by the Spaniards in the 1500s.

Lady of the Lake: Celtic Goddess of the Waters, linked to the healing and cleansing power of the Divine Mother. It is from her that King Arthur first received his sword Excalibur, and to her that it was returned.

Lakshmi: Hindu Goddess of Abundance and Success, known for her generosity and goodness. She is the consort of Vishnu, the preserver aspect of God.

Ma'at: Egyptian Goddess of Truth, to whom all gods, goddesses, and pharaohs are sworn. She is the cosmic law by which all the pharaohs of Egypt were expected to rule. Some believe that it was she who first emerged from the Cosmic Egg, for without divine law nothing could be created.

Maia: Roman maiden Goddess of May. Maia rules the season of spring and the Maypole.

Mary Magdalene/Maryam/Mary Sophia: The female aspect of the Christ, the Daughter principle that came to Earth with Yeshua to express the loving nature of partnership. Long maligned by the church fathers, Mary Magdalene taught the Way of the Chalice as the path of the return, a path that taught the balance of the male and female in perfect harmony.

Mary the Mother/Mary Anna: The human mother of Yeshua whose spirit was so pure that she was said to have been impregnated by the spirit of God, linking her to the Virgin Goddess of Creation. Later she was called the Virgin Mary. Mary is known to have appeared around the world for centuries in her Spirit form. The love, patience, and compassion of the Divine Mother is beautifully expressed in her.

Matronit/Matron: The maiden expression of the Divine Mother that was honored by troubadours and Kabbalists throughout the Middle Ages.

Her reemergence was linked to the hidden legacy of Mary Magdalene.

Medusa: A human woman seduced by Poseidon in Athena's Temple. Because of that sacrilege, Medusa was turned into a monstrosity, with snakes for hair, who could turn all who looked on her to stone. According to legend, she lived out her days in the ruins of Athena's Temple until Perseus slew her to defeat the Kraken and prevent the destruction of the city of Argos.

Mercury: *See* Hermes Trismegistus/Thoth/Ningishzidda/Mercury

Nannar/Sin: Sumerian and Akkadian names, respectively, for the son of the ruling Anunnaki god Enlil; Nannar was a benevolent moon god in Mesopotamia. He was also the father of Inanna/Ishtar. Ninurta, his jealous half-brother, later sought to wipe out Nannar's followers, who were called "sinners."

Neith: Egyptian Goddess of Wisdom and Battle. Her prophetic temples were at Sais on the Nile delta.

Nepthys: Egyptian half-sister to Isis and Osiris, full sister and wife to Typhon or Set. Nepthys represents the lunar energies of the moon and the subconscious realms. She is also associated with the "Watchtower" of the Magdalene Order that was sworn to protect the mission of the next Horus king, whether it be Horus, Jesus, or another. Her chief temple was located at Heliopolis.

Ningishzidda: *See* Hermes Trismegistus/Thoth/Ningishzidda/Mercury

Ninmah (Ninharsag)/Hathor: Sumerian and Egyptian names, respectively, for the Mother of Humanity; Goddess of Healing, Music, and Sound. It is from her original Sumerian name Ninmah that we get the word Ma or Mama today. As the chief medical officer of the Anunnaki gods, she was assigned to Earth. Her half-brothers were Enlil, the King of the Gods, and Enki, the Humanitarian. According to the Sumerian records, Ninmah is one of the three gods responsible for the genetic engineering of humankind. As the peacemaker between her two half-brothers' kingdoms, Ninmah oversaw the Levant for centuries. Her main temple was high up on Mount Sinai, and in her guise as Hathor, her healing temple was located in Denderah, Egypt, a temple dedicated to the healing power of sound as well as the celestial movements of the spheres. Hat-Hor means "house of Horus" or "house of the god of truth," making Hathor an overseeing grandmother energy of the Egyptians after Horus retook the throne of Egypt.

Nuit: Goddess of the Stars, said to have been the mother of Isis, Osiris, Set, and Nepthys, and the wife of Geb, the Earth god. Nuit was more than likely an Anunnaki astronomer and aerial navigator, but she became the embodiment of the heavenly worlds. It is said that the Goddess Nuit carries the soul through the heavens on her back in the Boat of a Million Years, perhaps a euphemism for an Anunnaki spaceship. Nuit thus came to represent the celestial majesty of the stars and heavens. Her chief temple was at Heliopolis, a temple dedicated to the study of the stars, which at one time had as many as thirteen thousand astronomers.

Odin: Norse Father God of the North, undoubtedly one of the many Anunnaki gods. He may have been the God Enlil, lord of the command, who moved farther north after the destruction of the Anunnaki homes in Mesopotamia around 2200 BCE.

Osiris: Egyptian God of Love, Life, and Resurrection. Osiris was one of the most beloved of all of the Anunnaki gods for his humanitarian work after the Flood. Husband of Isis, father of Horus, Osiris expressed the Christ consciousness of his day. His followers were called KRST, or Christians. Like Tammuz, Osiris was an earlier template for the life, death, and resurrection of Jesus. His chief temples were at Heliopolis and Abydos, Egypt. He is one of the Four Great Kumaras.

Parvati: Hindu Goddess of Creation, wife of Brahma, the Creator God, and an aspect of Devi, the Supreme Mother.

Persephone (Koré): The daughter of Demeter who was captured by Hades and eventually returned to the light. Her story is a metaphor for the human condition of our descent into the Underworld of mortal experience, and our eventual return to the Celestial Worlds. The story of Demeter and Persephone was intrinsic to the first level of the Mystery Schools in Greece.

Perseus: Greek demigod, son of Zeus, who was known for his heroic exploits. Perseus is best known for killing Medusa and saving the city of Argos.

Psyche: Greek maiden who was rescued by Cupid and eventually became his wife in Heaven.

Ptah: *See* Enki/Ptah

Quan Yin: Lady of Compassion, Healing, and Children, she is a bodhisattva who is committed to relieving the suffering of all people. She is said to have been born from the tears of Avalokiteshvara, a bodhisattva of compassion.

Ra: Egyptian God of the Sun, representing light and illumination. His chief temple was at Heliopolis.

Rama: Incarnation of Vishnu the preserver, who fought the forces of darkness in the famous saga the *Ramayana*.

Rhiannon/Epona: Celtic Horse Goddess who appears in the form of a white horse with three singing bluebirds. She rules all the phases of the moon, and is one of the members of the elves, or Shining Ones, who came from the fairy kingdom.

Rigel: Divine Father of the Universe whose wings turn the galaxies. Also known as Horus or Heru the Elder in Egypt, the Spirit of God the Father that is beyond this world.

River Woman: Native American Goddess of the Flowing Waters.

Sarasvati: Hindu Goddess of Music and Arts.

Sekhmet: Egyptian cat-headed Goddess of Healing and War. Her chief temples were at Memphis and Karnack.

Shakti: Hindu Goddess of the Kundalini Life Force and the consort of Shiva the transformer.

Shamash/Utu: Hebrew and Sumerian names, respectively, for the Sun God, known for his fiery flying sun chariot. He was the brother of Inanna/Ishtar and the son of Nannar/Sin.

Shekinah: The Holy Spirit, the Comforter, or the Hebrew Goddess whose breath moves the universe.

Shelia Na Gig: Celtic Goddess of Fertility, a comical figure whose image is placed over the doorway of homes for good luck.

Shiva: Hindu God of Transformation and Change.

Sophia the Daughter: Greek and Hebrew name for the Daughter principle that created the physical universe and continues to incarnate again and again for the redemption of the world.

Sophia the Mother: Greek and Hebrew name for the Divine Mother of Wisdom.

Spider Woman: Native American Goddess of the Universal Energy Field behind the Visible Worlds. Spider Woman sits at the center of the cosmos, connecting all things.

Tammuz: Mesopotamian grain God of Agriculture and Fertility. The noble king who was one of the most beloved of the Anunnaki gods, Tammuz is the forerunner of the dying and resurrected god whose full expression was found in Jesus.

Tara: Hindu Goddess of the All. Various colors express the many attributes of the Divine Mother: For example, Green Tara is about creating action, Red Tara is good for grounding, White Tara is known for her healing abilities, and many others.

Thoth: See Hermes Trismegistus/Thoth/Ningishzidda/Mercury

Uatchet Buto: Egyptian Goddess whose symbol is the snake, or the Uraeus of Enlightenment.

Venus/Aphrodite: *See* Aphrodite/Venus

Vesta: Roman Goddess of Illumination. Her priestesses were vestal virgins in Rome who kept the flame of knowledge alive for centuries.

Vishnu: Hindu name for the Preserver of the Universe. Krishna and Rama were two of Vishnu's many incarnations.

White Buffalo Calf Woman: Native American Goddess who brought the seven sacred rites to the Sioux Indians. These include the pipe ceremony, the sundance ceremony, the Inipi or sweat lodge ceremony, the vision quest ceremony, the making of relatives, the keeping of the soul of the dead, and tapa wankaye, or the throwing of the ball ceremony, which represents our connection with the Great Spirit.

Yahweh: *See* Jehovah (Yahweh)/Jupiter (Jove)/Zeus

Zeus: *See* Jehovah (Yahweh)/Jupiter (Jove)/Zeus

Notes

CHAPTER 3.
THE FEATHER OF TRUTH

1. Edmond Bordeaux Szekely, *The Essene Gospel of Peace, Book 4: The Teachings of the Elect* (Nelson, British Columbia: International Biogenic Society, 1981), 57.
2. Joseph Bharat Cornell, *Aum the Melody of Love: The Spirit Behind All Creation* (Nevada City, Calif.: Crystal Clarity Publishers, 2013), 75–76.
3. Manly P. Hall, *The Secret Teachings of All Ages* (New York: Penguin, 2003), 142.
4. Quoted in Ibid.
5. Tau Malachi, *The Gnostic Gospel of St. Thomas* (Wheaton, Ill.: Llewellyn Publishing, 2004).
6. Barbara Walker, *The Woman's Encyclopedia of Myths and Secrets* (New York: HarperCollins, 1983), 561.
7. Ibid.
8. John Anthony West, *The Traveler's Key to Ancient Egypt* (Wheaton, Ill.: Quest Books, 1985), 374–75.
9. Carmen Boutler, *Angels and Archetypes: An Evolutionary Map of Feminine Consciousness* (Rapid City, S.D.: Swan Raven Company, 1997), 208.

CHAPTER 4. THE GREAT MEDICINE CIRCLE AND THE FOUR GATES OF HEAVEN

1. Mary Jane Sherfey, M.D., *The Nature and Evolution of Female Sexuality*

(New York: Random House, 1973), 153–54. Dr. Sherfey writes that published reports in the medical literature in 1951 state that "all mammalian embryos, male and female are anatomically female during the early stages of fetal life." In Stephen Jay Gould's book, *Further Reflections in Natural History* (New York: Penguin, 1984), he writes, "The female course of development is, in a sense, biologically intrinsic to all mammals. It is the pattern that unfolds in the absence of any hormonal influence. The male route is a medication induced by secretion of androgens from the developing testes" (154).

2. Muata Ashby, *Mysteries of Isis* (Miami: Cruzian Mystic Books/Sema Institute of Yoga, 1996), 33.

3. Lynn Picknett, *Mary Magdalene* (New York: Carroll & Graf, 2003), 169.

CHAPTER 5.
THE CIRCLE CONVENES

1. Alan Jacobs, *The Gnostic Gospels: The Gospel of Philip* (London: Watkins Publishing, 2006), 90.

2. Wellspring Media, *The Burning Times* documentary, Part 2 of a three-part series on women and spirituality (New York: 1999).

3. Vicki Noble, *Shakti Woman: Feeling Our Fire, Healing Our World* (New York: HarperCollins, 1991), 3.

4. Jacquelyn C. Campbell, "If I Can't Have You, No One Can: Power and Control in Homicide of Female Partners," in Jill Radford and Diana E. H. Russell, eds., *Femicide: The Politics of Woman Killing* (New York: Twayne Publishers, 1992), 99–113; and Linda Langford, Nancy Isaac, and Stacey Kabat, "Homicides Related to Intimate Partner Violence in Massachusetts," *Homicide Studies* 2, no. 4 (1998): 353–77, www.ncjrs.gov/pdffiles1/jr000250.pdf (last accessed November 12, 2014).

CHAPTER 6.
REWRITING RELIGIOUS HISTORY

1. Joyce and River Higginbotham, *Christ to Paganism: An Inclusive Path* (Woodbury, Minn.: Llewellyn Publications, 2009), 112.

2. Cited in ibid.

3. Ibid., 110.

4. Richard Elliott Friedman, *The Hidden Book in the Bible* (New York: HarperOne, 1998), 5.

5. Anne Baring and Jules Cashford, *The Myth of the Goddess: Evolution of an Image* (London: Arkana Penguin Books, 1993), 418.

6. Raphael Patai, *The Hebrew Goddess* (Detroit: Wayne State University Press, 1990), 116.

7. Hall, *Secret Teachings of All Ages*, 391–94.

8. Higginbotham, *Christ to Paganism,* 110.

9. Quoted in Joe Lewels, Ph.D., *Rulers of the Earth: Secrets of the Sons of God* (Lakeville, Minn.: Galde Press, 2007), 137.

10. Ibid., 107.

11. William G. Dever, *What Did the Biblical Writers Know and When Did They Know It? What Archaeology Can Tell Us about the Reality of Ancient Israel* (Grand Rapids, Mich.: Wm. B. Eerdmans Publishing Co., 2001), 100.

12. Riane Eisler, *The Chalice and the Blade: Our History, Our Future* (San Francisco: Harper & Row, 1988), 86.

13. Quoted in Higginbotham, *Christ to Paganism,* 111.

14. Ibid.

15. William G. Dever, *Who Were the Early Israelites and Where Did They Come From?* (Grand Rapids, Mich.: Wm B. Eerdmans Publishing Co., 2003), 123.

16. William Whiston, *The Works of Josephus* (Peabody, Mass.: Hendrickson Publishers, 1988), 788.

17. Ibid.

18. Ibid.

19. Ibid., 791.

20. Ibid.

21. Ibid.

22. Helen Strudwick, *The Encyclopedia of Ancient Egypt* (London: Amber Books, 2006), 63–64.

23. Whiston, *Works of Josephus,* 788.

24. Ibid., 789.

25. Ibid.

26. Higginbotham, *Christ to Paganism,* 96.

27. Delores Cannon, *Jesus and the Essenes* (Bath, UK: Gateway Books, 1993), 159–62.

28. Baring and Cashford, *Myth of the Goddess,* 468.

29. Cited in Ibid., 466.

30. Dorothy Leon, *Was Jehovah an ET?* (Huntsville, Ark.: Ozark Mountain Press, 2003), 146.

31. Baring and Cashford, *Myth of the Goddess,* 427–28.

32. Quoted in Higginbotham, *Christ to Paganism,* 100.

33. Quoted in Ibid., 100–1

34. Baring and Cashford, *Myth of the Goddess,* 448.

35. Ibid.

36. Higginbotham, *Christ to Paganism,* 99.

37. Dever, *Who Were the Early Israelites and Where Did They Come From?,* 110–14.

38. Quoted in Higginbotham, *Christ to Paganism,* 99.

39. Christian and Barbara Joy O'Brien, *The Shining Ones* (Kemble, Cirencester, UK: Dianthus Publishing Company, 1997), 222–23.

40. Carl Jung, *Letters,* vol. 2 (Princeton, N.J.: Princeton University Press, 1973), 434.

41. Edmond Bordeaux Szekely, *The Essene Gospel of Peace,* Book 2 (Nelson, British Columbia: International Biogenic Society, 1981).

CHAPTER 7.
GODDESSES IN HEBREW HISTORY

1. Higginbotham, *Christ to Paganism,* 115.

2. Quoted in Baring and Cashford, *Myth of the Goddess,* 456.

3. Patai, *Hebrew Goddess,* 25–26.

4. Ibid., 120.

5. Malcolm Godwin, *Angels: An Endangered Species* (New York: Simon and Schuster, 1990), 36.

6. Baring and Cashford, *Myth of the Goddess,* 458.

7. Walker, *Woman's Encyclopedia of Myths and Secrets,* 66.

8. Ibid., 30.

9. Merlin Stone, *Ancient Mirrors of Womanhood* (Boston: Beacon Press, 1979), 119.

10. Walker, *Woman's Encyclopedia of Myths and Secrets,* 66.

11. Ibid.

12. Stone, *Ancient Mirrors of Womanhood,* 119.

13. Patai, *Hebrew Goddess,* 121.

14. Noble, *Shakti Woman,* 34.

15. Ibid.

16. Baring and Cashford, *Myth of the Goddess,* 454.

17. Patai, *Hebrew Goddess,* 67–68.

18. Ibid., 41.

19. Stone, *Ancient Mirrors of Womanhood,* 120.

20. Patai, *Hebrew Goddess,* 50.

21. Quoted in Higginbotham, *Christ to Paganism,* 102.

22. Patai, *Hebrew Goddess,* 117.

23. Ibid., 116.

24. Ibid., 61.

25. Joan Norton and Margaret Starbird, *14 Steps to Awaken the Sacred Feminine: Women in the Circle of Mary Magdalene* (Rochester, Vt.: Bear & Company, 2009), 30–31.

26. Jean-Yves Leloup, *The Sacred Embrace of Jesus and Mary: The Sexual Mystery at the Heart of the Christian Tradition* (Rochester, Vt.: Inner Traditions, 2005), 81.

27. Patai, *Hebrew Goddess,* 71.

28. Ibid., 68.

29. Quoted in Ibid., 450–51.

30. Ibid., 108–9.

31. Victoria LePage, *Mysteries of the Bridechamber: The Initiation of Jesus and the Temple of Solomon* (Rochester, Vt.: Inner Traditions, 2007), 47.

32. Philip Davies, "In Search of Ancient Israel," *Journal for the Study of the Old Testament* Supplement Series 148 (Sheffield, UK: Sheffield Academic Press, 1992), 116.

33. Quoted in Higginbotham, *Christ to Paganism,* 109.

34. Ibid.

35. Baring and Cashford, *Myth of the Goddess,* 449.

CHAPTER 8.
FOOTPRINTS OF THE MOTHER

1. Merlin Stone, *When God Was a Woman* (New York: Harcourt Brace & Company, A Harvest Book, 1976), xii–xiii.

2. Sjöö, Monica, and Barbara Mor, *The Great Cosmic Mother: Rediscovering*

the Religion of the Earth (San Francisco: Harper San Francisco, 1991), 49.

3. Ibid., 7.

4. Quoted in Noble, *Shakti Woman,* 228.

5. www.marijagimbutas.com/archeology.html (last accessed November 12, 2014).

6. Stone, *When God Was a Woman,* 47.

7. Noble, *Shakti Woman,* 228.

8. Stone, *When God Was a Woman,* 3.

9. Ibid., 47–48.

10. LePage, *Mysteries of the Bridechamber,* 215.

11. Ibid., 215–16.

12. "Interview with Marija Gimbutas," www.sibyllineorder.org/history/hist_marija.htm (last accessed November 12, 2014).

13. Quoted in Noble, *Shakti Woman,* 232.

14. Joseph Campbell, *Masks of God: Primitive Mythology* (London: Penguin Books, 1991), 313.

15. Stone, *When God Was a Woman,* 15.

16. Ibid., 3.

17. Noble, *Shakti Woman,* 234.

18. Ibid., 233.

19. Ibid., 16.

20. Baring and Cashford, *Myth of the Goddess,* 60.

21. Noble, *Shakti Woman,* 47.

22. Leonard Swidler, *Jesus Was a Feminist* (Lanham, Md.: Sheed & Ward, an imprint of Rowman & Littlefield Publishers, Inc., 2007), 106.

23. Quoted in Jennifer Barker Woolger and Roger J. Woolger, *The Goddess Within: A Guide to the Eternal Myths That Shape Women's Lives* (New York: Fawcett Columbine, Ballantine Books, 1987), 274–75.

24. Sjöö and Moor, *Great Cosmic Mother,* 131–32.

25. Joseph Campbell, *The Hero with a Thousand Faces* (Princeton, N.J.: Princeton University Press, 1949), 113.

26. Ibid, 114.

27. Christopher L. C. E. Witcombe, "Venus of Willendorf," http://witcombe.sbc.edu/willendorf/willendorfgoddess.html (last accessed November 12, 2014).

28. Baring and Cashford, *Myth of the Goddess,* 25–29.

29. Ailton Krenack, from the Krenacki Indian nation. Personal conversation, Altamira, Brazil, February 1989.

30. William Carl Eichman, "Catal Huyak: The Temple City of Prehistoric Anatolia," *Gnosis* 15 (Spring 1990): 52–53.

31. Walker, *Woman's Encyclopedia of Myths and Secrets,* 148.

32. Apurva Beniwal, "Gavushala," http://theindianmythology.wordpress .com/2012/03/25/gavushala (last accessed November 11, 2014).

33. "Sacred Animals," http://theindianmythology.wordpress.com/tag/cow-2 (last accessed November 12, 2014).

34. Noble, *Shakti Woman,* 89.

35. Marija Gimbutas, *The Goddesses and Gods of Old Europe, 7000–3500 B.C.* (Berkeley: University of California Press, 1982), 93.

36. Noble, *Shakti Woman,* 46–47.

37. Ibid., 47.

38. Joseph Campbell, *The Mythic Image* (Princeton, N.J.: Princeton University Press, 1974), 294.

39. Sjöö and Mor, *Great Cosmic Mother,* 34.

40. Stone, *When God Was a Woman,* 19.

41. Ibid., 18.

42. Woolger and Woolger, *Goddess Within,* 21.

43. Joseph Campbell, *Masks of God: Occidental Mythology* (London: Penguin Books, 1991), 7.

44. Baring and Cashford, *Myth of the Goddess,* 155–56.

45. Ibid., 157.

46. Noble, *Shakti Woman,* 236.

47. Joseph Campbell, *Masks of God:Occidental Mythology,* 21–22.

48. Baring and Cashford, *Myth of the Goddess*, 159.

49. Woolger and Woolger, *Goddess Within,* 23.

50. Noble, *Shakti Woman,* 33.

51. Ibid., 29.

52. Woolger and Woolger, *Goddess Within,* 17.

53. Ibid., 16.

CHAPTER 9.
THE FOUR MALE AND FEMALE POLARITIES

1. Child Welfare Information Gateway, "Child Maltreatment 2012: Summary of Key Findings," Child Abuse and Neglect Statistics, U.S. Department of Health & Human Services, 2012; "64 Facts about Child Sexual Abuse,"

http://facts.randomhistory.com/child-sexual-abuse-facts.html (last accessed November 11, 2014); and "Child Maltreatment 2012," www.acf.hhs.gov/programs/cb/resource/child-maltreatment-2012 (last accessed November 12, 2014).

2. Carolyn Rebecca Block, Ph.D., "How Can Practitioners Help an Abused Woman Lower Her Risk of Death?" *National Institute of Justice Journal,* no. 250 (November 2003), www.ncjrs.gov/pdffiles1/jr000250c.pdf (last accessed November 12, 2014).

3. Philo Judaeus, *Hypothetica,* chapter 11, verses 14–17; cited in F. H. Colson and G. H. Whitaker, trans., *Philo,* vol. 10; quoted by John A. Phillips, *Eve: A History of an Idea* (San Francisco: Harper & Row, 1984), 58.

4. The Testament of Reuben; cited in H. F. D. Sparks, ed., *The Apocryphal New Testament* (Oxford, UK: Clarendon Press, 1984), 519.

5. Sherfey, *Nature and Evolution of Female Sexuality,* 46.

6. Ibid., 48.

7. Stephen Jay Gould, *Hen's Teeth and Horse's Toes: Further Reflections in Natural History* (New York: Penguin, 1984), 154.

CHAPTER 10.
IMMANENCE AND TRANSCENDENCE

1. Elaine Pagels, *Adam, Eve and the Serpent* (London: Weidenfeld and Nicolson, 1988), 99.

CHAPTER 11.
THE DIRECTIONS OF TIME AND SPACE

1. This story comes from the Gnostic teachings and can be found in Tau Malachi's book *St. Mary Magdalene: The Gnostic Traditions of the Holy Bride* (Woodbury, Minn.: Llewellyn, 2006), 39. This book contains the Secret Gospel of Mary Magdalene.

2. Walker, *Woman's Encyclopedia of Myths and Secrets,* 663.

3. Zsuzsana E. Budapest, *The Grandmother of Time: A Women's Book of Celebrations, Spells, and Sacred Objects for Every Month of the Year* (New York: HarperCollins Publishers, 1989), 223.

4. Ibid., 160.

5. Ibid., 101.

CHAPTER 13.
JESUS AND THE LOST GOSPELS

1. Hall, *Secret Teachings of All Ages*, 600.

2. Higginbotham, *Christ to Paganism*, 72–79.

3. Paul Perry, *Jesus in Egypt* (New York: Ballantine Books, 2003), 5.

4. Ibid., 9.

5. Rev. Gideon J. Ouseley, *The Gospel of the Holy Twelve* (London: Edson Publishers Limited, 1923), ix–x.

6. Leloup, *Sacred Embrace of Jesus and Mary*, 6.

7. Ibid.

8. Ibid., 7.

9. Swidler, *Jesus Was a Feminist*, 180.

10. Pagels, *Adam, Eve and the Serpent*, 46–47.

11. Ibid.

12. James Robinson, editor, Nag Hammadi Library, quoted in "Secrets of the Da Vinci Code," *U.S. News & World Report* (2004): 42.

13. Swidler, *Jesus Was a Feminist*, 139.

14. Elaine Pagels, "The Treasure of Nag Hammadi: Secrets of the Da Vinci Code," *U.S. News & World Report* (2004): 38–43.

15. Ahmed Osman, *Jesus in the House of the Pharaohs: The Essene Revelations on the Historical Jesus* (Rochester, Vt.: Bear and Company, 2004), 7.

16. Quoted in Pagels, "The Treasure of Nag Hammadi," 41.

17. Osman, *Jesus in the House of the Pharaohs*, 11.

18. Ross, *Gospel of Thomas*, 49.

19. Ibid., 11.

20. Jean-Yves Leloup, *The Gospel of Mary Magdalene* (Rochester, Vt.: Inner Traditions, 2002), 27.

21. Ross, *Gospel of Thomas*, 11.

22. Malachi, *St. Mary Magdalene*, 167.

23. Pagels, *Gnostic Gospels*, 123.

24. Ibid., 143.

25. Leloup, *Gospel of Mary Magdalene*, 25.

26. Malachi, *St. Mary Magdalene*, quoting from the Secret Teachings of Mary Magdalene, 130.

27. Ibid., 134.

28. Ibid., 130.

29. Baring and Cashford, *Myth of the Goddess,* 618.

30. Malachi, *Gnostic Gospel of St. Thomas,* xii.

31. Higginbotham, *Christ to Paganism,* 42–43.

32. Malachi, *Gnostic Gospel of St. Thomas,* 5.

33. Lewels, *Rulers of the Earth,*11.

34. Godwin, *Angels,* 138.

35. Malachi, *St. Mary Magdalene,* 129–164.

36. Ibid., 130.

37. Ibid., 137.

38. Ibid., 135.

39. Ibid., 141.

40. Ibid., 134.

41. Quoted by Elaine Pagels, *The Gnostic Gospels* (New York: Vintage Books, A Division of Random House, Inc., 1989), 60.

42. Ibid., 61.

43. Pagels, *Gnostic Gospels,* 57.

44. Ibid.

45. Walker, *Woman's Encyclopedia of Myths and Secrets,* 610.

46. Pagels, *Gnostic Gospels,* 135.

47. Ibid., 140.

48. Malachi, *Gnostic Gospel of St. Thomas,* xiii.

49. Lewels, *Rulers of the Earth,* 152.

50. Pagels, "The Treasure of Nag Hammadi," 43.

51. Ross, *Gospel of Thomas,* 65.

52. Zecharia Sitchin, *The Wars of Gods and Men* (New York: Avon Books, 1985), 117.

53. Godwin, *Angels,* 111–13.

54. M. Don Schorn, *Legacy of the Elder Gods* (Huntsville, Ark.: Ozark Mountain Publishing, 2009), 129–30.

55. Malachi, *St. Mary Magdalene,* 138.

56. Valentinian Exposition 22.19–23, from the Nag Hammadi texts; cited in Pagels, *Gnostic Gospels,* 37.

57. Watkins, *Gospel of Truth,* 190.

58. Malachi, *Gnostic Gospel of St. Thomas,* x.

CHAPTER 14.
THE MANY FACES OF MARY THE ETERNAL ONE

1. Z. Budapest, *Grandmother of Time,* 101.

2. Walker, *Woman's Encyclopedia of Myths and Secrets,* 23, 626–27.

3. Ibid., 611.

4. Cardinal Tarcisio Bertone with Giuseppe De Carli, "The Mystery of Fatima," *U.S. News & World Report* (March 2010): 82–88.

5. Ibid., 86.

6. Courtney Roberts, *Visions of the Virgin Mary: An Astrological Analysis of Divine Intercession* (St. Paul, Minn.: Llewellyn Worldwide, 2004), xv.

7. Ibid.

8. Ibid.

9. *The Lost Books of the Bible and the Forgotten Books of Eden,* Introduction by Dr. Frank Crane (New York: World Press, 1926), 24.

10. Janice T. Connell, *Meetings with Mary: Visions of the Blessed Mother* (New York: Ballantine Books, 1994), xvii.

11. Stuart Wilson and Joanna Prentis, *Power of the Magdalene: The Hidden Story of the Women Disciples* (Huntsville, Ark.: Ozark Mountain Publishing, 2009), 42.

12. Margaret Starbird, *Mary Magdalene: Bride in Exile* (Rochester, Vt.: Bear and Company, 2005), 52–55. "Under close scrutiny, the fact emerges that the town now known as Migdol, situated on the Sea of Galilee, just north of Tiberias and accepted as Mary Magdalene's hometown, was known by an entirely different name in the first century AD. . . . According to Flavius Josephus, the first-century Jewish author . . . the town now called Migdol was known in his day as Taricheae" (53).

13. Jacobs, *Gnostic Gospels,* 82.

14. Starbird, *Mary Magdalene,* 21.

15. Malachi, *Gnostic Gospel of St. Thomas,* 353.

16. Ibid., 352.

17. The details about this story are well documented, but I wish to acknowledge Joanne K. McPortland's wonderful article, "Meeting the Lady of Guadalupe," in the spring 1995 edition of *Gnosis* magazine, 40–43.

18. Walker, *Woman's Encyclopedia of Myths and Secrets,* 490.

19. Ibid., 491.

20. Ibid., 615.

21. Ibid.

22. Ibid.

23. Wilson and Prentis, *Power of the Magdalene,* 127–30.

24. Willis Barnstone, *The Other Bible* (San Francisco: Harper San Francisco, 1984), 589–91.

CHAPTER 15.
THE LOST TEACHINGS OF JESUS

1. Quoted in Ouseley, *Gospel of the Holy Twelve,* ix–x.

2. M. Don Schorn, *Reincarnation: Stepping Stones of Life* (Huntsville, Ark.: Ozark Mountain Press, 2006), 23–34.

3. Ronald J. McMillan, *We Are Forever Voyageurs of Space* (Nashville, Tenn.: Scythe Publications, Inc., 1995), 239.

4. Cited in Hans Holzer, *Life Beyond: Compelling Evidence for Past Lives and Existence after Death,* (Chicago: McGraw Hill Publishing, Contemporary Books Imprint, 1994), 166–74.

5. Elizabeth Clare Prophet, *Reincarnation: The Missing Link in Christianity* (Corin Springs, Mont.: Summit University Press, 1997), 52.

6. Joseph Head and Sylvia Cranston, *Reincarnation*: *The Phoenix Fire Mystery* (San Diego: Point Loma Publications, 1991), 132–33.

7. Quran, Sura 39, The Crowds, Verse 42. Cited in Joseph Head and Sylvia L. Cranston, *Reincarnation: An East-West Anthology* (Pasadena, Calif.: Theosophical Publishing House, 1961), 56.

8. Quran, Sura 11, Rome, Verse 38. Cited in Thomas Cleary, *The Essential Koran* (San Francisco: Harper San Francisco, 1993), 97.

9. Quran, Sura 2, The Cow, Verse 28. Ibid., 89.

10. Schorn, *Reincarnation* (Huntsville, Ark.: Ozark Mountain Publishing, 2009), 38–39.

11. Prophet, *Reincarnation,* 18.

12. Walter Semkiw, M.D., *Return of the Revolutionaries* (Charlottesville, Va.: Hampton Roads, 2003), 24.

13. Head and Cranston, *Reincarnation,* 36.

14. Semkiw, *Return of the Revolutionaries,* 24.

15. W. Y. Evans-Wentz, trans., *Bardo Thodal* (London: Oxford University Press, 1927), 234.

16. Schorn, *Reincarnation,* 36.

17. Malachi, *Gnostic Gospel,* 26.
18. Ouseley, *Gospel of the Holy Twelve,* 32.
19. Ibid., 39.
20. www.subtleenergies.com (last accessed November 11, 2014).
21. Ibid.
22. "The Anathemas against Origen," attached to the decrees of the Fifth Ecumenical Church Council, 553 CE, in Alexander Roberts, James Donaldson, Philip Schaff, Henry Wace, eds., *Nicene and Post Nicene Fathers,* First Series (Peabody, Mass.: Hendrickson Publishing, 1996).
23. Semkiw, *Return of the Revolutionaries,* 25.
24. Ouseley, *Gospel of the Holy Twelve,* 32.

CHAPTER 16.
THE TEACHINGS THAT MUST BE SUPPRESSED

1. Swidler, *Jesus Was a Feminist,* 28.
2. Stone, *When God Was a Woman,* 56.
3. Quoted in Ibid., 55.
4. Eisler, *Chalice and the Blade,* 129–30.
5. Higginbotham, *Christ to Paganism,* 45.
6. Pagels, *Gnostic Gospels,* xxiv.
7. Starbird, *Mary Magdalene,* 73.
8. Baring and Cashford, *Myth of the Goddess,* 611.
9. Jacobs, *Gnostic Gospels,* 110.
10. Pagels, *Gnostic Gospels,* quoting Hippolytus, 50–51.
11. Ibid., 51.
12. Pagels, *Gnostic Gospels,* quoting Hippolytus, 49.
13. Malachi, *St. Mary Magdalene,* 131.
14. Pagels, *Gnostic Gospels*, 51–52.
15. Barnstone, *Other Bible,* 588.
16. Ibid., 592.
17. Malachi, *St. Mary Magdalene,* 147.
18. Ibid., 157.
19. Ibid., 142.
20. Ibid., 134–35.
21. Nicholas Notovitch, *The Unknown Life of Jesus the Christ* (Joshua Tree, Calif.: Tree of Life Publications, 1996), 21.

22. Ibid., 38.
23. Ibid., 41.

CHAPTER 17. THE DIVINE DAUGHTER AND SON

1. Malachi, *St. Mary Magdalene,* 141.
2. Malachi, *St. Mary Magdalene,* 148.
3. Ibid., 157.

CHAPTER 18.
MARY MAGDALENE AND THE DIVINE SOPHIA

1. Susan Haskins, *Mary Magdalene: Myth and Metaphor* (New York: Penguin, Riverhead Books, 1993), 93.
2. Leloup, *Gospel of Mary Magdalene,* xvi–xvii.
3. Pagels, *Gnostic Gospels,* 22.
4. Margaret Starbird, *The Goddess in the Gospels: Reclaiming the Sacred Feminine* (Rochester, Vt.: 1998), 26.
5. Leloup, *Sacred Embrace of Jesus and Mary,* 9.
6. Ibid., 13.
7. Jacobs, *Gnostic Gospels,* 90.
8. Karen L. King, *The Gospel of Mary of Magdala: Jesus and the First Woman Apostle* (Santa Rosa, Calif.: Polebridge Press, 2003), 3–4.
9. Leloup, *Gospel of Mary Magdalene,* 29.
10. Ibid., 31.
11. Pagels, *Gnostic Gospels,* 13–14.
12. Leloup, *Gospel of Mary Magdalene,* 39.
13. Malachi, *St. Mary Magdalene,* 150.
14. Ibid.
15. Ibid., 142.
16. Starbird, *Mary Magdalene,* 23.
17. Ibid., 43.
18. Sir Lawrence Durdin-Robertson, *The Goddesses of Chaldea, Syria and Egypt* (Enniscorthy, Ireland: Cesara Publications, 1975), 126.
19. Starbird, *Woman with the Alabaster Jar,* 29.
20. Starbird, *Mary Magdalene,* 49.
21. Ibid., 48.

22. Ibid., 51–52.

23. Ibid., 48.

24. Mark B. Woodhouse, *Paradigm Wars: Worldviews for a New Age* (Berkeley, Calif.: Frog, Ltd., 1996), 543.

25. Ibid.

26. Starbird, *Mary Magdalene,* 68–69.

27. Walker, *Woman's Encyclopedia of Myths and Secrets,* 614.

28. Baring and Cashford, *Myth of the Goddess,* 629.

29. Hall, *Lectures on Ancient Philosophy* (New York: Tarcher/Penguin, 2005), 82.

30. Quoted in Ibid.

31. Pagels, *Gnostic Gospels,* 123.

32. Malachi, *St. Mary Magdalene,* 134.

33. Ibid., 130.

34. Ibid., 145–46.

35. Ibid., 137.

36. Ibid., 140.

37. Ibid., 146.

38. Ibid., 140–41.

39. Ibid., 146–47.

CHAPTER 19. IN THE NAME OF GOD

1. www.wayoflife.org/fbns/catholiccommission.htm (last accessed November 12, 2013).

2. Sjöö and Mor, *Great Cosmic Mother,* 298.

3. Eisler, *Chalice and the Blade,* 133.

4. Starbird, *Mary Magdalene,* 115.

5. James Sprenger and Heinrich Kramer, *Malleus Maleficarum* (New York: Dover Publications, 1971), 44.

6. Austin Clive, "A Woman's Place in Christianity," http://atheism.about .com/b/2013/11/11/a-womans-place-in-christianity.htm (last accessed November 12, 2014).

7. Ibid.

8. M. L. W. Laistner, *Christianity and Pagan Culture in the Later Roman Empire* (Ithaca, N.Y.: Cornell University Press, 1951), 112.

9. Cline, "A Woman's Place in Christianity." http://atheism.about .com/b/2013/11/11/a-womans-place-in-christianity.htm.

10. Walker, *Woman's Encyclopedia of Myths and Secrets,* 921.

11. Starbird, *Mary Magdalene,* 115.

12. Walker, *Woman's Encyclopedia of Myths and Secrets,* 910.

13. Wayne Shumaker, *The Occult Sciences in the Renaissance* (Berkeley: University of California Press, 1972), 95.

14. Walker, *Woman's Encyclopedia of Myths and Secrets,* 911.

15. Ibid., 921.

16. Wolfgang Lederer, *The Fear of Women* (New York: Harcourt Brace Jovanovich, Inc., 1968), 162.

17. Walker, 921.

18. Sherfey, *Nature and Evolution of Female Sexuality,* 38.

19. Walker, *Woman's Encyclopedia of Myths and Secrets,* 608.

20. Ibid., 912.

21. "Scary Quotes," www.positiveatheism.org/hist/quotes/scar_o.htm (last accessed November 12, 2014), from Joan Smith's *Misogynies* (New York: Ballantine, 1992).

22. Quoted in Elizabeth Cady Stanton, *The Original Feminist Attack on the Bible* (New York: Arno Press, 1974), 164.

23. Walker, *Woman's Encyclopedia of Myths and Secrets,* 912.

24. Ibid., 924.

25. Ibid., 608–9.

26. Ibid.

27. James Carroll, *Constantine's Sword: The Church and the Jews—A History* (Boston: Houghton Mifflin, 2003).

28. Dan Burstein, "The Church Triumphant: Was There a Coverup, or Just a Great Theological Debate?" *U.S. News & World Report* (May 2006): 48.

29. Bart D. Ehrman, "How the Battle for Scripture Was Won," *U.S. News & World Report* (May 2006): 52.

30. Burstein, "Church Triumphant," 48.

31. Timothy Freke and Peter Gandy, "The Origins of the Coverup," *U.S. News & World Report* (May 2006): 51, excerpted from *The Jesus Mysteries* (New York: Three Rivers Press, a division of Crown Publishing Group and Random House, 1999).

32. Hall, *Secret Teachings of All Ages,* 650.

33. Ibid.

34. Ibid.

35. Ibid., 651.

36. Eisler, *Chalice and the Blade,* 132–33.

37. Hall, *Secret Teachings of All Ages,* 651.

38. D. L. David Moore, *The Christian Conspiracy* (Atlanta, Ga.: Pendulum Press, 1994), 56–57.

39. John Holland Smith, *The Death of Classical Paganism* (New York: Charles Scribner's Sons, 1976), 155.

40. Walker, *Woman's Encyclopedia of Myths and Secrets,* 601.

41. Jonathan Riley-Smith, *The Oxford Illustrated History of the Crusades* (Oxford: Oxford University Press, 1995), 66.

42. "Albigensian Crusade," www.britannica.com/EBchecked/topic/12976/ Albigensian-Crusade (last accessed November 12, 2014)

43. Eisler, *Chalice and the Blade,* 133.

44. Starbird, *Mary Magdalene,* 104–8.

45. Sjöö and Mor, *Great Cosmic Mother,* 298–99.

46. Walker, *Woman's Encyclopedia of Myths and Secrets,* 437.

47. Ibid., 438.

48. Starbird, *Mary Magdalene,* 107.

49. Walker, *Woman's Encyclopedia of Myths and Secrets,* 438.

50. Wilson and Prentis, *Power of the Magdalene,* 136–37.

51. Henry Charles Lea, *The Inquisition of the Middle Ages* (New York: Macmillan, 1961), 224.

52. Rossell Hope Robbins, *Encyclopedia of Witchcraft and Demonology* (New York: Crown Publishers, 1959), 451.

53. Walker, *Woman's Encyclopedia of Myths and Secrets,* 439.

54. Ibid., 444.

55. Cyrus Adler and Isidore Singer, eds., *The Jewish Encyclopedia: A Descriptive Record of the History, Religion, Literature, and Customs of the Jewish People from the Earliest Times to the Present Day* (New York: Funk & Wagnalls, 1903–1906), 591.

56. "Burning Times," www.themystica.com/mystica/articles/b/burning_times .html (last accessed November 12, 2013).

57. Walker, *Woman's Encyclopedia of Myths and Secrets,* 444.

58. Ibid., 441.

59. Ibid., 444.

60. Sjöö and Mor, *Great Cosmic Mother,* 299.

61. Ibid., 298.

62. Larissa Tracy, *Torture and Brutality in Medieval Literature: Negotiations of*

National Identity (Manchester, UK: Boydell and Brewer Ltd., 2012), 22.

63. Sjöö and Mor, *Great Cosmic Mother,* 300.

64. Ibid., 300–1.

65. Mary K. Greer, *Women of the Golden Dawn: Rebels and Priestesses* (Rochester, Vt.: Park Street Press, 1995), 14, quoting Martha Vicinus's book *Suffer and Be Still: Women in the Victorian Age* (New York: Routledge Publishing, 1972), 131.

66. Walker, *Woman's Encyclopedia of Myths and Secrets,* 926.

67. Ibid.

68. Ibid., 926–27.

69. Martha Vicinus, *Suffer and Be Still: Women in the Victorian Age* (Bloomington and London: Indiana University Press, 1972), xiv; taken from "Principles of Education, Drawn from Nature and Revelations and Applied to Female Education in the Upper Classes," which first appeared in *The Mother's Companion* (1889).

70. Bram Dijkstra, *Idols of Perversity: Fantasies of Feminine Evil in Fin-de-Siècle Culture* (Oxford: Oxford University Press, 1984), 324–25.

71. "Switzerland's Long Way to Women's Right to Vote," www.history-switzerland.geschichte-schweiz.ch/chronology-womens-right-vote-switzerland.html (last accessed November 12, 2014).

72. Bootie Cosgrove-Mather, "Japanese Women Shun the Pill," www.cbsnews.com/stories/2004/08/20/health/main637523.shtml (last accessed November 12, 2014).

73. B. A. Robinson, "Debates about FGM in Africa, the Middle East and Far East," www.religioustolerance.org/fem_cirm.htm (last accessed November 12, 2014).

74. Bureau of Justice Statistics Crime Data Brief, Intimate Partner Violence, between the years 1993–2001, www.bjs.gov/content/pub/pdf/ipv01.pdf (last accessed October 2014).

75. I. H. Frieze and A. Browne, "Violence in Marriage," in L. E. Ohlin and M. H. Tonry, eds., *Family Violence* (Chicago: University of Chicago Press, 1989), National Domestic Violence Fact Sheet.

76. "Domestic Violence Facts," National Coalition Against Domestic Violence, www.ncadv.org/files/DomesticViolenceFactSheet%28National%29.pdf (last accessed November 12, 2014).

77. Patricia Tjaden and Nancy Thoennes, "Extent, Nature and Consequences of Intimate Partner Violence: Findings from the National Violence against

Women Survey" (Washington, D.C.: National Institute of Justice and the Centers of Disease Control and Prevention, 2000), www.ncjrs.gov/pdffiles1/nij/181867.pdf (last accessed November 12, 2014).

78. Federal Bureau of Investigation, Uniform Crime Reports, "Crime in the United States, 2000" (2001).

79. Jacquelyn Campbell, Doris Campbell, Daniel Webster, et al., "Assessing Risk Factors for Intimate Partner Homicide," *National Institute of Justice Journal* 250 (2003): 14–19.

80. Amaury de Reincourt, *Sex and Power in History* (New York: Dell Publishing, 1974), 258.

81. Dave Oester, "Christianity and Ghosts," www.ghostweb.com/christianity.html (last accessed November 12, 2013).

CHAPTER 21.
THE HERO'S JOURNEY

1. Jacobs, *Gnostic Gospels,* 75.

2. Neil Douglas Klotz, *Prayers of the Cosmos: Meditations on the Aramaic Words of Jesus* (New York: HarperCollins, 1990), 41.

3. Joseph Campbell, *Hero with a Thousand Faces,* 16.

4. Ibid., 20.

5. Ibid.

6. Ibid., 28.

7. Carol Pearson, *Awakening the Heroes Within* (New York: HarperCollins, 1991), 1.

CHAPTER 22.
THE POWER OF ARCHETYPE

1. James Hillman, *The Soul's Code: In Search of Character and Calling* (New York: Random House, 1996), 36.

2. Deepak Chopra, *The Spontaneous Fulfillment of Desire* (New York: Three Rivers Press/Random House, 2003), 148.

3. Ibid., 150–51.

4. Timothy Freke and Peter Gandy, *Jesus and the Lost Goddess* (New York: Three Rivers Press, 2001), 80.

5. Joseph Campbell, *Hero with a Thousand Faces,* 4.

6. Ibid., 3.

7. Hall, *Secret Teachings of All Ages,* 649.

8. Hall, *Lectures on Ancient Philosophy,* 99.

9. Plato, *The Republic,* translated by Benjamin Jowett (Mineola, N.Y.: Dover Publications, Inc., 2000), 272–74.

10. Quoted in Caroline Myss, *Sacred Contracts: Awakening Your Divine Potential* (Carlsbad, Calif.: Hay House, 2001), 108.

11. *The Portable Jung,* edited by Joseph Campbell, translated by R. F. C. Hull (New York: Penguin, 1976), xxi.

12. C. G. Jung, *The Archetypes and the Collective Unconscious* (Princeton, N.J.: Bollingen Paperbacks, 1981), 120.

13. Woolger and Woolger, *Goddess Within,* 11.

14. Michio Kaku, "The Universe in a Nutshell," *Evolve* 4, no. 1 (2005): 24–25. The words *mother* and *matter* are related to each other.

15. Quoted in Ervin Laszlo, *The Self-Actualizing Cosmos: The Akasha Revolution in Science and Human Consciousness* (Rochester, Vt.: Inner Traditions, 2014), 108.

16. Quoted in Ibid., 103.

17. Joseph Campbell, *Hero with a Thousand Faces,* 181–82.

CHAPTER 23.
A RETURN TO THE CIRCLE

1. Hall, *Lectures on Ancient Philosophy,* 190–91.

Bibliography

Adler, Cyrus, and Isidore Singer, eds. *The Jewish Encyclopedia: A Descriptive Record of the History, Religion, Literature, and Customs of the Jewish People from the Earliest Times to the Present Day.* New York: Funk & Wagnalls, 1903–1906.

"The Anathemas against Origen," attached to the decrees of the Fifth Ecumenical Council, 553 CE, in Alexander Roberts, James Donaldson, Philip Schaff, Henry Wace, eds., *Nicene and Post Nicene Fathers,* First Series. Peabody, Mass.: Hendrickson Publishing, 1996.

Ashby, Muata. *Mysteries of Isis.* Miami: Cruzian Mystic Books/Sema Institute of Yoga, 1996.

Baring, Anne, and Jules Cashford. *The Myth of the Goddess: Evolution of an Image.* London: Penguin Books/Viking Arkana, 1993.

Barnstone, Willis. *The Other Bible.* San Francisco: Harper San Francisco, 1984.

Bertone, Cardinal Tarcisio, with Giuseppe De Carli. "The Mystery of Fatima." *U.S. News & World Report* (March 2010): 82–88.

Boutler, Carmen. *Angels and Archetypes: An Evolutionary Map of Feminine Consciousness.* Rapid City, S.Dak.: Swan Raven Company, 1997.

Budapest, Zsuzsana E. *The Grandmother of Time, A Women's Book of Celebrations, Spells, and Sacred Objects for Every Month of the Year.* New York: HarperCollins, 1989.

Budge, E. A. Wallis. *The Gods of the Egyptians*, vol. I. New York: Dover Press, 1969.

Burstein, Dan. "The Church Triumphant: Was There a Coverup, or Just a Great Theological Debate?" *U.S. News & World Report* (May 2006): 48.

Campbell, Jacquelyn, Doris Campbell, Daniel Webster, et al. "Assessing Risk

Factors for Intimate Partner Homicide." *NIJ Journal* 250 (2003): 14–19.

Campbell, Joseph. *The Hero with a Thousand Faces.* Princeton, N.J.: Princeton University Press, 1973.

———. *Masks of God: Occidental Mythology.* London: Penguin Books, 1991.

———. *Masks of God: Primitive Mythology.* London: Penguin Books, 1991.

———. *The Mythic Image.* Princeton, N.J.: Princeton University Press, 1974.

Cannon, Delores. *Jesus and the Essenes.* Bath, UK: Gateway Books, 1993.

Chopra, Deepak. *The Spontaneous Fulfillment of Desire.* New York: Three Rivers Press/ Random House, 2003.

Cleary, Thomas. *The Essential Koran.* San Francisco: Harper San Francisco, 1993.

Connell, Janice T. *Meetings with Mary: Visions of the Blessed Mother.* New York: Ballantine Books, 1994.

Cornell, Joseph Bharat. *Aum the Melody of Love: The Spirit Behind All Creation.* Nevada City, Calif.: Crystal Clarity Publishers, 2013.

Cranston, Sylvia. *Reincarnation: The Phoenix Fire Mystery.* Pasadena, Calif.: Theosophical University Press, 1998.

Davies, Philip. "In Search of Ancient Israel." *Journal for the Study of the Old Testament* Supplement Series 148. Sheffield, UK: Sheffield Academic Press, 1992.

Dever, William G. *What Did the Biblical Writers Know and When Did They Know It? What Archaeology Can Tell Us about the Reality of Ancient Israel.* Grand Rapids, Mich.: Wm. B. Eerdmans Publishing Co., 2001.

———. *Who Were the Early Israelites and Where Did They Come From?* Grand Rapids, Mich.: Wm B. Eerdmans Publishing Co., 2003.

Dijkstra, Bram. *Idols of Perversity: Fantasies of Feminine Evil in Fin-de-Siècle Culture.* Oxford: Oxford University Press, 1984.

Durdin-Robertson, Sir Lawrence. *The Goddesses of Chaldea, Syria and Egypt.* Enniscorthy, Ireland: Cesara Publications, 1975.

Ehrman, Bart D. "How the Battle for Scripture Was Won." *U.S. News & World Report* (May 2006): 52.

———. *Jesus, Interrupted: Revealing the Hidden Contradictions in the Bible and Why We Don't Know about Them.* New York: HarperCollins, 2009.

Eichman, William Carl. "Catal Huyak: The Temple City of Prehistoric Anatolia." *Gnosis* 15 (Spring 1990): 52–53.

Eisler, Riane. *The Chalice and the Blade: Our History, Our Future.* San Francisco: Harper & Row, 1988.

Evans-Wentz, W. Y., trans. *Bardo Thodal.* London: Oxford University Press, 1927.

Freke, Timothy, and Peter Gandy. *Jesus and the Lost Goddess.* New York: Three Rivers Press, 2001.

———. "The Origins of the Coverup." Excerpted in *U.S. News & World Report* (May 2006): 51, from *The Jesus Mysteries.* New York: Crown Publishing Harmony Books, 1999.

Friedman, Richard Elliott. *The Hidden Book in the Bible.* New York: HarperOne, 1998.

Gimbutas, Marija. *The Civilizations of the Goddess: The World of Old Europe.* San Francisco: Harper San Francisco, 1974.

———. *Goddesses and Gods of Old Europe—6500–3500 B.C.: Myths, and Cult Images.* Berkeley: University of California Press, 1982.

———. *The Language of the Goddess.* London: Thames and Hudson, 2001.

———. *The Living Goddess.* Oakland: University of California Press, 1999.

Godwin, Malcolm. *Angels: An Endangered Species.* New York: Simon and Schuster, 1990.

Gould, Stephen Jay. *Further Reflections in Natural History.* New York: Penguin, 1984.

Graves, Robert. *The White Goddess.* New York: Vintage Books, 1958.

Hall, Manly P. *Lectures on Ancient Philosophy.* New York: Tarcher/Penguin, 2005.

———. *The Secret Teachings of All Ages.* New York: Penguin, 2003.

Haskins, Susan. *Mary Magdalene: Myth and Metaphor.* New York: Penguin/Riverhead Books, 1993.

Head, Joseph, and Sylvia L. Cranston. *Reincarnation: An East-West Anthology.* Wheaton, Ill.: Theosophical Publishing House, 1961.

Higginbotham, Joyce and River. *Christ to Paganism.* Woodbury, Minn.: Llewellyn Publications, 2009.

Hillman, James. *The Soul's Code: In Search of Character and Calling.* New York: Random House, 1996.

Holzer, Hans. *Life Beyond: Compelling Evidence for Past Lives and Existence after Death.* Chicago: McGraw Hill Publishers/Contemporary Books, 1994.

Jacobs, Alan. *The Gnostic Gospels: The Gospel of Philip.* London: Watkins Publishing, 2006.

———. *The Gnostic Gospels: Gospel of Thomas.* London: Watkins Publishing, 2006.

Jung, Carl. *The Archetypes and the Collective Unconscious.* Princeton, N.J.: Bollingen Paperbacks, 1981.

———. *Letters,* vol. 2. Princeton, N.J.: Princeton University Press, 1973.

Kaku, Michio. "God in a Nutshell." *Evolve* 4, no. 1 (2005): 24–25.

King, Karen L. *The Gospel of Mary of Magdala: Jesus and the First Woman Apostle.* Santa Rosa, Calif.: Polebridge Press, 2003.

Klotz, Neil Douglas. *Prayers of the Cosmos: Meditations on the Aramaic Words of Jesus.* New York: HarperCollins, 1990.

Laistner, M. L. W. *Christianity and Pagan Culture in the Later Roman Empire.* Ithaca, N.Y.: Cornell University Press, 1951.

Laszlo, Ervin. *The Self-Actualizing Cosmos: The Akasha Revolution in Science and Human Consciousness.* Rochester, Vt.: Inner Traditions, 2014.

Lea, Henry Charles. *The Inquisition of the Middle Ages.* New York: Macmillan, 1961.

Lederer, Wolfgang. *The Fear of Women.* New York: Harcourt Brace Jovanovich, Inc., 1968.

Leloup, Jean-Yves. *The Gospel of Mary Magdalene.* Rochester, Vt.: Inner Traditions, 2002.

———. *The Sacred Embrace of Jesus and Mary: The Sexual Mystery at the Heart of the Christian Tradition.* Rochester, Vt.: Inner Traditions, 2005.

Leon, Dorothy. *Was Jehovah an ET?* Huntsville, Ark.: Ozark Mountain Press, 2003.

LePage, Victoria. *Mysteries of the Bridechamber: The Initiation of Jesus and the Temple of Solomon.* Rochester, Vt.: Inner Traditions, 2007.

Lewels, Joe. *Rulers of the Earth: Secrets of the Sons of God.* Lakeville, Minn.: Galde Press, 2007.

The Lost Books of the Bible and the Forgotten Books of Eden. New York: World Press, 1926. *Note:* This is a collection of apocryphal and pseudepigraphal literature from earlier works. The first half of the book is called *Lost Books of the Bible* and is a reprint of a book published by William Hone in 1820, titled *The Apocryphal New Testament.* This, in turn, was a reprint of a translation of the *Apostolic Fathers,* written in 1693 by William Wake (who later became the archbishop of Canterbury), with a smattering of medieval embellishments on the New Testament from a book published in 1736 by Jeremiah Jones (1693–1724). The second half of the book, which is called *The Forgotten Books of Eden,* includes a translation originally published in 1882 of the *First and Second Books of Adam and Eve.* This was translated first from ancient Ethiopic to German by Ernest Trumpp, then into English by Soloman Cesar Malan, together with a number of items of Old Testament pseudepigrapha, like those reprinted in the second volume of R. H. Charles's *Apocrypha and Pseudepigrapha of the Old Testament* (Oxford, 1913).

Malachi, Tau. *St. Mary Magdalene: The Gnostic Traditions of the Holy Bride.* Woodbury, Minn.: Llewelyn, 2006.

McMillan, Ronald J. *We Are Forever Voyageurs of Space.* Nashville: Scythe Publications, Inc., 1995.

McPortland, Joanne K. "Meeting the Lady of Guadalupe." *Gnosis* (Spring 1995): 40–43.

Moore, D. L. David. *The Christian Conspiracy.* Atlanta, Ga.: Pendulum Press, 1994.

Myss, Caroline. *Sacred Contracts: Awakening Your Divine Potential.* Carlsbad, Calif.: Hay House, 2001.

Noble, Vicki. *Shakti Woman: Feeling Our Fire, Healing Our World.* New York: HarperCollins, 1991.

Norton, Joan, and Margaret Starbird. *14 Steps to Awaken the Sacred Feminine: Women in the Circle of Mary Magdalene.* Rochester, Vt.: Bear & Company, 2009.

Notovitch, Nicholas. *The Unknown Life of Jesus the Christ.* Joshua Tree, Calif.: Tree of Life Publications, 1996.

O'Brien, Christian, and Barbara Joy. *The Shining Ones.* Kemble, Cirencester, UK: Dianthus Publishing Company, 1997.

Ohlin, L. E., and M. H. Tonry, eds. *Family Violence.* Chicago: University of Chicago Press, 1989.

Osman, Ahmed. *Jesus in the House of the Pharaohs: The Essene Revelations on the Historical Jesus.* Rochester, Vt.: Bear and Company, 2004.

Ouseley, Rev. Gideon J. *The Gospel of the Holy Twelve.* London: Edson Publishers Limited, 1923.

Pagels, Elaine. *Adam, Eve and the Serpent.* New York: Random House, 1988.

———. *The Gnostic Gospels.* New York: Vintage Books, 1989.

———. "The Treasure of Nag Hammadi: Secrets of the Da Vinci Code." *U.S. News & World Report* (2004): 38–43.

Patai, Raphael. *The Hebrew Goddess,* 3rd ed. Detroit, Mich.: Wayne State University Press, 1990.

Pearson, Carol. *Awakening the Heroes Within.* New York: HarperCollins, 1991.

Perry, Paul. *Jesus in Egypt.* New York: Ballantine Books, 2003.

Phillips, John A. *Eve: A History of an Idea.* San Francisco: Harper & Row, 1984.

Picknett, Lynn. *Mary Magdalene.* New York: Carroll & Graf, 2003.

Prophet, Elizabeth Clare. *Reincarnation: The Missing Link in Christianity.* Corin Springs, Mont.: Summit University Press, 1997.

Reincourt, Amaury de. *Sex and Power in History.* New York: Dell Publishing, 1974.

Robbins, Rossell Hope. *Encyclopedia of Witchcraft and Demonology.* New York: Crown Publishers, 1959.

Roberts, Courtney. *Visions of the Virgin Mary: An Astrological Analysis of Divine Intercession.* St. Paul, Minn.: Llewellyn Worldwide, 2004.

Ross, Hugh McGregor. *The Gospel of Thomas.* London: Watkins Publishing, 2002.

Schorn, M. Don. *Legacy of the Elder Gods.* Huntsville, Ark.: Ozark Mountain Publishing, 2009.

———. *Reincarnation: Stepping Stones of Life.* Huntsville, Ark.: Ozark Mountain Press, 2006.

Semkiw, Walter, M.D. *Return of the Revolutionaries.* Charlottesville, Va.: Hampton Roads, 2003.

Sherfey, Mary Jane, M.D. *The Nature and Evolution of Female Sexuality.* New York: Random House, 1973.

Shumaker, Wayne. *The Occult Sciences in the Renaissance.* Berkeley: University of California Press, 1972.

Sitchin, Zecharia. *The Wars of Gods and Men.* New York: Avon Books, 1985.

Sjöö, Monica, and Barbara Mor. *The Great Cosmic Mother.* San Francisco: Harper San Francisco, 1975.

Smith, John Holland. *The Death of Classical Paganism.* New York: Charles Scribner's Sons, 1976.

Sparks, H. F. D., ed. *The Apocryphal New Testament.* Oxford: Clarendon Press, 1984.

Sprenger, James, and Heinrich Kramer. *Malleus Maleficarum.* New York: Dover Publications, 1971.

Stanton, Elizabeth Cady. *The Original Feminist Attack on the Bible.* New York: Arno Press, 1974.

Starbird, Margaret. *The Goddess in the Gospels.* Rochester, Vt.: Bear and Company, 1998.

———. *Mary Magdalene: Bride in Exile.* Rochester, Vt.: Bear and Company, 2005.

———. *The Woman with the Alabaster Jar: Mary Magdalen and the Holy Grail.* Rochester, Vt.: Bear and Company, 1993.

Stone, Merlin. *Ancient Mirrors of Womanhood.* Boston: Beacon Press, 1979.

———. *When God Was a Woman.* New York: Harcourt Brace & Company, 1976.

Strudwick, Helen. *The Encyclopedia of Ancient Egypt.* London: Amber Books, 2006.

Swidler, Leonard. *Jesus Was a Feminist.* Lanham, Md.: Sheed & Ward, an imprint of Rowman and Littlefield Publishers, Inc., 2007.

Szekely, Edmond Bordeaux. *The Essene Gospel of Peace.* Nelson, B.C., Canada: International Biogenic Society, 1981.

Thomas, D. Winton, ed. *Documents from Old Testament Times.* New York: Harper Torchbooks, 1895.

Tjaden, Patricia, and Nancy Thoennes. "Extent, Nature and Consequences of Intimate Partner Violence: Findings from the National Violence against Women Survey." Washington, D.C.: National Institute of Justice and the Centers for Disease Control and Prevention, 2000.

Vicinus, Martha. *Suffer and Be Still: Women in the Victorian Age.* New York: Routledge Publishing, 1972.

Walker, Barbara. *The Woman's Encyclopedia of Myths and Secrets.* New York: HarperCollins, 1983.

Wellspring Media. *The Burning Times.* A three-part documentary on women and spirituality. New York: Wellspring Media, 1999.

West, John Anthony. *The Traveler's Key to Ancient Egypt.* Wheaton, Ill.: Quest Books, 1985.

Whiston, William. *The Works of Josephus.* Peabody, Mass.: Hendrickson Publishers, 1988.

Whitmont, Edward. *The Alchemy of Healing: Pysche and Soma.* Berkeley, Calif.: North Atlantic Books, 1993.

Wilson, Stuart, and Joanna Prentis. *Power of the Magdalene: The Hidden Story of the Women Disciples.* Huntsville, Ark.: Ozark Mountain Publishing, 2009.

Woodhouse, Mark B. *Paradigm Wars: Worldviews for a New Age.* Berkeley, Calif.: Frog, Ltd., 1996.

Woolger, Jennifer Barker, and Roger J. Woolger. *The Goddess Within: A Guide to the Eternal Myths That Shape Women's Lives.* New York: Fawcett Columbine/Ballantine Books, 1987.

Index

Page numbers in *italic* refer to illustrations.

About the Author

Tricia McCannon is a renowned American mystic, symbologist, historian, and teacher who has traveled the world in search of answers to the greatest Mysteries of the Ages. Trained as an initiate of many ancient streams of knowledge, including mystical Christianity, Native American wisdom, the Masters of the Far East, and the wisdom of the Goddess, she is known as "the Mysteries Expert." She is the founder of the Phoenix Fire Lodge Mystery School and has led hundreds of workshops worldwide. She has also appeared on over 175 radio and TV shows, including *Coast to Coast AM, Strange Universe,* and *Dreamland.* She is the author of over thirty DVDs, as well as the acclaimed books *Dialogues with the Angels* and *Jesus: The Explosive Story of the 30 Lost Years and the Ancient Mystery Religions.* She speaks on a variety of subjects from the Lost Years of Jesus to the Quest for the Philosopher's Stone. She is the founder of the UFO Forum in Atlanta, and for the past two decades she has been a headliner at conferences around the world. She is a practicing clairvoyant and hypnotherapist and has given Soul readings for over six thousand people worldwide, tracing their unique individual journeys from their celestial origin into their present-day life. She lives with her two cats at home in Atlanta. She can be reached at www.triciamccannonspeaks.com.

BOOKS OF RELATED INTEREST

The Angelic Origins of the Soul
Discovering Your Divine Purpose
by Tricia McCannon

Lessons from the Twelve Archangels
Divine Intervention in Daily Life
by Belinda J. Womack
Foreword by Catherine Shainberg

The Healing Wisdom of Mary Magdalene
Esoteric Secrets of the Fourth Gospel
by Jack Angelo

The Gospel of Mary Magdalene
by Jean-Yves Leloup

Womb Awakening
Initiatory Wisdom from the Creatrix of All Life
by Azra Bertrand, M.D., and Seren Bertrand

The Council of Light
Divine Transmissions for Manifesting the Deepest Desires of the Soul
by Danielle Rama Hoffman

Bringers of the Dawn
Teachings from the Pleiadians
by Barbara Marciniak

The Pleiadian Agenda
A New Cosmology for the Age of Light
by Barbara Hand Clow
Introduction by Brian Swimme, Ph.D.

Inner Traditions • Bear & Company
P.O. Box 388
Rochester, VT 05767
1-800-246-8648
www.InnerTraditions.com

Or contact your local bookseller